WITHDRAWN
UTSA LIBRARIES

AFRICAN HISTORICAL DICTIONARIES
Edited by Jon Woronoff

1. *Cameroon,* by Victor T. LeVine and Roger P. Nye. 1974
2. *The Congo,* 2nd ed., by Virginia Thompson and Richard Adloff. 1984
3. *Swaziland,* by John J. Grotpeter. 1975
4. *The Gambia,* by Harry A. Gailey. 1975
5. *Botswana,* by Richard P. Stevens. 1975
6. *Somalia,* by Margaret F. Castagno. 1975
7. *Dahomey,* by Samuel Decalo. 1975
8. *Burundi,* by Warren Weinstein. 1976
9. *Togo,* by Samuel Decalo. 1976
10. *Lesotho,* by Gordon Haliburton. 1977
11. *Mali,* by Pascal James Imperato. 1977
12. *Sierra Leone,* by Cyril Patrick Foray. 1977
13. *Chad,* by Samuel Decalo. 1977
14. *Upper Volta,* by Daniel Miles McFarland. 1978
15. *Tanzania,* by Laura S. Kurtz. 1978
16. *Guinea,* by Thomas O'Toole. 1978
17. *Sudan,* by John Voll. 1978
18. *Rhodesia/Zimbabwe,* by R. Kent Rasmussen. 1979
19. *Zambia,* by John J. Grotpeter. 1979
20. *Niger,* by Samuel Decalo. 1979
21. *Equatorial Guinea,* by Max Liniger-Goumaz. 1979
22. *Guinea-Bissau,* by Richard Lobban. 1979
23. *Senegal,* by Lucie G. Colvin. 1981
24. *Morocco,* by William Spencer. 1980
25. *Malaŵi,* by Cynthia A. Crosby. 1980
26. *Angola,* by Phyllis Martin. 1980
27. *The Central African Republic,* by Pierre Kalck. 1980
28. *Algeria,* by Alf Andrew Heggoy. 1981
29. *Kenya,* by Bethwell A. Ogot. 1981
30. *Gabon,* by David E. Gardinier. 1981
31. *Mauritania,* by Alfred G. Gerteiny. 1981
32. *Ethiopia,* by Chris Prouty and Eugene Rosenfeld. 1981
33. *Libya,* by Lorna Hahn. 1981
34. *Mauritius,* by Lindsay Rivière. 1982
35. *Western Sahara,* by Tony Hodges. 1982
36. *Egypt,* by Joan Wucher-King. 1984
37. *South Africa,* by Christopher Saunders. 1983
38. *Liberia,* by D. Elwood Dunn and Svend E. Holsoe. 1985
39. *Ghana,* by Daniel Miles McFarland. 1985
40. *Nigeria,* by Anthony Oyewole. 1985

Historical Dictionary of GHANA

by
DANIEL MILES McFARLAND

African Historical Dictionaries, No. 39

The Scarecrow Press, Inc.
Metuchen, N.J., & London
1985

Library of Congress Cataloging in Publication Data

McFarland, Daniel Miles.
  Historical dictionary of Ghana.

  (African historical dictionaries ; no. 39)
  Bibliography: p.
  1. Ghana--History--Dictionaries. I. Title.
II. Series.
DT510.5.M38   1985   966.7'003'21   84-22186
ISBN 0-8108-1761-6

Copyright © 1985 by Daniel Miles McFarland
Manufactured in the United States of America

CONTENTS

Editor's Foreword, by Jon Woronoff	v
Preface	vii
Abbreviations and Acronyms	ix
Chronology	xix
Introduction	1
THE DICTIONARY	13
Bibliography	199
Appendixes	
A. List of Ghanaian People	290
B. Rulers of Asante	292
C. British Administrators of the Gold Coast	293
D. Ghanaian Leaders from 1951	295
E. European Posts on the Gold Coast	296

MAPS

Fig. 1 Physical Regions	2
Fig. 2 Political Regions	4
Fig. 3 Rivers (John T. Kress)	6
Fig. 4 People	8

EDITOR'S FOREWORD

There have been few more encouraging events in modern African history than the independence of Ghana, which accelerated the decolonization of the continent. There have also been few African states which, on the eve of independence, looked as promising as Ghana. It had long been Britain's model colony. It was led by one of the most charismatic figures ever to emerge, Kwame Nkrumah. The country itself was fairly well endowed geographically and economically and, even more significant, it possessed a relatively well educated and dynamic population.

Yet, few countries have been more disheartening to distant admirers and few have actually fulfilled the hopes and aspirations of their people less. Ghana has, in some ways, again become the epitome of the African experience. But this time it is to ask the very sad question, What went wrong?

Just before independence, Kwame Nkrumah travelled to the Ivory Coast where he made a wager with that country's then and still present leader, Houphouet Boigny. Each was to try his own methods and the two would compare the results of their respective experiments later. Nkrumah took the path of political radicalism and stress on the political kingdom; Houphouet was a moderate, probably even a conservative, and he put economics first. The outcome is well enough known not to require repetition.

Still, when trying to figure out where Ghana, under its various leaders, went wrong, it is hard to attach this to a given type of regime. Ghana has tried just about every type of regime, civilian and military, radical and conservative, and not one has given it satisfaction. So, if the fault does not lie with the type of regime, perhaps it is connected to something else, namely the heavy emphasis on politics. By overlooking the economic kingdom, by not meeting the more immediate and vital needs of the population, it is possible that all the leaders failed to achieve what was desired most. If the economy had received top priority, if it had been reinforced consistently, Ghana might be a happier country now with a society that is far easier to govern under any type of regime.

Such weighty considerations, however, are not of the kind that can be elucidated in a brief foreword. Nor will they be adequately pondered in this book. The purpose of both is to show that what was once Africa's future, and has since become its past, was nowhere near as simple as many Africans and foreigners assumed. Hopes and aspirations could not be fulfilled merely because they were deep-rooted or intensely held. Leaders could not succeed merely because they meant well or seemed to enjoy public support. Everything was much more difficult and complicated. That, at least, will be demonstrated by this volume.

This Historical Dictionary will also provide a wealth of other material about this crucial country. There are indications about its political leaders and parties, about major events and institutions, about essential policies and activities in assorted fields. Of special note is the extremely comprehensive chronology which makes it far easier to follow the twists and turns of history. Finally, an extensive bibliography indicates other sources for more specialized information.

That the author of this book, Daniel McFarland, was concerned with more than just collecting useful facts and figures is obvious from the book's contents. He, too, was taken by the basic decency and kindness of the Ghanaians. He also was amazed to find that, after so many efforts, the results were painfully modest. And he, like so many others, still has the faith that eventually the country will succeed. That is a precious addition to the ample academic qualifications which enabled him to engage in such thorough research. We are therefore particularly indebted to him for this volume which follows his earlier contribution on Upper Volta.

Jon Woronoff
Series Editor

PREFACE

Ghanaians whom I have known are admirable people--warm, courteous, and intelligent. I spent the summer of 1973 at the Institute of African Studies at Legon. There it was my privilege to associate with a group of distinguished scholars who stimulated my interest in their culture and helped me appreciate the richness of their history. I acknowledge my debt to Jones Ofori-Atta, E.O. Apronti, R. Addo Fening, Kofi Frimpong, S.K.B. Asante, J.F. Fynn, J.H. Nketia, Kofi Drah, and J.F. Dwamena. They were a constellation of stars that made Mensah Sarbah Hall an exciting place to be that summer, a decade ago. A country which can produce such gentlemen must have a future.

An author always has certain sources that are especially valuable. I depended heavily on the research of Robert S. Rattray, Ivor Wilks, Albert Adu Boahen, John Kofi Fynn, David Kimble, Dennis Austin, Naomi Chazan, Kwame Arhin, John D. Fage, Kwamina B. Dickson, James Anquandah, and Christian C. Aguolu.

Geographic coordinates came from the U.S. Department of Interior Board on Geographic Names gazetteer: <u>Ghana, Official Standard Names Approved by the United States Board on Geographic Names</u>, Washington, D.C., 1967. I also constantly referred to the last two official censuses of Ghana, for 1960 and 1970. Frequent reference was made to Survey of Ghana, 1969, maps.

The system of spelling used is not consistent with that used anywhere else. I have used initial vowels and nasal consonants in alphabetizing entries. I hope this avoids the confusion that is often created for the average reader in English who knows nothing of Akan (Twi) orthography. I have tried to be consistent in the ways I spell words, giving alternate versions in parentheses. But I am certain some different spellings have escaped my proofreading.

At James Madison University I have been helped by many of my colleagues. To single out just a few, I am especially indebted to Debra Baker Ryman, Marcia E. Grimes, Gordon Miller, John T. Kress, Raymond Dingledine, and Paula See. And, most important of all, I owe the most to the calm endurance of my wife. She never bargained for so much Ghana when we made our vows.

Daniel Miles McFarland
Bridgewater, Virginia
January 1984

ABBREVIATIONS AND ACRONYMS

AAPO	All-African Peoples' Organization
AASU	All-African Student Union
AATUF	All-African Trade Union Federation
ABEDA	Arab Bank for Economic Development in Africa
AC	Asanteman Council
ACC	Asante Confederacy Council
ACDC	Army Central Defense Committee
ACP	Action Congress Party
ACP	African, Caribbean and Pacific (nations)
ACSOG	Association of Civil Servants of Ghana
ACSU	Agricultural Colleges Students' Union
ADAF	African Descendants Association Foundation
ADB	African Development Bank
ADB	Agricultural Development Bank
ADC	Agricultural Development Corporation
ADF	African Development Fund
AEC	All Ewe Conference
AFDC	Armed Forces Defense Committee
AFRC	Armed Forces Revolutionary Council
AGC	Ashanti Goldfields Corporation
AGCC	African Gold Coast Company
AGHANA	Association of Ghanaians in North America
AHCUG	Ad Hoc Committee on Union Government
AKS	Asante Kotoko Society
ALU	Association of Local Unions
AMB	Agricultural Marketing Board
AMEZ	African Methodist Episcopal Zion Church
AOC	Associated Overseas Countries (of the European Economic Community)
APB	Association of Professional Bodies
APP	All-People's Party
APRP	All-People's Republican Party
APS	Adabraka Progressive Society
ARGS	Annual Report Geological Survey
ARPB	Association of Recognized Professional Bodies
ARPS	Aborigines' Rights Protection Society
ATP	African Timber and Plywood, Ltd.
ATUC	African Trade Union Confederation
AWAM	Association of West African Merchants
AYA	Asante Youth Association

Abbreviations

AYB	African Youth Brigade
AYO	Anlo Youth Organization
BARADEP	Brong-Ahafo Regional Agricultural Development Program
BARDEC	Brong-Ahafo Regional Development Corporation
BASCOL	Bauxite Alumina Study Company, Ltd.
BASU	Brong-Ahafo Students' Union
BATO	Britain-African Trade Organization
BBC	British Broadcasting Corporation
BBWA	Bank of British West Africa
BCEAO	Central Bank of the West African States
BHC	Bank for Housing Construction
BIAS	Bulletin of Institute of African Studies (Legon)
BKF	Brong-Kyempem Federation
BNI	Bureau of National Investigation
BOAC	British Overseas Airways Corporation
BSL	Black Star Line
CAST	Consolidated African Selection Trust
CAYC	Continental African Youth Command
CC	Chief Commissioner
CCE	Center for Civic Education
CCG	Christian Council of Ghana
CCTA	Commission for Technical Cooperation in Africa
CDC	Commonwealth Development Corporation
CDC	Constitutional Drafting Commission
CDS	Chief Defence Staff
CEAO	Economic Community of West Africa
CECEC	Committee for Economic Co-operation with Eastern Countries
CFAO	French West African Company
CID	Criminal Investigation Department
CIDA	Canadian International Development Agency
CMB	Cocoa Marketing Board
CME	Council of Muslim Elders
CMG	Companion of the Order of St. Michael and St. George
CMS	Church Missionary Society
CO	Colonial Office
COV	Companion of the Order of the Volta
CPA	Cocoa Producers' Alliance
CPC	Cocoa Purchasing Company
CPP	Convention People's Party
CRIG	Cocoa Research Institute of Ghana
CRO	Chief Regional Officer
CRS	Catholic Relief Services
CSD	Cocoa Services Division
CSIR	Council for Scientific and Industrial Research
CUT	Committee for Togolese Unity
CVC	Citizens' Vetting Committee

Abbreviations

CYO	Catholic Youth Organization
CYO	Committee on Youth Organization
DAO	District Administrative Officer
DC	District Commissioner
DEC	District Executive Committee
DPO	District Political Officer
DRB	District Record Book
DYLG	Democratic Youth League of Ghana
ECA	Economic Commission for Africa (UN)
ECGD	Export Credits Guarantee Department (British)
ECOWAS	Economic Community of West African States
EDF	European Development Fund
EEC	European Economic Community
EIB	European Investment Bank
EPC	Ewe Presbyterian Church
ERDC	Empire Resources Development Committee
EREDEC	Eastern Regional Development Corporation
ESA	Early Stone Age
FAO	Food and Agricultural Organization (UN)
FDC	Food Distribution Corporation
FINCO	First International Natura Corporation (Diamonds)
FPD	Front for the Prevention of Dictatorship
FYO	Federated Youth Organization
GA	Government Agent
GAAS	Ghana Academy of Arts and Sciences
GAC	Ghana Airways Corporation
GAL	Ghana Academy of Learning
GAMEFA	Ghana-American Friendship Association
GAS	Ghana Academy of Sciences
GATT	General Agreement on Tariffs and Trade
GAW	Ghana Association of Writers
GAWU	Ghana Agricultural Workers Union
GAYC	Ga-Adangbe Youth Command
GBA	Ghana Bar Association
GBC	Ghana Broadcasting Corporation
GBO	G.B. Ollivant, Ltd.
GC	Gold Coast
GCARPS	Gold Coast Aborigines' Rights Protection Society
GCD	Ghana Consolidated Diamond, Ltd.
GCE	General Certificate of Education
GCEU	Gold Coast Exservicemen's Union
GCFA	Gold Coast Farmers' Association
GCHC	Ghana Cargo Handling Company

Abbreviations

GCL	Ghana Confederation of Labor
GCMA	Ghana Co-operative Marketing Association
GCP	Ghana Congress Party
GCR	Gold Coast Review
GCTUC	Gold Coast Trade Union Congress
GDP	Gross Domestic Product
GES	Ghana Education Service
GET	Ghana Educational Trust
GFDC	Ghana Food Distribution Corporation
GFIC	Ghana Film Industry Corporation
GH	Ghana
GHA	Ghana Highway Authority
GHAPSO	Ghana People's Solidarity Organization
GIC	Ghana Investment Center
GIHOC	Ghana Industrial Holding Corporation
GIMPA	Ghana Institute of Management and Public Administration
GJA	Ghana Journalists' Association
GJS	Ghana Journal of Science (Accra)
GMA	Ghana Manufacturing Association
GMA	Ghana Medical Association
GMNOA	Ghana Merchant Navy Officers' Association
GMS	Ghana Medical Services
GMT	Greenwich Mean Time
GNA	Ghana National Archives
GNA	Ghana News Agency
GNAT	Ghana National Association of Teachers
GNCC	Ghana National Construction Corporation
GNFC	Ghana National Farmers' Council
GNPA	Ghana National Procurement Agency
GNPC	Ghana National Petroleum Corporation
GNQ	Ghana Notes and Queries
GNTC	Ghana National Trading Corporation
GOIL	Ghana Oil Company
GPM	Ghana Patriotic Movement
GPP	Ghana People's Party
GPPF	Ghana Progressive Popular Front
GPSC	Ghana Peace and Solidarity Council
GPTU	Ghana Private Transport Union
GSFNB	Geological Survey of the Gold Coast Field Notebooks
GSK	Ga Shifimo Kpee (Ga Standfast Organization)
GSMC	Ghana State Mining Corporation
GTA	Ghana Timber Association
GTMB	Ghana Timber Marketing Board
GTPCWU	General Transport, Petroleum and Chemical Workers Union
GUNSA	Ghana United Nations Student Association
GUP	Ghana Universities Press
GWSC	Ghana Water and Sewerage Corporation
HSWU	Health Service Workers Union

Abbreviations

IAEA	International Atomic Energy Agency
IAS	Institute of African Studies (Legon)
IASAR	Institute of African Studies, Arabic Records (Legon)
IASB	International African Service Bureau
IBA	International Bauxite Association
IBM	International Black Market
IBRD	International Bank for Reconstruction and Development
ICC	Industrial Co-operative Corporation
ICCO	International Cocoa Organization
ICFTU	International Confederation of Free Trade Unions
ICGWU	Industrial and Commercial General Workers Union
ICO	International Coffee Organization
IDA	International Development Association
IDA	Irrigation Development Authority
IDB	Islamic Development Bank
IDC	Industrial Development Corporation
IFAD	International Fund for Agricultural Development
IFC	International Finance Corporation (World Bank)
IGP	Inspector-General of Police
ILO	International Labor Organization
IMC	Interim Management Committees
IMF	International Monetary Fund
INCC	Interim National Co-ordinating Committee
ITCZ	Inter-tropical Convergence Zone
ITF	Inter-tropical Front
JAH	Journal of African History (London)
JAS	Journal of the African Society (London)
JFM	June Fourth Movement
JHSN	Journal of the Historical Society of Nigeria (Ibadan)
JP	Justice Party
JPC	Joint Provincial Council of Chiefs
JWAC	Joint West Africa Committee
KBE	Knight of the British Empire
KCT	Kumasi College of Technology
KMAC	King's Medal for African Chiefs
KNRG	Kwame Nkrumah Revolutionary Guards
KYA	Kwahu Youth Association
LCP	League of Coloured Peoples
LDC	Less Developed Countries
LI	Legislative Instrument
LSNA	Legon Society on National Affairs
MAC	Military Advisory Council
MAP	Muslim Association Party

MATS	Military Academy and Training School
MBE	Member Order of the British Empire
MI	Military Intelligence
MLA	Member of Legislative Assembly
MLC	Member Legislative Council
MOH	Ministry of Health
MOV	Member of the Order of Volta
MP	Member of Parliament
MSA	Middle Stone Age
MYC	Muslim Youth Congress
NA	Native Authority
NADECO	National Development Company
NAG	National Archives of Ghana
NAL	National Alliance of Liberals
NAO	Native Administration Ordinance
NASSO	National Association of Socialist Students Organizations
NCBWA	National Congress of British West Africa
NCD	National Commission for Democracy
NCGW	National Council of Ghana Women
NDC	National Defence Council
NDC	National Development Commission
NDF	National Democratic Front
NDM	New Democratic Movement
NEB	National Energy Board
NERC	National Economic Review Committee
NES	National Employment Service
NGP	New Ghana Party
NHC	National House of Chiefs
NIB	National Investment Bank
NIC	National Investigations Committee
NJO	Native Jurisdiction Ordinance
NLC	National Liberation Council
NLCD	National Liberation Council Decree
NLM	National Liberation Movement
NORRIP	Northern Regional Rural Integrated Program
NPA	National Procurement Agency
NPP	Northern People's Party
NR	Northern Region
NRC	National Redemption Council
NSC	National Security Council
NSC	National Service Corps
NSC	National Sports Council
NSS	National Service Scheme
NT	Northern Territories
NTC	Northern Territories Council
NTTC	National Teacher Training Council
NUGS	National Union of Ghanaian Students
NUGSE	National Union of Ghanaian Students in Europe
NUS	National Union of Seamen

NYA	Northern Youth Association
NYC	National Youth Council
NYOC	National Youth Organizing Committee
OAC	Organization for African Community
OATUU	Organization of African Trade Union Unity
OAU	Organization of African Unity
OBE	Order of the British Empire
OCCGE	Organization of Coordination and Cooperation in the Fight Against Major Endemic Diseases (West Africa)
OCDR	Organizing Committee for the Defense of the Revolution
OECD	Organization for Economic Cooperation and Development
OFY	Operation Feed Yourself
ONUC	United Nations Organization in the Congo
OOV	Officer of the Order of Volta
OSA	Omnibus Services Authority
OTDC	Overseas Trade Development Council
PANA	Pan African News Agency
PAP	People's Action Party
PBD	Produce Buying Division (of Cocoa Marketing Board)
PC	Provincial Commissioner
PDA	Preventive Detention Act
PDC	People's Defense Committees
PEA	People's Educational Association
PFP	Popular Front Party
PG	Prison Graduate
PID	Produce Inspection Division
PMFJ	People's Movement for Freedom and Justice
PNDC	Provisional National Defense Council
PNP	People's National Party
POEU	Post Office Employees Union
POGR	President's Own Guard Regiment
POYA	Popular Youth Association
PP	Progress Party
PPC	Petroleum Promotion Council
PPF	People's Popular Front
PPP	People's Popular Party
PRAG	Public Relations Association of Ghana
PRELOG	People's Revolutionary League of Ghana
PRO	Public Record Office
PSWU	Public Services Workers' Union
PTP	Togolese Party of Progress
PTWU	Posts and Telecommunications Workers' Union
PUWU	Public Utility Workers' Union
PVA	Party Vanguard Activists
PWD	Public Works Department

Abbreviations

RAC	Royal African Company
RC	Regional Commissioner
RDC	Regional Development Corporation
RWAFF	Royal West African Frontier Force (WAFF before 1928)
SAT	Swiss African Trading Company
SBWA	Standard Bank of West Africa
SCIAO	Commercial and Industrial Society of West Africa
SCMB	State Cocoa Marketing Board
SCOA	Commercial Society of West Africa
SCOLMA	Standing Conference on Library Materials on Africa
SDF	Social Democratic Front
SDMC	State Diamond Marketing Corporation
SFC	State Farms Corporation
SG	Self-government
SGMC	State Gold Mining Corporation
SHC	State Housing Corporation
SIB	Special Investigative Board
SIC	State Insurance Corporation
SMC	Supreme Military Council
SMCD	Supreme Military Council Decree
SNA	Secretary for Native Affairs
SPG	Society for the Propagation of the Gospel
SRC	Students' Representative Council
SSB	Social Security Bank
SSNIT	Social Security and National Insurance Trust
STAFAMS	State Farms Corporation
STC	State Transport Corporation
STCC	State Tele-communication Corporation
TC	Togoland Congress
TCOR	Trusteeship Council Official Records
TCP	Togoland Congress Party
TDC	Tema Development Corporation
TFP	Third Force Party
TGCTHS	Transactions of the Gold Coast and Togoland Historical Society (Achimota and Legon)
THSG	Transactions of the Historical Society of Ghana (Legon)
TMB	Timber Marketing Board
TOLIMO	National Liberation Movement of Western Togo
TUC	Trades Union Congress
TVT	Transvolta Togoland
UAC	United Africa Company
UAF	United Action Front
UAS	Union of African States
UAT	United Africa Trust
UCC	University of Cape Coast

UGCC	United Gold Coast Convention
UGFC	United Ghana Farmers' Council
UGFCC	United Ghana Farmers' Council of Cooperatives
UMOA	West African Monetary Union
UNC	United National Convention
UNDP	United Nations Development Program
UNEF	United Nations Emergency Force (Zaire, 1960-)
UNESCO	United Nations Educational, Scientific and Cultural Organization
UNIDO	United Nations Industrial Development Organization
UNP	United Nationalist Party
UP	United Party
UR	Upper Region
URADEP	Upper Regional Agricultural Development Program
USAID	United States Agency for International Development
UST	University of Science and Technology (Kumasi)
UTAG	University Teachers' Association of Ghana
UTC	Union Trading Company (Swiss)
VALCO	Volta Aluminum Company
VBRP	Volta Basin Research Project
VGK	Records of the Danish West Indies and Guinea Company
VORADEC	Volta Regional Development Corporation
VORADEP	Volta Regional Agricultural Development Project
VR	Volta Region
VRA	Volta River Authority
VRF	Volta River Federation
WAAC	West African Airways Corporation
WABA	West African Bankers' Association
WACB	West African Currency Board
WACRI	West African Cocoa Research Institute
WAEC	West African Economic Community
WAEC	West African Examinations Council
WAFF	West African Frontier Force
WAPCB	West African Produce Control Board
WARDA	West African Rice Development Association
WARO	West African Research Organization
WASA	West African Science Association (London)
WASC	West African Shipping Conference
WASU	West African Students' Union
WATP	West African Trade Project
WAYL	West African Youth League
WDC	Workers' Defense Committees
WFP	World Food Program
WFTU	World Federation of Trade Unions (Communist)
WHO	World Health Organization
WR	Western Region
WREDEC	Western Regional Development Corporation

WTO	World Tourism Organization
WYA	Wassa Youth Association
YPM	Young Pioneers Movement
YSG	Youth Study Group

CHRONOLOGY

c. 10,000 B.C.	Probable human habitation at Jiman on the Oti River (8° 37'N, 0° 06'E) is earliest recorded site located within modern Ghana.
c. 8000 B.C.	There was probably human habitation around Lake Bosumtwi in modern Asante.
c. 4000 B.C.	Oldest date for pottery found at the Stone Age site on Gao Lagoon near Accra.
c. 3300 B.C.	Late Stone Age site at Bosumpra Rockshelter, Abetifi, Kwahu.
c. 1500 B.C.	The beginnings of Kintampo Culture.
c. 900-500 B.C.	Stone hoes were introduced from the northeast.
c. 100 B.C.	Early Iron Age at Tema.
c. 150 A.D.	Early Iron Age at Kpone.
c. 700	Iron technology had developed around New Buipe.
c. 1000	An iron technology existed at Bonoso in the nuclear area of the Brong.
1076-1077	The Almoravids conquered ancient Ghana on the edge of the Sahara.
c. 1200	The Guan began to move down the Volta from the Gonja area toward the Gulf of Guinea.
1235	The battle of Kirina marked the final end of ancient Ghana.
c. 1298	Asaman founded the Bono (Brong) kingdom.
c. 1364-1384	The French claim to have made settlements at Mina and Takoradi during this period.

Chronology

c. 1400	The Dyula (Dioula, Juula) founded Begho.
c. 1450	The Guan had reached the coast west of modern Accra and had settled the Akuapem area.
1472	The Portuguese had reached the Gold Coast and were trading for gold at Shama near the Pra.
1475	Flemish ships were trading for gold along the Gold (Mina) Coast.
1479	Castilian, English and Italian ships had joined the Flemish and Portuguese on the Gold Coast.
c. 1480	Dagomba, Mamprusi and Nanumba were created.
19 Jan. 1482	A Portuguese squadron under Diogo de Azambuja reached the Benya and soon began construction of the Fort of San Jorge, Elmina.
15 Mar. 1486	John II of Portugal gave Elmina the status of a Municipality and took the title "Lord of Guinea."
7 June 1494	The Treaty of Tordesillas recognized Portuguese claims to the coast of West Africa.
c. 1500	Adanse and Akwamu, early Akan states, were founded. The Ga, under Ayi Kushi, had settled in the Accra Plains by this time.
1503	The Portuguese began Fort San Antonio at Axim. (Fort St. Anthony to the English.)
25 July 1503	The paramount chief of Efutu and a thousand others were baptised on Santiago Hill outside Elmina.
1536	The Portuguese began a factory at Shama which they called San Sebastian.
c. 1550	The Mande began the conquest of Gonja.
1553	Englishmen were contesting the Portuguese monopoly of trade on the Gold Coast.
Mar. 1557	The Portuguese burned Accra because the Ga were trading with the English and French.
c. 1565	The Portuguese built a base at Accra. This was destroyed by the Ga in 1576.

1580	The French set up a factory at Accra, taken by the Portuguese in 1583.
16 Apr. 1581	Philip of Spain became King of Portugal. After this the Portuguese began to lose control of their Gold Coast trade.
1595	Dutch vessels were trading on the Gold Coast.
1591	The battle of Tondibi, in modern Mali, marked the end of the power of the Songhai.
1598	The Dutch established posts at Mouri and Butri.
1615	A violent earthquake did great damage along the Gold Coast.
c. 1620	The Gonja attacked Dagomba at Daboya and the Dagomba were forced to move their capital to Yendi.
1623	The Portuguese established a base up the Ankobra River and named it Fort Duma.
1624	The Fante and Dutch formed an alliance against the Portuguese.
c. 1630	Oti Akenten began his leadership of the Asante.
1631	The English built a lodge at Kormantin.
16 June 1633	The Dutch estimated five tons of gold being brought from the Gold Coast annually.
Dec. 1636	A violent earthquake was reported on the coast.
1637	The Portuguese built a lodge at Osu.
26 Aug. 1637	A Dutch force landed at Cabo Corso (Cape Coast) and began a final push against the Portuguese.
29 Aug. 1637	San Jorge Castle was surrendered to the Dutch and the Dutch moved their headquarters there from Mouri.
c. 1640	Tobacco was introduced from America.
1641	The Dutch founded a school for Africans at Elmina, but the school lasted only a short time.
8 Feb. 1642	The Dutch took Fort Saint Anthony at Axim, the last Portuguese post on the Gold Coast.

Chronology

20 Aug. 1642	The Accra gave the Dutch permission to build a post near Osu.
1645	Swedes captured the old Portuguese base at Osu.
c. 1646	By this date the Akwamu had conquered the Guan in the Akuapem area.
1650	The Swedes established themselves at Cabo Corso (Cape Coast) and Takoradi.
1652	The Swedes began Fort Carlsborg at Cabo Corso, and established themselves at Osu. The Dutch base at Accra was named Fort Crevecoeur.
1653	The Dutch began Fort Ruychaver on the Ankobra River sixty miles above the sea. The fort was destroyed a few years later.
1657-1658	Denkyira defeated Adansi and emerged the major Akan power in the west. Danes arrived on the Gold Coast and began to take Swedish posts.
1661	The Ga ceded the beach at Osu to the Danes, who began Christiansborg Castle.
1662	The Company of Royal Adventurers was organized in England to trade on the coast of Africa.
1663	The English established a base at Komenda.
1664-1665	The Anglo-Dutch War resulted in conflicts between those two nations on the Gold Coast. In May of 1664 the English took Cabo Corso from the Dutch, who had taken it from the Swedes the year before. The English called the place Cape Coast. It would be their headquarters for two hundred years.
1665	The Dutch took Kormantin from the English and named it Fort Amsterdam.
1672	The Royal African Company replaced the Company of Royal Adventurers as the English agents of the Gold Coast trade. The English began James Fort at Little Accra.
1677	The Akwamu under Ansa Sasraku sacked and burned the Ga capital at Great Accra (Ayawaso) and killed the Ga ruler and his eldest son.
1679	The Akwamu moved east from Great Accra into

	Ladoku. The English began a fort at Anomabo. The Portuguese took Christiansborg Castle, but returned it to the Danes in 1683.
c. 1680	Kumasi emerged as capital of Asante with the beginning of the reign of Osei Tutu.
1681	Akwamu burned Little Accra and Osu.
1682	Brandenburgers began to build a series of posts at Prince's Town, Takrama, and Akwida, but these Germans didn't stay long.
1688	The Akwamu conquered Ladoku. The French established themselves at Komenda, but soon left. The Dutch began Fort Vredenburg at Komenda. The Dutch began to sign alliances with peoples along the west coast.
1689	Ansa Sasraku of Akwamu died, leaving Basua as regent for young Ado.
c. 1691	The Adom-Ahanta war, which was to last many years, began about this time.
1691	The English established Fort Metal Cross at Dixcove.
1693	An Akwamu freebooter, Asameni, captured Fort Christiansborg, Osu, from the Danes. It was returned the following year.
1694	A war of the Komenda against the Dutch began. The English built a fort at Winneba.
1698	Denkyira defeated Assin.
1699	Basua of Akwamu died, leaving Ado to rule. Akyem attacked Akwamu.
c. 1700	The Mamprusi court moved from Gambaga to Nalerigu.
1701	The Akwamu under Ado crossed the Volta and advanced eastward into modern Benin (Dahomey). Osei Tutu and the Asante defeated Ntim Gyakari and the Denkyira in the Battle of Feyiase.
1702	The Asante defeated the Akyem Kotoku, allies of Denkyira. The Akwamu army pulled out of the

	area between the Volta and Whydah. Akwono became leader of Akwamu.
1707	The Akwamu army conquered the Ewe of Krepi, but failed in an invasion of Kwahu. The advance carried the Akwamu to Ho and Kpandu.
1708-1710	Akwamu campaigned against Kwahu and was finally successful.
1711	The Asante defeated Wenchi and destroyed Ahwene, the Wenchi capital. The Fante defeated Efutu.
c. 1713	Yendi Dabari, seat of the Dagomba, fell to the Gonja under Kumpatia.
11 Apr. 1713	The Treaty of Utrecht granted the English a contract to supply slaves to Spanish America, initiating the most active period of slave trade on the Gold Coast.
1715	Asante defeated the Aowin. The Akyem and Akwamu began a war.
1717	At Koromante on the Pra river the Akyem inflicted a costly defeat on the Asante army. Details are obscure, but the Asantehene, probably Osei Tutu, was killed.
1720	After a period of confusion in Asante, Opoku Ware became Asantehene.
13 Aug. 1720	The Dutch West India Company acquired claim to all Brandenburg (Prussian) properties on the Gold Coast.
1721	The Asante conquered Aowin, Sefwi and Nzema.
1723	Asante conquered Techiman (Bono-Mansu).
1724	The Akwamu and Fante campaigned against Agona. The Dutch took Gross Friedrichsburg, at Princestown, from John Konny, an Ahanta chief and merchant.
1726	The Asante began a war with Wassa.
1730	The Akyem and their allies defeated Akwamu and forced the Akwamu across the Volta.
1731	The Concord of Abotakyi created the state of Akuapem (Akwapim).

4 Dec. 1731	Ada swore allegiance to Denmark.
1734	The Danes began Fort Fredensborg at Ningo.
1735	The Akyem and Akwamu skirmished along the Volta.
1737	Troops from Dahomey (modern Benin) raided the area about Keta.
1742	Opoku Ware of Asante defeated the Akyem forces, making Asante the major power on the Gold Coast.
1744	Gonja became a tributary state to Asante.
1745	Dagomba became tributary to Asante.
1748	An attempted coup against Opoku Ware failed.
1750	Opoku Ware died and civil war broke out on the succession of Kusi Obodum as Asantehene. A war between Anlo on one side and Ada, Akuapem and Akyem Abuakwa began.
Apr. 1752	The Royal African Company was replaced by The Company of Merchants Trading to Africa.
May 1752	The Rev. Thomas Thompson arrived at Cape Coast as a missionary for the SPG.
1757	The French failed in an attempt to take Cape Coast.
1764	The Asante army crossed the Volta and was almost wiped out in an ambush by Oyo and Dahomey troops. Kusi Obodum was destooled, several tributary states rebelled against Asante, and Osei Kwadwo became the new Asantehene.
1765	Asante forces came within a few miles of Anomabo and Cape Coast, establishing a camp at Abora in Fante territory, but a shortage of food forced an Asante retreat. Coastal states formed an alliance against Asante.
1766	Philip Quaque began his missionary career for the SPG at Cape Coast.
1767	The Akyem, Akuapem and Krobo crossed the Volta to join Ada in a war with Akwamu and the Anlo.
1768	The English began Fort Apollonia at Beyin.

14 Feb. 1769	Keta and allies destroyed Ada and sold many of its people as slaves.
1772	The Asante became allies of Akwamu and Anlo in the war near the Volta.
1775-1783	The American Revolution caused conflict between the English and Dutch on the Gold Coast.
1776	The Anlo-Ada war devastated the lower Volta area.
1777	Osei Kwadwo died and was replaced by a minor, Osei Kwame, as Asantehene. A new civil war began in Asante.
26 Oct. 1780	The Anlo burned Ada, killed many people, and sold others into slavery.
Jan. 1782	Accra, Osu, Labadi, Krobo, Tema, Ningo, Ada and others along the eastern coast recognized Danish authority.
18 Apr. 1782	The English captured Fort Crevecoeur from the Dutch and demolished it.
15 Oct. 1783	The Danes began a fort near the Volta at Ada.
25 Mar. 1784	The Danes and their allies began a campaign against the Anlo, whom they defeated at Atocco on the 30th.
18 June 1784	The Danes signed a peace treaty with the Anlo.
22 June 1784	The Danes began a fort at Keta.
1785	The Asante fought Wassa, Nzema and Aowin.
1786	The Danish Governor murdered the Chief of Keta, and in return the Keta people killed the governor's assistant. Paul Erdmann Isert explored Akuapem.
1787	The Danes built a fort at Teshi, completing their control of trade along the eastern coast between Accra and the Volta.
21 Dec. 1788	Paul Erdmann Isert for Denmark signed a treaty with Akuapem by which the Danes gained use of all unused land in Akuapem. Dr. Isert founded a plantation in Akuapem, but the plantation did not last long after Isert's death.

1789	During a smallpox epidemic at Cape Coast a British surgeon inoculated over seventeen hundred persons.
1792	The Popo defeated the Anlo and killed most of the Anlo leaders.
16 Mar. 1792	The Danish King ordered an end to the slave trade by his subjects after 1 January 1803.
31 Mar. 1792	Archibald Dalzel arrived as Governor at Cape Coast Castle, a position he was to hold until 1802.
1800	Osei Tutu Kwame (Osei Bonsu) replaced Opoku Fofie as Asantehene.
1802	Denmark became the first nation to outlaw the Atlantic slave trade.
1804-1805	In a war between Akuapem and Akyem on one side and Accra and Fante on the other side, Akuapem and Akyem were victorious.
1805	The Asante defeated Assin at Kyikyiwere in the Moinsi hills. The Assin chiefs fled to the Fante.
7 Feb. 1805	George Torrane arrived at Cape Coast Castle as Governor for the Company of Merchants.
1806	The British paid Asante rent for Cape Coast and Anomabo.
1806-1807	The Asante army occupied much of the territory between Accra and the Volta. They also invaded Fante territory in pursuit of two fugitive Assin chiefs. The Dutch surrendered Fort Amsterdam at Kormantin to the Asante. Mankesim was destroyed and the British base at Anomabo was attacked.
1807	After doing great damage along the coast, the Asante army, under Osei Bonsu, was forced to retreat due to smallpox and dysentery.
March 1807	The British and the United States outlawed all dealing and trading in slaves in Africa and their transport elsewhere was declared unlawful after 1 January 1808.
1809	The Fante and their allies attacked Elmina and Accra without success.

1811	Two Asante armies marched to the coast to aid Accra and Elmina. Akuapem, Wassa, Akyem and the Fante fought the Asante forces. Fighting took place from the Pra to the Volta.
1814-1816	Fighting between Asante and her enemies on the coast continued. The Asante generally had the upper hand and allied strength weakened.
19 May 1817	An English expedition under Frederick James and Thomas Edward Bowdich, nephew of the Governor of Cape Coast Castle, reached Kumasi to negotiate with Osei Bonsu.
7 Sept. 1817	An agreement was reached between the English and Asante to maintain peace between the two nations. A British officer would reside at Kumasi and some children of the Asantehene would be educated at Cape Coast.
1818	Denmark offered to sell its posts on the Gold Coast to the United States.
1819	Joseph Dupuis went to Kumasi to negotiate an agreement with the Asantehene.
17 Sept. 1819	The Awuna and Keta fought a battle.
23 Mar. 1820	An agreement reached by Joseph Dupuis with the Asantehene provided that the Asante and English would share jurisdiction on the coast. The English officials at Cape Coast repudiated the agreement.
7 May 1821	An Act of the English Parliament abolished the Company of Merchants Trading to Africa and transferred all its property to the crown.
3 July 1821	British posts on the Gold Coast were placed under the Governor of Sierra Leone.
April 1822	Sir Charles Macarthy arrived at Cape Coast and began to prepare for war with Asante.
Feb. 1823	A policeman under British command was executed by the Asante for insulting the Asantehene.
4 June 1823	The Asante army crossed the Pra to begin a campaign against Denkyira, Wassa, Fante and the British.
Oct. 1823	Osei Bonsu died and the Golden Stool was seized by Osei Yaw Akoto.

21 Jan. 1824	Between Bonsaso and Nsamankow in Wassa the Asante and a British force under Sir Charles Macarthy accidently met. Macarthy and eight other officers were killed and most of their soldiers also died.
May-July 1824	Fighting went on around Cape Coast.
Aug. 1824	Smallpox forced the Asante to retreat from the coast.
1825	There were frequent clashes between Asante and Akyem during the year.
7 Aug. 1826	The Asante army under Osei Yaw Akoto suffered a serius defeat at Katamanso, near Accra. The battle is sometimes called the Battle of Dodowa. The victorious forces were made up of Ga, Fante, Denkyira, Akyem, Akwamu and British forces.
1828	The British government transferred control of Gold Coast British interests to a committee of London merchants. At Cape Coast and Accra the English merchants were to elect a council, which in turn would choose a president.
Jan. 1828	Henrik Gerhard Lind was leader of a Danish expedition up the Volta.
18 Dec. 1828	The first Basel Mission arrived at Osu.
1829	Asante forces crushed a rebellion against Asante rule in Dwaben. The town was destroyed.
15 Feb. 1830	George Maclean assumed duties as President of the Council of Merchants at Cape Coast.
27 Apr. 1831	Asante agreed to peace terms with the English and English allies on the coast. Peace between Asante, and Denmark and its allies was reached during the summer.
1833	The first Methodist missionaries arrived in the Gold Coast.
1834	There was a mass migration of people from Dwaben (Juaben) into Akyem.
1 Aug. 1834	Slavery was abolished in the British Empire. The Act passed Parliament in August 1833.
1835	Assin reaffirmed its allegiance to Asante.

Chronology

11 Jan. 1835	George Maclean began a military campaign into Nzema territory.
21 Mar. 1835	Andreas Riis began work for the Basel Mission in Akuapem.
12 Jan. 1836	Akuapem defeated Krobo in a battle.
Jan. 1838	Thomas Birch Freeman began his long missionary career for the Wesleyans at Cape Coast.
1839	Thomas Birch Freeman established a Wesleyan mission at Kumasi. It lasted until 1872.
1841-1844	The Asante conducted a campaign against Gonja.
1843	The Basel Mission established schools at Osu and Akuropon. The Mission imported 24 people from Jamaica as a nucleus for a Christian community in Akuapem. At the same time the missionaries introduced coffee seeds from the West Indies into Akuapem. The British government resumed control of English posts on the Gold Coast from the Committee of Merchants.
1844	Danish posts east of the Volta were besieged by the Anlo.
6 Mar. 1844	Eight coastal groups signed the Bond of 1844 by which they recognized jurisdiction of the British and outlawed human sacrifice and panyarring. More groups signed the Bond by the end of the year.
1847	The Bremen Mission (German) began work on the Gold Coast.
1848	The Basel Mission opened a seminary at Akuropon.
16 Feb. 1848	The last slaves in the Danish Gold Coast were freed by order of the King of Denmark.
1850	During the year Denmark turned over all its interests on the Gold Coast to the British.
24 Jan. 1850	Queen Victoria issued a charter to the forts and settlements on the Gold Coast which provided for a Governor and Legislative Council to govern the area between 10 degrees west and 10 degrees east longitude, subject to the Queen and her Council.

28 Jan. 1852	Aflao ended slave trading and human sacrifice.
19 Apr. 1852	A number of chiefs and elders under English jurisdiction agreed to a poll tax under what was known as the Poll Tax Ordinance of 1852. Opposition to the tax developed quickly and no real effort was made to collect the tax after 1862.
1853	The Asante invaded Assin.
26 Apr. 1853	The British established a system of courts to deal with civil and criminal cases in areas under their control.
1854	During the year there were frequent demonstrations against attempts to collect the British poll tax.
1856	The British expanded their protectorate to include Akuapem, Krobo and Krepi.
1857	Charles Bannerman established the <u>Accra Herald</u> (later the <u>West African Herald</u>) at James Town, Accra. This was the first newspaper run by Africans on the Gold Coast.
1858	There was a civil war among the Krobo. The Basel Mission attempted a cocoa crop in Akuapem.
10 May 1858	The Municipal Corporations Ordinance provided for municipal government with power to assess house taxes in British areas. The Poll Tax Ordinance was amended in a vain attempt to make it more acceptable to Africans. The District Assemblies Ordinance established District Councils in the British Protectorate. The Ordinance was disallowed the next year.
1860	Akyem Abuakwa defeated Akyem Kotoku in a war over mining rights.
10 July 1862	Accra was almost totally destroyed by an earthquake.
Mar. 1863	The Asante invaded the British Protectorate in a dispute over extradition of two fugitives from Asante territory. Economic activities along the coast were severely dislocated.
25 Oct. 1864	People in the Cape Coast area protested to the British Governor that they were not British subjects

	and should not be subject to British tax without their consent.
1865	John Zimmerman finished a translation of the Bible into Ga. Ada and Anlo began a war which lasted for several years, with the British eventually siding with Ada and the Asante supporting Anlo.
14 Apr. 1865	The leader of Winneba and other Africans petitioned the British for continued British protection.
24 Aug. 1865	A British Parliamentary Report recommended gradual British withdrawal from the Gold Coast.
1866	The Ada-Anlo War was general in the Volta area.
19 Feb. 1866	British Gold Coast interests were returned to the jurisdiction of authorities in Sierra Leone.
5 Mar. 1867	The British and Dutch agreed to exchange their posts on the Gold Coast to separate their jurisdictions at the Sweet River, just east of Elmina. They also agreed to establish common tariffs. The transfer would take place at the start of the next year.
21 Mar. 1867	The British deposed King John Aggery of Cape Coast, abolished his position, and announced that in the future the people of Cape Coast would elect a headman, who would have to swear allegiance to England.
27 Apr. 1867	Asantehene Kwaku Dua I died. His successor was thirty-five year old Kofi Karikari.
28 Aug. 1867	Akwamu and England reached an agreement of amity and commerce.
1868	Attempts to transfer English posts at Komenda to Dutch control raised a storm of protest. A meeting at Mankesim formed an alliance of Africans to resist transfer of Komenda, Dixcove, Sekondi and Beyin to the Dutch. The alliance became the Fante Confederation.
1 Feb. 1868	The Dutch bombarded Komenda.
Fall 1868	The Asante army crossed Akyem and invaded Krepi.
1869	The Asante armies threatened the whole coastal area.

17 May 1869	British officials warned that they were not responsible for the defense of peoples outside their coastal posts.
9 June 1869	The Asante captured Anum and Ho and took several Europeans prisoner.
13 Aug. 1869	A meeting was held in Accra to try to form an alliance with the Fante to resist Asante expansion.
25 Aug. 1869	The Fante Confederation held a meeting in Mankesim to discuss the Asante threats.
Oct. 1869	An Asante army reached the coast at Axim. The Krepi held out on Gemi hill against Asante, Akwamu and Anlo forces.
Nov. 1869	The Dutch proposed to turn over all their Gold Coast interests to the British.
19 Dec. 1870	African leaders in Elmina protested proposed transfer of Elmina from the Dutch to British.
18 Nov. 1871	Fante leaders adopted a constitution for a Fante Confederation at Mankesim.
30 Nov. 1871	British authorities at Cape Coast arrested a number of Fante leaders who had played a role in the creation of the Fante Confederation. The British Colonial Office later ordered the release of these persons.
12 Feb. 1872	British authorities at Cape Coast issued a proclamation warning against anyone taking office under the Fante Confederation and condemning the Constitution of the Confederation.
17 Feb. 1872	The Dutch agreed to turn over their Gold Coast possessions to the English.
20 Feb. 1872	The Asante demanded that the British pay a ransom for the release of European hostages held in Kumasi.
6 Apr. 1872	Elmina Castle was transferred to the British by the Dutch. Within a short time Axim, Dixcove and Sekondi were also transferred to English control.
30 July 1872	Fante leaders, meeting at Mankesim, selected their leaders.

9 Dec. 1872	The Asante army left Kumasi in a move to protect their interests on the coast.
9 Feb. 1873	The Asante defeated an allied army in Assin and continued their advance toward the coast.
6 June 1873	Fante leaders appealed for British protection.
2 Oct. 1873	Major General Sir Garnet Wolseley (called "Sagrenti" by Africans) arrived at Cape Coast to organize forces against the Asante.
22 Dec. 1873	The Asante army began a retreat to Kumasi.
Jan. 1874	Forces under Wolseley began the advance toward Kumasi.
1 Feb. 1874	Bekwai was destroyed by forces under Wolseley.
4 Feb. 1874	The allied army entered Kumasi. The next day the palace was blown up and Kumasi was burned. By the 19th Wolseley was back at Cape Coast, and on 4 March he sailed for England.
13 Feb. 1874	A treaty of peace was signed at Fomena between the Asante and British.
22 June 1874	By the Treaty of Dzelukofe Anlo recognized British control east of the Volta.
July 1874	During the summer many areas began to resist Asante rule.
24 July 1874	The British established the Gold Coast Colony (including Lagos) under a governor, executive council and legislative council. The seat of government was established at Accra.
6 Aug. 1874	An Order in Council empowered the Gold Coast Legislative Council to legislate for all areas on the Gold Coast under British protection.
21 Oct. 1874	Kofi Karikari was deposed as Asantehene. Later in the year Mensa Bonsu, a younger brother of Kofi Karikari, was elected Asantehene.
17 Dec. 1874	The British Gold Coast government emancipated all pawns and slaves in areas under their jurisdiction.
12 Sept. 1875	The Asante army attacked Dwaben, which had broken from Asante control.

3 Nov. 1875	The Dwaben were defeated by Asante and fled southward to refuge in Akyem Abuakwa, where they settled about Koforidua.
7 Dec. 1875	Marie-Joseph Bonnat set out up the Volta with five canoes and twenty-seven men on a journey to Salaga. Bonnat was an Asante agent.
1876	The Wesleyans opened a secondary school at Cape Coast. In time this school would unite with other schools to become Mfantsipim.
30 Jan. 1876	Marie-Joseph Bonnat and British Special Commissioner Dr. V.S. Gouldsbury reached Salaga. Each man hoped to control trade through Salaga.
8 Mar. 1876	Dr. Gouldsbury signed a commercial treaty for the British with Kete Krakye.
1877	Marie-Joseph Bonnat joined a company to prospect for gold along the Ankobra river. Geraldo de Lema and the Anlo were active in resistance to British control of trade in the Ada-Keta area. Geraldo de Lema had been active along the lower Volta since 1862.
19 Mar. 1877	The British formally moved their seat of government from Cape Coast to Christiansborg.
1878	Tetteh Quashie introduced cocoa seedlings from Fernando Po to Akuapem. His first harvest was in 1883.
Jan. 1878	A.B. Ellis was appointed District Commissioner of the Keta District with orders to stop the smuggling activities of Geraldo de Lema and the Anlo.
Dec. 1879	The British extended their jurisdiction around the Keta Lagoon as far as Aflao.
2 Sept. 1880	The British created the Volta River District with jurisdiciton over Krobo, Akuapem, Shai and Krepi.
1881	The British protected a member of the Gyaman royal family against the Asante, causing Asantehene Mensa Bonsu to lose face.
May 1881	A Roman Catholic Mission was established at Elmina.
15 Oct. 1881	Captain R. La Touche Lonsdale began his trip to Kumasi, Salaga and Yendi. He reached Salaga on Christmas Day and continued on to Yendi.

1882	A District Commissioner was assigned to keep order in the gold fields around Tarkwa by the British.
May 1882	The British provided for general and local boards of education, and for inspectors of schools for the Gold Coast.
1883	The Public Labor Ordinance provided powers for the British to recruit paid African labor.
15 Jan. 1883	A reenactment of the Native Jurisdiction Ordinance of 1878 based the powers of African chiefs and tribunals on English authority.
8 Mar. 1883	Mensa Bonsu was destooled and banished from Kumasi. This touched off a long period of anarchy in Asante.
1884	Germans entered eastern Dagomba.
27 Apr. 1884	Kwaku Dua II was enstooled as Asantehene, but he died of smallpox seventy-one days later.
24 June 1884	Former Asantehene Kofi Karikari died suddenly.
5 July 1884	The Germans announced a protectorate over Togoland.
1885	The first cocoa was exported from the Gold Coast. By 1911 the Gold Coast was the world's largest producer of cocoa.
7 Jan. 1885	The British arrested Geraldo de Lima. He was rescued by Anlo friends but soon recaptured. The British held him at Elmina from May 1885 to the end of 1893.
Dec. 1885	Adansi was restored to Asante rule. They rebelled early the next year and were forced to flee south of the Pra for British protection.
1886	The Liverpool-Accra submarine cable began operation.
13 Jan. 1886	Lagos was separated from the Gold Coast. Organization of the Legislative Council was changed to allow for four nominated unofficial members, two European and two African.
12 May 1886	Gottlob Adolf Krause left Accra on his northward trip, which would take him almost to the Niger river.

14 July 1886	The British and Germans reached an agreement on the border between the Gold Coast and Togoland.
24 July 1886	Edmund Bannerman and others began a campaign in Accra to raise funds to send a deputation to London to protest actions of the colonial officials in Gold Coast.
27 July 1886	Akwamu became part of the protectorate as part of the Gold Coast.
7 Oct. 1886	Krepi formally submitted to Gold Coast rule.
Dec. 1886	Anti-Christian riots occurred in Akyem Abuakwa.
1887	A civil war created anarchy in Asanteland.
18 Feb. 1887	Sefwi signed a treaty for protection with the British at Wiawso.
1888	John M. Sarbah became the first African member of the Gold Coast Legislative Council. Captain Kurt Von François visited Yendi, Karaga, Gambaga and other places north of Salaga for the Germans.
14 Mar. 1888	The English and Germans agreed upon a neutral zone north of the Daka river.
26 Mar. 1888	Agyeman Prempe was elected Asantehene, ending a four-year interregnum. He could not be formally installed as Kwaku Dua III (Prempe I) until 1894.
5 May 1888	Kwahu submitted to British protection by a treaty signed at Abetifi.
11 May 1888	A Gold Coast police officer was killed in Tavievi country. A British force caused the Tavievi to surrender on 23 June.
8 Oct. 1888	Louis Binger, a French explorer, reached Salaga from the north.
1889	The Fante National Political Society was formed at Cape Coast. This was one of the earliest nationalist movements on the Gold Coast.
10 Aug. 1889	The French and British reached their first agreement defining the boundary of the Gold Coast and Ivory Coast.
1890	A Department of Roads and a Department for Education were created by the Gold Coast Colony.

1 July 1890	The Heligoland Agreement between Germany and England further demarked the boundaries between Togo and the Gold Coast, leaving Ho, Kpandu and part of Peki in German hands.
25 Nov. 1890	Atebubu recognized British protection.
1891	The first Gold Coast census showed a population of 764,185 for the Colony. A Department of Telegraph and a Department of Prisons were established.
26 June 1891	The British and French extended the Gold and Ivory Coast border to 9 degrees north latitude.
1892	Asante began a campaign against Nkoranza. A civil war took place in Salaga. The Krobo moved off Krobo Mountain.
25 Apr. 1892	George Ekem Ferguson began his trip into the territory north of Salaga to secure British interests in that area.
26 Aug. 1892	Nanumba signed a treaty of friendship and trade at Bimbila with the British.
12 July 1893	England and France divided Gyaman, with the chief city of Gyaman, Bonduku, going to the Ivory Coast.
Aug. 1893	The Asante defeated Nkoranza, Mo, and Abease in a battle near Kintampo.
Nov. 1893	The Asante invaded Atebubu in an attempt to destroy the Brong Confederation and open the route to Salaga for Asante traders again.
15 Nov. 1893	The British extended an offer of aid to the Brong Confederation in case of Asante threats.
1894	During the year many groups in the north signed agreements with the British. The Trade Roads Ordinance authorized chiefs to require up to six days of labor per quarter on the public roads of all their people. Coastal towns from Axim to Lome were connected by a telegraph line. The Town Councils Ordinance provided for municipal governments for Accra, Cape Coast and Sekondi, to be financed by a house tax. A bill to vest all "waste lands" in the Crown was introduced into the Legislative Council, but was withdrawn due to the great protest.

23 Feb. 1894	The British warned Asante about military operations against her neighbors and offered the Asantehene a liberal stipend to allow a British mediator to live in Kumasi and settle disputes between Asante and neighbors.
12 Apr. 1894	Bona signed a trade and friendship treaty with the British.
4 May 1894	The Dagaba (Dagarti) signed a treaty with the British at Wa.
28 May 1894	The Mamprusi signed a treaty with the British at Gambaga.
4 June 1894	Kwaku Dua III (Prempe I) was enstooled.
2 July 1894	The Mossi signed a treaty with the British at Ouagadougou (Upper Volta).
25 Nov. 1894	The Germans executed the chief priest of Dente in Krakye.
1895	The Wesleyans opened a secondary school for girls at Aburi.
28 Mar. 1895	A delegation from Asante left the Gold Coast for England to protest British policy against Asante. The Asante delegation was not received in London.
8 Apr. 1895	William Edward Maxwell replaced Brandford Griffith as governor of the Gold Coast.
23 Sept. 1895	Governor Maxwell sent an ultimatum to the Asantehene demanding that the Asante consent to a British resident in Kumasi.
18 Oct. 1895	The Adansi signed a treaty for protection with the British.
17 Jan. 1896	British forces occupied Kumasi.
20 Jan. 1896	The Asantehene and many of his chiefs were arrested. Prempe and many of those close to him were soon sent into exile.
14 Aug. 1896	The British established a garrison of African soldiers at Kintampo.
16 Aug. 1896	The British proclaimed a protectorate over Asanteland.

Chronology

1 Dec. 1896	A demonstration against the house tax took place in Accra.
4 Dec. 1896	The Germans defeated a Dagomba army at Adibo, and the following day the Germans destroyed Yendi.
24 Dec. 1896	British troops under Donald Stewart occupied Gambaga.
1897	The Obuasi gold mines were opened. The Bank of British West Africa opened a branch in Accra. A branch in Kumasi was opened in 1908. The British tried again to get a bill to vest unused lands in the Crown through the Legislative Council, but opposition again forced the measure to be withdrawn. The debate gave rise to the Aborigines' Rights Protection Society (ARPS).
14 Mar. 1897	The French and their allies defeated Babatu and his Zabrama (Zabarima) forces at Gandiaga.
29 Mar. 1897	British forces under Francis B. Henderson clashed with the forces of Samori Toure. Troops of Samori had been along the Black Volta over a year.
7 Apr. 1897	George E. Ferguson was killed near Wa during a battle between the British and Samori's forces.
20 Apr. 1897	The French and British at Yariba reached a temporary agreement on boundaries for their spheres of control in what would become Upper Volta and the Northern Territories of Gold Coast.
May 1897	The Aborigines' Rights Protection Society was organized at Cape Coast.
23 June 1897	French forces defeated Babatu at Doucie.
Oct. 1897	The British began a campaign to end the influence of the Zabrama. By June of the following year Zabrama power had been broken.
1898	The African Methodist Episcopal Zion Church was founded in Cape Coast. It was the first independent Christian denomination on the Gold Coast run solely by Africans.
1 Jan. 1898	The Aborigines' Rights Protection Society began to publish The Gold Coast Aborigines at Cape Coast.

4 May 1898	A mass meeting to oppose the house tax was held in Accra.
24 May 1898	The ARPS sent a delegation to London to protest land policy of the government of the Gold Coast.
14 June 1898	The French and British reached an agreement on the northern limits of British control behind the Gold Coast. Formal ratification of the agreement took place in 1899.
13 July 1898	Africans of the western Gold Coast petitioned for representation on the Legislative Council.
Aug. 1898	Construction of a railroad from Sekondi to the north began. It reached Tarkwa in 1901, Obuasi in December 1902, and Kumasi in October 1903.
5 Aug. 1898	The Colonial Office in London received the ARPS delegation protesting land policy.
14 Nov. 1899	Germany and England agreed on their borders in the north. The neutral zone was abolished. Mamprusi went to England, Dagomba was split, and Chakosi went to Germany.
5 Feb. 1900	Cecil Hamilton Armitage arrived in Asante with Hausa troops in search of the Golden Stool, which could not be found.
25 Mar. 1900	Governor Frederic Mitchell Hodgson arrived in Kumasi.
28 Mar. 1900	Governor Hodgson announced that the Asantehene would never be allowed to return to Kumasi, that the Asante were responsible for public work, and the Governor demanded the Golden Stool.
31 Mar. 1900	The Asante went to war with the British in what is called the Yaa Asantewa War, after the queenmother of Ejisu who was one of the leaders against Hodgson and the British occupation of Asante.
15 Apr. 1900	The chiefs of Kumasi demanded a return of Prempe, restoration of the slave trade, an end to conscript labor and the expulsion of all foreigners from Kumasi.
25 Apr. 1900	The siege of the British fort in Kumasi began.
23 June 1900	Governor Hodgson and others escaped from Kumasi.

15 July 1900	The siege of the fort at Kumasi was broken and most of the rebellion collapsed but some resistance continued until the end of the year.
26 Sept. 1901	Asante and the Northern Territories were annexed to the British crown under the Governor of the Gold Coast effective as of 1 January 1902.
1902	A Department of Native Affairs was created in the Gold Coast Colony administrative organization. Governor Matthew Nathan imported a steam automobile, the first to be used on the Gold Coast. The next year the first gasoline internal combustion engine was introduced.
1 Jan. 1902	The Gold Coast officially became the Colony, Asante and the Northern Territories.
May 1906	The White Fathers began their mission at Navorongo. They opened a school the following year.
1907	Tamale and Wa were connected to the coast by telegraph. British headquarters in the Northern Territory was moved from Gambaga to Tamale and changed from a military to civil status. At the time Tamale had a population of 1,435.
11 Nov. 1907	The first Motor Traffic Ordinance was enacted for the Gold Coast.
1908	There was an outbreak of bubonic plague in Accra.
1909	A government Training College for Teachers and a government Technical School were opened in Accra. Government schools were opened at Kumasi and at Tamale.
21 Sept. 1909	The official date for the birthday of Kwame Nkrumah in Nkroful, Nzema (Apollonia). In his autobiography Nkrumah says the date was 1912.
1910	The first public water hydrants were installed in Accra.
13 Sept. 1911	A bill to establish forest reserves was enacted by the Legislative Council, but dropped because of ARPS opposition.
1912	Government schools were opened in Gambaga and at Sunyani. A railroad was completed between Tarkwa and Prestea.

1914	Prophet Harris spent three months preaching in Nzema. Manganese was discovered at Nsuta.
4 Aug. 1914	Britain declared war on Germany.
14 Aug. 1914	Yendi, capital of Dagomba, was occupied by the Northern Territories Constabulary.
26 Aug. 1914	German forces in Togoland surrendered to an Anglo-French force. The area was divided between the two allied powers.
Sept. 1916	Governor Hugh Clifford announced the "Clifford Constitution." The Legislative Council was enlarged to twenty-one members: twelve official and nine unofficial members. Three of the unofficial would be paramount chiefs, and three others would be Africans.
2 Feb. 1918	The Gold Coast Leader issued the call which was to bring about the organization of the National Congress of British West Africa (NCBWA).
11 Nov. 1918	World War I ended.
1919	An influenza epidemic, which had started in Europe in 1918, killed thousands on the Gold Coast. Diamonds were discovered near the Birim River not far from Kibi. Electricity was installed at Sekondi. Accra got electricity in 1921 and Kumasi in 1927.
6 May 1919	The Supreme Council of the League of Nations assigned Togoland as a mandate to the British and French. This action was confirmed by the whole League 20 July 1922.
28 June 1919	Germany renounced its claims to Togoland when it signed the Treaty of Peace at Versailles.
10 July 1919	The Milner-Simon Declaration fixed the boundary between British and French Togoland. The English-mandated part covered 13,000 square miles.
9 Oct. 1919	Frederick Gordon Guggisberg arrived in Accra as the new Governor of the Gold Coast.
30 Oct. 1919	Governor Guggisberg met in Kumasi with the Kumasi Council of Chiefs and listened sympathetically to their requests that Prempe be returned from exile.

17 Nov. 1919	Governor Guggisberg presented his Ten Year Development Program to the Legislative Council. He called for improved transportation, education, health care, utilities, port facilities, prisons, and for more Africans in government service.
1920	Sampson Opon, from near Dormaa, began a religious revival in Asante which caused great excitement.
15-28 Mar. 1920	The National Congress of British West Africa held its first conference in Accra.
23 Feb. 1920	Governor Guggisberg outlined his educational reforms to the Legislative Council.
5 Mar. 1920	The Governor's Committee on Educational Matters recommended that education at the local level on the Gold Coast be in the local vernacular.
1921	An Anthropological Department was organized for Asante under Robert S. Rattray.
23 June 1921	Governor Guggisberg announced a plan to speed replacement of Europeans by Africans in government service.
1923	The railroad from Accra to Kumasi was completed. Construction had started in 1905.
11 Oct. 1923	The northern part of the Togo mandate was placed under the Northern Territories for administration and the southern part of the mandate was to be administered as part of the Colony.
1924	Wesleyan College was opened at Kumasi. Korle Bu Hospital was opened in Accra.
11 Nov. 1924	Prempe returned to the Gold Coast from exile.
8 Apr. 1925	The Constitution of 1925 provided for fifteen official and fourteen unofficial members for the Legislative Council. Accra, Cape Coast and Sekondi each were allowed to elect a member. Six paramount chiefs were to be selected by provincial councils--nine elected Africans. The Provincial Councils of Chiefs were officially created for the three provinces of the Colony. The Constitution was published in the <u>Gold Coast Gazette</u> on 10 December 1925.
1926	The British Under-Secretary for Colonies recom-

	mended that the railroad be extended from Kumasi to Navrongo.
17 May 1926	The Provincial Councils of Chiefs met for the first time in face of considerable opposition from educated Africans.
11 Nov. 1926	Prempe was installed as Kumasihene.
1927	The Central Province railroad from the Sekondi-Tarkwa line in Huni Valley to Kade was completed. A new road from Krakye to Atebubu was finished.
Jan. 1927	Prince of Wales (Achimota) College was opened, offering courses from kindergarten through college. Work on the school had begun in 1924.
19 Apr. 1927	Nana Ofori Atta introduced the Native Administration Ordinance in the Legislative Council. This was the first time that a bill had been offered by an unofficial member. The bill defined powers of chiefs, stool councils, and the Provincial Councils of Chiefs. The bill aligned the Chiefs with the British government against nationalist leaders on the Gold Coast.
1928	The new harbor at Takoradi was opened.
1929	The British government established a Colonial Development Fund. The United Africa Company was created as a subsidiary to Lever Brothers. A world economic depression began.
17 Apr. 1930	The Youth Conference held its first conference at Achimota. This group would play a major role in maintaining the momentum of nationalism during the 1930s.
Fall 1930	Cacao farmers organized a boycott of the cacao market to try to keep up prices.
12 May 1931	Prempe I (Kwaku Dua III) died.
22 June 1931	Kwame Kyeretwie was elected as Kumasihene.
24 Sept. 1931	A call for an income tax to meet the financial crisis was answered with new demands for equal representation in the government and with demonstrations in several coastal towns.
1932	Chiefs and councilors in the Northern Territories became salaried officials of the government.

20 Sept. 1932	Various Wesleyan groups combined to form the Gold Coast Methodist Church.
24 Apr. 1933	The Kumasihene was installed as Asantehene Osei Agyeman Otumfuo, Prempe II.
23 June 1933	The Accra Brewery was opened to produce Club Beer. This was the first brewery in all West Africa. It was also the first nontraditional industry to open on the Gold Coast.
1934	The Chief Commissioner of the Northern Territories became a member of the Gold Coast Executive Council. The Waterworks Ordinance and the Sedition Ordinance both passed in the Legislative Council with a clear division of African and European members on the votes. Both laws stirred up widespread protests.
1935	Station ZOY, Accra, became the first radio station on the Gold Coast. The Executive Council of Gold Coast Colony was empowered to act for Asante and the Northern Territories. Achimota produced its first university graduates. The Asante Confederacy was restored.
Oct. 1937	Cacao farmers began a boycott of European firms buying cacao. The hold-up lasted until the next April in Akuapem and Akyem Abuakwa.
1938	A research station to combat cacao diseases was established at New Tafo.
1939	An earthquake did much damage in the Accra area.
3 Sept. 1939	World War II began in Europe.
21 June 1940	France fell to Germany. The Ivory Coast, Upper Volta and Togoland declared their loyalty to the Vichy government in France, and all the land borders of the Gold Coast were closed.
1941	The United States Army Air Force established an air base at the Accra airport.
1942	Ofori Atta I of Akyem Abuakwa and Kobina Arku Korsah of Saltpond were appointed the first Africans on the Governor's Executive Council.
1943	The Dunkwa to Awaso railroad was finished. It served bauxite and gold mines.

20 Aug. 1943	An Income Tax Ordinance finally was enacted by the Legislative Council.
1944	A teacher training college was opened in Tamale. The Youth Conference launched a major campaign for changes in the Gold Coast Constitution.
4 Oct. 1944	Governor Alan Burns announced planning for a new constitution after the war.
7 May 1945	World War II ended in Europe.
26 July 1945	The Labor Party won a landslide victory in the British elections.
29 Mar. 1946	The Burns Constitution was announced. The Gold Coast became the first British African colony with a majority for Africans in the Legislative Council. The Asanteman council of chiefs would elect four members, and Kumasi would elect a member.
23 July 1946	Governor Burns opened the new Legislative Council.
Dec. 1946	A council of chiefs was established in the Northern Territories for the first time.
13 Dec. 1946	The UN approved the British Togoland Trusteeship.
24 Mar. 1947	Three men were executed for their 1944 role in a ritual murder on the occasion of the funeral of Sir Ofori Atta at Kibi.
4 Aug. 1947	The United Gold Coast Convention (UGCC) was inaugurated at Saltpond.
16 Dec. 1947	Kwame Nkrumah returned to the Gold Coast after many years' absence in the US and England to become general secretary to the UGCC.
1948	The University College of the Gold Coast was established with classes to be held at Achimota until a campus was built at Legon.
26 Jan. 1948	A boycott of imported goods from Europe was initiated under the leadership of Nii Bonne. The boycott climaxed at the end of February with riots and the looting of stores. Several people were killed, many were injured, and much property was damaged or destroyed.

20 Feb. 1948	J.B. Danquah and Kwame Nkrumah spoke to a mass rally at the Palladium Cinema in Accra.
28 Feb. 1948	Rioting began along Christiansborg Road in Accra and spread throughout the Gold Coast. It did not subside until the middle of March. On the first day of the riots Sergeant Cornelius F. Adjetey and two other veterans were killed by police.
12 Mar. 1948	Six leaders of the UGCC were arrested and sent to the Northern Territories. Nkrumah and Danquah were among the arrested.
15 Apr. 1948	J.B. Danquah proposed that the name of the country be changed from the Gold Coast to Ghana.
June 1948	A British commission under the direction of Andrew Aiken Watson issued a report on the causes of the February riots. It recommended that the people of the Gold Coast be allowed to write their own constitution and that educational developments be greatly accelerated.
3 Sept. 1948	Kwame Nkrumah established the <u>Accra Evening News</u>.
Jan. 1949	An All-African committee under Sir Henley Coussey was established to prepare new constitutional recommendations.
14 Mar. 1949	The Coussey Committee began its meetings.
12 June 1949	After a conflict with the leadership of UDCC, Nkrumah announced the formation of the Convention People's Party (CPP). Nkrumah called for "Self-Government Now."
29 June 1949	Charles Arden-Clarke was appointed Governor of the Gold Coast.
10 Oct. 1949	Governor Arden-Clarke appointed Emmanuel Charles Quist as President of the Legislative Council of the Gold Coast Colony and Asante.
23 Oct. 1949	Nkrumah addressed a crowd at the West End Arena in Accra on "What I Mean by Positive Action."
26 Oct. 1949	The Coussey Committee plan for a new constitution was made public. It recommended a larger Legislative Council of two houses, an Executive Council which would be responsible to the legislature and

	on which a majority of the members would be African, a new organization of local government, and a voting age of twenty-five.
20 Nov. 1949	Nkrumah convened a massive assembly at the West End Arena. He called the group the Ghana People's Representative Assembly. The group rejected the Coussey recommendations, called for the election of a constituent assembly to write a constitution and demanded immediate self-government as a British Dominion.
7 Jan. 1950	The Trades Union Congress began a strike.
8 Jan. 1950	In the West End Arena Nkrumah announced the beginning of his Positive Action campaign, calling for a general strike, a boycott of foreign business and non-cooperation with the government. Within a short time public services began to be disrupted in the larger towns of the Gold Coast.
11 Jan. 1950	Governor Arden-Clarke proclaimed an emergency.
12-13 Jan. 1950	Many demonstrators were arrested in Accra and in Sekondi-Takoradi.
17 Jan. 1950	Two policemen were killed trying to halt a march of ex-servicemen on Christiansborg.
19 Jan. 1950	The leaders of the TUC called off the General Strike.
21 Jan. 1950	Police took over CPP headquarters and arrested a number of CPP leaders. The CPP press had been banned by this time.
22 Jan. 1950	Nkrumah was arrested.
14-22 Feb. 1950	Nkrumah was tried and sentenced to three one-year terms in prison.
22 Mar. 1950	An appeal of Nkrumah's sentence was dismissed by the High Court.
Apr. 1950	The CPP won all seven seats in the Accra Municipal Council elections.
Nov. 1950	The CPP won all the seats in the Kumasi Town Council elections.
30 Dec. 1950	The new Gold Coast Constitution was published by

Chronology

                      the government. The new Legislative Assembly would have 84 members, 75 of whom would be Africans. The new Executive Council would consist of eight Africans responsible to the Assembly and three ex-officio European members.

5-10 Feb. 1951   Elections were held for the Legislative Assembly. The CPP won 34 of the 38 popularly contested seats.

12 Feb. 1951   Sentences of Nkrumah and six other members of the CPP were remitted.

13 Feb. 1951   Nkrumah was called to Christiansborg Castle and met with Governor Arden-Clarke, who told Nkrumah to form a government.

20 Feb. 1951   The new Legislative Assembly met with Nkrumah as Leader of Government Business. E.C. Quist was selected as President of the Assembly.

26 Feb. 1951   The new Executive Council was appointed. Kwame Nkrumah was Leader of Government Business and Minister without Portfolio. Six seats were alloted to members of the CPP.

4 June 1951   Nkrumah and Kojo Botsio began a visit to the US. During the visit Nkrumah received an honorary doctorate from his alma mater, Lincoln University.

Nov. 1951   The Local Government Ordinance ended most of the powers of chiefs over local affairs.

1952   The College of Arts, Science and Technology was established at Kumasi. The Gold Coast began a program to build sixteen new teacher-training colleges.

10 Mar. 1952   The Constitution was amended to provide for a prime minister, to be nominated by the governor and confirmed by the Assembly. The Executive Council would become a Cabinet with the governor to serve as president of the Cabinet.

21 Mar. 1952   In a secret ballot Nkrumah was elected Prime Minister by the Assembly, 45-31, with eight abstentions.

19 Oct. 1952   The Gold Coast Legislative Assembly voted to create the Bank of the Gold Coast.

10 July 1953   Nkrumah made his "Motion of Destiny" to the As-

	sembly. The Assembly approved the motion requesting independence within the Commonwealth "as soon as the necessary constitutional arrangements are made."
7-8 Dec. 1953	The Sixth Pan-African Conference met in Kumasi to consider speeding the liberation of Africa and the creation of a West African Federation. Nkrumah and Nnamdi Azikiwe attended the conference.
10-11 Apr. 1954	The Northern People's Party was created.
28 Apr. 1954	Constitutional changes were announced. Indirect elections were ended and seats in the Legislative Assembly were increased to 104. There would be an all-African Cabinet.
11 May 1954	The railroad from Achimota to Tema and from Tema to the Shai Hills was formally opened.
15 June 1954	The first elections under the 1954 Constitution were held. The CPP won 72 out of 104 seats in an election contested by seven parties.
12 Aug. 1954	The Legislative Assembly called the government to ban all political parties based on racial or religious principals.
14 Aug. 1954	An Act fixing the price of Cocoa passed the Assembly, causing great discontent in Asante.
19 Sept. 1954	The National Liberation Movement (NLM) began in Asante.
21 Oct. 1954	The Asantehene and his Council adopted a resolution endorsing the idea of a federal form of government for the Gold Coast.
17 Dec. 1954	The Asante Council rejected an offer by Nkrumah to hold a round-table conference on federalism.
Jan. 1955	Several people were killed and many arrested in acts of violence in Kumasi.
7 Jan. 1955	The Governor banned carrying arms in Asante.
9 Mar. 1955	The Northern People's Party endorsed the concept of federalism.
27 July 1955	A select committee appointed by the government in April to study the form of government the Gold

	Coast should have after independence rejected federalism in favor of a centralized form of government. The Assembly endorsed this report on 9 August.
12 Aug. 1955	Asante and the Northern Territories submitted proposals for a federal constitution to the Governor.
26 Sept. 1955	Sir Frederick Bourne arrived in Accra to advise the government on organization of constitutional matters.
9 Oct. 1955	An official of the CPP killed an official of the NLM in Kumasi, touching off violence which lasted in Asante for many weeks.
16 Nov. 1955	The Legislative Assembly gave lesser chiefs in Asante the right to appeal from the Asante Council direct to the Governor in constitutional disputes.
23 Dec. 1955	Sir Frederick Bourne recommended that the independence constitution should provide a "substantial transfer of power from the centre to the regions."
1956	The opening of the railroad from Achiasi, on the Central Province line, to Kotoku, on the Accra-Kumasi line, made it possible to go from Tema and Accra to Sekondi-Takoradi without going by Kumasi.
1 Jan. 1956	Nkrumah called for a conference to study the report made by Sir Frederick Bourne on the new constitution.
17 Feb. 1956	The Achimota Conference on the Bourne Conference began. It lasted until 16 March. The Asante Council and the NLM refused to take part in the meeting.
18 Apr. 1956	Sir Kobina Arku Korsah became the first African Chief Justice of the Gold Coast.
19 Apr. 1956	Nkrumah published his blueprint for an independence constitution. He suggested that the new nation should be called "Ghana," that there should be a centralized form of government, and that Brong should be separated from Asante.
9 May 1956	A plebiscite on union with the Gold Coast was held in the British-mandated section of Togo. The voters approved unification by overwhelming margins everywhere except in the southern Ewe section.

11 May 1956	The British Secretary for Colonies called for a general election to resolve the constitutional impasse in the Gold Coast. After the election the question of the form of government would be left to the new Assembly.
17 July 1956	In general elections the CPP won 71 of 104 seats in the new Assembly.
3 Aug. 1956	The Legislative Assembly voted for independence within the Commonwealth under the name of Ghana by a vote of 72 out of 104.
23 Aug. 1956	Nkrumah requested that the British government set a date for independence.
18 Sept. 1956	The British Colonial Secretary announced that independence would be granted 6 March 1957.
16 Oct. 1956	A conference in Accra on the form of government for independent Ghana could reach no agreement. Asante and the Northern Territories now demanded a federal form that would recognize their separate identities.
15 Nov. 1956	The Assembly endorsed Nkrumah's unitary form of constitution by 70 to 25 votes.
20 Nov. 1956	The NLM and NPP sent a resolution to the Secretary for Colonies demanding separate independence for Asante and the Northern Territories.
10 Dec. 1956	The British Colonial Office issued a statement in opposition to the division of the Gold Coast.
18 Dec. 1956	The Ghana Independence Bill passed in the British House of Commons. It became law 7 February 1957.
Jan. 1957	The Bridge at Adomi became the first to span the main Volta.
26 Jan. 1957	The Secretary for Colonies came to the Gold Coast in an attempt to resolve the constitutional predicament. Before he left he talked to all the major factions.
8 Feb. 1957	The Colonial Office published the draft of a compromise constitution.
12 Feb. 1957	Both Nkrumah and Busia endorsed the draft as proposed by the British government.

13 Feb. 1957	It was announced that the Queen would appoint Governor Charles Arden-Clarke as first Governor-General after independence.
21 Feb. 1957	Prime Minister Harold Macmillan announced that all Commonwealth prime ministers had approved of independence and membership in the Commonwealth for Ghana.
22 Feb. 1957	The Queen approved the new constitution, to become effective 6 March.
6 Mar. 1957	Independence Day. The Gold Coast Colony became the independent nation of Ghana within the British Commonwealth.
8 Mar. 1957	Ghana became the 81st member of the United Nations.
11 June 1957	Kojo Botsio announced the formation of a national merchant marine line, the Black Star Line.
22 July 1957	The Deportation Act gave the government power to deport any foreigner whose presence in Ghana was not conducive to the public good.
7 Sept. 1957	Geoffrey Bing, former Labor member of the British Parliament, was appointed Attorney-General of Ghana.
13 Oct. 1957	Three opposition parties and several regional groups joined in forming the United Party (UP) under the leadership of Kofi Busia, Simon Dombo, Joe Appiah and Joseph Danquah.
Nov. 1957	All local and ethnic organizations were made illegal and tribalism was declared a criminal offence.
13 Nov. 1957	William Francis Hare, Earl of Listowel, member of the British Labor party, and Minister of State for Colonial Affairs, was sworn in as Ghana's second and last Governor-General.
Dec. 1957	The Avoidance of Discrimination Act outlawed all parties based on religious considerations.
30 Dec. 1957	Kwame Nkrumah married an Egyptian student, in part a symbolic gesture of unity with Muslims.
14 Mar. 1958	The government approved a new national anthem selected from entries in a national competition.

15-22 Apr. 1958	The first Conference of Independent States of Africa met in Accra.
21 May 1958	The government announced a new issue of coins and currency in which the likeness of Nkrumah would replace that of the Queen.
30 May 1958	Nkrumah left Accra on a tour of the seven independent African states.
16 July 1958	Ghana Airways began international flights to London.
18 July 1958	The Preventive Detention Act gave the Government power to detain persons up to five years without trial or appeal for conduct prejudicial to the security of the state or its foreign relations.
23-26 July 1958	Nkrumah visited the United States and addressed the US Congress on the 25th.
3-7 Aug. 1958	Nkrumah visited England.
3 Sept. 1958	The government announced the Asante Stool Lands Act, which gave the central authorities in Accra control of all Asante lands and left the Asantehene a mere figurehead.
24 Sept. 1958	Ofori Atta II of Akyem Abuakwa was arrested and was forced to live in Accra until 1966.
10 Nov. 1958	Arrests of many members of the opposition United Party under the Preventive Detention Act began. They were accused of a plot to overthrow the government.
23 Nov. 1958	Nkrumah and Sekou Toure announced the formation of the Ghana-Guinea Union.
5-13 Dec. 1958	Kojo Botsio served as Chairman of the first All-African People's Conference, which met in Accra. The conference was organized as the successor to the Pan-African meetings of earlier times.
24 Dec. 1958	Nkrumah left for a tour of India.
26 Jan. 1959	Nkrumah began a tour of Nigeria that lasted until 6 February.
21 Feb. 1959	The government introduced an amendment to the Constitution dissolving regional assemblies.

Apr. 1959	The Brong-Ahafo Region was created from Asante.
6 Apr. 1959	A law expelled any member of the National Assembly who was detained under the Preventive Detention Act.
May 1959	Nkrumah and Sekou Toure announced the Ghana-Guinea Union. Mali would join later.
29 June 1959	A Stool Lands Act took over all stool lands in Akyem Abuakwa. Kofi A. Busia reached England and exile. Later he was expelled from the Assembly and S.D. Dombo became leader of the opposition.
19 July 1959	Ghana, Guinea and Liberia signed an agreement to create the Community of Independent African States.
25 Sept. 1959	A Bureau of African Affairs was created in Accra.
4 Oct. 1959	George Padmore, Nkrumah's adviser on African Affairs who had died 23 September, was buried at Christiansborg Castle.
10 Nov. 1959	A number of the leaders of the UP in Asante, including the senior linguist to the Asantehene, were detained under the Preventive Detention Act.
Mar. 1960	Frantz Fanon was named representative of the Algerian Provisional Government in Accra.
6 Mar. 1960	Nkrumah announced plans for a new constitution which would turn Ghana into a republic. The draft provided for eventual surrender of Ghanaian sovereignty to a union of African States.
15 Mar. 1960	The draft republican constitution was approved by the National Assembly, 75 votes to 10.
19, 23, 27 Apr. 1960	A presidential election and plebiscite on the new constitution took place. Nkrumah, as CPP candidate, defeated J.B. Danquah, UP candidate, 1,016,076 to 124,623. The republican constitution was ratified overwhelmingly.
29 June 1960	The Regions of Ghana Act adjusted the boundaries of all the regions and created the Central Region from the Western Region and the Upper Region from the Northern Region.
30 June 1960	Ghana established a special office in Leopoldville

	(Kinshasa), the Congo (Zaire), from which to oversee the birth of the new nation.
1 July 1960	The Ghanaian Republic was inaugurated with Kwame Nkrumah as first President.
16 July 1960	Ghanaian troops joined other UN troops in the Congo. In five weeks 2,394 Ghanaians were in the Congo.
8 Aug. 1960	Patrice Lumumba visited Accra and he and Nkrumah formed an alliance and vowed to fight on together against Belgium if the UN withdrew from the Congo.
25 Aug. 1960	Accra attempted to establish a policy for succession to the skin (throne) of Dagomba.
23 Sept. 1960	Nkrumah addressed the UN on the Congo and other world problems.
1 Oct. 1960	The President's Own Guard Regiment was established.
6 Dec. 1960	Ghana broke diplomatic relations with Belgium on the Congo issue.
24 Dec. 1960	Mali announced that it had joined Ghana and Guinea in their union.
Jan. 1961	The Third Battalion of the Ghanaian Army in the Congo mutinied and its Commander, Colonial David Hansen, was severely beaten.
3-7 Jan. 1961	Presidents Nkrumah of Ghana, Toure of Guinea and Keita of Mali met with North African leaders at Casablanca to develop a strategy in support of Patrice Lumumba as opposed to Joseph Kasavubu in the Congolese struggle.
17 Jan. 1961	Lumumba died near Elizabethville in the Congo.
15 Feb. 1961	Ghana recognized the Stanleyville government of Antoine Gizenga in the Congo.
7 Mar. 1961	Nkrumah addressed the General Assembly of the UN in New York on the Congo situation.
8 Apr. 1961	Nkrumah, in a famous Dawn Broadcast, promised to clean the CPP of corruption. This marked the beginning of a campaign against the old guard of the CPP.

22 Apr. 1961	Nkrumah made an address to the CPP Study Group on Building a Socialist State.
27-29 Apr. 1961	The presidents of Ghana, Guinea and Mali met in Accra and agreed to create a union to be known as the Union of African States.
28 Apr. 1961	Ghanaian troops at Port Francqui in the Congo were attacked by Congo troops of Joseph Mobutu. Forty Ghanaian soldiers were killed.
1 May 1961	Nkrumah took full control of the CPP, assuming the offices of General Secretary, Life Chairman, and Chairman of the Central Committee.
5 May 1961	Komla Gbedemah was demoted from Finance Minister to Minister of Health. Ako Adjei signed the protocol of the African Charter for Ghana.
13 June 1961	Nkrumah began a five-day visit to Upper Volta to try to persuade President Maurice Yameogo to join the Ghana-Guinea-Mali union.
7 July 1961	A bitter battle over the new budget began in the National Assembly. The "Austerity Budget" called for higher prices, increased taxes and forced savings. Wages were to be frozen.
10-25 July 1961	Nkrumah and a large retinue visited the Soviet Union at the start of a visit to most of the communist bloc of nations.
25-28 July 1961	Nkrumah's group was in Poland.
28 July 1961	Nkrumah visited Hungary, Czechoslovakia, East Germany, Yugoslavia, Rumania, Bulgaria and Albania between 28 July and 12 August.
14-19 Aug. 1961	Nkrumah and group were in China.
21 Aug. 1961	Nkrumah began a vacation in the Crimea which lasted to the first of September.
29 Aug. 1961	A law made it an offense to insult President Nkrumah in writing, print or speech subject to imprisonment for up to three years.
1-6 Sept. 1961	Nkrumah attended a meeting of nonaligned nations in Belgrade.
4 Sept. 1961	Attempts of the government to deduct five percent

	compulsory savings from worker's wages led to a general strike. The strike began among the railway and dock workers in Sekondi-Takoradi.
6-7 Sept. 1961	The strike spread to municipal bus workers in Accra.
7-15 Sept. 1961	Nkrumah continued his vacation in the Crimea.
9 Sept. 1961	A limited state of emergency was declared in Sekondi-Takoradi.
10 Sept. 1961	Emergency crews took over trains on Kumasi routes.
12 Sept. 1961	J.B. Danquah and the Executive Committee of the United Party called upon the government to modify its economic policy.
16 Sept. 1961	Nkrumah returned to Ghana after an absence of more than two months.
17 Sept. 1961	Nkrumah ordered all striking workers back to work.
18 Sept. 1961	Petrol and motor workers in Accra went on strike.
22 Sept. 1961	The strike came to an end. Nkrumah became Supreme Commander of the Ghanaian armed forces, and all non-Ghanaian officers attached to the Ghanaian forces were relieved of their commands.
28 Sept. 1961	Nkrumah dismissed Komla Gbedemah, Kojo Botsio and other old comrades from his government and replaced them with people from the left wing of the CPP.
3 Oct. 1961	J.B. Danquah, Joe Appiah and other UP leaders plus many of the recent strike leaders were detained under the Preventive Detention Act.
10 Oct. 1961	It was announced that four hundred Ghanaian cadets would be sent to the USSR for officer training.
16 Oct. 1961	Komla Gbedemah denounced Nkrumah in the National Assembly. A few days later he and his family went into exile.
25 Oct. 1961	Ghana recognized the government of Cyrille Adoula in the Congo.
30 Oct. 1961	A special criminal division of the High Court was

	created to try offences against the safety of the State at the discretion of the President. Verdicts of this division were not subject to appeal.
4 Nov. 1961	Two bombs exploded in Accra, one damaging the statue of Nkrumah in front of Parliament House.
7 Nov. 1961	Hundreds of opponents of the CPP were arrested all over Ghana.
9-20 Nov. 1961	Queen Elizabeth visited Ghana. While in Ghana she made trips to Tamale, Kumasi, Tema, Akosombo, Aburi, Cape Coast, Elmina, and Sekondi-Takoradi.
8 Jan. 1962	Ghana and Canada concluded an agreement by which Canadian officers would advise the Ghanaian army.
10 Feb. 1962	The new harbor at Tema, begun in 1954, was officially opened. The old roadstead ports at Cape Coast, Winneba, Accra and Keta were closed.
14 Apr. 1962	Nkrumah made a speech at the Kwame Nkrumah Institute of Ideology in Winneba denouncing the civil service for obstruction and red tape.
30 Apr. 1962	The USSR awarded Nkrumah the Lenin Peace Prize for 1961.
5 May 1962	Nkrumah released many of those held under Preventive Detention and offered an amnesty to political exiles.
20 June 1962	A group of political detainees, including J.B. Danquah and Victor Owusu, were released from prison.
July 1962	The CPP's eleventh congress met in Kumasi and adopted Nkrumah's "Plan for Work and Happiness." The aim of the plan was to create "a socialist pattern of society adapted to African conditions according to the principles of Nkrumaism."
31 July 1962	Yameogo and Nkrumah met at Tenkodogo in Upper Volta.
1 Aug. 1962	At Kulungugu a grenade was thrown at Nkrumah. The explosion killed several and injured many others, but the President was not seriously hurt.
29 Aug. 1962	Foreign Minister Ako Adjei, Information Minister Tawia Adamafio, and the Executive Secretary of the

	CPP, Cofie-Crabbe, were all arrested under the Preventive Detention Act and dismissed from their posts, charged with the Kulungugu incident.
7 Sept. 1962	The National Assembly proclaimed Nkrumah to be President for life.
9 Sept. 1962	A bomb exploded near Flagstaff House, where the President lived, killing one person and injuring others. Shortly afterwards Nkrumah surrounded himself with security guards from communist bloc nations.
11 Sept. 1962	The National Assembly adopted a resolution calling for a one-party system in Ghana.
14 Sept. 1962	The death penalty for possession of unlawful firearms or explosives was voted for by the National Assembly.
18 Sept. 1962	Warrant Officer Edward Tetteh, charged with supplying the grenade used in the Kulungugu attempt on Nkrumah, committed suicide.
20 Sept. 1962	Two bombs exploded in Accra killing and injuring several persons.
22 Sept. 1962	Bombs exploded in Accra. A state of emergency with dusk to dawn curfew was imposed in Accra and Tema.
28 Sept. 1962	All news leaving Ghana was subjected to censorship.
12 Dec. 1962	Nkrumah spoke at the opening session of the First International Congress of Africanists at the University of Ghana, Legon.
8 Jan. 1963	A bomb exploded in Accra stadium shortly after Nkrumah left a CPP rally there. Over twenty were killed and more than four hundred were injured in the blast.
11 Jan. 1963	A Special Court was established to hear cases involving crimes against the security of the state. There would be no appeal from verdicts.
Mar. 1963	The National Assembly adopted a Seven-Year Development Plan for 1963-1970. This was to be the first stage of a program that would establish a full socialist state in two decades.

17 Mar. 1963	Kojo Botsio was appointed Foreign Minister. In September 1961 Botsio had been dismissed as Minister of Agriculture, and he had been obliged to resign from the National Assembly in February 1962.
17 Apr. 1963	Five persons were sentenced to be hanged for treason for the bombings of August and September 1962.
25 May 1963	Ghana became one of the charter members of the Organization of African Unity in Addis Ababa.
9 Aug. 1963	The treason trial of Ako Adjei, Tawia Adamafio, Hugh Horatio Cofie-Crabbe, and two others began before the Special Court on treason cases.
27 Aug. 1963	William E.B. Du Bois died and was buried near the wall of Christiansborg Castle.
Sept. 1963	The last Ghanaian troops were removed from the Congo.
25 Oct. 1963	Nkrumah gave the address at the opening of the Institute of African Studies at Legon.
4 Nov. 1963	The Preventive Detention Act of 1958 was extended for five more years, after heated debate, in the National Assembly.
9 Dec. 1963	Chief Justice Arku Korsah delivered the judgment of the Special Court which acquitted Ako Adjei, Tawi Adamafio and H.H. Cofie-Crabbe of charges that they were involved in the attempt to kill Nkrumah in August 1962. Two other defendants were convicted and sentenced to death.
11 Dec. 1963	Nkrumah dismissed Chief Justice Arku Korsah from office.
23 Dec. 1963	The National Assembly gave the President authority to override decisions of the Special Court.
24 Dec. 1963	Nkrumah set aside the verdict of the Special Court in the case of Adjei, Adamafio and Cofie-Crabbe and ordered a new trial.
31 Dec. 1963	Nkrumah announced a referendum would be held to make Ghana a one-party state, adopt the CPP party flag as the national flag, and give the President power to dismiss judges.

Chronology

2 Jan. 1964	Police Constable Seth Ametewee fired five shots at President Nkrumah in Flagstaff House. Nkrumah was not hurt, but a security guard was killed.
8 Jan. 1964	J.B. Danquah was arrested under the Preventive Detention Act.
24-31 Jan. 1964	A national referendum overwhelmingly approved a new flag, making Ghana a one-party state, and giving the President power to dismiss judges.
27 Jan. 1964	Nkrumah notified the University of Ghana that he was assuming full jurisdiction over the University.
8 Feb. 1964	Six members of the University of Ghana faculty, four of them Americans, were expelled from Ghana.
21 Feb. 1964	Ghana became the Convention People's Republic, a one-party state. The CPP party flag, overprinted with a black star on the center stripe, replaced the old national banner.
1 Oct. 1964	The Special Branch of the Ghana police was dissolved and its security functions were placed under the President's Security Service.
4 Feb. 1965	Dr. Joseph B. Danquah, 69, former leader of the UP and opponent of Nkrumah in the presidential election of 1960 died in prison, where he had been for more than a year.
8 Feb. 1965	The five defendants in the Kulungugu bomb attempt on Nkrumah were all sentenced to death. On 26 March, Nkrumah commuted the sentences to twenty years.
9 June 1965	CPP candidates for membership in the National Assembly were returned without contest. The membership in the Assembly was increased from 104 to 198.
10 June 1965	The new National Assembly unanimously elected Nkrumah for a second five-year term as President. Construction was begun on the 2,162-foot long bridge on the lower Volta at Sogakofe.
19 July 1965	Ghana adopted a decimal currency based on the cedi, which replaced the Ghanaian pound.
31 July 1965	The Ghana Broadcasting Service began its television transmission. Shirley Du Bois, widow of W.E.B. Du Bois, was first director of the service.

12 Aug. 1965	Professor W.E. Abraham, adviser and speechwriter to Nkrumah, became Pro Vice Chancellor of the University of Ghana, Legon.
30 Aug. 1965	The Report of the Commission of Enquiry into Trade Malpractices (The Abraham Report) was released.
31 Aug. 1965	President Nkrumah took over direct command of the armed forces and all senior officers were required to take an oath of allegiance to the President. Major Generals S.J.A. Otu and J.A. Ankrah were retired.
10 Sept. 1965	The National Assembly passed a provision which provided that any member of the Assembly that lost the support of Nkrumah could be recalled.
17 Sept. 1965	The Volta River Project began to generate electricity.
27-29 Oct. 1965	President Gamal Abdul Nasser of Egypt paid a visit to Ghana.
5 Nov. 1965	Nkrumah assumed personal charge of the Kwame Nkrumah Ideological Institute at Winneba.
22 Nov. 1965	The Ghana Trading Corporation was created.
26 Nov. 1965	The National Assembly unanimously gave Nkrumah permission to use the Ghanaian armed forces against Ian Smith's government, which had been proclaimed 11 November.
3 Dec. 1965	The $10,640,000 Accra-Tema superhighway was opened to traffic.
15 Dec. 1965	Radio Ghana reported rallies throughout the country calling for a "people's militia" to crush the white government of Rhodesia.
16 Dec. 1965	Ghana broke diplomatic relations with the United Kingdom because the British would not use military force to crush Ian Smith's government in Rhodesia.
3 Jan. 1966	A military coup occurred in Upper Volta.
15 Jan. 1966	A military coup occurred in Nigeria.
22 Jan. 1966	Nkrumah inaugurated the Volta River project at Akosombo, 65 miles (104 km) northeast of Accra.

Chronology

1 Feb. 1966	Nkrumah made what would be his last address to his National Assembly. It was his usual appeal for African unity and socialism.
21 Feb. 1966	Nkrumah left Accra for a trip to Peking and Hanoi, hoping to bring peace to Vietnam.
24 Feb. 1966	The Convention People's Republic of Ghana was overthrown by a military coup. A National Liberation Council (NLC) was established with Major-General Joseph A. Ankrah as Chairman and Commissioner of Police John W.K. Harley as Deputy Chairman. The CPP and the National Assembly were dissolved. Colonel Emmanuel K. Kotoka was promoted Major-General and became Commander of the Ghanaian Army. Nkrumah learned of his removal from office in China.
26 Feb. 1966	The NLC promised that as soon as practicable it would appoint a committee to prepare a new constitution.
1 Mar. 1966	Political parties were banned by the NLC. The NLC began to expel all Soviet and Chinese personnel from Ghana.
2 Mar. 1966	Nkrumah was welcomed to Guinea by President Sekou Toure who proclaimed Nkrumah to be co-President of Guinea.
7 Mar. 1966	The Young Pioneer Youth Movement was outlawed by the NLC.
19 Mar. 1966	Kofi Busia returned to Accra after seven years of exile.
24 Mar. 1966	The NLC placed local government in the hands of management committees which began a purge of CPP sympathizers.
5 Apr. 1966	The Preventive Detention Act was revoked.
16 June 1966	K.A. Gbedemah returned to Ghana after more than four years of exile.
23 June 1966	The NLC announced that it would dispose of many of the state corporations and farms founded in the Nkrumah period.
30 June 1966	The NLC established an advisory Political Committee with Edward Akufo-Addo as Chairman and Kofi

	Busia as Vice Chairman. Joe Appiah, Simon Dombo, William Ofori-Atta, Joseph A. Braimah and other anti-Nkrumah political figures were appointed to the committee.
1 Sept. 1966	The NLC established a Constitutional Commission to prepare proposals for a new constitution.
28 Sept. 1966	The Jiagge Commission was established to investigate assets of former members and officials of the CPP. Mrs. Annie Jiagge, Chairman, was a High Court Justice.
1 Dec. 1966	The NLC removed all chiefs enstooled during the Nkrumah period by the CPP.
15 Jan. 1967	The Apaloo Commission issued a 154-page report charging that Nkrumah accumulated assets of 2,300,000 pounds between 1951 and 1966.
30 Jan. 1967	The bridge across the lower Volta at Sogakofe was opened to traffic.
23 Feb. 1967	A new cedi was placed in circulation.
17 Apr. 1967	An attempted coup took place. A reconnaissance regiment from Ho came to Accra with plans to take over the government. Lt. General E.K. Kotoka and several other soldiers were killed before order was restored.
9 May 1967	Lieutenants Samuel Arthur and Moses Yeboah were executed at Teshie for their roles in the attempted coup of 17 April.
30 June 1967	The NLC established a twenty-one-member Executive Committee responsible for the general direction of the government. Two-thirds of the Committee were civilians, most former civil servants, educators or technocrats.
8 July 1967	The cedi was devalued in an attempt to improve Ghana's export position and to discourage imports. In relation to the US dollar the devaluation was from $1.40 for a cedi to $.98 to the cedi. This was a 33 percent drop in its value.
11 July 1967	The NLC established a National Advisory Committee to replace the earlier Political Committee. K.A. Busia was Chairman of the new Committee.

8 Dec. 1967	The Legon Observer published an article critical of the length of time courts took to hear cases.
22 Jan. 1968	Staff members of the Legon Observer were convicted of contempt of court for an article of 8 December. They were fined and released after an apology for the article.
26 Jan. 1968	The Constitutional Commission, chaired by Justice Edward Akuffo-Addo, presented its draft constitution.
27 Jan. 1968	Lt. General Joseph A. Ankrah flew to Upper Volta for a five-day official visit.
29 Jan. 1968	The NLC announced that a 140-seat Constituent Assembly would be established to debate the constitutional proposals of the Akuffo-Addo Commission. The Elections and Public Disqualification Decree banned many former CPP members from public office for ten years.
27 Mar. 1968	Head of State Ankrah paid an official visit to Togoland.
24 Apr. 1968	Most of the officials held after the coup of 24 February 1966 were released.
22 May 1968	Ankrah promised to return to civilian rule "not later than 30 September 1969."
17-25 Aug. 1968	President Sangoule Lamizana of Upper Volta paid an official visit to Ghana.
4 Sept. 1968	A nationwide strike of ports and railroad workers began.
5-10 Sept. 1968	Ankrah paid an official visit to the Ivory Coast.
10 Oct. 1968	The Ghanaian Navy seized two Soviet fishing trawlers off the coast west of Takoradi. The Russians were suspected of smuggling arms to help restore Nkrumah. The ships and crews were held until the end of February.
10-13 Oct. 1968	Ankrah paid an official visit to the United States.
12 Oct. 1968	Krobo Edusei, former minister under Nkrumah, was sentenced to eighteen months hard labor for perjury before the Jiagge Assets Commission.

28 Oct. 1968	Ankrah announced that each of the country's 49 administrative districts would elect a member of a constituent assembly through local councils, 91 members would be elected by occupational and civic groups, and 10 members would be appointed by the NLC.
7 Nov. 1968	The funeral of Abudulai III, Ya Na of Yendi, touched off a struggle for the skin (throne) of Dagbon (Dagomba). An Exemptions Commission announced that Komla A. Gbedemah was exempted from the decree that kept former CPP members from being candidates for public office.
19 Nov. 1968	Air Marshal Otu was arrested on charges of complicity in subversive activities against the state.
Dec. 1968	Elections were held for members of the Constituent Assembly.
6 Jan. 1969	The Constituent Assembly began work on a new constitution. The Assembly rejected a motion to have their work approved by a national referendum and adopted a motion that their approved draft would become the constitution of the second Ghana republic.
2 Apr. 1969	Lt. General Joseph A. Ankrah was forced to resign as Head of State after admitting that he had received money for political purposes. Brigadier Akwasi Amankwa Afrifa became the new Chairman of the NLC and Head of State.
28 Apr. 1969	A decree prohibited political parties based on tribal or religious grounds.
1 May 1969	The NLC lifted the ban on political activity.
12 May 1969	The Jiagge Commission recommended that one and a half million cedis be recovered from twenty-one top former members of the CPP.
6 June 1969	A decree prohibited the reorganization of the CPP as the People's Popular Party.
16 Aug. 1969	The Constituent Assembly approved a new Constitution of the Second Republic.
22 Aug. 1969	Togo, Dahomey and Ghana signed an agreement with the Volta River Authority for the purchase of power produced at Akosombo. A Presidential Commission

Chronology

was established to oversee the transition to civilian government.

29 Aug. 1969	A national election was held for a new National Assembly. K.A. Busia's Progress Party (PP) defeated K.A. Gbedemah's National Alliance of Liberals (NAL), winning 59 percent of the popular votes. Gbedemah won a seat from Keta, but later the courts ruled that he was not eligible. The PP won 105 and the NAL 29 seats in the Assembly.
3 Sept. 1969	Akwasi Afrifa, J.W.K. Harley and A.K. Ocran of the NLC took oaths as the Presidential Commission. K.A. Busia was sworn in as Prime Minister.
6-9 Sept. 1969	Riots between rival factions in Dagomba resulted in many deaths.
30 Sept. 1969	Air Marshall Michael Otu was absolved of subversion and reinstated in the armed forces. Ghana officially returned to civilian rule.
16 Oct. 1969	Prime Minister Busia departed on a trip to the US and Europe to try to find help with the Nation's debts. While in New York he addressed the UN.
18 Nov. 1969	The government ordered the expulsion of all aliens in Ghana without residence permits. This created major problems between Ghana and her neighbors.
Feb. 1970	The government began a purge of the civil service. Renewal of appointments was denied to 568 (the "Apollo 568") persons who had served during the Nkrumah period. E.K. Sallah appealed to the courts against dismissal and won his case. Busia refused to reemploy him.
May 1970	Asantehene Osei Agyeman Prempe II died and J. Matthew Poku became Asantehene Opoku Ware II.
7-11 July 1970	At a London meeting with fifteen creditor nations Ghana was able to refinance most of the debt from the Nkrumah period with a two-year moratorium on 50 percent of the amounts due.
30 July 1970	The National Assembly voted to abolish the Presidential Commission created the year before.
28 Aug. 1970	Edward Akufo-Addo was elected President of the Second Republic by an Electoral College, made up of members of the National Assembly plus twenty-four chiefs.

20 Oct. 1970	Three opposition parties combined as the Justice Party (JP).
Dec. 1970	General Albert K. Ocran demanded that all members of the Assembly declare their assets as required by the Constitution. Many members refused to make the declarations.
Mar. 1971	The government announced increased rent on government housing.
Apr. 1971	The National Union of Ghanaian Students demanded free education, wholesale nationalization of business and amnesty for political exiles.
27 July 1971	The government published its austerity budget. Public services and benefits for public employees were to be cut and taxes were to be raised.
Aug. 1971	All "direct or indirect" mention of Nkrumah or the CPP was outlawed.
3 Sept. 1971	The Labor Minister announced firm action to prevent the Trade Union Congress from initiating strike action in opposition to the new taxes.
10 Sept. 1971	The National Assembly dissolved the TUC.
27 Dec. 1971	The cedi was devalued by 43.9 percent, dropping from $.98 to $.55 in relation to the US dollar.
8 Jan. 1972	Prime Minister Busia left Accra on a flight to London for treatment of an eye condition.
13 Jan. 1972	A military coup ended the Second Republic and established a government of the National Redemption Council (NRC) under Lt. Colonel Ignatius Kutu Acheampong as Chairman.
15 Jan. 1972	Akwasi Amankwaa Afrifa was arrested at Busia's Odorkor house and charged with plotting against the NRC. He was released a few days later.
4 Feb. 1972	Acheampong announced the revaluation of the cedi from $.55 per cedi to $.78 per cedi. This was a 42 percent increase in the value of the cedi.
5 Feb. 1972	The NRC repudiated part of the foreign debt of Ghana.
27 Apr. 1972	Kwame Nkrumah died in Bucharest, Rumania, where he was undergoing treatment for cancer.

31 Apr. 1972	The body of Nkrumah was flown from Rumania to Conakry, Guinea.
7 July 1972	The body of Nkrumah was flown to Accra, and the next day it lay in state in the Conference Hall of the State House.
9 July 1972	Nkrumah was buried at Nkroful.
16 July 1972	The NRC announced that it had foiled a plot to overthrow the government and that many people had been arrested.
18 July 1972	The NRC issued a decree making it a capital offense to attempt to overthrow the NRC.
14 Aug. 1972	The Aidoo Assets Commission began to investigate the assets of K.A. Busia and the ministers in his administration.
12 Sept. 1972	The NRC abolished the Supreme Court.
13 Nov. 1972	The 96-day trial of persons accused in July of trying to restore Busia to power ended. Eight persons were sentenced to death by firing squad. Sentences were later commuted to life.
18 Nov. 1972	Cape Coast University was formally opened.
3 July 1973	The last political detainees of the Busia government were freed.
31 Aug. 1973	Kojo Botsio, one of Nkrumah's lieutenants, was arrested and charged with plotting to overthrow the NRC.
Dec. 1973	A plot by former Nkrumah supporters to replace the NRC was uncovered. Death sentences were imposed and later commuted to life.
1974	The world oil price crisis and inflation began to seriously erode standards of living in Ghana.
13 Jan. 1974	Acheampong announced a National Economic Planning Council to create a national self-reliance program.
11 Feb. 1974	The three universities were closed for more than a month because of subversive activities on the campuses.
13 Mar. 1974	A Debt Settlement Agreement was reached with

	Western creditors by which many debts were rescheduled at lower rates of interest with longer periods for repayments.
23 Apr. 1974	The central government deposed the Ya Na of Yendi installed during the Busia period.
31 May 1974	Yakuba II, a member of the Andani family, was recognized by the NRC as paramount chief of the Dagomba.
4 Aug. 1974	Ghana changed its traffic pattern from left to right side driving. Ghana was the last West African country to drop the British pattern.
7 Aug. 1975	The NRC announced an amnesty for all secessionists in the Volta Region.
9 Oct. 1975	A seven-member Supreme Military Council (SMC) was established as the highest legislative and administrative organ of the state. A reorganized NRC continued as an executive council.
7 Mar. 1976	Ignatius Kutu Acheampong was promoted to the rank of general.
30 June 1976	A SMC decree became effective which limited foreign control of many business activities and required foreign companies to sell part (30 to 50 percent) of their stock to Ghanaians.
28 July 1976	Five Ewe soldiers were sentenced to death for subversion.
1977	Economic conditions deteriorated rapidly. Near-famine conditions existed in the Upper Region, and food shortages were common all over Ghana.
10 Jan. 1977	The SMC announced creation of the Koranteng-Addow Committee to prepare proposals for a union form of government. Dr. Gustav G. Koranteng-Addow, SMC Attorney-General and Commissioner of Justice, would be Chairman of the committee.
June 1977	The Ghana Bar and Medical associations threatened to strike if the SMC did not hand power over to civilians. Pharmacists, engineers, accountants and teachers joined in protests in July.
1 July 1977	General Acheampong, in a dawn broadcast, announced that power would be transferred to an elected government as soon as practicable.

9 July 1977	All army leaves were cancelled in the face of a national crisis because of professional strikes.
13 July 1977	General Acheampong promised to transfer power to an elected government with a new constitution and general elections by 15 June 1979 and return to elected government two weeks after the election.
4 Oct. 1977	The Koranteng-Addow Committee made its report, proposing a constitution with a president and a legislature selected "on merit" without resort to political parties. The proposed constitution was publically known as the "Union Government" plan.
11 Jan. 1978	The Bar Association denounced the campaign being waged by the SMC for Union Government.
13 Jan. 1978	Police broke up mass meetings of university students who opposed Union Government. Many students were sent to jail.
27 Jan. 1978	The People's Movement for Freedom and Justice (PMFJ) was organized to oppose Union Government. Komla Gbedemah, Akwasi Afrifa and William Ofori-Atta were among the leaders of the movement.
4 Feb. 1978	A large meeting in Kumasi in opposition to Union Government was broken up. Several were killed.
29 Mar. 1978	Ghana and Upper Volta agreed on joint construction of hydroelectric projects at Bui and Koulbi-Noumbiel.
30 Mar. 1978	The Union Government Referendum was held with low voter turnouts and bitter disputes about the validity of SMC reports of the results. Brong-Ahafo, Asante and the Eastern regions all opposed Union Government, yet the SMC reported 60.1 percent for Union Government to only 39.9 against.
3 Apr. 1978	All organized groups which had opposed the Union Government plan in the referendum were banned.
5 Apr. 1978	Many of the leaders in opposition to Union Government were placed in detention. Among them were Gbedemah, Ofori-Atta, Victor Owusu, John Bilson and Adu A. Boahen. Many others went into exile or hiding.
30 Apr. 1978	A Constitutional Drafting Commission was named by the SMC. The Commission was headed by Thomas

	A. Mensah. It began work on 31 May and was scheduled to finish its work by October.
19 June 1978	The cedi was floated and immediately declined in value 14.8 percent.
5 July 1978	General Acheampong was forced to resign and he was replaced by Lt. General Frederick W.K. Akuffo, who had been Acheampong's deputy since 1977.
Aug-Nov. 1978	Widespread labor unrest and strikes disrupted the Ghanaian economy.
28 Aug. 1978	Kofi Busia died in exile in England.
2-4 Nov. 1978	Accra was without water or electricity due to strikes.
6 Nov. 1978	The SMC imposed a state of emergency as strikes and unrest spread.
7 Dec. 1978	A Constituent Assembly was announced. New district councils elected 64 delegates, the SMC appointed 29 members, and 27 persons were nominated by various interest groups.
21 Dec. 1978	The Constituent Assembly convened to approve a draft constitution.
30 Dec. 1978	The SMC published a list of 105 persons it disqualified from holding public office.
1 Jan. 1979	The ban on political activities was lifted. Within a month almost twenty parties were organized, but by April only six of these groups were really viable.
12 Mar. 1979	New cedis were issued at seven new cedis for ten old cedis on amounts up to 5,000. Above that amount the rate was five new for ten old cedis.
15 May 1979.	The Constituent Assembly presented its approved draft for a constitution and adjourned. An attempted coup by junior officers was suppressed and several were arrested, including an Air Force officer named Jerry John Rawlings.
4 June 1979	A group of junior officers seized control of the government, released Flight Lieutenant Jerry Rawlings, arrested General Frederick Akuffo, and replaced the SMC with the Armed Forces Revolutionary Council under Rawlings.

12 June 1979	The AFRC began trials of former government officials and others for corruption and crimes against Ghana.
16 June 1979	General Ignatius Kutu Acheampong and General E.K. Utuka, former commander of the border guard, were executed by the AFRC for squandering government funds.
18 June 1979	Elections for president and a new National Assembly were held. The People's National Party (PNP) gained 71 seats to 42 seats for the Popular Front Party (PFP), 13 for the United National Congress (UNC), and 10 for the Action Congress Party (ACP). Dr. Hilla Limann of PNP and Victor Owusu of PFP were ahead of several other candidates in the presidential race, and they had to face each other in a runoff.
26 June 1979	Former heads of state and generals Frederick W.K. Akuffo and Akwasi A. Afrifa were executed by the AFRC. Former Foreign Minister Roger Felli, Major General Robert Kotei, former Chief of Defense Staff, Air Marshal George Yaw Boakey, and Admiral Joy Amedune were also executed.
9 July 1979	Hilla Limann of PNP was elected president in a runoff election against Victor Owusu of PFP. Limann got 62 percent of the vote. Limann belonged to the old Nkrumah legacy and Owusu represented the old Busia tradition.
18 Aug. 1979	The Makola Market in central Accra was bulldozed by troops of the AFRC.
5 Sept. 1979	The markets of Kumasi were destroyed by troops of the AFRC.
24 Sept. 1979	Hilla Limann and Joseph William Swain de Graft-Johnson were inaugurated as president and vice-president of the Third Republic for four-year terms. The AFRC warned that if the civilian officials used their positions for self-interest they would be unseated. A Special Tribunal took over all cases of corruption still pending before People's Revolutionary Courts set up by the AFRC. Transitional provisions placed this Special Tribunal above control by the National Assembly.
27 Nov. 1979	Rawlings was retired from the army on the grounds that his position was not compatible with his status as former head of state.

29 Mar. 1980	A number of soldiers were arrested and charged with an attempt to start a mutiny. AFRC supporters claimed the arrests were an attempt to discredit the AFRC.
June 1980	The government closed down the University at Legon after teachers and workers went on strike.
11 June 1980	Military Intelligence (MI) began surveillance of Captain Kojo Tsikata, an Ewe who was one of the founders of the June 4 Movement and an associate of Rawlings. The June 4 Movement was a group founded to support Rawlings.
Summer 1980	The economy declined steadily and popular discontent mounted during the summer.
Aug. 1980	Parliament rejected two judges nominated by President Limann to the Supreme Court. This touched off a constitutional crisis which eroded the strength of the PNP.
Sept. 1980	The government warned that all public employees who resorted to strikes would be summarily dismissed.
15 Oct. 1980	Security forces raided the home of Rawlings and arrested a foreigner accused of being a left-wing radical in the country to train members of the June 4 Movement in political subversion. Rawlings was briefly detained on suspicion of subversive activities.
Nov. 1980	President Limann reshuffled the economic machinery of his government in an attempt to deal with the growing economic stagnation and inflation. Cocoa prices were only 33 percent of what they had been in 1963.
1 Apr. 1981	Imoru Egala, founding father of the PNP and the chief supporter of Limann, died.
31 May 1981	All military personnel associated with the AFRC were retired.
June 1981	Fighting between the Konkomba and Nanumba in the Nanumba area of the Northern Region resulted in the deaths of more than a thousand people.
4 June 1981	Over 5,000 persons attended a rally in Accra in celebration of the anniversary of the 4 June 1979

	coup. Flight Lieutenant Rawlings was the main speaker.
23 June 1981	Five opposition parties announced plans for a merger as the All People's Party (APP). The union did not hold together and during the year several small political groups tried to organize as parties.
30 June 1981	The Budget for 1981-1982 was announced, calling for cuts in expenditures, higher taxes and a large deficit. This touched off a parliamentary hassle and a revision of the budget.
July 1981	Inflation was running at 106.6 percent.
12 Aug. 1981	An Earth Satellite Station at Nkutunse, near Accra, was commissioned.
Oct. 1981	The June 4 Movement began to publish a weekly newspaper called The Workers' Banner.
6 Nov. 1981	The Limann government tripled the price paid to farmers for cocoa.
25 Nov. 1981	Nana Okutwer Bekoe III, National Chairman of the PNP, was forced to resign in face of a financial scandal involving kickbacks on contracts to print Ghanaian currency notes.
7 Dec. 1981	A High Court injunction forced the PNP to call off its National Convention, scheduled for 11-13 December.
31 Dec. 1981	A coup ended the Third Republic, and Flight Lieutenant Jerry John Rawlings again became head of state as head of the Provisional National Defense Council (PNDC).
1 Jan. 1982	The foreign debts of Ghana equalled twice the total value of 1981 exports. Annual inflation was running above 140 percent.
2 Jan. 1982	Rawlings announced suspension of the Constitution, dismissal of all the officers of the Third Republic, and he proscribed all political parties.
11 Jan. 1982	The PNDC resumed diplomatic relations with Libya, which became one of Rawlings' chief supporters.
18 Jan. 1982	Libya established a "People's Bureau" in Accra.

Chronology

21 Jan. 1982	The PNDC announced appointment of 17 secretaries as heads of ministries.
28 Jan. 1982	Demonstrations against the United States took place in front of the American Embassy. Jerry Rawlings spoke to a vast throng in Black Star Square, promising an economic revolution.
5 Feb. 1982	All 50-cedi notes were withdrawn from circulation.
6 Mar. 1982	Ghana celebrated its twenty-fifth anniversary of independence with a military and police parade and a speech by Chairman Rawlings.
15 Mar. 1982	The PNDC ordered all unions to withdraw demands for wage increases.
4 Apr. 1982	The PNDC organized the 31st of December Youth Brigade to create a program of national service for all Ghanaian youth.
28-29 May 1982	Chairman Rawlings left Ghana for the first time since taking power to attend the ECOWAS meeting at Cotonou, Benin.
4 July 1982	The bodies of three High Court judges and a retired army officer, abducted four days before, were discovered near Akuse.
21 Sept. 1982	All the borders of Ghana were closed indefinitely in a campaign to halt smuggling.
23 Oct. 1982	Prime Minister Robert Mugabe of Zimbabwe and his Ghanaian wife arrived for a visit in Ghana.
29 Oct. 1982	Rumors of an attempted coup in Burma Camp under the leadership of two members of the PNDC, Sgt. Alolga Akata-Pore and Chris Atim were general in Accra.
23 Nov. 1982	An attempted coup at Burma Camp was halted.
16 Dec. 1982	Chairman Rawlings announced the decision to split the Upper Region into Upper West Region and Upper East Region.
30 Dec. 1982	The PNDC announced its four-year economic program of austerity and sacrifice.
17 Jan. 1983	Nigeria ordered all aliens out of Nigeria. This order involved from one to two million Ghanaians.

29 Jan. 1983	The border at Afloa, closed in September, was opened to admit Ghanaians expelled from Nigeria. The Nigerian expulsion order had touched off a national emergency in Ghana.
27 Feb. 1983	A number of soldiers said to be plotting a coup and the assassination of members of the PNDC were arrested.
Apr. 1983	A drastic food crisis reached the point of desperation during April. Many commodities disappeared from markets. Prices for the few items that were available quadrupled from the start of the year.
23 Apr. 1983	Kwesi Botchway, Secretary for Finance and Economic Planning, presented the 1983 budget. It called for tight controls on spending and imports.
4 May 1983	Some 2000 workers from Obuasi occupied the campus of the University of Science and Technology in Kumasi.
6 May 1983	University students marched from Legon into Accra in a demonstration against the PNDC. Workers began a counter-demonstration and fighting ensued.
9 May 1983	Workers came to the campus at Legon to demonstrate against the students.
14 June 1983	Several persons were arrested for plotting to overthrow the government.
19 June 1983	Many persons died in an attempted coup. Prisons were opened and many opponents of the PNDC escaped.
21 June 1983	Members of the Workers' Defense Committees of Accra and Tema took over the Supreme Court, Cadbury Factory, and two presses in Accra.
1-27 July 1983	The National Defense Committee held a cadre training school for more than a thousand supporters of the PNDC on the campus of the University at Legon.
13 Aug. 1983	Four soldiers were executed for their part in an attempted coup in June.
17 Aug. 1983	Those convicted of the murders of the High Court judges and retired army officer the previous year were executed.

28 Aug. 1983	Chairman Rawlings warned that revolutionary rhetoric was no substitute for productive work.
30 Sept. 1983	Chairman Rawlings went to Po, Upper Volta, to meet the new head of state of Upper Volta, Captain Thomas Sankara. The new revolutionaries in Upper Volta were attempting to pattern their revolution after that of the PNDC.
11 Oct. 1983	The PNDC announced the most drastic devaluation of the cedi in the history of Ghana.
6 Nov. 1983	The head of the UN Food and Agriculture Organization reported massive hunger in Ghana.
4-8 Nov. 1983	Joint military exercises of the forces of Upper Volta and Ghana were observed by the heads of state of both countries in a demonstration of solidarity between the revolutionary governments of the two countries.
4 Aug. 1984	The name of Ghana's northern neighbor was changed from Upper Volta to Burkina Faso, meaning the land of incorruptible people.

INTRODUCTION

Ghana is a West African country which was created in 1957 from the British Gold Coast Colony, Asante, the Northern Territories Protectorate, and the United Nations Trust Territory of Togo. Roughly rectangular in shape, it has an area of 92,100 square miles (238,539 sq km), which is twice the size of Pennsylvania, and slightly smaller than the United Kingdom. Located on the Gulf of Guinea, Ghana is bordered by three Francophone nations: the Ivory Coast and Upper Volta* on the west, Upper Volta on the north, and Togo on the east. The southern coastline, on the Gulf of Guinea, is 344 miles (554 km) wide, and the north-south length averages 522 miles (840 km). The total borders total 1,280 miles (2,060 km).

Ghana is located barely 400 miles (644 km) north of the equator. Its climate is determined by its position between the Atlantic and the Sahara. The southwest monsoon, with its cool, moist breezes coming in across the Gulf of Guinea, brings rain to the southwestern part of the country, while the northeast Harmattan, with its desiccating gales from the desert, brings periods of drought to the Upper and Northern regions. North of the Mampong-Koforidua Scarp the Harmattan is dominant from November to April. In this savanna area the rainy season is from May to October, when violent storms often flood lower elevations. Below the Mampong-Koforidua watershed there are rains much of the year, with peaks in June and October, and less moisture in August and January. The greatest rainfall is recorded each year in the Western Region, and the least precipitation is usually registered in the southeast plain between Accra and Akosombo. January is the coolest month, except in the Volta Region, where August is the most moderate. March is uniformally the warmest month everywhere. The mean maximum temperature south of the Mampong-Koforidua line is 86°F (30°C), while the minimum is 82°F (28°C). North of the watershed the maximum is 6° higher, and the minimum is 20° lower. The highest temperature ever recorded in Ghana was 109°F (43°C) at Navrongo, in the Upper Region, while the lowest on record was 51°F (11°C) at Kumasi.

The continental shelf off Ghana is narrow, the coastal zone is faulted and subject to severe earthquakes. There are no good natural harbors. The heavy surf makes landing from the sea hazardous, but good artificial harbors were opened at Takoradi in 1928, and at Tema in 1962. Cape Three Points is the southernmost pro-

---
*Upper Volta was renamed Burkina Faso on 4 August 1984.

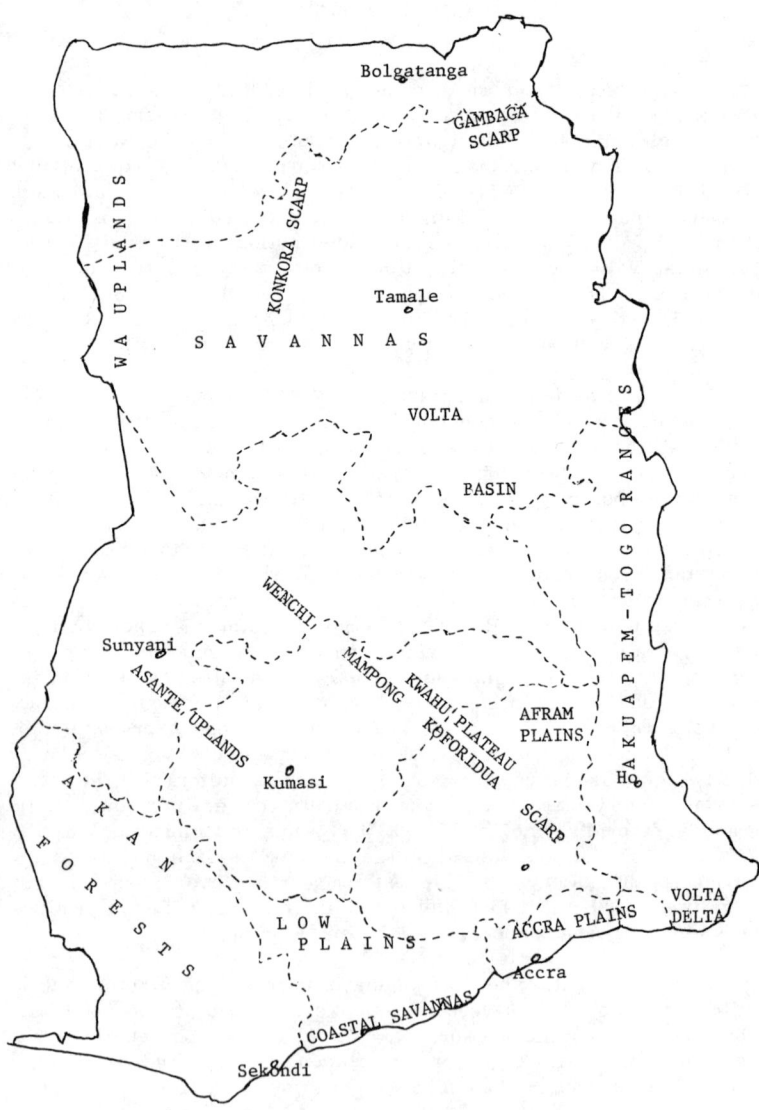

Fig. 1: Physical Regions of Ghana (Sherry L. Coakley)

jection of Ghana. The littoral is lined with old trade castles, built by Europeans in the days of the gold and slave trade. The beach is flat and sandy, backed by frequent saltwater lagoons and occasional rocky projections. The strand is lined with scrub, mangroves, and coconut and oil palms. There are larger lagoons, some of them freshwater, in the Volta Delta.

The Forest Zone is a great triangle southwest of the Mampong-Koforidua Scarp. It is broadest along the border with the Ivory Coast, and narrows to the east. The Forest covers most of Asante, all of the Western and Central regions, and a part of the Eastern Region. The Forest is the homeland of the Akan people, and it is by far the most productive part of the country. The forest, mineral, and agricultural wealth of Ghana is concentrated in this zone.

The Voltaic Basin occupies much of Brong-Ahafo and the Northern Region. It includes 45 percent of Ghana's area. There is evidence that the region once supported a much larger population, but today it is thinly settled. The poor soils, long dry seasons, periodic storms and floods, the diseases which plague both humans and animals make it an unattractive place in which to live. The Volta Basin has been drastically changed since 1965 by the creation of Lake Volta behind the Akosombo Dam. Begun in 1961, the dam is 350 feet (113 m) high, and 2,100 feet (640 m) long. The lake covers 3,276 square miles (8,485 sq km), is 250 miles (402 km) long, and has a shoreline of 4,500 miles (7,241 km). The project was the pride of Nkrumah, who dedicated it just days before he was deposed in 1966. It is the most ambitious project ever undertaken in Ghana, and it may one day improve the quality of life in the Volta Basin.

The Upper Region (divided in 1983 into Upper West and Upper East) is separated from the Northern Region by a line of escarpments running from the Togo border in the northeast, the Gambaga Scarp, and picking up across the White Volta as the Konkori Scarp. The area is moister and the soils are a bit more fertile than in the Northern Region, so there is a much greater population density. The border of Upper Volta encircles the Upper regions on the west and north, and there is a close affinity of peoples on each side of the border.

The Volta Region is a thin strip along the Togolese border, once ruled by Germany. It is separated from the rest of Ghana by the Volta. The people are related to the ethnic groups in Togo. The northern part is heavily forested, and it has the highest elevations in Ghana. The south is marshy and there are many lagoons.

There are two major drainage systems in Ghana. They are divided by the Wenchi-Mampong-Koforidua watershed. North and east of this line the Volta system drains more than two-thirds of the country. This basin includes the Black Volta, forming part of the border with Upper Volta and the border with the Ivory Coast before

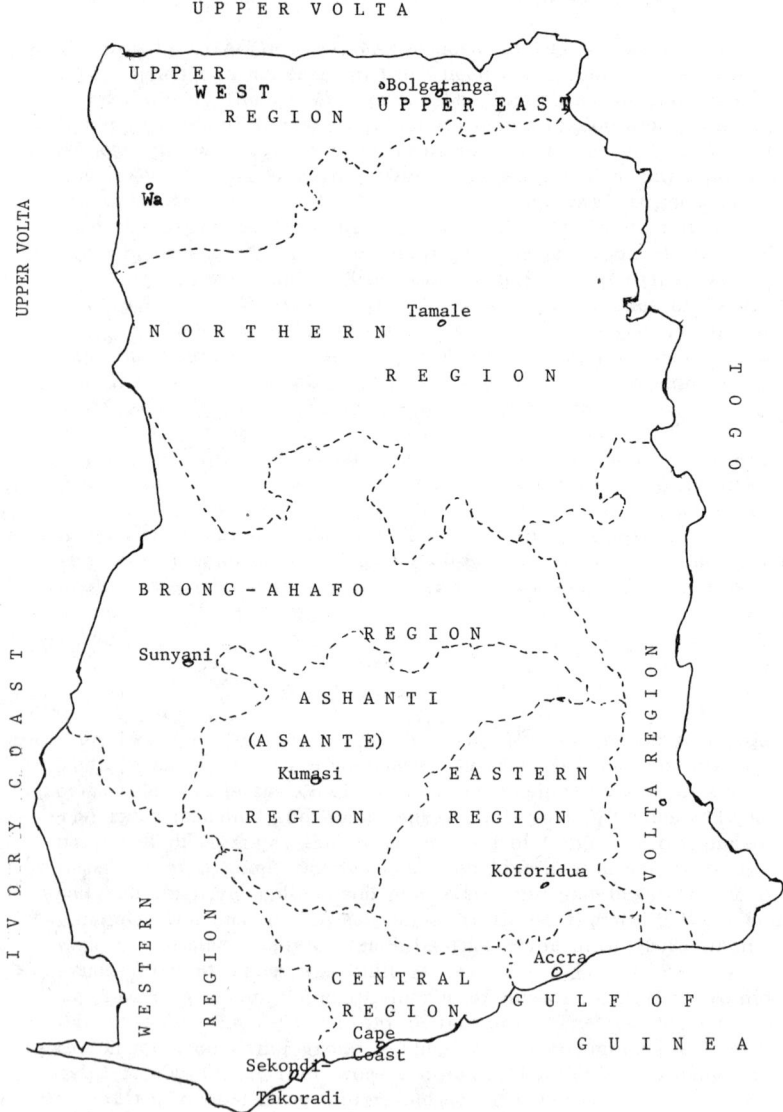

Fig. 2: Political Regions of Ghana (Sherry L. Coakley)

turning east to join the White Volta. The White and Red Voltas enter Ghana from Upper Volta, are deflected westward by the Gambaga Scarp after joining in the Upper Region, and then as one they flow down the center of the country into Lake Volta. The Tain, Mole, Kulpawn, Sisili, Daka, Oti, Pru, Sene, and Afram are among the more important tributaries of the Volta. All the drainage of this whole network is now impounded by Lake Volta. Below Akosombo Dam there is now another barrage at Kpong before the Volta turns sharply southeast to flow into the Atlantic near Ada.

Southwest of the Wenchi-Mampong-Koforidua divide, a number of separate rivers drain the forest zone from north to south. The longest and most western of these streams is the sacred Tano. It rises near Techiman, in Brong-Ahafo, and flows through Asante and the Western Region, forming the border with the Ivory Coast for a short distance before entering the Aby Lagoon. The Ankobra is next. It enters the ocean west of Axim. The Pra, with its Ofin, Oda, Anum, and Birim branches, drains much of the Akan-Asante heartland and enters the Gulf of Guinea near Shama. The Densu flows from the Atewa Hills in the Akyem lands into the Sakumo Lagoon west of Accra.

Elevations within Ghana are generally under 1,000 feet (305 m). The highest elevations are in the Akuapem (Akwapim)-Togo Range. Mount Afadjoto in the Volta Region, at 2,905 feet (885 m), is the highest point in the whole land. Occasional points in the Wiawso, Mpesao, Moinsi, Atewa, Banda, and Zabzugu (Shiene) hills reach 2,000 feet (610 m). The Konkori and Gambaga scarps rarely top 1,000 feet (305 m).

Ghana is potentially self-sufficient in agriculture. Cassava (manioc), cocoyam, coffee, cotton, cowpeas, maize (corn), millet, peanuts (groundnuts), pineapples, rice, sorghum, sugarcane, tomatoes, tobacco, yams, and a number of other crops do well in Ghana. Oranges, limes, grapefruit, avocado, mango, papaya, shea, baobab, oil palm, banana, plantain, cocoa, coconut, kola (cola), and many other items enrich the diets of Ghanaians. Chickens, guinea fowl, goats, cattle, rabbits, and pigs add protein. Fishing is of major importance. If the nation has a future it will come from food production. But less than 20 percent of the soil is utilized, methods of cultivation are basically primitive, obstacles common to the tropics seem sometimes to be intractable, and to date government policy has never stimulated farm incentives to break age-old patterns of subsistence production. Population growth continually outstrips food production, and Ghana is forced to import food. Cocoa and timber are major exports, but production of both has actually been declining in recent years.

Over 300 species of birds have been reported in Ghana, including eagles, parrots, herons, swallows, and vultures. Many kinds of monkeys inhabit the forests. Rodents abound. Wild pigs, leop-

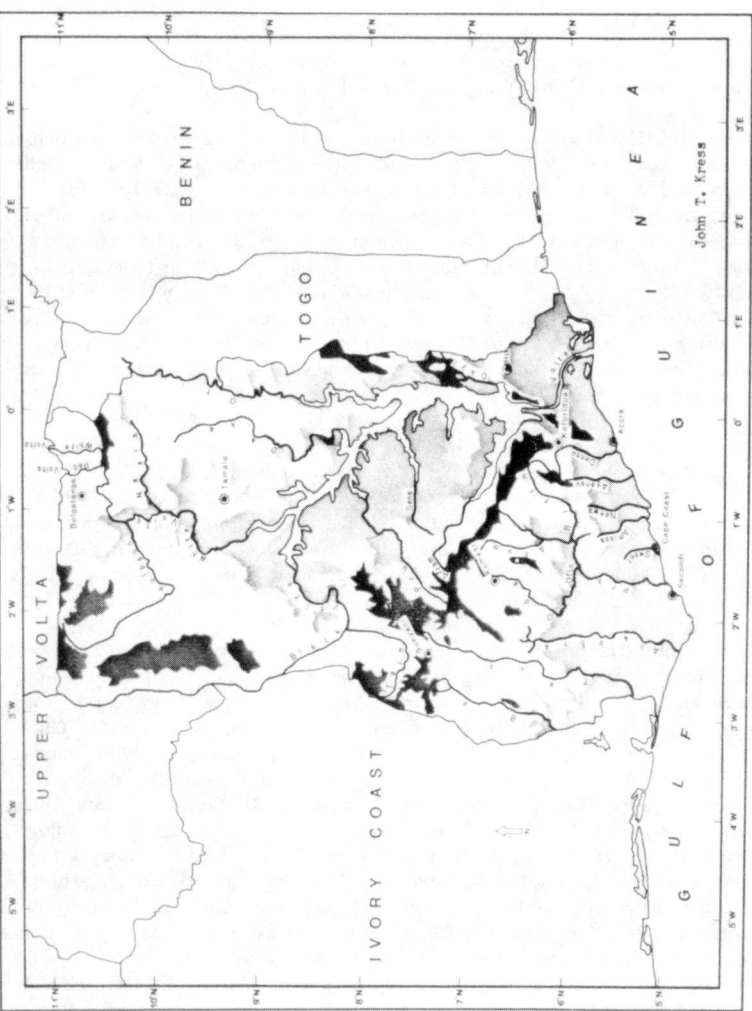

Fig. 3: Rivers (by John T. Kress)

ards, antelopes, buffaloes, hyenas, porcupines, and lesser game are still sighted. Lions and elephants are rare, but still reported. Crocodiles and hippopotamuses sun themselves on river banks. Manatees and a variety of fish swim in the rivers. Snakes include pythons, cobras, adders, mambas, and boomslangs. Lizards are omnipresent. And there are thousands of insects, many the vectors for deadly tropical organisms. The Mole and Kujani Game Reserves are the two largest conservation projects in Ghana.

Europeans first came to Ghana in search of gold, and gold is still found today. Industrial diamonds, manganese, and bauxite are also there in significant quantitites. Most mineral wealth is confined to the south. There is some iron ore, chromite, asbestos, kaolin, limestone, and marble, probably not in exportable quantities. In recent years there have been wistful predictions of offshore gas and petroleum. Traces have been found here and there. Some is being pumped off Saltpond. But at best there probably is not enough to last for long.

There was notable industrial development for a short time after independence. Most industry is located near the coast, especially in the Accra-Tema, and Sekondi-Takoradi urban areas. The Valco Aluminum smelter at Tema, in production since 1968, is the largest plant in Ghana. A petroleum refinery opened at Tema in 1963. Food processing, tobacco, textiles, wood products (furniture, veneers, plywood, pulp), cement, beverages, ceramics, vehicle assembly, batteries, and tires are some examples of Ghanaian enterprise. By African comparison this is an impressive list, but Ghanaian industry has never operated at full capacity, and it depends heavily upon foreign capital, management, technology, and parts. Products all too frequently are expensive and are not competitive. The hydroelectric projects at Akosombo and Kpong, and the projected dam at Bui, also on the Volta, will help furnish the energy necessary for industrial development. But at present the whole industrial sector is stagnant.

Ghana has around 2,500 miles (4,023 km) of paved highways, including a short superhighway from Tema to Accra. Over 6,000 miles (9,656 km) of gravel and laterite surface roads exist. Beyond that there may be 12,000 miles (19,308 km) of indifferent, sometime roads and trails, serviceable only in dry seasons. The triangle from Accra and Tema to Sekondi to Kumasi, with a route length of 592 miles (953 km) of track, is serviced by a reasonably efficient, but deteriorating, rail system. There are no railroads above Kumasi. There are major airports at Accra, Kumasi, Takoradi, and Tamale. Minor airstrips are located at Damongo, Navrongo, Ho, Wa, Kete Krakye, and Sunyani. Modern ports are operated at Takoradi and Tema. Lake Volta offers prospects of an opening to the north, but this potential has yet to be realized. As of 1983 the whole Ghanaian transport system is in a state of decline.

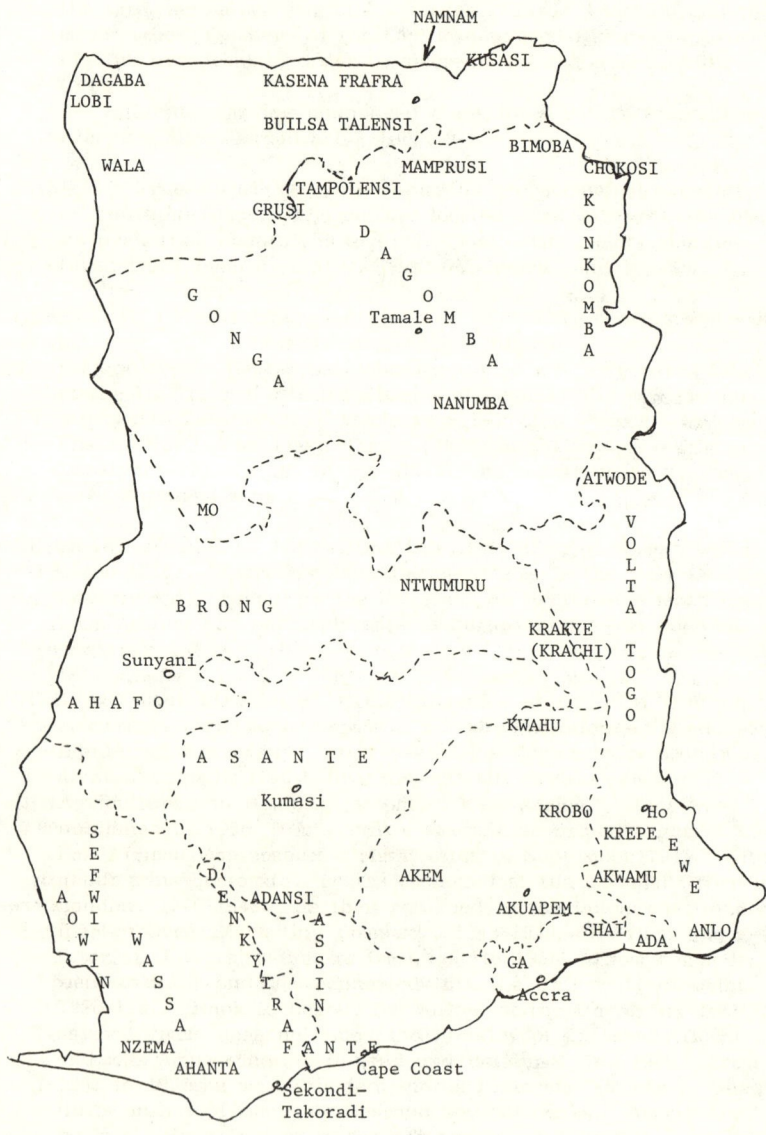

Fig. 4: People of Ghana (Sherry L. Coakley)

An estimated 14,000,000 people lived in Ghana in 1984, an average of 152 per square mile. This roughly compares with the figures for Pennsylvania. In West Africa only the census of Nigeria is larger. The heaviest concentration of people is in the triangle between Accra, Kumasi, and Takoradi. Most of the rest of the country is thinly inhabited, except for the Upper Region along the Upper Volta border. The average annual growth rate is 3.4 percent. By 1990 the population may be 16,000,000; by 2000 it may have passed 23,000,000. These figures will pose disastrous problems. The major urban centers are Accra, the nation's capital, and the regional capitals at Cape Coast, Takoradi, Kumasi, Koforidua, Tamale, and Bolgatanga. Tema is a part of the Accra metropolitan area. All these places are lodestones which attract the most ambitious citizens only to leave most of them disappointed.

There are over fifty distinct ethnic groups listed in the census of Ghana. Most people come from Akan, Ewe, or Voltaic backgrounds. But the country has always attracted migrants from all of West Africa, so almost every West African group is present in the heterogeneous population. At the end of World War II there were 108 traditional states in the Gold Coast. Thirteen of these were in the Upper and Northern regions, 24 were in Asante, and no fewer than 71 were in what was called the Colony. The official language of Ghana is English, but Twi, Ga, Fante, Hausa, Dagbani, Ewe, Nzema, and many other dialects are used. Traditional religion is practiced by about 38 percent of Ghanaians, predominantly in the rural areas. Islam is professed by about 12 percent of the people, mostly in the north. Christianity, in one of its variants, is listed in the census as the faith of 43 percent of the population. These are concentrated along the coast and in urban areas. Secularism is confined to urban areas and is a product of European influences.

Since independence Ghana has tried three republican constitutions and been ruled by several combinations of soldiers. It has counted itself as nonaligned, and it has leaned toward the East, the West, and Libya. It is a member of the Economic Community of West Africa, the British Commonwealth, the Organization of African Unity, and the United Nations. Its chief trade partners are the Western nations--the United Kingdom, the United States, West Germany, and the Netherlands. Nigeria, Russia, and Japan are also important commercial partners. Since the Rawlings coup, Libya is playing an important role in Ghanaian trade.

The flag of Ghana has red, gold, and green horizontal stripes with a five-pointed black star centered on the gold stripe. The national motto is "Freedom and Justice." In 1982 the national anthem was "God Bless Our Homeland Ghana," composed by Philip Gbeho. Rawlings has proposed finding a new anthem. The currency is the national cedi, divided into 100 pesewas.

In 1982 Ghana had more than fifteen thousand persons in its

armed forces, not counting five thousand in the paramilitary forces. This was more than twice the size of the armed forces of the Ivory Coast, and it totals more than the number of all three countries on the Ghanaian borders.

Humans have lived on the land today known as Ghana for at least twelve millennia. There is evidence for human habitation on the Oti River by 10,000 B.C., around Lake Bosumtwi by 8000 B.C., and on the Accra Plains by 4000 B.C. A neolithic culture with agriculture, domesticated animals, community life, pottery, and iron technology existed along the Volta by the time the Anglo-Saxons arrived in England. But these ancient people left only the vaguest traces of their existence. Archaeology has unearthed enough to give a hint of what the earliest Ghanaians were and how they lived.

The record begins to come into focus about 1400 A.D. By then there may have been 200,000 people. Trade networks were operating to Sahel areas north and east of the Niger. Cola, salt, and gold were attracting outsiders from beyond the Niger, and Ghanaians were making their first contacts with Islam. Textiles, musical instruments, jewelry, tools, weapons, furniture, and minerals were all produced in Ghana by the time the first Europeans reached the coast.

Europeans first ventured down the Guinea coast trying to find a route to Asia. They saw little in Africa to hold them until they reached that stretch of coast between the Tano and Volta rivers. Here they heard rumors of gold, and they found Africans with peppercorn, coconut, palm oil, ivory, gold, and slaves that they would exchange for European textiles, guns, beads, metals, and alcohol. In time the Europeans also introduced a whole complex of new agricultural products to the Gold Coast--sugar cane, maize, manioc (cassava), pineapples, tomatoes, peanuts, beans, squash, and tobacco. These new crops changed African life irrevocably. The plethora of new foods caused a nutritional revolution. Trade with the Sahel in the north continued to grow even after the coastal trade began, but by 1600 the southern commerce was by far the most important.

Portugal built lodges at Elmina, Axim, Shama, and Accra, and dominated the Gold Coast trade until the end of the sixteenth century. In the seventeenth century the Dutch and English replaced the Portuguese. Sweden, Denmark, France, and Brandenburg joined the Dutch and English. The Europeans on the coast, and the Africans in the interior squabbled continuously for control of the trade on the coast throughout the sixteenth, seventeenth, eighteenth, and into the nineteenth centuries. As this competition reached a climax in the eighteenth century, Asante emerged as the power in the interior, just as England came to dominate the coast.

The crucial year in the relations between the Africans and Europeans on the Guinea coast was 1807. By that year the gold deposits accessible to the technology of that time seemed to be nearly exhausted, and many of the Europeans committed themselves to end the slave trade. Export trade began to diminish rapidly during the next three decades. A few enterprising people experimented with coffee and other tropical crops in desperate attempts to keep the connection intact, but nothing seemed to work. Trade dwindled. A committee of the British Parliament recommended withdrawal. The Danes surrendered their interests in 1850--the Dutch pulled out in 1872. But there were Englishmen with a mission; Englishmen who felt an obligation to develop the whole world in a British matrix. By 1850 the advocates of the white man's burden in England had persuaded the Colonial Office to stay, and in 1872, when Asante seemed ready to contest the British decision to remain, the British sent Major General Sir Garnet Wolseley to settle the issue once and for all. In 1874 the British Gold Coast Colony with a seat of government at Accra was established. Asante quivered in impotent frustration for awhile longer, and indecisiveness on the part of England prolonged a settlement. Then in 1883 the first harvest of cocoa offered new economic prospects, and late in the next year the European powers gathered in Berlin to open a scramble for West Africa. By 1902 the British flag waved from Keta to Bawku, from Newtown to Hamale. That flag remained for just over half a century.

In the first half of the twentieth century the English introduced much of the world to industrial civilization and all that that implied. It meant new modes of communication and transportation; canned food, beer, soda pop, electricity, and running water. It included banks, paper money, the consumer society, high expectations for a better life in terms of material goods, and taxes. It introduced ideas of equality, individualism, political competition, literary education, Jesus, Karl Marx, and alienation from traditional ways of life. In Ghana all this was to be built on a foundation of cocoa and dreams--a lick and a promise.

Two world wars ended British commitment to empire. A nation no longer able to solve its own problems, no longer able to satisfy the expectations of its own citizens, could hardly be expected to carry the rest of the world on its shoulders. The end came quickly. In 1957 the British flag was lowered from Christiansborg Castle to the thunderous sound of celebrations all over Africa. Kwame Nkrumah joyfully assumed the burden the white man put aside. "Seek ye first the political kingdom and all things will be added unto it." March 1957 was a heady time, and there was scarcely a cloud in the sky.

Eight men have headed the government of Ghana since independence. And the dream of 1957 began to fade. The political kingdom has proved to be an illusion as anticipation has given way to acrimony. A quarter of a century has not brought the promised glory. Each year saw Ghana sink deeper into her doldrums. Where did the plan go wrong? Is neocolonialism the culprit? Is African disunity the villain? Or is Ghana trapped in a Malthusian predicament from which there is no escape?

THE DICTIONARY

ABANKESIESO. The first Denkyira capital. It was located not far from modern Obuasi, in Adansi, the modern Asante Region.

ABBOTT LABORATORIES CASE. In June of 1967 Abbott Laboratories of Chicago signed a deal with the NLC to rehabilitate a pharmaceutical plant, which had been built as one of Nkrumah's state-owned enterprises. A new corporation was created with Abbott holding 45 percent and Ghana 55 percent of the stock for ninety-nine years. Abbott would manage the concern, which would have a virtual monopoly of the drug market in Ghana. Public objections to the deal in Ghana were so great that Abbott withdrew from the agreement.

ABENE. 6°42' N, 0°47' W. The old chief town of Kwahu in what is today the Eastern Region northwest of Mpraeso.

ABETIFI. 6°40' N, 0°45' W. Kwahu town in the Eastern Region. Archaeologists have unearthed neolithic remains at Bosumpra Cave near here. Abetifi was an important mission center in the colonial period. The population was about 4,200 in 1950, 5,000 in 1960, and 6,000 in 1970.

ABIREWA CULT. "Old woman's fetish." A cult which originated in the north during the colonial period and spread to Asante and southern areas by 1910. The "high priest" of the cult lived in Bondoukou, Gyaman, in the Ivory Coast. The cult was suppressed by the British in 1910.

ABONSE (Abonce). The old market town of Great Accra, located inland from modern Accra. This Ga market was frequented by merchants from the interior, who brought gold, ivory, and slaves to trade for salt and European goods. It appears on a 1629 Dutch map as "A.B.C."

ABORA (Abura and other spellings). 5°17' N, 1°07' W. One of the main Fante divisions. In the Central Region some 16 miles (26 km) north of Saltpond. The population was about 1,400 in 1960 and 2,100 in 1970.

ABORIGINES RIGHTS PROTECTION SOCIETY (ARPS). A group organized at Cape Coast in 1897 to conduct a campaign of opposition to the Lands Bill of that year. The Lands Bill threatened traditional land tenure by proposing that all land not in actual use be in the control of the British government. Jacob Wilson Sey of Cape Coast and Anomabo was first head of the ARPS.

ABOSO. 5°22' N, 1°55' W. An important mining town in the Western Region just above Tarkwa.

ABOSOM. The higher gods of the Akan. These divinities have personalities and come and go freely. They live in rocks, caves, and special places, where their shrines are attended by priests and priestesses.

ABOTAKYI, CONCORD OF. An alliance of Guan, Akyem and others to unite against Akwamu and create Akuapem (Akwapim). The agreement was reached about 1731.

ABRADE. The people who founded the Akwamu state with a center at Nyannaoase about 1600.

ABRAHAM, WILLIAM E. Onetime head of the philosophy department at the University of Ghana who was a confidant and speechwriter of President Nkrumah. He was author of The Mind of Africa. In November of 1964 Nkrumah appointed him as chairman of a committee of nine to purge the country of literature critical of socialism. The next year he became a member of the State Publishing Corporation board, a group established to control all publishing and distribution of printed materials in Ghana. In 1965 he also became Pro-Vice Chancellor of the University at Legon. After the 1966 coup he spent about nine months in prison, and when released he became a priest.

ABRAMBO (Abramboe, Abrem, Abrembo). An Etsi state north of Komenda which appears on a 1629 Dutch map. It was east of the Pra.

ABREM see ABRAMBO

ABREMPON. The first chiefs of the Asante confederacy.

ABRON see BRONG

ABRUQUAH, JOSEPH WILFRED. Native of Saltpond, born in 1921. He was educated at Mfantsipim and in England and served as Headmaster of Mfantsipim for a time. He was a teacher in Cape Coast and at Keta between 1949 and 1963. After the fall of Busia he moved to the United States. He wrote The Catechist in 1965 and The Torrent in 1968.

ABUAKWA AKYEM (Abuaswa Akim). The eastern and largest branch of the Akyem. Their origins are traced to the Adansi, one of the earliest Akan groups. During their earliest history they were settled about a place called Kokobiante. Under Ofori Panin they migrated from Adansi to the Atewa hills. Kibi is their chief city today. It was founded around 1700.

ABUMA. An area between the Tano and Ankobra rivers in the Western Region.

ABURA see ABORA

ABURI. 5°51' N, 0°11' W. Located in the Eastern Region at the edge of the Akuapem Ridge, the village is some 20 miles (32 km) north of Accra. It is shown on a 1729 map as Abura and was known to the Dutch as Aboera. The population was 3,142 in 1948, 4,715 in 1960, and 7,656 in 1970. The Basel missionaries began a school for girls here in 1847, and it has been an educational center since then. A nursery for cacao pods was started in 1886, and this developed into the present Botanical Gardens. The town has long been a resort for bureaucrats escaping the heat and bustle of Accra.

ABUSA. The farm contract system by which farm laborers served as tenants in exchange for one-third the produce of the land.

ABUSUA. Akan matrilineal clans in which members trace their lineage from a common ancestress and blood. There are seven (or eight) Akan clans. The Aduana and Oyoko trace their origin to a hole in the ground at Asantemanso, the nuclear point from which one tradition traces Akan beginnings.

ACCANY see AKANNY

ACCRA. 5°33' N, 0°13' W. One of the original Ga coastal settlements, first known as Small Accra. It became the Ga capital in 1677 after Akwamu destroyed Great Accra, located some 10 miles (16 km) inland. Accra became an important trade center during the Atlantic slave trade era, especially after several European posts were built. In 1876 it replaced Cape Coast as the British administrative center, and in 1957 it became capital of Ghana. The population was about 16,000 in 1891, 19,600 in 1911, 38,000 in 1921, 60,700 in 1931, 135,000 in 1948, 348,000 in 1960, and 565,000 in 1970. It is by far the largest urban area in Ghana.

ACCRA CAPITAL DISTRICT. The area is part of the Eastern Region of Ghana, but it has a separate administration. It covers much of the Accra Plain, and fronts on the Gulf of Guinea for about fifty miles (80 km).

ACCRA PLAINS. The flat, dry triangle between Accra, Ada, and Akosombo. Kpesi people lived in the area from early times.

Ga, Adangbe, and Ewe moved in at later dates. The Plains have the lowest rainfall in Ghana, but the region is fairly free of tsetse, and therefore it is suitable for livestock.

ACHEAMPONG, IGNATIUS KUTU. Head of State. Born 23 September 1931; died 16 June 1979. Educated at Catholic schools in Kumasi and Ejura, and Central College of Commerce, Agona-Swedru. Teacher and principal, 1949-1952. Commissioned in the army in 1959. Attended military training programs in England and Kansas. Leader of the military coup in 1972. Head of State and Chairman of the National Redemption Council, 1972-1978. Removed from his offices by his colleagues in the Supreme Military Council 5 July 1978. After being held in custody for a time, he was released, dismissed from the army without benefits, and disqualified from holding office again. In June 1979 he was arrested by the AFRC and executed by firing squad.

ACHIMOTA. 5°37' N, 0°14' W. A town in the Accra Capital District six miles (10 km) north of Accra where Achimota School is located. It had a population of 1,765 in 1948, and 3,450 in 1970.

ACHIMOTA SCHOOL. The foundation stone for Achimota was placed in 1925 and unveiled by the Prince of Wales, for whom the school was at first named. Prince of Wales' College was formally opened in January 1927. The school was conceived by Governor Frederick G. Guggisberg, and it became one of the finest schools in Africa under the administration of A.G. Fraser. For many years it took male and female students from kindergarten through college. In 1948 it was decided to build a college campus nearby Achimota at Legon.

ACRON see AKRON

ACTION CONGRESS PARTY (ACP). A political party organized to contest the 1979 elections. Retired Colonel Frank Bernasko, once agricultural minister under Acheampong, was leader and presidential candidate of the party, and Kofi Awooner, famous author, was general secretary. Most of the support for the party came from the Fante area of the Central and Western regions. They won ten seats in the assembly in the June 1979 elections. The ACP was known as the party of "progressive intelligentsia."

ACULO. Grusi-speaking group in the Upper Region who are closely related to the Sisala and Kasena.

ADA (Addah). 5°47' N, 0°38' E. Coastal town on the right bank of the Volta. It is about 71 miles (114 km) east of Accra. The Volta is about a mile wide at this point. Constantly shifting sand impedes navigation, but navigation in small launches is possible from here up the river 50 miles (80 km) to Akuse most of

the year, and to the Senchi Rapids in the rainy seasons. The
town was an important trade center for slaves from up the Volta
River in the eighteenth century. A ferry crosses the river
from Ada to Anyanui, on the left bank of the Volta.

The Danes built Fort Kongensten at Ada in 1784. Eight
years later they outlawed the slave trade in the area, a dictate
often ignored by many of the traders on the lower Volta. Palm
oil, hides, ivory, and salt were the main commodities traded
here during the nineteenth century. In 1850 the Danes sold
out to the English, who finally crossed the dreaded Ada bar in
the steam launch Eyo in 1868. For a time the community became
a busy place. During the British-Asante War of 1873, Captain
John Glover established his headquarters there. G.A. Henty
and Henry Stanley visited Glover there that year. Robert Bannerman,
M.J. Bonnat, Alexandre Dumas, Geraldo de Lima, and
other famous traders operated in the region during the last three
decades before 1900. Commander Paget Jones set out from Ada
in 1899 to explore the Volta.

Ada is actually two towns: Ada Foah (Ada proper) and
Big Ada. In 1948 their combined census was 4,349. By
1960 the total was 6,330, and in 1970 there were 8,529
in the two parts.

ADAE. Akan national festivals which are observed twice in every
forty-three days on Sundays (Great Adae) and Wednesdays (Little
Adae). These are days of rest when the ancestors are remembered,
their spirits are propitiated, and the royal ancestors
are honored and solicited for mercy.

ADALI-MORTTY, GEORMBEEYI. Poet and educator. He was born
about 1920 in Gbogame, Northern Eweland, and was educated at
Achimota and Cornell University. After spending many years
as a government official, and slowly building a reputation as a
poet, he was asked to join the faculty of the University of
Ghana, Legon. He is now recognized as one of Ghana's best
poets.

ADAMAFIO, TAWIA. Ga political leader. At birth he was christened
as Joseph Tawia Adams, but he changed his name in 1946 while
a clerk for the Supreme Court in Accra. At first he opposed
Nkrumah and the CPP, but he was finally won over and began
writing for the Evening News. In 1956 he went to England to
study law, and while there he organized the National Association
of Socialist Students Organizations (NASSO) to support the CPP
in London. After he returned to Accra he became General Secretary
of the CPP for seventeen months. By the middle of 1961
Adamafio was Minister of Presidential Affairs with an office in
Flagstaff House. He was an ally of John Tettegah of the TUC,
one of the leaders of the left wing of the CPP, and he was often
spoken of as Nkrumah's heir. During this period he became
Minister of Information and Broadcasting, and in this role he is

credited with beginning the campaign to exalt Nkrumah. He also was active in a Study Group which attempted to work out a new socialism as the program for the CPP. After an attempt on Nkrumah's life in August 1962, Adamafio and some friends were charged with the assassination attempt. He was arrested 29 August 1962, tried by a special court, found not guilty, but held in preventive detention by Nkrumah until the coup in 1966. Adamafio returned to favor in 1972 when the military ended the Second Republic. In 1977 he headed the Continental African Youth Command, and in 1978 he was active in the SMC campaign of Union Government. Adamafio produced his memoirs in 1982.

ADAMANSO. 5°16' N, 1°52' W. Place in the Western Region in Wassa country near which the British Governor, Sir Charles MacCarthy, was killed in a skirmish with the Asante, 21 January 1824. The skirmish is also called Bonsaso or Nsamakow by different authorities.

ADAMPAS see ADANGBE

ADANGBE (Adampa, Adangme, Dangme). People associated with the Ga in southeastern Ghana. Many of these people live along the coast and on inselbergs in the Accra Plain. Ada, Kpong, Krobo, Ningo, Shai, Prampram, and Osudoku are identified as Adangbe. They are closely related to the Ewe.

ADANSI. One of the earliest Akan states, probably founded in the first half of the sixteenth century. It was located between the Oda and Fum tributaries of the Pra in the Kwisa and Moinsi hills, also known as the Adansi hills. It was astride the major north-south trade route. The traditional founder was Opon Enim. The first capital was at Adansimanso, which was destroyed in a war with Denkyira about 1657. A new capital was built at Dompoase, not far from Adansimanso. Later Fomena became the Adansi capital.

ADANSI HILLS (also Moinsi). A ridge running from Lake Bosumtwi across a strip of the Central Region to the Huni Valley and Tarkwa.

ADANSIMANSO. 6°18' N, 1°33' W. The earliest Adansi capital, located southwest of Lake Bosumtwi about 15 miles (24 km). This is the Heartland of the Akan people.

ADDO, EDWARD AKUFO. Attorney, President of the Second Republic, Chief Justice. He was born in Akropong-Akuapem in 1906 and was educated in Presbyterian schools, Achimota, and Oxford. He was a brother-in-law to William Ofori Atta and son-in-law of Sir Ofori Atta I. In 1940 he received his law degree, and soon after he returned to Ghana he became active in politics. He was a founding member of the UGCC in 1947, and the follow-

ing year he was one of the "Big Six" arrested by the British
authorities in connection with the riots. In the elections of
1951, 1954, and 1956, he was an anti-Nkrumah candidate. In
spite of his opposition to Nkrumah, he was appointed to the Supreme Court and was one of the judges in the treason trial of
Adamafio and Ako Adjei in 1963. After the court found the defendants in the treason trial innocent, Nkrumah dismissed Addo
from the Supreme Court. After the coup of 1966 which toppled
Nkrumah, Addo became an important figure in the National Liberation Council as Chairman of the Political Committee, Chairman
of the committee that drafted the constitution for the Second Republic, and Chief Justice. In the elections for the chief executive of the Second Republic he was elected as president by the
electoral commission as the candidate of the Progress Party.
Soon thereafter he suffered a stroke. After the 1972 military
coup he was allowed to retire to his home in Nima and was not
arrested.

ADDO-DANKWA I. Died 1838. Ruler of Akuapem, 1816-1836. He
was a member of the alliance that defeated Asante at Katamanse
(Dodowa) in 1826. Near the end of his reign the Basel Mission
began its work in Akuapem. In 1836 he was deposed by a pro-
Danish faction, and he died two years later.

ADELE. Small group in the Volta Region on the Togo-Ghana border
to the northeast of Krakye.

ADERE. Name sometimes used for the Volta river and its affluents.

ADEROSO RAPIDS (Aderessa). Rapids on the Black Volta from Bui
Gorge for a distance of some 10 miles (16 km).

ADIBO. 9°18' N, 0°01' E. A village in the Northern Region in
Dagomba just south of Yendi. Here in 1896 the Germans defeated the Dagomba before moving on to sack Yendi.

ADINKRA CLOTH. Cotton cloth stamped with various designs. The
stamps were once made from pieces of calabash. The dye came
from the bark of the badie tree. Each design has a special
meaning to the Akan.

ADISADEL. A school started as the Church of England Grammar
School in Cape Coast in 1910; it became one of Ghana's most
prestigious secondary schools.

ADJEI, AKO. Born 1915. A Ga attorney who was a student with
Nkrumah in the United States and London. In 1947 he was offered the secretaryship of the UGCC, but suggested Nkrumah
instead of himself. He was arrested during the 1948 riots, and
became one of the famous "Big Six" imprisoned with Nkrumah,
Danquah, and others. Adjei joined the CPP in 1952, and joined

Nkrumah's government in 1954. He was the Foreign Minister
from 1959 to 1962. In 1962 he was arrested and charged with
complicity in the attempt to murder Nkrumah. Acquitted by the
court, he still was held in prison by Nkrumah under preventive
detention until released after the 1966 coup.

ADJETEY, CORNELIUS FREDERICK. 1893-1948. Veteran soldier
and Ghanaian martyr. A native of Labadi, near Accra, who was
educated at Osu Presbyterian Primary School and served in the
Gold Coast forces from World War I through World War II, with
service in East Africa in the first World War and in Burma during
the second World War. On 28 February 1948 he was killed
leading a group of ex-servicemen towards the Castle at Osu in
protest against conditions in the Gold Coast. His death touched
off the chain of events which would lead to the British decision
to withdraw from the Gold Coast.

ADO. Ruler of Akwamu from 1699 to 1702, he extended the rule of
Akwamu far to the east of the Volta into modern Togo and Benin.

ADOM. Gold-producing area shown on a Dutch map of 1629 just
south of Wassa and north of Ahanta in what is now the Western
Region. About 1691 the inhabitants fought with those in Ahanta
in a campaign in which many people were killed. A 1702 report
described Adom as "bandit-infested."

ADOMI (Adome). 6°14' N, 0°06' E. Place on the Volta just north
of Senchi and south of Akosombo where a single-span steel arch
bridge, built between 1955 and 1957, takes the Accra-Ho highway
across the Volta River. The bridge replaced the ferry at Senchi
and was the first bridge built across the Volta proper.

ADONTEN. The main body of an Akan army, it is under the command
of the Adontenhene.

ADUANA (Abrade). One of the principal Akan clans.

ADU BOFFO. Died 1883. Asante General and Royal Treasurer.
Adu Boffo commanded the Asante army of the east in 1868 which
occupied the trans-Volta area and took the Basel missionaries
F.A. Ramseyer and J. Kuhne and the French trader Marie
Joseph Bonnat prisoners. In the Asantehene's council, he was
a leading opponent of any détente with the Europeans. In 1873
he commanded the west wing of the Asante forces attacking the
coast toward Elmina. When the British captured Kumasi, he retired
back to Asante.

ADUMFO. An Akan state executioner.

AFADJOTO, MOUNT. 7°02' N, 0°34' E. At 2,905 feet (885 m), this
peak in the Volta Region on the Togo border is the highest point
in Ghana.

AFLAO. 6°07' N, 1°11' E. The most eastern town in Ghana, this coastal border town is the last stop before entering Togo and is only a few miles from the Togo capital city of Lome. It is a major point for smuggling activities. It had a population of 2,485 in 1948, 7,439 in 1960, and 11,397 in 1970.

AFRAM. A western tributary of the Volta river which rises northwest of Mampong in the northern part of the Asante Region and flows into Lake Volta.

AFRAM PLAINS. Large area of underdeveloped land between the Afram and Sene arms of Lake Volta. The plains are sparsely settled by Guan-speaking people who mainly support themselves by fishing. Soils are frequently flooded in the wet season and parched the rest of the year. The savanna woodland is spotted with red ironwood and shea trees. Here and there baobabs grow. Tall elephant grass grows near the water. It was once an important hunting area, but much of the game, especially the elephants, is gone. Part of the area is set aside as a game reserve. Tsetse flies are a major problem.

AFRICAN COMPANY OF MERCHANTS. A British company organized to replace the Royal African Company for trade on the coast of Africa in 1750. Membership in the new company was open to all British merchants who paid a forty-shilling fee. Parliament made an annual grant to help maintain trade posts for the company on the coast of Africa.

AFRICAN MORNING POST. An Accra newspaper which Nnamdi Azikiwe edited in the early 1930s. The journal was the mouthpiece of the West African Youth League, an early nationalist group.

AFRICAN STEAMSHIP COMPANY. A merchant marine company chartered in 1852 for the purpose of trading with West African ports. It carried the mail to the Gold Coast for many years. In 1891 it became part of the Elder-Dempster Lines. The British and African Steam Navigation Company, organized in 1869, also became part of Elder-Dempster by 1894.

AFRIFA, AKWASI AMANKWAA. 1936-1979. Asante soldier and politician who was born in Mampong. He attended Adisadel in Cape Coast before joining the army in 1956. The army sent him to England, where he went to Officer Cadet School at Aldershot, and the Royal Military Academy at Sandhurst. After returning to Ghana in 1961 he was sent to the Congo as a member of the UN peacekeeping force. It was during this tour of duty that he became convinced that Nkrumah's international aspirations were a threat to Ghana.

Not long after the end of Ghanaian involvement in the Congo, Nkrumah began to plan Ghanaian intervention in Rhodesia. During this period, Afrifa became associated with Kotoka and other officers who opposed the direction of Nkrumah's policies. These officers directed the coup of 24 February 1966 which ended the reign of Kwame Nkrumah and established the National Liberation Council. Afrifa tells the story of these events in his <u>The Ghana Coup: 24th February 1966</u>, published in 1967. In the NLC Afrifa was a member of the Executive Council and Minister of Finance, Economic Affairs, and Trade. In 1969 he became NLC Chairman and Head of State. In his position of leadership he engineered the return to civilian rule under Busia and the Second Republic.

Though disappointed with progress under Busia, Afrifa defended the Second Republic against another military coup, and when the army again returned to power, as the National Redemption Council, at the beginning of 1972, Afrifa was arrested, and spent more than a year in detention. After his release, he lived in retirement for some time, returning to active participation in public life during the referendum on Union Government in 1978, as a member of the People's Movement for Freedom and Justice (PMFJ). In 1979 he helped organize the United National Convention Party, and was elected to Parliament on that ticket in the election held 18 June that year. Just a week later, he was executed by Rawlings and his AFRC cohorts.

AFUTU   see   EFUTU

AGAVE (or Crophy). An Ewe group who live in the eastern Accra Plain just west of the Volta River and north of the Songaw Lagoon and Ada.

AGBOSOME (Somme). 6°05' N, 1°02' E. Area northeast of the Keta Lagoon near the border of Togo. This territory came under British control in 1879. Smuggling has long been a problem in this region.

AGGREY, JAMES EMMAN KWEGYIR. 1875-1927. Educator. Born in Anomabo, Aggrey was educated in the Methodist school at Cape Coast. He was one of the early members of the Aborigines' Rights Protection Society. In 1898 he went to Salisbury, North Carolina, where he attended Livingstone College for four years. After his graduation he married a lady from Virginia, received a doctorate in divinity, and remained a member of the faculty of Livingstone until 1924. In October 1924 he returned to the Gold Coast to become vice-principal of Achimota. In 1927 he returned to the United States to study at Columbia in New York, but died suddenly on 30 July 1927.

AGGREY, JOHN. 1809-1869. Fante Ruler of Cape Coast, 1865-1866. As ruler of Cape Coast, Aggrey claimed sovereignty to the walls of the English Castle. He petitioned the British to respect his authority in Cape Coast, a request the English took to be a chal lenge to their prerogatives. The British arrested Aggrey in December 1866 and sent him into exile in Sierra Leone. In 1869 he was allowed to return to Cape Coast, but he died shortly after his homecoming. In Ghana he is honored as the first traditional ruler on the Gold Coast to resist colonial rule.

AGOGO. 6°48' N, 1°05' W. Town in the Asante Region, about 40 miles (64 km) east of Kumasi. It was an early mission center. In 1948 it had a population of 4,744, which increased to 10,356 in 1960 and to 14,710 in 1970.

AGONA. One of the Akan Abusua clans.

AGONA ASANTE. 6°56' N, 1°29' W. Town in the Asante Region on the Great Northern Road between Kumasi and Mampong. It was one of the principal divisions of the Asante Confederation. Its paramount chiefs are the descendants of Okomfo Anokye.

AGONA STATE (Agua, Aguna, Agwano, Agonna, Janconcomo). One of the larger states shown on a 1629 Dutch map located between Fante and Accra. On the 1729 Anville map it is shown between Akron and Akra, with a note that it was "very powerful." It was conquered by Akwamu in 1689. Nsaba (5°39' N, 0°45' W) in the Central Region was the seat of the omanhene of Agona from 1693 to 1931. Senya Beraku and Winneba are the important ports of the area, and Swedru is the most important inland city today.

AGUAFO (Eguafo, Guaffo, Komenda). Area between the Pra and Elmina. See also EGUAFO and KOMENDA.

AGUNA see AGONA STATE

AHAFO. Sefwi territory between the Bia and Tano rivers which was conquered by Opoku Ware of Asante about 1721. The name means "hunting ground of the Asantehene." Today the region is part of the Brong-Ahafo Region.

AHANTA (Anda, Anta, Hanta). Coastal area of the Western Region between the Ankobra and Pra rivers. Busua (4°48' N, 1°56' W) is the center. Ahanta was shown on the 1629 Dutch map as Anta, and the Anville map of 1729 as Hante. The state runs inland from the coast for a short distance. Sekondi, Takoradi, Dixcove, Cape Three Points, Prince's Town, and Axim were some of the important outlets to the area. The Prussians, Portuguese, Dutch, and English all vied for trade here.

AHASIA see GREAT INKASSA

AHEMA (Ahemaa, Hemaa). Plural of Ohema. Akan for queen mothers. The Queen Mother of Asante would be the Asantehemaa.

The queen mother in Asante and Akan society is the second most important person. She nominates the candidate for chief, and if the council does not select her choice she can veto anyone of whom she disapproves. She can give advice to the chief, she sits next to the ruler in court, and she alone can rebuke the chief. She can also hold her own court, and she selects the chief's senior wife.

AHENE (Ahenfo, Afahene). The plural of ohene. Asante courtesy title. The Asantehene's agents. The political-military bureaucracy or elite. The upper class. Custodians of state lands. Captain.

AHENEMMA. Princes of the Golden Stool.

AHIAFO. The Akan poorer class.

AHMADIYYA. A Muslim brotherhood founded in India in the late nineteenth century. It appeared in the Gold Coast during World War I. They are fundamentalist missionaries who claim to be the only true believers, denouncing all persons who do not agree with them. They conduct an aggressive educational program. The Ahmadis publish thousands of religious tracts.

AHUBAW. The Yam Custom or "Black Christmas." A popular Akan festival. During the colonial period, celebrations would frequently get out of hand due to public drunkenness and disorder. The 1892 Native Customs Ordinance tried, unsuccessfully, to limit excesses in the celebrations in the major coastal cities.

AHWENE KOKO (Affindio Coco, Old Wankyi). The traditional first capital of Wenchi. It was destroyed by the Asante around 1712.

AIDOO, CHRISTINA AMA ATA. Born 1940. Author. Aidoo was born near Saltpond in the Central Region; she was educated in Methodist schools, and graduated from the University of Ghana, Legon. She has also studied in England and the United States. She is author of many poems and short stories. Her collection of short stories, No Sweetness Here, published in 1970, received acclaim the world over. In 1982 she became Secretary for Education in the PNDC government, a position she held until June 1983.

AIRPORTS. Kotoka International Airport in Accra is the major air terminal for Ghana. All international flights into and out of Ghana use this field. Kumasi, Tamale, Takoradi, and Sunyani have airports for internal flights.

AJAMI SCRIPT. Arabic script modified for writing Hausa as used in Northern Ghana.

AJENA GORGE. 6°16' N, 0°03' E. Place where the Volta once broke through the Akuapem-Togo (Akwapim-Togo) range of Mountains. The narrow gorge was only 30 yards (28 m) wide. The gorge is now the location of the Akosombo Dam, completed in 1965. Akosombo village is just south of the dam.

AKAN (Akanny, Akani, Acanjj, Hecanny, etc.). One of the major ethnic groups of West Africa, the majority living in Ghana. They are grouped around a number of clans, most of them having traditions of origins in the Adanse region around Lake Bosumtwi. They have matrilineal systems of descent.

AKAN CLANS. The Abusua (blood) clan is matrilineal. The Fante seem to have seven female clans and the Asante seem to have eight. The Asante clans are: Aduana (Aduena), Agona, Asinie (Asena), Asokore, Asona, Oyoko; and, depending on sources, Abrade, Beretuo, and Ekuana. These are totemic clans. All Akan belong to one of them. The totem of the Oyoko is a parrot, of the Aduana is a frog, of the Asona is a crow, etc. Every Akan also belongs to his father's family, called the ntoro or spirit family.

AKAN DIVISIONS. There are a number of divisions of the Akan: Akuapem, Akyem, Kwahu, Ahafo, Asante, Brong, Denkyira, Assin, Nzema, and Fante.

AKAN LANGUAGE. The language is today known as Akan. It was once known as Twi. The Akan of the Asante is the most widely used. The Akuapem dialect was the first to be written. Fante is the third dialect, and is more distinct. The Brong (Abron) and Bawle (Baule) of the Ivory Coast speak Akan. The language is a tone language and each syllable has its own tone or pitch.

AKANNY (Akanni, Acanny, Hacany, etc.). The old Akan state around Lake Bosumtwi and southward to the Pra. Adansi and other Akan now occupy the area.

AKANTAMANSU (Akantamanso, Katamanso). 5°44' N, 0°05' W. Akantamansu is the Akan name, and Katamanso is the Ga name for the place where the great battle took place in August 1826 which marked the start of the decline of Asante power. The British called the battle Dodowa. Dodowa and Akantamansu are eight miles (13 km) apart.

AKIM   see   AKYEM

AKOAPA (Ahoba ni). Pawns who became slaves.

AKONNO. Akwamuhene, 1702-1725, at the peak of Akwamu power. During his reign slave raiders terrorized the country and carried off thousands to the coast for sale to the Europeans. In 1708 he attacked Kwahu, but got the worst of it. In 1717 he betrayed his Asante allies to Akyem. By the end of his reign Akwamu had few friends.

AKOSOMBO. 6°18' N, 0°03' E. Village in the Eastern Region near the Ajena Gorge and the Akosombo Dam. The year before the dam project began there were only 52 people at Akosombo. By 1970, when the hydroelectric project on the Volta was in full operation, there were 7,716 living at Akosombo. There is a fine hotel at Akosombo. It is now a port from which boats go northward to Kete-Krakye, Kpandu, Yeji, and Yapei (Tamale Port). The town is 65 miles (104 km) northeast of Accra.

The Akosombo power project was started in 1961 and was operational by the end of 1965. The dam was an earth and rock fill type structure 370 feet (113 m) high, and 2,100 feet (640 m) long at its crest. When the reservoir behind the dam was completely filled, Lake Volta extended 250 miles (402 km) into the north, forming one of the largest man-made lakes in the world. James Moxon's Volta: Man's Greatest Lake, published in 1969, is a fascinating account of this great engineering feat.

AKPAFU. Small Volta-Togo group living in the Volta Region.

AKPOSO. Small Volta-Togo group who live in the Volta Region.

AKRAMAN see GOMOA

AKRON (Acron, Akrong). A polity on the coast between Fante and Agona in what is now the Central Region. On the 1729 Anville map it is shown as Great Akron, in the interior, and Akron, on the coast. Apam was the chief town. Akron was in the Fante orbit.

AKROPONG see AKUROPON

AKUA BA (pl. Akuamma). An Akan doll carved of wood with flat oval head, long neck, and small round body. It gives an overall impression of a fan. They are often called "fertility dolls," and are sometimes carried by pregnant women. It has come to be one of the symbols of Asante.

AKUAPEM (Akwapim, Aquapim). An Akan polity in the Eastern Region northeast of Accra on the Akuapem Ridge. It covers about 330 square miles (855 sq km). The area was once part of the Akwamu empire from around 1680 to 1730, but it then gained its independence. The seat of the paramount chief was first at Asamankese, then Nyanaoase, and today at Akuropon (Akropong). There are some nineteen towns in the polity. Aburi, Dawu, Mampong-Akuapem, and Akuropon are among the more important.

Its healthy climate, good land, industrious people, and proximity to Accra make Akuapem one of the most progressive areas of Ghana.

AKUAPEM-TOGO RANGE. (Akwapim-Togo) Folded hills that run from the mouth of the Densu river in a northeasterly direction to the Togo frontier. They are cut by the Volta at the Ajena Gorge. In Togo they continue as the Togo-Atakora Mountains. In Ghana their average height is 1,500 feet (457 m).

AKUFFO, FREDERICK W.K. 1937-1979. Soldier, Head of State. Native of Akuropon in Akuapem. He joined the army in 1957, was trained at Sandhurst in England, was commissioned in 1960, and served in the UN peacekeeping force in the Congo. At the time of the coup against Busia and the Second Republic, Akuffo was a colonel. By 1976 he was a member of the Supreme Military Council and Chief of the Defense Staff. On 5 July 1978 he seized power from Acheampong, becoming Chairman of the Supreme Military Council. Less than a year later, 4 June 1979, Akuffo was overthrown by Jerry Rawlings. He was executed 26 June 1979.

AKUMADAN (Akomada, Akomadan). 7°24' N, 1°57' W. Town on the Western Road from Kumasi to Wenchi near the northern border of the Asante Region. It is 56 miles (90 km) northwest of Kumasi. There were 2,342 people living in Akumadan in 1948. By 1970 the census showed 7,310 persons.

AKUROPON (Akropon, Akropong). 5°58' N, 0°05' W. Seat of the Okuapemhene of Akuapem. Town in the Eastern Region, on the Akuapem Ridge, about 32 miles (51 km) northeast of Accra. Akuropon was an early site of educational and agricultural activities of the Basel missionaries, and later of similar activities of the Presbyterians. One of the earliest training colleges for teachers was founded here. Head of State Frederick W.K. Akuffo was a native of Akuropon. In 1911 the town had 6,218 inhabitants. By 1948 the population was down to 4,150, which climbed to 5,606 by 1960 and had reached 7,426 persons in 1970.

AKUSE. 6°06' N, 0°08' E. River port on the west side of the Volta some 55 miles (88 km) above Ada. It is on the tidal limit of the river, and navigation generally ends here except in the rainy season from August to December. It was one of the earliest inland trading centers depending on river transport from Ada, and a ferry still plies the Volta from here. The Basel Mission once had a station at Akuse. The British had a District Commissioner here as early as 1895, one of two on the Gold Coast. The town is in the Eastern Region and is part of Manya (Eastern) Krobo. There were 3,084 persons at Akuse in 1911, 4,704 in 1948, and 3,791 in 1970.

AKWAMU (Aquamboe, Oquie). One of the early Akan kingdoms. Traditions claim an origin in the north, but by the early sixteenth century the kingdom was in the Atewa Hills with a capital at a place called Asamankese. Later the capital was moved to Nyanaoase, near modern Nsawam, not far above Accra. Akwamu conquered the Akuapem (Akwapim) area by 1646, Accra by 1681, and Agona by 1689. By 1702 the armies of Akwamu held power all the way to Ouidah (Benin) in the east. Kwahu fell to Akwamu in 1710. That was to be the point of greatest expansion. From 1729 a series of reverses contracted the limits of Akwamu power to a small area north of Krobo. They submitted to the British on 27 July 1886.

AKWAMUFIE. 6°17' N, 0°05' E. The Akwamu capital. A town in the Eastern Region near the Volta and the Akosombo Dam. The Akwamu moved here after a defeat by the Akyem and Akuapem in 1730.

AKWAPIM see AKUAPEM

AKWAPIM-TOGO RANGE see AKUAPEM-TOGO RANGE

AKWATIA. 6°03' N, 0°48' W. Town in the Eastern Region that is the center of diamond mining. Population was 4,457 in 1948 and 12,177 in 1970.

AKWAWA, MOUNT. 6°27' N, 0°25' W. Peak on the Mampong-Koforidua Scarp near Begoro in the Kwahu part of the Eastern Region. It is 2,585 feet (788 m) high.

AKWIDA (Akoda). 4°45' N, 2°01' W. Coastal village on Cape Three Points between Prince's Town and Dixcove in the Western Region. The Brandenburgers built Fort Dorothea here in 1685. This post was later taken over by the Dutch. Only the ruins of Fort Dorothea remain today.

AKYEASE (Achiasi). 5°50' N, 1°00' W. Town on the railroad below Oda in the southwestern corner of the Eastern Region. It had a population of 4,991 in 1948 and 8,466 in 1970.

AKYEM (Akim, Achim). One of the major Akan groups of Ghana. Akyem tradition traces their origin as a state to the modern Adansi area in the sixteenth century. Pressure from the Denkyira in the seventeenth century forced Akyem movement eastward into the area of the Atewa Hills and the Birim River between the modern towns of Kibi and Oda. Reindorf says Akyem means "salt trader." At one time they were also active in the gold and slave trade. The Akyem are divided into three major divisions: the Akyem Abuakwa, the Akyem Bosume, and the Akyem Kotoku.

AKYEM ABUAKWA. The senior and largest Akyem division. These

Akyem migrated into the Atewa Hills around Kibi in the late seventeenth century from the Adansi area. They established their capital at Banso, near their modern center at Kibi. By 1960 there were some 114,220 Akyem Abuakwa.

AKYEM BOSUME. The southernmost and smallest Akyem division. These Akan moved from Adansi into their present position as a result of pressure from the Asante early in the eighteenth century. Their chief town today is Akyem Swedru. The 1960 census showed 12,140 Akyem Bosume.

AKYEM KOTOKU. The middle Akyem division. When they first moved into the Atewa Hills they established a capital at Jedem (Jyadem, Gyadam), only a short distance from their present capital at Oda (Nsuaem). The 1960 census showed 45,550 Akyem Kotoku.

AKYEM SWEDRU. 5°54' N, 1°01' W. The capital of Akyem Bosume, located near Oda in the Eastern Region.

AKYERE. A person or animal killed to accompany a dead person into the spirit world.

ALEXANDER, HENRY TEMPLER. 1911-1977. British officer, Scottish Rifles. He served as Nkrumah's Chief of Defense Staff from January 1960 to September 1961 during the early stages of the UN Congo operations. He wrote of his experiences in Ghana and the Congo in African Tightrope, published in 1965.

AMANFU (Amanfro, Amanfur, Amanful, Mount Manfro). A place just a few hundred yards east of the Castle at Cape Coast. The Danes built Fort Fredriksborg here around 1660, but sold their claims to the British in 1685. About 1699 the English rebuilt the fort and named it Fort Royal. Almost no traces of the fort are there today.

AMANHENE. The plural of Omanhene. Akan paramount chiefs.

AMANKWATIA (Amankwa Tia, Aman Quatia, Amanquattiah). Ca. 1833-1874. Bantamahene and Commander of the Asante army against the British, 1872-1873. Amankwatia owed his position to Asantehene Kofi Karikari, and he became one of his master's closest advisers. He belonged to the group that counselled a hard line against British pretensions on the Gold Coast. During 1872 he persuaded the Asantehene to allow him to occupy the trade routes as far as the Fante borders. Permission was granted, and on 9 December 1872 Amankwatia left Kumasi at the head of an Asante army. By the middle of 1873 the army was within a few miles of Cape Coast. But anti-war sentiment in Kumasi in the second half of 1873 undermined Kofi Karikari's resolution, and in November Amankwatia was ordered to retreat back to Asanteland. A British and Fante army followed under Wolseley. Amankwatia died in defense of Kumasi in January 1874.

AMANSIE (Amanse, Amansi). The area around Lake Bosumtwi, between the upper Oda and Anum rivers, which is the Asante heartland. The territory was settled by members of the Oyoko clan from Adansi around 1600. According to Asante tradition, the first Asantes came out of the ground at Asantemanso.

AMANTOO STATES. The chief states forming the Asante Confederation. They are Kumasi, Dwaben, Mampong, Nsuta, Kokofu, and Bekwai.

AMARIA (Hamaria, Amariya). Zabrama-Grusi leader who was born in Santijan, in the Sisala-Builsa area 50 miles (80 km) southwest of Bolgatanga (Santijan is located at 10°32' N, 1°32' W). When Amaria was about seven he was captured by Alfa Hano, first of the Zabrama leaders. In the following years he distinguished himself as a leader under Alfa Gazare and Babatu. In 1894 he broke from his allegiance to the Zabrama, allied himself with the Europeans, and helped break the power of the Zabrama in the Volta area.

AMEDUME, J.K. Naval officer who was a close associate of Acheampong 1975 to 1978. During this time he was Minister of Labor, Social Welfare, and Cooperatives. In the last year of SMU rule he was promoted to Rear Admiral and naval chief. He was executed by the AFRC in June 1979.

AMEDZOFE (Amedzope). 6°51' N, 0°26' E. Old German mission station in the Volta Region Avatime section midway between Ho and Hohoe. It is a beautiful mountain town in the Togo hills in the shadow of Mt. Gami and in sight of the Biakpa, Kabakaba, and Peki hills. There are several interesting waterfalls near Amedzofe.

AMETEWEE, SETH. A police constable who was assigned to guard duty at Flagstaff House. On New Year's Day, 1964, he attempted to kill President Nkrumah. Ametewee was Ewe.

AMOKU. A small village six miles (ten km) east of Anomabo, near Saltpond and Ankoful, where the French maintained a small thatched mud hut as a trade post from 1786 to 1807.

AMSTERDAM, FORT. 5°12' N, 1°05' W. A fort near Kormantin (Kromanti, Kormantine) on the coast in the Central Region near Saltpond. It was started by the English in 1638. The Dutch took the place in 1665, and gave it the name by which it is still known. It changed hands between the English and Dutch several times. The Asante took it in 1807, and in 1811 Anomabo held it a short time. The British held it after 1868. In 1951 a restoration project was undertaken, but this was not completed.

ANAMOBO or ANOMABU   see ANOMABO

ANANSE, KWAKU. The legendary spider of Ghanaian folk tales.

ANASHAN (Anashun). 5°09' N, 1°09' W. Place near Cape Coast in the Central Region. The British had a fort here in the seventeenth century. Nothing is left of the original lodge. Today the place is called Biriwa.

ANKOBEA. (Amkobia) The Asantehene's personal security force and bodyguard. These persons were appointed by and only responsible to the Asantehene.

ANKOBRA RIVER. River which rises near Bibiani and flows through the Western Region to reach the Gulf of Guinea just west of Axim. It flows through Ghana's gold-producing region. In October 1983 a modern bridge near Axim replaced the old one-vehicle ferry. The new bridge will be a part of the Pan-African highway. The Ankobra is navigable in small boats for 50 miles (80 km). The Mansi and the Bonsa are the major tributaries.

ANKRAH, JOSEPH ARTHUR. Soldier and Head of State. A Ga, born in Accra during World War I, Ankrah was educated in the schools of Accra. After school he joined the army, and by the start of World War II he was a warrant officer. During the war he took officer training in England and became a commissioned officer. He served in the UN forces in the Congo and afterwards had reached the rank of Deputy Chief of Defense Staff when, in July 1965, Nkrumah retired him from the armed forces. After the 1966 coup he was reinstated in the army with the rank of Lieutenant General, appointed Commander of the Armed Forces, and named Chairman of the National Liberation Council. As Head of State, Ankrah was largely a figurehead, but he apparently had ambitions to keep his job. He accepted money from foreigners to conduct a poll to determine his chances if he should become a candidate when popular elections were allowed again. This touched off a scandal, and Ankrah resigned his public offices.

ANLO (Awuna). An Ewe group who live along the coast to the east of the Volta River. Other peoples in the area called them the Awuna. The legendary founders of Anlo are said to have come from Notsie in the area of modern Togo in the second half of the seventeenth century. There were two founding fathers, Sri and Wenya. From the settlement of the Anlo around the Keta Lagoon there were wars between Anlo and Ada and Accra over fishing rights and the salt and slave traffic. More than half the population of Anloland are said to have been killed in fighting in 1776.

Later the Danes joined Ada and the allies of Ada in a war with
Anlo, and on 18 June 1784 the Anlo had to submit to Danish rule.
It was an uneasy relationship, and the Danes surrendered their
prerogatives to the English in 1850. The fierce competition with
Ada continued, and England frequently resorted to military force
to subdue the Anlo. In June 1874, with the Treaty of Dzelukofe,
Anlo surrendered. But they soon allied themselves with the
notorious slave trader Geraldo de Lima (Lema) and resumed their
conflict with the English. In 1884 the British burnt the Anlo
capital town of Anloga and once again forced the Anlo into submission.

ANLOGA (Awunaga). 5°48' N, 0°54' E. Capital of the Anlo, located
11 miles (18 km) southwest of Keta on the spit of land between
the Keta Lagoon and the Gulf of Guinea. Zion College of West
Africa was opened here in October 1937. It is the oldest secondary school in the Volta Region. In 1911 the population of
Anloga was 2,115. By 1948 the census showed 6,358, by 1960
it was 11,038, and in 1970 there were 14,032 people in Anloga.

ANOKYE, OKOMFO (Anonkye, Anotche, Anotchi). National hero of
the Asante. Okomfo (or Komfo) means priest. Kwame Frimpong
Anokye was an Akwamu priest who helped Osei Tutu establish
the traditions of the Asante Union, including the Golden Stool,
soul of the Asante nation. He helped work out the Asante Constitution, and the tradition of the Odwira Festival. Francis
Fuller called Anokye the "Cardinal Wolsey" of Asante. Anokye
lived in the second half of the seventeenth century. His descendants sit on the stool of Agona.

ANOMABO (Anamobo, Anomabu). 5°10' N, 1°07' W. Fante town in
the Central Region ten miles (16 km) east of Cape Coast. It was
founded in the sixteenth century as a fishing village. The name
means "bird rock." The Dutch built a lodge to trade here about
1640, and the town was in turn captured by Danes, Swedes, and
English. It was bombarded by the French in 1794, and attacked
by the Asante in 1807. The English built Fort Charles at Anomabo in 1679, and in the 1750s built another fort called Anomabo
Fort. This was restored in the 1950s. Anomabo was a major
British commercial depot for many years.

ANOUFOU or ANUFO   see   CHOKOSI

ANSA SASRAKU. Ruler of Akwamu in the latter part of the seventeenth century. He defeated the Ga in 1677, and by the time
of his death in 1689 he ruled the coast from the Volta to Agona.

ANTHONY, SETH. Attended Sandhurst, England, and became first
Gold Coast commissioned officer, 1945. Admitted to Civil Service. In 1957 he became one of Ghana's first senior diplomats.

ANTOR, SENYO GATROR. Born 1913. Ewe political leader in the
Volta Region. Educated in Bremen Mission at Amedzofe, the
Presbyterian Training College, Akuropon, and the Theological
College at Ho. Editor, UN Newsletter, 1949-1953. One of the
leaders in the formation of the Togoland Congress Party in 1951.
He wanted an Ewe homeland under Ewe control and was opposed
to the integration of British Togo into the Gold Coast. He was
a member of the Legislative Assembly, 1954-1957. After independence he was arrested in connection with unrest in the Volta
Region. He was sentenced to six years, but released after appeal. He served in the National Assembly, 1958-1961. In 1961
he was detained by Nkrumah and was left in prison without trial
until the coup in 1966. Under the NLC he served as a member
of the Political Committee, and he was a member of the Constituent Assembly, 1968-1969. In the Second Republic he was ambassador to Togo, 1970-1972.

ANUM. A tributary of the Pra which rises northeast of Kumasi,
near Efiduasi, in the old Dwaben area of the Asante Region, and
flows southward until it joins the Pra at 6°12' N, 1°12' W.

ANUM-BOSO. A Guan group that lives mostly in the Eastern Region.

ANYAKO. 6°00' N, 0°55' E. An Anlo village in the Volta Region
near the Keta Lagoon where there was much fighting between the
Anlo and Danes in the 1840s over the slave trade. Anyako had
a population of 4,700 in 1970.

AOWIN (Awowin). An Anyi-Bawle group of Akan who live along the
Ivory Coast border in the Western Region between the Nzema
and Sefwi.

APAM (Appam). 5°17' N, 0°44' W. Coastal city just to the west of
Winneba and 43 miles (69 km) west of Accra. The Dutch began
Fort Leydsaamheid here in 1697. It was taken briefly by the
Akyems in 1811 and by the British in 1868. In the present cen-
tury the fort became a police station.

APO CEREMONY. An eight-day holiday when all Akan are supposed
to clear their souls (sunsum) of evil by saying and doing what is
on their minds.

APOLLO 568. In 1970 Prime Minister Kofi Busia dismissed 568 civil
servants who had served while Nkrumah was president, and who
still seemed to be loyal to the former president. This caused a
clash with the judiciary, which ruled that one of the dismissed,
E.K. Sallah, could not be dismissed. Busia refused to obey a
court order ordering him to reemploy Sallah.

APOLLONIA (Appolonia, Amanahia, Apolonia). Name the early missionaries gave to all the Nzema country. The British built a

fort at Beyin in 1768-1770 which they called Fort Apollonia. This was transferred to the Dutch in 1868. It is in ruins today.

APPIAH, JOSEPH MANUEL. Born 1918. Political leader from Kumasi. Educated at Wesleyan Primary School in Kumasi, and Mfantsipim at Cape Coast. Worked for United Africa Company in Accra, Takoradi, and Freetown (Sierra Leone). In 1943 he went to England to study law. There he became a friend of Kwame Nkrumah, and they both attended the Pan African Conference in Manchester in 1945. He did not pass the bar until 1954, but in the meantime he married Peggy Cripps, daughter of Sir Stafford Cripps, Labor Chancellor of Exchequer. While still in England he was one of the founders of the West African National Secretariat. After his return to the Gold Coast Appiah was at first a member of the CPP, but in early 1955 he quit the CPP and joined the opposition NLM. Elected to the Legislative Assembly in 1956, he became head of the opposition in 1957. His bitter opposition to Nkrumah's "cult of personality" landed him in prison in October 1961. He was not released from Ussher Fort Prison until December 1962.

After the coup of 1966 Appiah was made a roving ambassador for the NLC, and was later placed on the Political Committee. In the 1969 elections he organized the United Nationalist Party, but was defeated in an attempt to get a seat in National Assembly. During the Second Republic he joined the Justice Party, and was active in opposition to Busia. With the NRC coup in 1972 he returned to favor once again. He became a close adviser to Acheampong. He was given the job of roving ambassador again, and represented Ghana in the UN for a time. He was active in the campaign for Union Government in 1978. Then when the SMC was replaced with the AFRC, he found himself in prison once more.

APPOLONIA   see   APOLLONIA

AQUAMBOE   see   AKWAMU

AQUAPIM   see   AKUAPEM

AQUOWOA   see   KWAHU

ARCANIA or ARCANES   see   AKANNY

ARDEN-CLARKE, CHARLES NOBLE. 1898-1962. Colonial officer. After service in the army, 1917-1920, Arden-Clarke joined the Colonial Service: Nigeria, 1920-1936; Bechuanaland, 1936-1942; Basutoland, 1942-1946. He was then elevated to Governor of Sarawak, 1946-1949; Governor of the Gold Coast, 1949-1957; and first Governor-General of Ghana, March-May 1957, when he was replaced by a Labor peer, the Earl of Listowel. As the last British Governor of the Gold Coast, Arden-Clarke worked unusually well with Kwame Nkrumah in the transfer of power from Great Britain to Ghana.

ARGOTIME. Old name for an area east of the Volta in the Volta Region in what is the general area of Krepi.

ARMAH, AYI KWEI. Born 1939. Author. Armah is from Takoradi in the Western Region. He was educated at Achimota, Groton (Massachusetts), and Harvard University. His BA degree was in sociology. After graduation he worked briefly as a translator in Algiers. Then he taught English at Navrongo and got a job writing scripts for Ghana Television. In 1967 he studied briefly at Columbia and wrote for a few months for Jeune Afrique. Then he lectured on African Literature at the University of Massachusetts and since 1972 he has been teaching at the University of Tanzania, Dar es Salaam. He is Ghana's most prolific novelist. His first novel was The Beautyful Ones Are Not Yet Born, published in 1968. This was followed by Fragments, 1970; Why Are We So Blest?, 1972; Two Thousand Seasons, 1973; and The Healers, 1978. Armah has also published short stories and poems. He is the subject of several interesting monographs.

ARMED FORCES OF GHANA. In July 1981 there were 15,300 in the Ghanaian Armed Forces. The army had 12,700, divided into two brigades of eleven battalions. The navy had 1,200 sailors with bases at Secondi and Tema. The air force had 1,400 airmen divided into five squadrons. There were 5,000 persons in the paramilitary forces, counting the border guards. The Military Academy was located at Teshi, near Accra.

The Ghanaian armed forces were in a sad state at the end of 1983. Most equipment was worn out. There was almost a complete lack of discipline, and the officer corps had been decimated in the political turmoil of the preceding five years. The officers still in service were afraid of the men under them. Esprit de corps was almost nonexistent. And worst of all, the military terrorized the civilians they were supposed to protect. By the end of 1983 Rawlings was in the process of organizing a Peoples' Militia to advance the cause of his revolution.

ARMED FORCES REVOLUTIONARY COUNCIL (AFRC). A group of junior officers and enlisted soldiers, led by Jerry John Rawlings, which overthrew the Supreme Military Council on 4 June 1979 with the avowed purpose of conducting a "house-cleaning" exercise. Eight high-ranking officers (including three former heads of state: Afrifa, Acheampong, and Akuffo) were found guilty of corruption and executed. Many other persons were sentenced to long terms at hard labor and had their property confiscated. After four months in power, during which elections were held, the AFRC surrendered power to a civilian government under Hilla Limann, 24 September 1979.

ARMITAGE, CECIL HAMILTON. 1869-1933. Colonial officer. Armitage entered Gold Coast service in 1894 and was part of the Asante expedition of 1895-1896. He was secretary to Governor Frederic Hodgson for a time, and in 1900 he was sent to Kumasi to find the Golden Stool, a mission in which he failed. He was acting Resident of Kumasi during the siege of the Fort in Kumasi in 1900.

Armitage was Chief Commissioner, Northern Territories, 1910-1920, during which time he was criticized by Governor Hugh Clifford for his failure to prevent excesses in the way his subordinates sometimes dealt with people under their control. While in the North, Armitage wrote The Ashanti Campaign of 1900 and made several valuable reports on conditions in the Northern Territories.

Cecil Armitage became Governor of the Gambia in 1920 and held the position until 1927, when he retired.

ART. Ghana is famous for its wood carvings, especially stools, oware boards, and Akua ba dolls. Masks and human or animal figures in wood are not traditional in most Akan societies. Drums, combs, and other objects made of wood are often decorated with designs.

Brass ceremonial vessels (kuduo) and brass boxes and containers are sometimes interesting. Metal-casting by the lost-wax method is developed to a fine art, especially among the Asante, known for their gold weights, ornaments, and jewelry.

Ghanaian pottery is generally undistinguished. Most pots are blackened after firing by placing the hot pot in leaves. Smoke then turns the pot black. Some pots are decorated with interesting designs. Terracotta heads were once used in funerals.

Contemporary Ghanaian artists compare favorably with any in Africa. Saka Acquaye excels in music, writing, and art. He is a sculptor of note, and his wood panel inlay murals grace a number of public buildings in Accra. Oku Ampofo, Kofi Antubam, and Vincent Kofi are other important sculptors. Among Ghana's notable painters are: Kobina Bucknor, A.O. Bartimeus, Alex Amofa, and Sylvanue Amenuke. W.C. Owusu and Daniel Cobblah are ceramists. S.K. Prah, S.H. Kyei, S.K. Nkansah, and J.C. Okyere are among the better-known wood-carvers. The Gold Coast Society of Artists was formed in 1946, and Ghana today continues to have an active community of talented and skilled artists.

ASAFO. Communal or militia groups organized for defense or group enterprises. Asafo companies often ruled sections of villages or towns, and they often fought pitched battles against each other, as in Cape Coast in 1859. The companies were sometimes a disrupting force used by young men against the chief and elders.

ASAFOHENE. Captain of an Asafo Company, or a ceremonial head of a group of kinsmen.

ASAFU-ADJAYE, EDWARD OKYERE. 1903-1976. Lawyer and political leader. Educated in Kumasi, at Adisadel, and the University College of London. Passed his bar examination in 1926. He and F.V. Nanka-Bruce represented the Gold Coast at the coronation of George VI in 1937. Member of the Legislative Assembly from 1946 to 1956, and member of the National Assembly 1956. Minister of Local Government in 1951, and of Trade and Labor in 1955. One of the Gold Coast representatives at the coronation of Elizabeth II in 1953, and Ghana's first High Commissioner to the Court of St. James, 1957-1961. He resumed his law practice in 1961.

ASAMAN (1). The traditional founder of Bono-Manso. The date for the foundation of Bono-Manso is disputed. Some authorities say between 1297 and 1329, and others give a date as late as 1400. The settlement was near Techiman.

ASAMAN (Asamang) (2). 6°29' N, 1°30' W. A village in the Asante nuclear area. Rattray says that a hunter from this village first discovered Lake Bosumtwi in "the time of Oti Akenten."

ASAMANKESE. 5°52' N, 0°40' W. An old capital of Akwamu, it is a large town in the Eastern Region about 50 miles (80 km) northwest of Accra. It had a population of 3,319 in 1911, 8,856 in 1948, 16,718 in 1960, and in 1970 the census was 16,905.

ASAMENI (Asomani, Asemmani). An Akwamu merchant who learned several European languages to deal with the Europeans at Accra. In June of 1693 he overpowered the Danish garrison of Christiansborg, and he ruled that post as governor for about a year, trading with the English, French, and Dutch. After Christiansborg was restored to the Danes, Asameni continued to play an important role in Akwamu affairs.

ASANTE (Ashanti). A region, people and Akan nation. Asante is the proper Akan spelling, and Ashanti is the English spelling. The divisions of Asante are Kumasi (Kumase in Akan), Mampong, Bekwai, Kokofu, Nsuta, Dwaben (Juaben), Effiduase, Asokore, Ejisu (Edweso), Bonwire, Assumigya, and Senfi.

The Asante kingdom was formed in the seventeenth century by Akan who came from the Adansi area around Lake Bosumtwe to the neighborhood of the trading town of Tafo. The Asante leader was Obiri Yeboa, a member of the Oyoko lineage. The date for the hegira was the 1670s. By 1690 Osei Tutu was the Asante leader. He formed the alliance with Mampong, Bekwai, Kokofu, Dwaben, Nsuta, and others which became the Asante Confederation or Union. With the aid of Okomfo Anokye, he established the traditions of the Golden Stool, the Odwira, and the Asante Constitution.

The eighteenth century saw the steady expansion of Asante influence. Denkyira fell in 1701; Assin, Aowin, Amanahia, Wassa, Twifo, and Wenchi by 1720; Techiman, Banda, Gyaman, and Western Gonja by 1740; Kete Krakye, Central and Eastern Gonja, Dagomba, Akyem, and Akwamu by 1755. By 1760 all Asante's neighbors save the Fante were under the spell of the Golden Stool. The Fante were vulnerable too, but they were in the British sphere.

As the Asante attempted to open routes to the coast, it was perhaps inevitable that they would come into conflict with the Europeans and the European allies on the coast. From 1807, when Asante pushed hard toward the coast, clashes began to occur. In 1826 the Asante army was defeated at Katamanso (Dodowa). That battle proved to be the beginning of the decline of Asante. In 1874 the British marched into Kumasi, leaving it a city of ashes. In 1896 the British returned again, and this time they sent the Asantehene into exile. He was allowed to return again only in his old age, in 1924. By then the power of Asante was no more. But they were still a proud people. In 1935 the British allowed the Asante Union to be recreated, but it would never again be a sovereign power.

ASANTE, DAVID. 1834-1892. A Basel missionary. He was educated in the Basel school in Akuropon, and in Basel, Switzerland. After he returned to Akuapem, he gained some note as a writer on African religion, travel, and as a translator. He helped J.G. Christaller with a translation of the Bible into Twi or Akan, and he translated John Bunyan's Pilgrim's Progress into Twi.

ASANTEHEMAA. Akan Queen-mother. She was not actually the mother of the Asantehene, but the personification of motherhood. See AHEMA.

ASANTEHENE. The Omanhene of Kumasi and head of the Asante Union. He is the keeper of the Golden Stool.

ASANTE-KOTOKO-UNION SOCIETY. A society founded in Kumasi in 1916 as a patriotic Asante association of middle class Asante merchants, clerks, and teachers. J.E. Bandoh was the first president of the society, and J.W.K. Appiah was the first secretary. E.P. Owusu, who later became Prempe II in 1931, was a charter member.

ASANTEMANHYIAMU. The High Council or Assembly of the Asante Union. It served as the highest tribunal of the nation. All the provincial rulers, the senior Kumasi officials, and the queen-mother were members. It held regular annual sessions at the time of the Odwira Festival, and held extraordinary sessions in times of emergency.

ASANTEMANSO. (Santemanso) Place where Asante traditions say the first of their ruling clans came from the ground. R.S. Rattray called the spot the "most hallowed spot in all their territory." The grove where Asante history is supposed to have begun is not far from Lake Bosumtwi.

ASASE YAA (Asase Ya, Asase Efua). The earth-goddess. Thursday is the day set aside by the Akan to honor mother earth. The soil is not tilled on Thursday, it is a day of rest from farm work. Asase Yaa is not regarded as a divinity. There are no priests, shrines, or temples, but Asase Yaa is recognized as the source of truth. Offerings are sometimes placed upon the ground for the earth spirit.

ASEBU (Saboe, Sabu, Sabou, Sabue). 5°13' N, 1°12' W. Village in the Central Region. A 1629 Dutch map shows Saboe (Asebu) as a coastal state with Futu to the west and Fante to the east. The locality was known for its salt. Mouri is an Asebu village. The Dutch dominated the trade of this place from the 1590s. It was also subject to Fante domination by 1725.

ASENE. 5°55' N, 0°56' W. The Battle of Asene took place here in 1824. Asene Krofoso is on the north bank of the Pra near Obogu and Dampon. Here a two-day battle was fought in 1824 between the Akyem-Akuapem allies on one side, and an Asante army on the other side. As a result of their victory, Akyem Kotoku gained freedom from Asante rule.

ASENIE (Asinie). One of the principal Akan clans.

ASESEWA. 6°23' N, 0°08' W. Famous Manya Krobo market in the Eastern Region some 30 miles (48 km) northeast of Koforidua and near Lake Volta. The population was 1,468 in 1948, 4,282 in 1960, and by 1970 the population was up to 6,111.

ASHANTI see ASANTE

ASHANTI CONFEDERACY COUNCIL. Group created by the British at Kumasi in January 1935 to represent the Asante people in the revived Asante Union. It was assigned only limited powers in keeping with the policies of Indirect Rule proclaimed by the British at the time. By the end of the second World War in 1945 it had been called together only 11 times.

ASHANTI GOLDFIELDS CORPORATION. A corporation organized in 1897 with E.A. Cade as the chief figure. The corporation gained a 100-square-mile (259-sq-km) concession for mining, trading, rubber and timber extraction, and road building. It opened its first mine at Obuasi in 1898. In 1975 the NRC took over 55 percent ownership of Ashanti Goldfields Corporation.

ASIKAFO (sing. is sikani). The Asante bourgeoisie. People of wealth in Asante were allowed to have an elephant's tail carried before them as a mark of status.

ASIN see ASSIN

ASOFO. Fetish priests.

ASOKO. Also Assini. A state along the lower Tano basin and the Aby Lagoon, much of it in the area of the modern Ivory Coast. Assini was the chief town, and Asoko the state capital. Canoe construction and salt production were the chief products of the area. Asoko is on an island in the Aby Lagoon.

ASOKORE. One of the Akan clans.

ASOMFO. Akan bureaucrats.

ASONA. One of the Akan clans, called the "fox" clan.

ASSEYDOU. Area in Northern Ghana in the Grusi Sisala River region.

ASSIN (Asen, Asin). Akan group that today is found in the Central Region east of the Pra with the Denkyira and Twifo to the west, the Adansi to the north, the Akyem to the east, and the Fante to the south. They have been intermediaries in the trade between the north and the coast, and have often been subject to pressures from their more powerful neighbors. Both Denkyira and Asante have ruled them at different times. The Assin have frequently allied themselves to Wassa, Twifo, and Fante, and their lands were frequently devastated in wars between these people and the Asante.
   The Assin are divided into two groups. The Assin Apemanim (Apimenem) are mostly on the east side of the Cape Coast-Kumasi highway, with a capital at the old slave depot of Manso. The Assin Attendansu (Atandanso) are mainly to the west of the road, with a capital at Nyankumasi.

ASSOCIATION OF WEST AFRICAN MERCHANTS (AWAM). A group of European businesses which united during the depression of the 1930s to fix prices and divide markets in West Africa. Their agreement about the Gold Coast markets was reached in July 1934.

ASSUMIGUA (Asumegya). One of the original Metropolitan states of Asante, but it was never very important.

ASUMAN see SUMAN

ASUMEGYA see ASSUMIGUA

ATABIA. Died ca. 1742. Mamprusi ruler. His reign of half a century, from about 1688, saw a great expansion of Mamprusi in what is now the Northern and Upper regions. At first his capital was located at Gambaga, but about 1700 he moved to Nalerigu, seven miles (11 km) to the east of Gambaga.

ATEBUBU (Tebu). 7°45' N, 0°59' W. An old capital of the Brong, the town is on the Great Northern Road 85 miles (136 km) northeast of Kumasi. It is the western end of an old road that used to go off to the ferry at Kete-Krakye, but now goes to Lake Volta. It is a stopover for the cattle drivers from the north. In 1948 it had a population of 2,391, which grew to 4,216 by 1960, and had reached 6,630 by 1970.

ATEWA HILLS. 5°59' N, 0°40' W. Hills in the center of the Eastern Region. The Birim River rises in this area, and the Akyem capital of Kibi is located in these hills. Diamonds were discovered in the hills in 1919, and there is also bauxite. Altitudes rise to 2,400 feet (732 m) on these densely forested slopes.

ATTOH-AHUMA, SAMUEL RICHARD BREW. 1863-1921. Methodist minister, nationalist, author. He was an officer in the Aborigines' Rights Protection Society. He worked hard to persuade Africans to reject European names and to adopt African names.

ATWIA. Early inhabitants of what became the Akyem area between the Pra and the Densu. It is said that these people in the Atewa Hills were people who lived alone and were subject to no one.

ATWODE. Guan group in the Volta Region who have a culture much like the Ewe. They are sometimes called Atyoti.

AUGUSTABORG, FORT. A Danish fortification built on the location of an earlier Dutch post in 1787. It was bought by the British in 1850. The ruins are to be seen today at the modern town of Teshi.

AVATIME (Afatime). Central Togo people who form an enclave in Ewe territory in the Volta Region. The paramount chief lives at Vane. Amedzofe is the more important town. The area is in one of Ghana's most beautiful mountain districts.

AVOLIENU see NEWTOWN

AWASO (Awaaso). 6°14' N, 2°16' W. Town in the Western Region. It is the terminal of a rail line from Dunkwa, built at the end of World War II to bring out bauxite. The area is also an important timber source. The population was 1,049 in 1948, 3,548 in 1960, and 5,449 in 1970.

AWHAITEY, BENJAMIN. Adangbe military officer who in December 1958 was commander of Giffard Camp at Accra. He was arrested for being involved with others in a plot to overthrow or assassinate Nkrumah. From this point the government began to use the Preventive Detention Act of 18 July 1958 against its opposition. Awhaitey was convicted and dismissed from the army.

AWONA (Anwona). Akan name for Ewe.

AWOONER, KOFI (George Awooner-Williams). Born 1935 at Wheta, Anlo South, Volta Region, near Keta. One of Ghana's best known writers. He received his education at Achimota, Legon, London, and Stony Brook, New York. He was managing director of Ghana Film Industries, 1965-1967, and has held several academic appointments in the United States and Ghana. Awooner is best known as a poet, but he is author of a novel, This Earth, My Brother (1971) and a survey of the history, culture, and literature of Africa south of the Sahara, The Breast of the Earth (1975). In 1975, while on the faculty of the University of Cape Coast, he was arrested by the military government for helping Brigadier Alphonse Kattah, accused head of an Ewe plot to overthrow the government, escape into Togo. He was held in prison eleven months before being convicted and sent to prison. In 1983 Awooner was appointed ambassador to Brazil by the PNDC.

AWOONER-RENNER, KWEKU BANKOLE (Kweku Awuno-Bankole). 1898-1970. Journalist and politician. Born at Elmina, and educated in Catholic school at Cape Coast, in the 1920s he went to the United States and attended Tuskegee (Alabama), and Carnegie Institute (Pennsylvania). While in the US he was once secretary of the African Student's Association, and he wrote for the NAACP Crisis. From the US he went on to Russia, where he attended the University of Toilers of the East in Moscow. In 1928 he published a book of poems, This Africa, in Moscow. An English version of this book was published in 1943.

Back in the Gold Coast by 1931, Awooner-Renner edited the Gold Coast Leader (Sekondi) for awhile, and then moved to Accra and became active in the Gold Coast Youth Conference. He helped organize the Asante Freedom Society, an attempt to block recreation of the Asante Union. He also became the most vocal Communist in the Gold Coast, and joined the Accra Muslim Party. In 1942 he was elected to the Accra Town Council. By the last year of World War II he went to London to study law. There he was quickly involved in the West African National Secretariat, where he got to know George Padmore and Kwame Nkrumah. He attended the Pan-African Congress at Manchester in 1945. The following year he published a pamphlet, "The West African Soviet Republic."

Awooner-Renner was back in Ghana during the heady days of the organization of the Convention Peoples' Party. He was an active supporter of Nkrumah, and he was sent to James Fort Prison with Nkrumah, Kojo Botsio, and other CPP leaders in 1950. While Nkrumah and Awooner-Renner were in prison,

Awooner-Renner's wife was elected to the Accra Council on the CPP ticket. Once the CPP achieved power, though, Awooner-Renner separated himself from his CPP comrades. For a time he devoted his energies to the Muslim Association Party, and in 1957 he joined other opposition leaders in the United Party. But poor health curtailed his political activities after 1957.

AWOWA (Ahoba ni). Pawns. Persons held as collateral for debts or obligations. Often applied to all persons in servitude.

AWOWIN see AOWIN

AWUNA. English for the Anlo people.

AWUNA. A northern group located in the area between the Kasena and Sisala, and identified as Grusi. They are sometimes called the western Kasena. The Awuna are divided into the Fera and the Nagwa. Pina is their most important settlement.

AWUTU (Obutu). A Guan group, most of whom live in the Gomoa area.

AXIM (Axem, Atsyn). 4°52' N, 2°14' W. Coastal town in the Nzema area of the Western Region just to the east of the Ankobra River, and 40 miles (64 km) west of Takoradi. It is on a beautiful, small bay, and just offshore is Bobaysi Island with its lighthouse. The Portuguese first reached Axim in 1472 and had a small base there by 1503. They began Santo Antonio de Axem in 1515. The fortress was erected on a bluff above the small harbor. The Portuguese evacuated their fort 8 February 1642 in the face of a Dutch attack. In 1872 the Dutch ceded Antonio to the British. The fort was restored in the 1950s, and it is now used for government offices. The town had a population of 4,635 in 1948, 5,619 in 1960, and 8,107 in the 1970 census.

AYAWASO (Ayaso). 5°40' N, 0°17' W. A small village just out of Accra on the Nsachi river where King Ayite of the Ga Asere dynasty established the Ga capital about the middle of the sixteenth century. The place was sacked and burned by the Akwamu in 1677. In 1970 the village reported a population of just 72 persons.

AYEKE, KOJO. Ewe leader. Ayeke was elected as a member of the Legislative Assembly in 1954 and the National Assembly in 1956. He was one of the leaders in the creation of the Togoland Congress Party in 1951, and he favored Ewe unification in a separate state. In 1957, after Ghana became independent, Ayeke was arrested in connection with unrest in the Volta Region. He was sentenced to six years, but released after appeal.

AYENSU RIVER. 5°22' N, 0°35' W. A river which rises in the

Atewa-Atwiredu hills south of Kibi and flows into the Gulf of Guinea just east of Winneba. It is the major source of the water supply of Winneba.

- B -

BAAH, KWAME R.M. Born 1938. Soldier. Native of Dormaa Ahenkro in the Brong Ahafo Region. He attended secondary school in Kumasi, joined the army in 1959, and was commissioned in 1962, after cadet training at Teshi and in India. He saw duty in the Congo under command of Acheampong, and then was assigned to the Ghanaian embassies in London and Washington. In 1972 he joined Acheampong and the NLC in the coup which ended the Second Republic. He was Commissioner of Lands and Mineral Resources in 1972 and was promoted to Commissioner of Foreign Affairs from 1973 to 1975. After the creation of the Supreme Military Council, Baah was dropped from the Cabinet and retired from the army. In 1979 AFRC trials he got a fifty-year sentence.

BAAKO, KOFI. Politician from Saltpond. An early nationalist, he was a founding member of the Committee of Youth Organization and the League of Ghana Patriots. From the creation of the CPP he was one of the key members of that party and one of Nkrumah's closest confidants. In 1949 Baako became editor of the CPP Cape Coast Daily Mail, and he soon joined other nationalists in prison for his opposition to colonial rule. He was elected to the Legislative Assembly in 1954 from Saltpond and represented his home town until the coup of 1966 ended the rule of Nkrumah and the CPP. He became the leader of the CPP in the National Assembly in July 1961. He became Minister of Information and Broadcasting in 1958, then Minister of Parliamentary Affairs, and finally Minister of Defense. At one time he was the General Secretary of the CPP, and he was long a member of the Central Committee of the CPP. He was identified with the left or socialist wing of the party, and was the person who recruited Tawia Adamafio into the party. He favored a one-party state, and the exaltation of Nkrumah beyond criticism.

BABATU (Babato, Baba, Mahama dan Issa). Zabrama (Zabarima or Zerma) leader who followed his father, Alfa Gazari, as leader of a band which dominated a large area of what is now northern Ghana and central Upper Volta. He succeeded his father in 1883. The Grusi people under Amaria (Hamaria) rebelled against Babatu and joined the French in destroying Zabrama suzerainty. Babatu was defeated at Gandiaga in March 1897 and at Doucie (Ducie) in June. With his forces decimated, Babatu retreated into Dagomba, where he joined the Dagomba in resistance to British incursions. Babatu died about 1900.

BADU, KOFI. Born 1935. Journalist and politician. A native of the Asante Region, Badu was an active member of the CPP and the editor or reporter for several Accra papers during the Nkrumah period. He also served in the National Assembly during the First Republic. After the 1966 coup he continued his newspaper career, and his biting editorials in The Spokesman against Busia were a factor in destroying the Second Republic. He enthusiastically supported the NRC after the 1972 coup, was a close adviser to Acheampong after the SMU was established in 1975, and became Commissioner for Consumer Affairs in 1978.

BAGALE (Bagele). 10°12' N, 0°22' W. A village in the Northern Region where the mausoleum of the Dagomba Nas is located. The spirits of all the dead Dagomba Nas are said to live in the Spirits' Room at Bagale.

BALME, DAVID MOWBRAY. Born 1912. Classical Scholar. Graduate of Cambridge and Halle (Germany), who after service in World War II, became a lecturer in classics at Jesus College, Cambridge. From 1948 to 1957 he was the Principal of the University College of the Gold Coast, Legon. In that position he did much to determine the basic direction of the University along Cambridge lines with residence halls, faculty rule, and intellectual elitism. The library at the University of Ghana is named for Balme. After leaving Legon Balme taught classics at Queen Mary College, London, from 1957 until he retired in 1978.

BALMER, WILLIAM TURNBULL. An English minister who taught at Mfantsipim, Cape Coast, from 1907 to 1911. In 1925 he published A History of the Akan Peoples, in which he advanced the idea that the Akan peoples had moved south from ancient Ghana after that old Sahel kingdom had come to an end in the thirteenth century. J.B. Danquah picked up the idea of dispersion from Ghana in his 1928 Akim Abuakwa Handbook, and then later Danquah proposed that the name of the Gold Coast be changed to New Ghana.

BAMBOI. 8°10' N, 2°02' W. Village in the Northern Region on the Black Volta. It is the site of the ferry on the Wenchi-Bole road, located 25 miles (40 km) northwest of Kintampo. There were only 438 people there in 1948, up to 815 in 1960, and 1,117 in 1970.

BANDA (Banna). 8°10' N, 2°22' W. Village in the extreme northwestern corner of the Brong-Ahafo Region about ten miles (16 km) from Bui and the Black Volta. This was once an important stopping point for traders from the north and south.

BANDA HILLS. Hills along the border of the Ivory Coast to the west of Bamboi and Wenchi.

BANKAM STOOL. The Beaded Stool. The symbol of the royal power of Denkyira.

BANKESIESO. An old Denyira capital near Obuasi on the route from Kumasi to Elmina in the modern Asante Region.

BANNERMAN, CHARLES EDWARD WOOLHOUSE. 1884-1943. First African to become a judge of the Supreme Court of the Gold Coast. He was one of the founders of the National Congress of British West Africa.

BANNERMAN, EDMUND. 1832-1903. Grandson of an Asantehene, and son of Lieutenant-Governor James Bannerman. He was educated in England as a lawyer. He held a number of positions in the Gold Coast government during his lifetime and was one of the leaders in the movement to have Africans serve on the Legislative Council. In 1886 he was a leader in a movement to send a delegation to England to protest British policy on the Gold Coast.

BANNERMAN, JAMES. 1790-1858. Son of a Scottish commandant at Cape Coast Castle and of an Akan mother. He married a daughter of the Asantehene. By 1850 he was one of the leading merchants in Accra, and in that year he was appointed a member of the first Gold Coast Legislative Council and became civil commandant of Christiansborg Castle. At the end of the year he became Lieutenant-Governor of the Gold Coast, a position he held until October 1851. James Bannerman established a family which has long been one of the most prominent in the country.

BANTAMA. An important section of Kumasi, it is in the northwestern section of town, between Suntreso and the Mampong Road. The Asante Cultural Center, the Royal Mausoleum, the Okomfo Anokye Hospital, the Public Library, the Zoo, and the city Race Course are all in the vicinity. The chief of Bantama was the traditional military commander of the Asante armies in time of war.

BAOBAB (<u>Adansonia digitata</u>, monkey-bread tree). One of West Africa's most useful trees. Its seeds have medicinal value, its bark is used to make rope, it is a reservoir for water, its fruit has a pleasing lemon taste, and its leaves, when ground, provide a flour which is used in sauces.

BAOULE see BAWLE

BARROS, JOAO DE. 1496-1570. Portuguese factor at Elmina in 1532, treasurer from 1522-1525, commander at Elmina from 1525 to 1528. He wrote one of the earliest accounts of the Gold Coast.

BASARE (Kyamba, Tchamba). A Gurma group who today are scattered all over Ghana and Togo.

BASEL MISSION SOCIETY. A missionary society founded in 1815 in Basel, Switzerland. It began its work on the Gold Coast in 1827. Many of the early missionaries who came to Africa died in their first year in the tropics, but they persisted in their evangelical, educational, medical, agricultural, and vocational endeavors in spite of all odds. Of nine sent to Christiansborg between 1828 and 1840, not one made a convert. After 1835 the Akuapem (Akwapim) area became the center of their enterprises. A boys' school was founded there in 1843, followed by a girls' school four years later. By 1881 they had almost fifty schools, mostly in the Eastern Province, and in 1890 there were almost 2,000 students enrolled in their care. By 1900 they operated two Teacher Training schools in the Gold Coast. Since the Basel missionaries used German, they were deported during World War I and were not allowed to return until 1926. After that the Basel Mission Church became known as Presbyterian. Kwamena-Poh says that the work of the Basel Mission in Akuapem "shook the bases of traditional life."

BATENSTEYN, FORT. 4°49' N, 1°55' W. A European fort which once stood at Butri, in the Western Region. The Swedes established a trade post there about 1650, but the Dutch built the fort in 1656. The British gained the area in 1872. Today the fortifications are in ruins.

BAWA. The progenitor of the Mole-Dagbani peoples. Tradition says that he came from Gurma and settled at Pusiga, in the Upper Region East, near the borders of Upper Volta and Togo. The Mossi call him Nedega, and Dagomba traditions call him Gbewa.

BAWKU. 11°03' N, 0°15' W. An important town in the Upper Region East near the border with Upper Volta. It is the principal town of the Kusasi people. The market at Bawku has long been famous, and it is an important contact with the Muslim Sahel to the north. It is about 170 miles (274 km) to Tamale, and 43 miles (69 km) to Bolgatanga. In 1911 the population was only 1,466, by 1948 it was 6,888; in 1960 the census was 12,719, and by 1970 some 20,567 people lived there.

BAWLE (Baoule, Baule, Bahure). The Anyi-Bawle are the most western Akan group. Most of them live on the border of the Ivory Coast or in the Ivory Coast. They are most closely related to the Sahwi and Aowin.

BEGHO (Bahaa, Bighu, Bitu, Insokka, Insoko, Nsoko, Socco). Begho is one of many enigmas in the Ghanaian past. There is evidence of iron smelting there as early as the third century of our era, but the important period in the history of the place probably began when the Dyula established themselves here toward the end of the fourteenth century. Begho became the southern depot of a long caravan route that stretched to Kong (Ivory Coast), Bobo Dioulasso (Upper Volta), Jenne, and the Niger River (Mali). Trade in kola, gold, textiles, and slaves flourished through over four hundred years until the Asante conquered the area about 1730. By that time the community was already weakened by internal tensions between the Muslim and Animist population. Before the eighteenth century ended the settlement was in ruins.

In recent years the locality of old Begho has attracted many archaeologists. The site is near the Nimpeni, a branch of the Tain River. The modern villages of Hani (7°51' N, 2°29' W) and Nsawkaw (7°52' N, 2°19' W) are nearby.

BEGORO. 6°23' N, 0°23' W. Town in the Eastern Region 20 miles (32 km) northeast of Kibi and on the edge of the Kwahu Scarp. It was once an important missionary center. The Begoro Falls is not far away. The census in 1948 was 5,061, by 1960 that was up to 9,289, and in 1970 the population had grown to 11,043.

BEKWAI (Bekwae). 6°27' N, 1°35' W. One of the original members of the Asante Confederation. It is located just 15 miles (24 km) south of Kumasi and is about the same distance to the west of Lake Bosumtwi. It was at the crossroads where the Kumasi road separated on the way to Obuasi and to Fomena. Its population was 4,477 in 1948, up to 9,093 by 1960, and 11,287 in 1970.

BENKUM. The Left Wing of an Akan army.

BEREKUM. 7°27' N, 2°35' W. Town in the Brong-Ahafo Region some 20 miles (32 km) west of Sunyani, and 80 miles (128 km) northwest of Kumasi. It is said that the town was founded by refugees from Dormaa when that town was sacked by the Asante during the time of Osei Tutu. There were 5,378 people in Berekum during the 1948 census. The figure was 11,148 in the 1960 count, and 14,296 in 1970.

BERETUO. One of the Asante abusua or clans. The rulers of Mampong are identified with the Beretuo (Bretuo). The stool of Mampong is called the Silver Stool, and it is the second most important stool in the Asante Union. In Fante this clan is called Twidan.

BERNASKO, FRANK G. Born 1931. Military officer, lawyer, politician. Bernasko is a Fante, born at Cape Coast. He was educated in Presbyterian schools, at Adisadel College, and at the University in Legon, where he graduated in 1960. He later was awarded a law degree from the university. Joining the army, he served a term as Commandant of the Military Academy at Teshi, and after the 1966 coup he was Director of Education in the Ministry of Defense. With the 1972 coup he was first appointed Commissioner of the Central Region under the NRC, and in January 1973 he became Commissioner of Agriculture. In this position he gained national attention as the dynamic director of the "Operation Feed Yourself" campaign. In February 1975 he also took charge of the newly created Ministry of Cocoa Affairs; but shortly thereafter he lost favor with Acheampong, and in August he resigned from the government and the army. In 1979 Bernasko was a leader in forming the Action Congress Party (ACP). In June he was presidential candidate of that party, coming in fourth in a field of ten. He was first in the Central Region count, but had little support elsewhere.

BESEASE (Bisiasi). 5°33' N, 1°11' W. Town in the Central Region on the Cape Coast-Kumasi highway below Foso. It had a population of 3,427 in 1948. By 1970 the census was up to 7,451.

BEYIN. 4°59' N, 2°35' W. Coastal town in the Nzema country of the Western Region about 50 miles (80 km) to the west of Dixcove. The Europeans called the area Apollonia. The Dutch built a lodge here about 1660. Between 1768 and 1770 the British built their last important fortification on the Gold Coast here. It is still standing today. The fort was transferred to the Dutch in 1868, but the English purchased it back in 1872.

BIA-TAWYA GAME RESERVE. A game reserve located on the Ivory Coast border in the Western Region.

BIBIANI. 6°28' N, 2°20' W. Town in the Sefwi area of the Western Region. This is in the gold mining country southwest of Kumasi. The population of the town in 1948 was 7,173. By 1960 the census had jumped to 12,942, but by 1970 it had declined to 9,691.

BIGHU   see   BEGHO

BIMBILA (Bimbla). 8°51' N, 0°04' E. The capital of Nanumba. It is located in the Northern Region about 40 miles (64 km) to the south of Yendi and 75 miles (120 km) north of Kete Krakye. There were just over 2,000 there in 1948. By 1970 the population had grown to 8,068.

BIMOBA (Bimawba, B'Moba, Moba). Gurma group who live along the Ghana-Togo border to the west of Sansanne-Mango. Many live in Togo. Of those who live in Ghana, almost all of them are in the Northern Region.

BINEY, ALFRED POBEE. Marxist ex-serviceman and locomotive driver who was an officer in the Trade Union Congress. He played an active role in the nationalist movement in the 1940s and was the leader in calling a general strike early in 1950. He was active in the Sekondi branch of the CPP and helped organize the CPP in the Denkyira region. Elected to the Assembly in 1951 as a CPP candidate, he was expelled from the party in 1954.

BING, GEOFFREY HENRY CECIL. 1909-1977. Radical legal adviser to Kwame Nkrumah. Bing was a left-wing Ulsterman, educated at Oxford and Princeton, and was a signal officer in World War II. He was a Labor member of the British Parliament from 1945 to 1955, and he helped finalize the terms for Gold Coast independence. After the creation of Ghana he went to Accra as Nkrumah's adviser on legal and constitutional affairs, and as liaison with the left wing of the British Labor Party. He was Attorney General of Ghana from 1957 to 1961. After the 1966 coup he spent a few days in prison, but was expelled from Ghana on 24 March 1966. Some months later he published <u>Reap the Whirlwind; An Account of Kwame Nkrumah's Ghana from 1950 to 1966</u>. It is a valuable inside story of the Nkrumah years. In 1977, just a few weeks before he died, he returned to Ghana for the first time in over ten years. He praised the Supreme Military Council for pursuing a policy of national reconciliation.

BINGER, LOUIS GUSTAVE. 1856-1936. French colonial officer. In 1887 he began a famous trip through Mali, Upper Volta, Ghana, and the Ivory Coast. During 1888 he crossed the Upper and Northern Region to Salaga, and from there went to Kong. In 1893 he became the French Administrator of the Ivory Coast. His account of his trip across West Africa was published in 1892.

BIRIFOR (Birifon). Lobi group who live in the Upper West Region around Nandom.

BIRIM RIVER. A stream which rises in the Atewa Hills near Kibi and runs in an arch northeast to the foot of the Kwahu Scarp and then bends sharply southwest, flowing across the Akyem country, past Oda, to join the Pra at 5°58' N, 1°13' W. The river's whole course makes a great bend through the center of the Eastern Region.

BITU see BEGHO

BLACK STAR LINE. The State Shipping Corporation was established 10 September 1957 with the aid of Israel. The ships were named for the rivers, lakes and lagoons of Ghana. The <u>Volta River</u>, built in 1940, was the first ship purchased for the line. The name "Black Star" came from the US shipping line formed in the 1920s by Marcus Garvey, one of the early Black nationalists.

BLACK VOLTA (Coumbo). Western tributary of the Volta system. It begins in Upper Volta near Bobo Dioulasso.

BLANKSON, GEORGE KUNTU. 1809-1898. Merchant, soldier, and member of the Legislative Council, 1861-1873. He was a native of Anomabo. Blankson played an important role in the wars against Asante, and negotiated with the Asante and the Dutch on behalf of the British. He was a loyal member of the Methodist Church, often serving as a minister.

B'MOBA see BIMOBA

BOAHEN, A. ADU. Historian. Adu Boahen attended Mfantsipim, the University of Ghana, and the School of Oriental and African Studies, London, where he received his doctorate in history. His academic career has been at Legon, where he has been a prolific writer on West African history. He was active in the campaign against the military government Union Government plan in 1978, spending several weeks in prison for his opposition to the SMC.

BOAKYE, GEORGE YAW. Air Force officer under the NRC who became the Acting Army Commander after the SMU was established in 1975. He was executed by Rawlings and the AFRC in June 1979.

BOBIKUMA. 5°33' N, 0°51' W. A town between Mankesim and Agona Swedru in the Central Region some 25 miles (40 km) northwest of Winneba. A battle between the Asante and people of the Ekumfi area took place here in 1863. The population of Bobikuma in 1970 was 5,097.

BOENOE (Bonnoe, Bunu). A small area above Accra and Ningo in the Accra Plain.

BOLE. 9°02' N, 2°29' W. A town on the Western Road in the Northern Region some 77 miles (124 km) south of Wa, and about 12 miles (19 km) east of the Black Volta. It was once a Dyula trade depot. The population in 1948 was just 1,811. By 1970 that had grown to 4,772.

BOLGATANGA. 10°47' N, 0°51' W. Important crossroads, administrative center, and marketplace in the Upper Region some 100 miles (160 km) north of Tamale, and 26 miles (42 km) from the border of Upper Volta just beyond Paga. The market is famous for its basketware and straw hats. The town has developed an important meat-packing industry since independence. The census was 3,645 in 1948, but by 1970 it stood at 18,896.

BOND OF 1844. An agreement signed by eight African leaders and the British Lieutenant Governor on 6 March 1844. It defined British legal jurisdiction in the area which came to be known as the Protectorate. This mutual protection alliance was later signed by additional Africans. There is dispute about the real meaning of the Bond.

BONGO. 10°55' N, 0°48' W. Town in the Upper Region near the Upper Volta border and just northeast of Bolgatanga. From April to June in 1916 there was much opposition to British-supported chiefs in the area. The disturbances were ruthlessly crushed by the English. The English officer in charge of the area at the time was C.H. Armitage. The town had a population of over 5,700 in 1911.

BONNAT, MARIE JOSEPH. 1844-1881. French adventurer. Bonnat was an agent for a French firm in the Volta area when captured by the Asante in 1869. He was held prisoner in Kumasi for four years. Finally released in 1874, he was back in Kumasi the following year. On 31 July 1875 Asantehene Mensa Bonsu appointed Bonnat as his governor of the area south of Salaga, giving him a monopoly of the commerce in that area for six years. He organized an expedition, which travelled most of the way in canoes up the Volta. He reached Salaga 30 January 1876, becoming the first known European to reach that town. In 1877 he led an expedition up the Ankobra River to prospect for gold. They discovered the Tarkwa reef. This resulted in the formation of a company to exploit the gold deposits at Awudua (5°26' N, 2°05' W) and later at Tarkwa. Bonnat died in this region 8 July 1881.

BONNOE see BOENOE

BONO. The Bono or Brong state is purported to be the oldest of the Akan states, but there is a debate about the time it was founded. It was sometime between 1297 and 1400, sometime in the fourteenth century. Colin Flight lists the first king as Asaman, and says that he reigned from around 1420 to 1430. It was at the southern end of the Dyula trade route from the north, and it was also located near the source of the Tano River. The first capital was at Tutena or Bono-Manso, in the area of modern Techiman. After Bono-Manso was captured and destroyed by the Asante in 1723, Techiman became the most important town of Bono. In 1897 Bono came under the protection of the British, and in 1935 it was attached to the Asante Confederacy.

BONO-MANSO. Capital of Bono.

BONSASO. 5°17' N, 1°50' W. Place southwest of modern Tarkwa in the Western Region near which a clash between a large Asante and small British force took place 21 January 1824. Charles Macarthy, British Governor of Sierra Leone and the Gold Coast, was killed in the skirmish. Some sources call the engagement the Battle of Nsamankow. Nsamankow (Nsamanko, Insamankow) is the name Africans used.

BONWIRE (Bonweri). 6°47' N, 1°28' W. A village in the Asante Region near Kumasi which is often called the capital of Kente cloth. There were 1,011 inhabitants in 1948 and 2,729 in 1970.

BORON see BRONG

BOSMAN, WILLIAM. A Dutch factor who was on the Gold Coast from about 1689 to 1702. He wrote a very good account of the Gold Coast during this period. The original version was letters, written between 1700 and 1702. They were published in Dutch in 1704, and in English in 1705 as <u>A New and Accurate Description of the Coast of Guinea</u>.

BOSOME AKYEM see AKYEM

BOSUMTWI, LAKE. 6°30' N, 1°25' W. A natural lake in the Asante Region some 21 miles (34 km) southeast of Kumasi, and at the northeastern end of the Moinsi Hills. There is a dispute about whether the lake filled a volcanic crater or resulted from the impact of an ancient meteorite. The caldron covers 19 square miles (49 sq km), reaches a depth of 230 feet (70 m), and has no outlet. It is regarded as a sacred place by the Asante.

BOTCHWAY, KWESI. Lecturer in Economics at the University of Ghana who became Secretary of Finance and Economic Planning for the PNDC in 1982.

BOTI FALLS. Falls on the Pawnpawn River 12 miles (19 km) from Koforidua.

BOTSIO, KOJO. Born 1916. Educated at Adisadel, Fourah Bay (Sierra Leone), and Oxford. First met Nkrumah in London in 1945. He taught at Akyem Abuakwa State College. Botsio was one of the founders of the CPP, and was its first general secretary. In 1950 he was in James Fort Prison with Nkrumah. Elected to Parliament in 1951, he became the first Minister of Education and Social Welfare in the new Cabinet. Except when out of favor between September 1961 and March 1963, he was in the Cabinet most of the time the CPP was in power. From November 1958 to April 1959, and from March 1963 to June 1965 he was Foreign Minister. In June 1965 he became Chairman, State Planning Commission.

After the 1966 coup, Botsio spent some time in custody. When finally released, Botsio joined Nkrumah and was with his former leader when Nkrumah died in Rumania in April 1972. It was Kojo Botsio who made the formal arrangements with the NRC to have the body of the former President returned to Nkroful. Botsio and Mrs. Nkrumah accompanied the body to its final resting place. The following year, Botsio was sentenced to death for plotting the overthrow of the NRC. In time this was commuted to life, and he was released from prison once again in January 1977. By 1979 he was again in politics, becoming Director of Operations and Chairman of the Campaign Committee of the People's National Party in spite of being banned from running for office.

BOURNE REPORT. During 1954 a stalemate developed over the question of what kind of government Ghanaians wanted. Frederick Chalmers Bourne (b. 1891) was called in to try and resolve the conflict. Arriving 26 September 1955 in Accra, Bourne held a series of meetings with local groups, but the NLM refused to participate. Bourne also held a conference at Achimota to discuss recommendations, but the NLM refused to discuss anything other than a federation. In the end the Bourne Report recommended against a federation, but did advocate regional assemblies responsible for local matters, although without taxing powers. They would be dependent on the central government for their funds.

BOWDICH, THOMAS EDWARD. 1790-1824. English writer in the service of the African Company of Merchants. He was a member of the first British group to reach Kumasi, 19 May 1817. Bowdich spent four months in Kumasi negotiating a treaty and collecting information on the Asante. The treaty was signed 7 September 1817, and soon after that Bowdich and his companions returned to the coast. In 1818 he returned to England, and the following year the account of his trip to Kumasi was published. Mission from Cape Coast to Ashantee is a valuable account of early Asante. After spending some time in Paris and Lisbon, Bowdich returned to Africa in 1823 and died at Bathurst, Gambia, the following year.

BOWLI. A Volta-Central Togo group who live east of Lake Volta in the Volta Region. Their language is called Bowiri.

BRAFFO (Brafo of Fantyn). The paramount chief of the Fante was the chief of Abora. He actually exercised little authority.

BRAIMAH, J.A. A member of the Gonja ruling dynasty, he was appointed Kabachewura in 1942 and has been secretary to the Gonja Native Authority. He became a member of the Legislative Council in 1950 and was elected to the Legislative Assembly in 1954 and to the National Assembly in 1956. In 1950 he joined Nkrumah's government as Minister of Communications and Works. In November 1953 he resigned with a confession that he had accepted money from an Armenian contractor working in the Northern Region. He broke with the CPP and in 1954 was one of the founders of the Northern People's Party (NPP). He continued to be a vocal parliamentary opponent of Nkrumah until the coup of 1966. Under the NLC he was a member of the Political Committee and the Constitutional Commission. Joseph Braimah is not only a politician, but he is also known as a Gonja historian. The Ashanti and the Gonja at War (1970) and The Two Isanwurfos (1967) are two of his works. Kabache, of which Braimah is chief, is a village to the north of Salaga.

BRACKEY see KRAKYE

BRANDENBURG. The German province which founded posts at
Pokoso, Takrama, and Akwida at the end of the seventeenth
century. Gross Friedrichsburg (Prince's Town), their largest
post, was started in 1683. These posts were at the southern
end of the western trade route to the Asante and Aowin gold
fields. The Brandenburg Company sold out to the Dutch West
India Company in 1717.

BREMEN MISSIONARY SOCIETY. A North German missionary society which began educational work on the Gold Coast in 1847.
In 1881 they had four schools in the Volta area. By 1890 most
of their work was among the Ewe. In June 1916 the Bremen
missionaries were deported, and their schools were taken over
by the British.

BRETUO see BERETUO

BREW, JAMES HUTTON (Prince Brew of Dunkwa). 1844-1915. Attorney, journalist, businessman, nationalist. He was the son of
Samuel Collins Brew (ca. 1810-1881), who was a member of the
Legislative Council, 1864-1866. In 1871 James Hutton Brew was
active in the Fante Confederation movement and is said to have
been the author of the constitution of the Fante Confederation.
He founded the Gold Coast Times at Cape Coast in 1874, and
during the 1880s was one of the leaders in trying to create a
national consciousness among the people of the Gold Coast. He
ran a folklore column on African culture in his newspaper, and
he conducted a campaign to get elected representation for Africans in the Legislative Council. In November 1885 he organized
another paper, The Western Echo. He suggested mass meetings
of Africans and deputations to England as methods by which
Africans could make their opinions known to the authorities in
England. In 1889 he went to England as a self-appointed embassy for African interests, and in 1895 he tried to get English
authorities to recognize him as an agent for the Asante.

BREW, OSBORNE HENRY KWESI. Born in 1928 at Cape Coast and
educated at schools at Cape Coast, Kumasi, Tamale, and Accra,
he became one of the early graduates of the new college at
Legon. He entered the Administrative Service of the Gold Coast
in 1953 and held posts as Assistant District Commissioner and
District Commissioner under the British. After independence he
joined the Diplomatic Service of Ghana. He is a poet and short
story writer of note.

BREW, RICHARD. Died 1776. An Irishman who spent thirty years
on the Gold Coast in the service of the Company of Merchants
Trading to Africa. He was also a private trader at Anomabo.
His wife was a Fante, and the famous Brew family of the Gold
Coast descended from this couple.

BRISCOE AFFAIR. One of the frequent examples of corruption during the NRC/SMC period. The R.T. Briscoe Company was charged with corruption in 1975, and its Ghanaian assets were seized by the government. The company was owned by the Danish East Asiatic Company. Two generals, Lawrence Okai, Chief of Defense Staff, and Charles Beausoleil, Air Force Commander, were implicated and lost their jobs.

BRONG (Abron, Boron, Borong, Bron, Bono). One of the Akan groups, most of whom live in the Brong-Ahafo region between the Ivory Coast border and the Volta River. Sunyani, Techiman, Kintampo, and Atebubu are major Brong towns.

BRONG-AHAFO REGION. The region between Asante and the Northern Region. It was created in 1958.

BRONG CONFEDERATION. A defensive alliance formed by the Dente Bosomfo of Krakye against the Asante in the late nineteenth century. The alliance lasted from about 1875 to 1895, by which time the British had established their control over much of the area and had limited the power of Asante to be a threat to the Brong.

BROWN, EMMANUEL JOSEPH PETER. 1875-1929. Lawyer and author. After teaching for some years in Methodist schools, he worked in the offices of John Mensah Sarbah, and then went to England to study law. In the years just before World War I he was a leader of the Aborigines' Rights Protection Society. He was a member of the Legislative Council from 1916 to 1927. His two-volume Gold Coast and Asianti Reader (1929) was a popular collection of folklore and local history.

BROWN, JOSEPH PETER. 1843-1932. Fante teacher and political leader. He was one of the founders of the Aborigines' Rights Protection Society, and he served on the Legislative Council from 1904 to 1909. In the 1920s he was active in the National Congress of British West Africa.

BUEM. One of the Volta-Central Togo groups of the Volta Region.

BUI. 8°16' N, 2°16' W. A small village on the Black Volta near rapids which offer possibilities for hydroelectric development. The project has been discussed since before independence. In 1982 the PNDC announced that Russia would help with the project. The population of Bui has changed little in recent times. In 1948 the census counted only 124. In 1970 there were 125 in Bui.

BUI NATIONAL PARK. The park runs along both sides of the Black Volta above Bui, and it extends to and along the border with Ivory Coast.

BUI RAPIDS. Between Bui and Bamboi there are two sets of rapids. Li Rapids is about two miles (three km) below the gorge and has a drop of 20 feet (six m). The Vilibalo Rapids are 11 miles (18 km) below the Bui Gorge, and the fall is about the same as for the Li. The gorge starts about two miles (three km) below Bui. The Bamboi ferry is 20 miles (32 km) below the Bui Gorge. There is no appreciable fall of the river in the gorge itself.

BUILSA (Bulse, Builse, Kangyaga, Kanjaga). One of the Mole-Dagbani groups in the Upper Region between the Sisala River and the Great Northern Highway. Their language is called Buli (Bulea). They call their land Bulugu. The Mamprusi are below them, Kasena above them, the Sisala to the west, and the Nankansi to the east.

BUIPE (Ghofe, Ghofon, Goaffi). 8°47' N, 1°32' W. A village in the Northern Region some 60 miles (96 km) southwest of Tamale, and just eight miles (13 km) northwest of a bridge across the Black Volta. This is one of the most important prehistoric sites in Ghana. There is evidence of iron technology in the area by the eighth century of our era. The town was a commercial center from very early times. The tomb of Sumaila Ndewura Jakpa, great ruler of Gonja, is located in Buipe, and the ruler, the Buipewura, is the traditional guardian of the tomb of Jakpa. Buipe lost importance after the chief trade center of Gonja moved to Salaga. In 1970 there were just 231 persons in Old Buipe and 894 in New Buipe.

BUKARI-ATIM, CHRIS. Radical student leader who was one of the founders of the June 4th Movement and one of the most aggressive left-wing supporters of Jerry John Rawlings. He was one of the seven members of the initial PNDC in 1982. He was dropped from the PNDC.

BULLER AFFAIR. In November 1980 the Limann government arrested several people at Jerry Rawlings' apartment and charged them with establishing camps to train enemies of the Third Republic, using Libyan money. Diplomatic relations with Libya were broken.

BUOYEM HILLS. Hills around Wenchi and Techiman in the Brong-Ahafo Region.

BURNS, ALAN CUTHBERT MAXWELL. 1887-1980. Governor of the Gold Coast, 1941-1947. Alan Burns' father was a colonial civil servant in the West Indies, and the son followed in his father's footsteps, assigned to the West Indies from 1905 to 1912. He then went to Nigeria (1912-1924), returned to the West Indies (1924-1928), was back in Nigeria (1928-1934), and was Governor of British Honduras from 1934 to 1940. He served as Governor of Gold Coast during the difficult years of World War II. During this time, in 1942, he also filled in as Acting Governor of Nigeria. From 1947 to 1956 he was British Representative on the UN Trusteeship Council. He retired in 1956. He published an autobiography, Colonial Civil Servant, in 1950. The most memorable accomplishment of his term as Governor of the Gold Coast was the Burns Constitution of 1946. This provided for an African majority of 18 out of 31 on the Legislative Council and united the Colony and Asante.

BUSANSI (Busanga, Bussansi). A Mande group who live in the extreme northeastern tip of the Upper East Region, and in Upper Volta and Togo. They use a Mande-Fu language called Busa.

BUSHAN (Busua). 4°48' N, 1°56' W. A coastal village in the Western Region where the English had a base from about 1660 to 1750. It is between Dixcove and Butri.

BUSIA, KOFI ABREFA. 1913-1978. Teacher, author, politician, Prime Minister. Busia was a member of the royal family of Wenchi, in the Brong-Ahafo Region. He was educated at the Methodist School in Kumasi, Mfantsipim, and Wesley College, Kumasi. In 1936 he was an instructor at Achimota. From there he went to London and Oxford, where he got a doctorate in Social Anthropology. He then became an officer in the Gold Coast Administration. In 1949 he joined the faculty of the new University College at Legon, where he remained until 1956. During his academic period he was the author of The Position of the Chief in the Modern Political System of Ashanti, 1951; and Report on a Social Survey of Sekondi-Takoradi, 1950.

Elected to the Legislative Assembly in 1951, Busia assumed his parliamentary duties while still teaching sociology at Legon. By 1957 he was the leader in organizing the United Party in opposition to Nkrumah's CPP. Busia and his allies wanted a maximum amount of local autonomy, while Nkrumah and the CPP wanted a highly centralized form of government for independent Ghana. In June 1959 Busia was forced into exile. For the next seven years he lived and worked in Holland, Mexico, the United States, and England. During this exile he produced several more books. At the time of the 1966 coup he was at Oxford.

Busia made a triumphant return to Accra a few days after the fall of Nkrumah. He held several important posts under the National Liberation Council. He was the most influential member of the Constituent Assembly which drew up the constitution for the Second Republic. And while he was working on the new constitution, he and his educated friends created the Progress Party, which won the elections of August 1969, gaining 105 seats to 35 for the National Alliance of Liberals and other parties. Busia became the Prime Minister of the Second Republic on 3 September 1969. As leader of the Republic, Busia was soon overwhelmed with intractable problems. The army, civil service, unions, and Nkrumah's supporters refused cooperation. Everyone demanded a larger portion of a shrinking national economy. Busia's suggestions for austerity won him no friends. Early in 1972, while Busia was in England getting medical treatment, the army staged another coup, 13 January 1972. The ousted Prime Minister again found himself in exile. He settled down once more to an academic life at Oxford. He died of a heart attack there 28 August 1978. A few days after his death his body was returned to Ghana for a state funeral.

BUTANE. An area shown on the 1729 Anville map between Insokko and Asante. This is the present Brong-Ahafo area. Butane is not shown on earlier or later maps.

BUTRI (Butre). 4°49' N, 1°55' W. A small coastal village in the Ahanta country of the Western Region just east of Dixcove and at the mouth of Butri Creek. The Swedes had a post here in the middle of the seventeenth century, but the Dutch forced them out and in 1656 began a fort on top of the high hill overlooking the small bay. The fort was called Batensteyn or Batenstein. Over the years the Dutch tried to develop the economy of the area by experimenting with cotton and sugarcane. They set up a rum factory there at the start of the eighteenth century. The Ahanta maintain a small boat industry at Butri. The fort was ceded to the British in 1872. Today the fortifications are in ruins.

- C -

CABO CORSO   see   CAPE COAST

CABOCEER. Corruption of a Portuguese word meaning head or captain. A title of respect. An important person. The leader of a community.

CADBURY BROTHERS. Famous British chocolate business which was founded by George Cadbury (1839-1922). In 1918 it joined with J.S. Fry and Son to become the largest British chocolate business. By 1914 it purchased most of the cocoa production of the Gold Coast. The firm encouraged the production of only the highest quality cocoa by paying higher prices for the best grades of cocoa.

CAPE COAST (Cabo Corso, Cap Corso, Oguaa, Ogua, Oegua). 5°06' N, 1°15' W. Fante fishing center which was subject to the Efutu before the eighteenth century. The Portuguese first traded here in the late fifteenth century. The Portuguese, English, Dutch and Swedes all vied for the trade of the town during the first half of the seventeenth century. About 1652 the Swedes began to build the modern Castle, which they called Carlsborg (Carolusburg). This structure changed hands several times during its first decade, but it was in the hands of the British by 1664, and most of the present fort was built by them. It was the British headquarters on the Gold Coast from 1664 to 1877.

Today Cape Coast is an important commercial, educational, and government center. Some of the best secondary schools of Ghana are located there, and one of Ghana's three universities is at Cape Coast. The city is steeped in history, it was the birthplace of Ghanaian nationalism, and it holds great attraction for tourists. It is just eight miles (13 km) east of Elmina, and the coast between these two historic places is one of the most attractive places in all of Africa.

Accra is 90 miles (144 km) to the east of Cape Coast, and Kumasi is 132 miles (212 km) to the north. In the triangle formed between these three cities lies the heart of Ghana. At the beginning of the twentieth century there were around 11,000 people in Cape Coast. By 1948 the census was 23,294, and in 1970 the population was 51,653.

CAPE SAINT PAUL. 5°49' N, 0°57' E. Promontory between Keta and Anloga, on the spit that separates the Keta Lagoon from the Gulf of Guinea.

CAPE THREE POINTS. 4°45' N, 2°06' W. The southernmost point in Ghana, it is located on the coast of the Western Region between Axim and Dixcove. Cape Three Points is 327 miles (526 km) north of the equator.

CARAMANSA. Portuguese name for Kwamina Ansah, ruler of Edina at the time the Portuguese began Elmina Castle in 1482.

CARDINALL, ALLAN. 1887-1956. British colonial officer. Cardinall joined the Gold Coast Service in 1914 and spent most of his tour in the Gold Coast in the north, especially at Yendi. He wrote many articles and several books about the Gold Coast. Natives of the Northern Territories of the Gold Coast (1920), A Gold Coast Library (1924), In Ashanti and Beyond (1927), Tales Told in Togoland (1931), and A Bibliography of the Gold Coast (1932) are his major contributions. Allan Wolsey Cardinall was Commissioner to the Cayman Islands from 1934, and Governor of the Falkland Islands, 1941-1946.

CARLSBORG (Carolusburg). The Swedish base built at Cape Coast about 1652. This was later expanded by the English into Cape Coast Castle.

CASELY-HAYFORD, ARCHIE. Fante from a Cape Coast family, but born at Axim, in the Western Region. He was educated at Mfantsipim, London, and Cambridge, receiving his law degree in London. He was a member of the Legislative Assembly, 1954-1956, and the National Assembly, 1956-1966. During the early days of the CPP he gained the title "Defender of the Verandah

Boys" for his defense of Nkrumah and other CPP members before the Gold Coast courts. Under Nkrumah he served as Minister of Agriculture and Natural Resources, Minister of Communications, and Minister of Interior.

CASELY-HAYFORD, JOSEPH EPHRAIM (Ekra Agyiman). 1866-1930. Author, lawyer, and politician. A Fante, born at Cape Coast, and educated at Fourah Bay College in Sierra Leone, and Cambridge. He became a lawyer in 1896. He was a member of the Legislative Council from 1916 to 1926, and municipal member of the Council from Sekondi from 1927 to 1930. He was a member of the Aborigines' Rights Protection Society, and one of the founders of the National Congress of British West Africa. He was the author of Ethiopia Unbound (1911) and Gold Coast Native Institutions (1903).

CASSAVA (Manioc). One of the basic staple foods of Ghana, it probably originated in Brazil. Its starchy root is highly poisonous until soaked for some time. Toasted cassava flour is called Gari. Dumplings made from the flour are Fufu (Foofoo). The leaves are a popular vegetable. Cassava is not harmed by locusts or other insects and will grow on poor soil.

CEDI. The official currency of Ghana. A cedi is divided into one hundred pesewas. On 1 January 1980 the official exchange rate was 2.75 cedi for $1 US. The unofficial rate at that time was 14 cedi to the dollar. On 23 November 1983 the Bank of America listed the exchange rate as 30 cedi to $1 US.

CENTRAL TOGO TRIBES. A group of tribes in the Volta Region between Lake Volta and the Togo border. The Avatime, Nyangbo, Tafi, Logba, Likpe, Lolobi, Santrokofi, Akpafu, Bowli, Buem, Akposo, Ntrubu, and Adele are the people so classified. They are remnants of the original inhabitants of the area and were there long before the Ewe moved into the Volta Region.

CHAKOSSI   see   CHOKOSI

CHEREPONG   see   KYEREPON

CHOKOSI (Chakossi, Kyokosi, Tschokossi). Akan group, similar to the Anyi-Bawle, Sefwi, and Aowin. These people live in the north, along the Togo border. They are partly Islamized. The French call them Tyokossi. They call themselves the Anufo. In the past they were mercenaries for the Dagomba and Konkomba. Their chief town is Sansanne-Mango in Togo. Many of them were under German rule from 1899 to 1914.

CHRISTALLER, JOHANN GOTTLIEB. 1827-1895. Basel missionary. He came to the Gold Coast in 1853 and was first stationed at Akuropon for five years. From 1862 to 1865 he was at Aburi, and from 1865 to 1867 he lived at Kibi. From 1867 to 1868 he was back at his first mission at Akuropon. He is best known for his translations of biblical and devotional materials into Akuapem Akan (Twi), and an Akan grammar and dictionary.

CHRISTIANSBORG CASTLE (Osu). One of the three most famous European structures on the Gold Coast. The Swedes first built a lodge at Osu, next to Accra, in 1652. The Danes then took the site. There were brief Dutch, Portuguese, and Akwamu interludes, with the Danes starting the present structure about 1661. Over the years it has been changed and enlarged many times. The British purchased it in 1850, and it served as the residence of British governors from 1877 to 1957. Since Independence it has been generally known as Government House. William E.B. Du Bois is buried against the outside wall of the Castle.

CHU MIENTWI. Died ca. 1599. Founder of the royal Oyoko dynasty of Asante.

CITIZENS' VETTING COMMITTEE (CVC). A committee established by the PNDC in 1982 to scrutinize large bank accounts to spot illegal income.

CLARIDGE, WILLIAM WALTON. 1874-1923. Author of one of the better known histories of the Gold Coast, A History of the Gold Coast and Ashanti from Ancient Times to the Commencement of the Twentieth Century (2 vols., 1915). Claridge was appointed a medical officer to the Gold Coast in 1903. He served in many places about the Gold Coast before he was senior medical officer in the invasion of Togoland in 1914. He retired in 1919 and died in 1923, less than 49 years of age.

CLIFFORD, HUGH CHARLES. 1866-1941. Colonial officer. Son of a major general, Clifford began his colonial service in the Malay States. By 1900 he reached appointment as Governor of North Borneo and Labuan. From there he went to the West Indies, 1903-1906, and Ceylon, 1907-1912. He became Governor of the Gold Coast in 1912 and held that position until after the end of World War I. In 1920 he published a history, The Gold Coast Regiment in the East African Campaign. While he was Governor the Legislative Council was enlarged to 21 members, six of whom would be Africans.

From the Gold Coast Clifford went to Nigeria as Governor (1919-1925), Ceylon as Governor (1925-1927), and his last appointment was as Governor of the Straits Settlements and High Commissioner of the Malay States (1927-1929).

COBRE RIVER see ANKOBRA

COCOA. Ghana's most famous crop. Until recent years, Ghana was the world's major producer of cocoa. Cocoa is native to Central America, and it was introduced to Africa in the 1820s. It was first exported from the Gold Coast in 1891. A major crop is harvested between October and March, and a minor crop is produced between May and August. Pods are formed on the tree. They contain beans, which are fermented and dried. The trees are subject to a number of diseases, especially swollen shoot (a virus carried by mealy bugs), a fungus called black pod, and capsid insects.

COCOA MARKETING BOARD. A board established in 1947 to buy and export all Gold Coast cocoa. Its chief objective was to protect African producers from unfair competition and fluctuating prices. The Board maintained a fund for research on cocoa. After 1951 the government absorbed more and more of the earnings of the CMB for general development plans. This created resentment against the government among the cocoa growers, and smuggling of cocoa into Togo and the Ivory Coast, where prices were higher, became a problem.

COCONUT. The coconut is common along the coast of the Central and Western regions. Every part of the tree is used for something.

COCOYAM. A tuber which is cheaper than yams, and thus popular among the poor in Ghana. They grow effortlessly and are easy to tend. The leaves are a rich source of minerals and vitamins, and they are prized as a vegetable.

COLA see KOLA

COLONY. In 1874 the British organized the coastal areas under their protection into the Gold Coast Colony. The "Colony" lasted until 1957.

COMMENDA see KOMENDA

COMMITTEE ON YOUTH ORGANIZATION (CYO). Group organized in Accra in August 1948 which favored a break from the UGCC and "Self-Government Now." K.A. Gbedemah, Kojo Botsio, and Krobo Edusei were the leaders of this movement. It was the progenitor of the Convention People's Party (CPP).

COMPANY OF LONDON MERCHANTS. Company organized during the Commonwealth period to trade with the Gold Coast, 1651-1658.

COMPANY OF MERCHANTS TRADING TO AFRICA. The successor to the Royal Africa Company. This company was a device for maintaining the British posts on the West African coast from 1751 to 1821. Any English merchant could belong for a small fee.

COMPANY OF MERCHANTS TRADING TO GUINEA. Company chartered to do business with the coasts of West Africa, 1632-1651.

COMPANY OF ROYAL ADVENTURERS. A British Company chartered by Charles II which managed trade on the Gold Coast from 1663 to 1672.

COMPULSORY LABOUR ORDINANCE OF 1895. An ordinance which required chiefs to provide workers for the government under certain circumstances. It was initially designed to obtain carriers for the Asante campaign, but maintenance of roads and telegraph lines soon became the chief form of public labor demanded by the British.

CONNY, JOHN   see   JOHN KONNY

CONSCIENCISM. Title of a book published for Kwame Nkrumah in 1964. This was Nkrumah's brand of socialism. He believed that traditional communalism of African society would make a natural transition to socialism in an evolutionary way. Parts of the book were written by the research sections of the departments of Economics and Philosophy at the University in Legon.

CONSTITUTION OF 1850. In 1850 the Gold Coast Colony was administered by a Governor who was assisted by an Executive and a Legislative Council. The Executive Council was made up of senior European officials. The Legislative Council was composed of the Executive Council plus unofficial members. The members of both councils were nominated by the Governor.

CONSTITUTION OF 1916. The Clifford Constitution. Hugh Clifford was British Governor from 1912 to 1919. Under Clifford the government of the Gold Coast was reorganized. The Executive Council was made up of the Governor, the Colonial Secretary, the Attorney-General, the Treasurer, the principal medical officer, and the Secretary of Native Affairs. The Legislative Council was composed of the Executive Council plus the Comptroller of Customs, Director of Public Works, General Manager of Railroads, commissioners of the Eastern and Western Provinces, and nine unofficial members appointed by the Crown on nomination by the Governor. Of these nine, three were Europeans, three paramount chiefs, and three other Africans.

CONSTITUTION OF 1925. This is sometimes called the Guggisberg Constitution, after Frederick Gordon Guggisberg, Governor from 1919 to 1927. The Legislative Council was increased to 15 official and 14 unofficial members. Provincial Councils of paramount chiefs were established for the western, central, and eastern provinces. These councils elected six unofficial members to the Legislative Council. The new Legislative Council touched off the first real political activity in the Gold Coast, because Accra,

Cape Coast, and Sekondi could each elect one unofficial member to the Council. The new enlarged Council met for the first time in August 1926.

CONSTITUTION OF 1946. This is sometimes called the Burns Constitution for Alan Burns, Governor, 1941-1947. This charter abolished the Central Province and provided for representation of Asante in the Legislative Council for the first time. The Legislative Council now had six ex-officio, six nominated, and eighteen elected members. For the first time there was provision for a clear African majority.

CONSTITUTION OF 1951. This charter is sometimes called the Arden-Clarke Constitution for Governor Charles Arden-Clarke, 1949-1957. This constitution was based on recommendations of a committee headed by J.H. Coussey. There was a Legislative Assembly of 84 members. Thirty-three members were elected in rural districts of the Colony and Asante by electoral colleges, 37 were elected by Territorial Councils of chiefs, 5 were elected from the towns of Accra, Cape Coast, Sekondi-Takoradi, and Kumasi, three represented the Chamber of Commerce, three the Chamber of Mines, and three were nominated by the Governor. The Executive Council had a majority of African ministers, responsible to the Governor and to the Assembly. The Northern Territories were now included in the Assembly. In the elections for members of the new Legislative Assembly, the CPP, in spite of being opposed to the Constitution, won two-thirds majority. Nkrumah became leader of government business and immediately set out to change the Constitution of 1951.

CONSTITUTION OF 1954. This is the first Nkrumah constitution. This charter ended the complicated electoral procedures of the 1951 charter. All members of the Legislative Assembly, 104 members, were popularly elected. The new Executive Council or Cabinet would be made up of eight members of the Assembly, appointed by the Governor on the advice of the Prime Minister. The Governor retained control of defense and external affairs and retained reserve powers.

CONSTITUTION OF 1957. The second Nkrumah Constitution. This was the independence Constitution of Ghana. The Queen would be Head of State, represented by a Governor-General. The Cabinet of Ministers would be members of the National Assembly, responsible to the National Assembly. A Prime Minister was selected by the National Assembly, and he was Head of the government. A vote of no confidence in the Prime Minister would force a new general election. The National Assembly was made up of 104 members, elected for five-year terms. The country was divided into five regions: Eastern, Western, Trans-Volta-Togoland, Ashanti, and Northern. Each region elected its own Regional Assembly for a term of three years.

CONSTITUTION OF 1960. The third Nkrumah Constitution. It established the First Republic. This constitution was approved by a plebiscite on 19, 23, and 27 April 1960. The post of Governor-General was abolished, and the Prime Minister became the President. Article 55 gave the President power to rule by decree, and Article 44 allowed the President to appoint and dismiss the Chief Justice.

CONSTITUTION OF 1969. The Constitution of the Second Republic. This constitution provided for a liberal parliamentary democracy. A President would be ceremonial Head of State. He was selected by an electoral college of members of Parliament plus members of regional assemblies. A Council of State would assist the President in his duties. A Prime Minister was Head of Government and appointed his own Cabinet. The Cabinet was required to resign if Parliament gave a vote of no confidence. The Constitution set up a National House of Chiefs, to meet in Kumasi, and a House of Chiefs for each region of the country. This constitution was promulgated on 22 August 1969, and the Second Republic took office on 1 October 1969.

CONSTITUTION OF 1979. The constitution of the Third Republic. This charter provided for a president and vice-president. They could serve not more than two four-year terms. They could be removed from office by a two-thirds vote of Parliament. Cabinet ministers were appointed by the President, but had to be confirmed by Parliament. Ministers could not sit in Parliament. Legislative power was vested in a unicameral Parliament of no fewer than 140 members elected for a normal term of five years. Parliament selected its own Speaker. A one-party state was unconstitutional. This charter went into force 24 September 1979.

CONSTITUTION OF THE FANTE CONFEDERATION, 1871. An agreement reached by 31 leaders of the Fante at Mankesim, signed 18 November 1871. It provided for an Executive Council of five elected officials, a Representative Assembly appointed by Kings and Chiefs, a National Assembly of Kings and principal Chiefs, and a King-President, elected by the kings in the National Assembly each year. The Confederation was a military alliance, but would also concern itself with internal improvements. A poll tax and import and export duties would be levied to pay expenses. The British refused to recognize the Fante Confederation and had many of its leaders arrested.

CONVENTION PEOPLE'S PARTY (CPP). This was the political party of Kwame Nkrumah. It was created in June 1949 in a break from the UGCC. It demanded "Self-government Now!" It won the elections of February 1951 and remained in power until 1966, when it was disbanded after Nkrumah was deposed.

COOMASSIE   see   KUMASI

CORMANTINE   see   KORMANTIN

COUMBO   see   BLACK VOLTA

COUNTERCOUP OF 1967. On 17 April 1967 a reconnaissance regiment that was stationed at Ho, Volta Region, marched on Accra and tried to take over the government. The coup was headed by Lieutenant Samuel B. Arthur, a Fante, and two other lieutenants. General E.K. Kotoka of the NLC was wounded and captured at Flagstaff House and was later killed at Accra Airport. Lieutenants Arthur and Moses Yeboah were executed for the attempted coup at Teshi 9 May 1967.

COUSSEY COMMITTEE, 1949. An all-African committee, chaired by Sir Henley Coussey, which was appointed to make recommendations for a new constitution. The committee made its report in October 1949, and the report was the basis for the 1951 Constitution.

COUSSEY, J. HENLEY. 1895-1958. Lawyer. Educated for the law in England, he became one of the foremost solicitors on the Gold Coast. During the twenties he was active in the National Congress of British West Africa. He became a judge on the High Court in 1943. He was made chairman of a committee to make recommendations on a new form of government to the British in 1949. The report of the Coussey Committee was approved by the Legislative Council in December 1949, touching off Nkrumah's Positive Action Campaign for immediate self-government.

COWPEAS. The most common legume in Ghana. There are several varieties, and they are often called "the poor man's meat." They are often eaten with corn or rice.

CRABBE, HUGH HORATIO COFIE-. A Ga leader who joined the CPP as a lieutenant of Tawia Adamafio. Crabbe served as executive secretary of the CPP in 1961-1962, but was arrested 29 August 1962 and charged with complicity in the Kulungugu bombing. He was tried in 1963 and was acquitted, but he was held in prison until after the 1966 coup.

CRACKEY   see   KRAKYE

CREASY, GERALD HALLEN. Born 1897. Governor. Educated at Rugby and King's College, Cambridge, he served in World War I, and joined the colonial service in 1920. By 1945 he was Chief Secretary of the West African Council, a post he held until he became Governor of the Gold Coast. He was Governor of the Gold Coast, 1948-1949, and of Malta from 1949 to 1954, when he retired. It was Creasy who sent the "Big Six" leaders of the UGCC--J.B. Danquah, Kwame Nkrumah, William Ofori Atta, Akufo Addo, Ako Adjei, and E. Obetsebi Lamptey--into detention in the Northern Territories after the 1948 riots.

CREPPEE see KREPI

CREVECOEUR, FORT. Fort built at Little Accra by the Dutch between 1642 and 1652. It was almost destroyed by an earthquake in 1862. The British gained the place in 1868, rebuilt it, and named it Fort Ussher. At present it is a prison.

CROWN LANDS BILL OF 1894. A proposal to vest all waste and forest lands and minerals in the Queen. All concessions were to be made by the Crown alone. The British meant the legislation to protect Africans against European exploitation, but Africans thought it was an attempt to take their land. The bill was withdrawn by Governor William Maxwell, and a new lands bill was introduced on 10 March 1897. This was designed to give the Crown control but not ownership. This did not calm African fears, and the outcome was the organization of the Gold Coast Aborigines' Rights Protection Society. The British retreated again, substituting the Concessions Ordinance of 1900. This provided that all concessions would be reviewed by the Supreme Court of the colony, which could modify concessions it found to be unreasonable. It also limited the size of concessions, and protected existing rights of Africans.

CRUICKSHANK, BRODIE. Died 1854. Scottish merchant and magistrate. He came to the Gold Coast in 1834, and in a short time rose to a position of great prominence. He was a member of the Legislative Council, Collector-General of the poll tax in 1853, and served briefly as the acting Lieutenant-Governor, 1853-1854. He was the author of Eighteen Years on the Gold Coast, published in 1853.

- D -

DABOYA (Wasape, Wasipe). 9°32' N, 1°23' W. Village on the White Volta in the Northern Region some 40 miles (64 km) northwest of Tamale. It is the chief town of the Wasipe Division of Gonja. The ruler is called the Wasipewura. Daboya is 70 miles (112 km) northeast of Nyanga, the former capital of Gonja. From ancient times the area about Daboya has been known as a source of rock salt, obtained by boiling soil and extracting salt crystals. The village is the limit of normal canoe traffic on the White Volta and was the terminal port for trade on that river until 1908, when Tamale Port at Yapei was built.

There is archaeological evidence of human habitation around Daboya since the first century of our era. The people belong to the Tampolensi-Grusi group. They were once under the Dagomba, but about 1620 they were conquered by Gonja. During this period the people came under Islamic influences, and a famous old Sudanic mosque is the most interesting edifice in the village today. Most of the village was destroyed by Babatu in 1890, but it was soon rebuilt. Ferguson persuaded the Wasipewura to sign a treaty of friendship with the British 8 July 1892. In 1948 there were 1,075 persons in Daboya. By 1970 the population was still just 1,872.

DABUNGA-GYIMATOR CATARACTS (Nsunua Rapids). The old Cataracts on the Volta at Kete-Krakye. They are now covered by Lake Volta.

DAGABA (Dagari, Dagarte, Dagati). A Mole-Dagbani group of people who live in the Upper Region-West between the Black Volta and Kulpawn. Some live in the Ivory Coast and in Upper Volta. Their neighbors are the Wala, Lobi, and Sisala. The singular of Dagaba is Dagao. Han (10°41' N, 2°27' W) is the chief town of the Dagaba.

DAGBANE. Language of the Dagomba.

DAGOMBA (Dagbon, Dagbong). A Mole-Dagbani kingdom in the Northern Region in the Oti plain below the Gambaga escarpment. The Mamprusi are to the north, and the Nanumba to the south. They call themselves the Dagbamba, their language Dagbane, and their country Dagbong. Tumo is western Dagomba, and Naja is eastern Dagomba. Tradition connects the royal family with the rulers of the Mossi, Mamprusi, and Nanumba. Yendi Dabari, on the White Volta, was the original town of the Ya Na, the ruler of Dagomba, but it was destroyed by the Gonja about 1713. Yendi is now the home of the Ya Na, but the largest and most important city in Dagomba today is Tamale.

Sitobu, son of Gbewa of Pusiga, is the traditional founder of the Dagomba dynasty. His son, Nyagse, founded Yendi Dabari. These two conquered the lands from the White Volta to the Oti from people ruled by earth priests (sing. tindana, pl. tindamba) during the latter part of the fifteenth and early part of the sixteenth centuries. In the early seventeenth century the Gonja took part of Dagomba's western lands, and they administered a severe defeat to Na Dariziegu at Yapei, on the White Volta. Yendi Dabari fell to Gonja in these campaigns, and the Dagomba capital had to be moved eastward to Yendi, a former Konkomba town. The wars with Gonja lasted a century, and hardly had these conflicts subsided before Asante raids began. From the 1740s to 1874 the Asante dominated Dagomba, and collected tribute there. By 1874 Dagomba was exhausted, split by factional disputes. The Ya Na Abudulai called in the mercenaries, the Zabrama, to try to restore order. And at this point incursions by the British, Germans, and French began. On 4 December 1896 the Germans defeated a Dagomba army at Adibo. The following day they destroyed Yendi. By an Anglo-German treaty 14 November 1899 Dagomba was partitioned; with Yendi and most of the eastern part of Dagomba going to the Germans, and the western part becoming part of the British Northern Territories. Then in 1914, at the start of World War I, England gathered all Dagomba under her rule.

Dagomba is a patrilineal society. The sub-chiefs are appointed by the Ya Na. The Ya Na in turn is selected from one of the chiefs of either Karaga, Savelugu, or Mion. These three towns are called the "gate skins."

DAILY ECHO. Accra newspaper published from 1937 to 1955.

DAILY GRAPHIC. Accra newspaper started in 1950 as a subsidiary of the London Daily Mirror group of papers. It was eventually taken over by the Ghanaian government. The Sunday Mirror is the Sunday edition.

DAILY MAIL. The CPP newspaper at Cape Coast. It was founded by Kwame Nkrumah in December 1949, and its first editor was Kofi Baako.

DAKA RIVER. A stream which rises southeast of Karaga and flows down across Dagomba, passing just west of Yendi, and then being joined by its major tributaries, the Jeba, Kumou (Kumbo), Kbongo, and Lumpe. It flows into Lake Volta almost across the Lake from where the Pru River flows into Lake Volta. By an Anglo-German agreement in November 1899, the point at which the Daka flowed into the Volta was the start of a line drawn north and dividing Dagomba into the British and German sections of Dagomba.

DAKE, MAWUSE. Professor and Civil Engineer who helped organize the Social Democratic Front (SDF), a northern and labor group for the 1979 elections. He was his party's vice-presidential candidate in the election that year. After the PNDC seized power he first held the position of Secretary of Works and Housing, and then became Secretary of the National Defense Committee.

DAMBA FESTIVAL. A festival at Wa which commemorates the birth of the Prophet Muhammad.

DAMONGO. 9°05' N, 1°49' W. Town in the Northern Region some 70 miles (112 km) southwest of Tamale. The Gonja capital was moved here from Nyanga in 1942. The paramount chief of Gonja is the Yagbumwura. The Gonja Development Company was established here in 1949. One of Ghana's most interesting mosques is located here. In 1948 the census showed only 921 inhabitants. That figure was 6,575 by 1960, and it was 7,760 in 1970.

DAMPONG (Dampon). 6°33' N, 1°03' W. Town in the Asante Region near the upper course of the Pra which was once the chief village of the Akyem Kotoku. About 1824 they moved to Gyadam (Jedem), near Oda.

DANKYIRA see DENKYIRA

DANQUAH, JOSEPH KWAME KYERETWI BOAKYE. 1895-1965. Lawyer and nationalist. Danquah was born in Bepong, Kwahu. He was half-brother of Nana Ofori-Atta, Paramount Chief of Akyem Abuakwa. He was educated in Basel Mission schools, and at the University of London, and read law at the Inner Temple. During his London days he published The Akim Abuakwa Handbook, Akan Laws and Customs and the Akim Abuakwa Constitution, and Cases in Akan Law, all three in 1928.

Returning home to the Gold Coast, in 1931 he founded the West African Times (later the Times of West Africa). He also became active in politics, and in 1947 he was one of the founders of the United Gold Coast Convention (UGCC). In March 1948 he was arrested with Nkrumah and others, but in the following year he was a member of the Coussey Committee on Constitutional Reform. But by this time he and Nkrumah had come to a parting of the ways. In 1951 Danquah was elected to the Legislative Assembly, and he became one of the leaders of the opposition to Nkrumah.

Danquah lost in the elections of 1954 and 1956. During this period he belonged first to the National Liberation Movement, and then the United Party. In 1960 he was the candidate of the United Party for president against Nkrumah. He received just 10 percent of the vote, winning only the Volta Region. Nkrumah never forgave him. He was imprisoned in 1961, released in June 1962, and arrested again in January 1964. He died in Nsawam Prison 4 February 1965.

DANQUAH, MABEL DOVE. Died 1984. Wife of Joseph Danquah, writer, editor. She was the first woman elected to an African legislature.

DARIZIEGU. The Eleventh Ya Na of Dagomba, fl. 1590-1620. He was the Ruler of Dagomba at the time Dagomba lost large areas in the west to Gonja, and at the time the Dagomba capital was moved to Yendi. Dariziegu was defeated and killed in a battle with Gonja at Yapei.

DASH. A gift, tip, or gratuity.

DATORLI (Datorle). The fourth Ya Na of Dagomba, he was a grandson of Nyagse, the first Ya Na.

DATSUTAGBA, BATTLE OF. Battle in the Volta Region about 40 miles (64 km) north of Ada between the British and British allies on one side and the Anlo and their allies on 12 April 1866. At first the Anlo had the advantage of surprise, but their ammunition gave out and Akuapem forces attacked the Anlo from behind, bringing defeat to Anlo.

DAWN BROADCAST. Dawn is the traditional time when the Akan

make important announcements. On 8 April 1961 Nkrumah made an important announcement which marked a change in the direction of his government. All officials of government, the CPP, and parliament who were in private business were called upon to resign their posts. K.A. Gbedemah and Kojo Botsio were the most famous victims of this order. Tawia Adamafio and the more radical members of the CPP maneuvered Nkrumah into making the broadcast in order to discredit the old guard of the CPP.

I.K. Acheampong announced plans for a return to civilian rule in a Dawn Broadcast 1 July 1977.

DAWU. 5°59' N, 0°05' W. Site of famous archaeological excavations of Thurstan Shaw. The culture located here was probably at its peak from about 1550 to 1700. The Guan society manufactured iron, bronze, textiles, pottery, ivory, and jewelry.

DE GRAFT, JOE COLIMAN. Born 1932. Novelist, short story writer, poet, and dramatist. He studied English at the University College of the Gold Coast, and for a time was a research fellow at the Institute of African Studies at Legon. His most famous works are <u>The Secret of Opokuwa</u> (1967) and <u>Visitor from the Past</u> (1968). <u>The Third Woman</u> (1943) and <u>Through a Film Darkly</u> (1970) are two of his plays. In recent years he has lived outside Ghana.

DE GRAFT-JOHNSON, JOHN COLEMAN, SR. Son of Joseph William (1860-1928). Secretary for African Affairs in the Gold Coast Government. Leader in the movement to preserve African customs against the encroachments of European ways in the Gold Coast.

DE GRAFT-JOHNSON, JOHN COLEMAN, JR. Born 1919. Author, economist, historian, diplomat. Educated at Mfantsipim and at Edinburgh University. He received his doctorate in Economics at Edinburgh in 1946 with a dissertation on "Cooperation in Agriculture and Banking in British West Africa." This was published in 1958. While still a student he helped organize the Pan-African Conference at Manchester in September 1945. After gaining his doctorate, he was employed at the Colonial Office in London, 1946-1948. He then returned to the Gold Coast to work for the Cocoa Marketing Company, 1948-1949. He then was a tutor at University College from 1950 to 1956. From Legon he went to India and was connected with the University of Delhi, 1956-1961. Back to Legon, he worked at the University for several years until he joined the Ministry of External Affairs and was Ambassador to Holland and Belgium, 1967-1970. From 1961 to 1967 he was President of the Historical Society of Ghana. He is author of many articles and several books. Among his books <u>An Introduction to the African Economy</u> (1959) is perhaps the best known. <u>African Glory: The Story of Vanished Negro</u>

Civilizations has gone through several editions since it was first published in 1954.

DE GRAFT-JOHNSON, JOSEPH WILLIAM, SR. 1860-1928. Cape Coast merchant and early nationalist. He was also known as Kwesi Johnson. He was a long-time leader in Cape Coast civic affairs, was a political associate of J.E. Casely Hayford and J.P. Brown, and was one of the co-founders of the Aborigines' Rights Protection Society (ARPS). Joseph William was son of Joseph Benjamin Johnson, who was a native of Sierra Leone, and of Betsey de Graft, daughter of Joseph de Graft (1756-1843). Joseph William was educated in Cape Coast by a maternal uncle, John Coleman de Graft. He was so attached to this uncle that he added his mother's family name to that of his father, and the famous De Graft-Johnson family was begun. At the start of his career, Joseph William worked for F. and A. Swanzy at Elmina, but he established his own business at Cape Coast in the 1890s. He was killed in 1928 while cutting down a tree.

DE GRAFT-JOHNSON, JOSEPH WILLIAM, JR. Son of Joseph William and brother of John Coleman, Sr. He was headmaster of the Wesleyan School at Cape Coast and author of Towards Nationhood in Africa (1928) and Historical Geography of the Gold Coast (1929).

DE GRAFT-JOHNSON, JOSEPH WILLIAM SWAIN. Born 1933. Member of the famous Cape Coast family, engineer, and Vice President during the Third Republic. He was educated at Mfantsipim, Leeds and Birmingham universities, and the University of California, where he received his doctorate. He became a member of the engineering faculty at the University of Kumasi in 1968. While on the faculty in Kumasi, he served on many important commissions and committees, including the one which drew up the constitution for the Third Republic. He was active in the creation of the People's National Party (PNP) and was nominated as the party's candidate for vice president at the party congress in Kumasi, 20 April 1979. He was elected on the ticket with Hilla Limann two months later. Deposed at the end of 1981, he was arrested a few days later and released from custody in September 1983.

DEH-SEKYI. The river god of the lower Volta. The high priest of Deh-Sekyi lived in a cave near where the present Akosombo Dam is located. The priest charged tribute of all persons who went up the river.

DEI-ANANG, MICHAEL FRANCIS. Born 1909. Writer from Mampong, Akuapem. He was educated at Achimota and at the University of London. He was employed in the British Civil Service in the Gold Coast before independence. During the Nkrumah period he was an adviser to Nkrumah on African and foreign affairs and was one of Nkrumah's ghostwriters. He is the author of <u>Ghana Resurgent</u> (1964), <u>Okomfo Anokye's Golden Stool</u>, a play published in 1960, <u>The Administration of Ghana's Foreign Relations, 1957-1965: A Personal Memoir</u> (1975), and several books of poetry. During the final year of Nkrumah's rule, Dei-Anang was Chairman of the State Publishing Corporation.

DE LIMA, GERALDO (de Lema). Died 1912. Trader. He was born in Dahomey (Benin) about 1835 and at a very early age went to work for a slave trader by the name of Casar Cenquira Geraldo de Lima. At that time his name was Adzoviehlo Atiogbe. When the master died in 1862, the employee took over the boss's business, wife, and name. In 1865 he was expelled from Ada for mistreatment of one of Ada's chiefs. He persuaded the Anlo to take up his quarrel, and the dispute kept the Volta region in turmoil for over twenty years. He opposed British expansion into the area of the Keta Lagoon because they were a threat to his business dominance of the area behind the Keta Lagoon. As the British moved in and suppressed the slave trade, de Lima was forced to turn to the palm oil trade. He was constantly at odds with the British, and he tried to organize resistance to British expansion. In 1871 the English bombarded his home in Anlo and offered a reward for his capture. For some time he evaded arrest, and he smuggled his goods past British officials. When the Germans arrived in 1884, de Lima supported the Germans. Finally the British captured him. They held him prisoner at Elmina from May 1885 until the end of 1893. By then he was broken and ruined. A few years later he went blind, and he finally died at Keta in 1912 as a result of tripping over a small child.

DENKYIRA (Dankyira, Denkera, Denkira, Denkyera). Akan state which before 1701 was the most powerful state in the Gold Coast hinterland. It controlled most of the gold traded to the Europeans from the area between the Tano and Pra rivers. The old capital was at Abankesieso or Bankesieso, on the Ofin, not far from the modern Obuasi. In the summer of 1701 Osei Tutu of Asante conquered Denkyira under Ntim Gyakari. Denkyira never recovered from the defeat in that battle of Feyiase. They attempted to rebel in 1711, but the rebellion was crushed. Many Denkyira people fled eastward into the lands of the Akyem. Today Denkyira is a small state in the Western Region.

DENSU RIVER. A river which rises in the Atewa-Atewiredu hills west of Koforidua and flows through the Sakumo Lagoon to reach the sea just west of Accra. It is a major source of the water used by Accra.

DEPORTATION ACT OF 1957. An act passed in July 1957 which allowed the government to void the citizenship of any person who was not born in Ghana of Ghanaian parents. Such persons could be deported if they did not give support to the CPP.

DEPUTATIONS. In 1868 the people of Elmina sent a deputation to the Netherlands to protest an ineffective governor. In 1871 they sent another deputation to protest plans of the Dutch to turn Elmina over to the British. After this example, people under British rule began to send deputations to England to demand representation in the Legislative Council and to oppose unpopular laws. In 1895 an Asante deputation went to London, but was not received. Deputations were a mild way to protest colonial rule.

DEVIL'S MOUNT (Monte da Diable, Mankwadi Hill, Ejisimanku Hill). 5°20' N, 0°41' W. A hill near Winneba which is the chief landmark on the coast between Accra and Apam. It is over 600 feet (183 m) high. It is believed to be the residence of the god Bobowisi.

DIPALI (Dipalli, Dapali, Yendi Dabari). 9°48' N, 0°57' W. A village in the Dagomba part of the Northern Region some 30 miles (48 km) north of Tamale and near Diari. It is also called Yendi Dabari and was once the capital of Dagomba before the Gonja invasion forced the Dagomba to establish a new capital at Yendi.

DISTRICT ASSEMBLIES ORDINANCE, 10 May 1858. An act establishing District Councils in the British Protectorate to supervise the collection of taxes. The Ordinance was disallowed in 1859.

DIXCOVE. 4°48' N, 1°57' W. A coastal village in the Ahanta part of the Western Region just west of Achowa point and east of Butre. It is only about 15 miles (24 km) west of Takoradi port. The English and Dutch built bases here in the seventeenth century. The Portuguese were there as early as 1503. The Dutch began Fort San Antonio beginning in 1642. It was turned over to the British in 1872. The fort was restored in the 1950s, and today is used as offices for the local authorities. The village is divided in two parts, Upper and Lower Dixcove. Together they had 2,269 persons in the census of 1970.

DJEBOBO, MOUNT. 8°20' N, 0°38' E (estimate). A mountain peak on the Togo border which the Survey of Ghana maps show as 2,873 feet (876 m) high. The little village of Kilinga is nearby.

DJERMA see ZABRAMA

DJOLETO, SOLOMON ALEXANDER AMU. Born 1929. Author. He was born near Odumase Krobo in the Eastern Region and educated in Presbyterian schools, St. Augustine's in Cape Coast, the University of Ghana, and the University of London. He became a teacher and editor of the Ghana Journal of Education. He is the author of The Strange Man (1967), Money Galore (1975), and other works.

DODOWA. 5°53' N, 0°07' W. Town in the Eastern Region about 25 miles (40 km) northeast of Accra, and just a short distance from Larteh. It was once the seat of the Joint Provincial Council of Chiefs, and it is the commercial center for the port of Prampram. In 1970 Dodowa had a population of 4,412.

DODOWA, BATTLE OF. Dodowa is the English name, Akantamasu is the Akan name, and Katamanso is the Ga name for a battle which took place eight miles (13 km) south of Dodowa on 7 August 1826. In the battle the Ga, Fante, Denkyira, Akyem, Akwamu, and British united to stop the Asante advance into the southeast. The Asante were badly defeated. It marked the beginning of the decline of Asante.

DOMBO, SIMON DIEDONG. Born 1923. Politician, traditional chief, and businessman. He is a native of Duori in the Upper Region West, near Lawra and Upper Volta. He was educated at Lawra and at Tamale. He represented the north in the Legislative Council in 1951. In April 1954 he founded the Northern People's Party. This group soon formed an alliance with the National Liberation Movement to demand a federal system of government. After Busia left the country in 1959, Dombo became leader of the opposition to the CPP. He served in the legislative branch of government until the coup of 1966 and was elected again during the Second Republic. In the Busia government he served as Minister of Health and as Minister of Interior. After the 1972 coup he returned to his duties as Duori Na, a position he had held since 1949.

DOMPOASE (Dompoasi). 6°18' N, 1°32' W. The second Adansi capital, established early in the seventeenth century on the Cape Coast-Kumasi road about 12 miles (19 km) south of Bekwai, and just above Fomena. Fomena became the third Adansi capital.

DONKO (Dunko, Duncoe, Donce, Odonko). Persons brought down from the north of Asante for use or sale as slaves. The term is sometimes used for anyone from north of Asante.

DORMAA AHENKRO (Domaa). 7°17' N, 2°53' W. A border town west of Sunyani in the Brong-Ahafo Region. At one time these people lived close to Kumasi, but they moved to their present location in an attempt to avoid Asante rule. Their original home was one of the first places captured by Osei Tutu. The population in 1948 was 2,179. By 1970 that figure had grown to 8,959.

DOROTHEA, FORT. 4°45' N, 2°01' W. A small fort located at Akwida in the Western Region near Cape Three points. The structure was first built by the Brandenburgers in 1685, but it was soon taken over by the Dutch. It is in ruins today.

DU BOIS, WILLIAM EDWARD BURGHARDT. 1868-1963. An American

Black leader who was one of the founders of the NAACP and the Pan-African Movement. He was the author of several books. In 1961 he joined the Communist Party, and at the invitation of Nkrumah, he moved to Ghana and became a Ghanaian citizen. He became the first director of the Encyclopaedia Africana and was awarded a doctorate by the University of Ghana just a short time before he died. He died on 27 August 1963, and is buried beside the western wall of Christiansborg Castle at Osu, Accra.

DUMA, FORT. A base built by the Portuguese in 1623 about 23 miles (37 km) up the Ankobra River from the coast. It was established to trade for gold thought to be in the area. The building was destroyed by an earthquake in 1636, and there is no trace of it today.

DUMPO (Kugulo, Kaala). Group of Guan who live in the Brong area. Their dialect is much like that used in Gonja.

DUNKWA (Abora or Abura Dunkwa). 5°20' N, 1°10' W. A village just above Anomabo, and about 20 miles (32 km) northeast of Cape Coast. On 8 April 1873 the Asante attacked an allied army of Assin, Fante, Denkyira, and British troops. The allies were forced to retreat.

DUNKWA-ON-THE-OFIN. 5°58' N, 1°47' W. Mining center on the railroad between Kumasi and Sekondi-Takoradi. It is 23 miles (37 km) south of Obuasi and 75 miles (120 km) north of Takoradi. It had a population of 15,437 in 1970.

DUPUIS, JOSEPH. A British official sent to Cape Coast in 1819 as consul to Kumasi. He did not go to Kumasi until he had spent a year at Cape Coast. While in Kumasi, Dupuis worked out a treaty with the Asantehene. It was signed on 23 March 1820. In the treaty, the Asantehene and his chiefs acknowledged themselves as British subjects, but claimed that all the Fante country was part of the Asante empire. The treaty was never ratified by the British. Dupuis returned to England, and in 1824 published Journal of a Residence in Ashantee, an account of his experiences on the Gold Coast.

DURBAR. A formal meeting of the elders, or a state occasion.

DWA. The Akan symbol of office. A stool is the equivalent of the European throne. In northern Ghana the symbol of office is a skin.

DWABEN (Juaben). 6°49' N, 1°26' W. A town 15 miles (24 km) to the northeast of Kumasi. It was one of the founding villages of the Asante Confederacy. It was once known as Apeayinase before its absorption into Asante. The Dwabenhene was one of the most powerful of the Asante chiefs, and at times the Asantehene considered Dwaben to be a threat to the central power. In 1831 Asantehene Yaw Akoto ordered a military occupation of Dwaben. Many of the people of Dwaben fled to Akyem Abuakwa to seek British protection. Many of these returned home after peace was restored in 1841. But in 1874 the Dwabenhene declared his independence of Asante, and he asked for British protection. The British did not respond to the pleas of Dwaben, and in October 1875 the Asante attacked. On 3 November the Dwaben gave out of ammunition. Hundreds were captured by the Asante and sold into slavery. Many others fled to Akyem and British protection again. These founded New Dwaben, with its capital at Koforidua. Some eventually returned to Old Dwaben. In 1948 Dwaben had a population of only 2,471 persons. By 1970 this had doubled to 5,018.

DYULA (Dioula, Juula, Wangara). Mande traders who came from Mali to trade along the Volta river. They helped spread Islam wherever they went.

DZODZE. 6°14' N, 1°00' E. Town in the Volta Region near the Togo border. Its population in 1970 was 10,390 persons.

- E -

EAST INDIA COMPANY. A British company formed in London in 1599 for trade with the East Indies. It controlled English trade with the Gold Coast from 1658 to 1663.

EDUCATION. Ghana has a system of education much like that of the British. Kindergartens take children 4 to 6 years old. There are six years of primary school and three years of junior secondary. In 1980 there were some 105 secondary schools, 11 technical institutes, 82 teacher training schools, and a number of commercial schools. Many secondary schools, such as Achimota, Mfantsipim, and Adisadel, are outstanding. Churches maintain a number of distinguished schools. Adult education is provided by the Institute of Public Education, founded in 1962. There are three universities. The University of Ghana is at Legon, the University of Science and Technology is located at Kumasi, and the third university is at Cape Coast. Ghana trains its nurses and physicians at teaching hospitals at Korle Bu, Accra, and Okomfo Anokye in Kumasi. There is a law school at Legon. In spite of tremendous public and private expenditure on education since 1957, Ghana still has an illiteracy rate of above 60 percent.

EDUSEI, KROBO. 1915-1984. Asante politician. Born in Kumasi in December 1915, he was educated at the government boys' school in Kumasi. For a time he was a reporter and debt collector for the

Ashanti Pioneer. In 1947 Edusei was one of the founders of the
Ashanti Youth Association, and he joined the CPP in 1949. He was
imprisoned in the Positive Action civil disobedience campaign in
1950, and as a Prison Graduate was elected to the legislative
assembly in 1951, becoming Minister of Justice in Nkrumah's
first government. For a time he was propaganda secretary of
the CPP. In 1957 he became Minister of Interior, and in that
position he was one of the leaders of the group which tried to
silence all opposition to Nkrumah. As a member of Nkrumah's
government, Edusei became wealthy. His generosity and extra-
vagant life-style made him one of the best known of Nkrumah's
circle. Between 1952 and 1966 he made over 40 trips to Europe.
In England in 1955 he married Mary Jackson, who later created
a sensation by buying a gold-plated bed. Edusei also served
terms as Minister of Industries and as Minister of Agriculture.

After the fall of Nkrumah in 1966, Edusei was imprisoned.
He was charged with holding illegal assets, but acquitted in
May 1970 after spending many months in prison. He was banned
from politics in the 1979 elections, but still was a member of the
Central Committee of the PNP and chairman of the Asante Region
branch of the PNP. After the fall of President Limann in 1981,
Edusei found himself in prison again. In October 1982 he was
sentenced to 11 years for accepting a large loan in the Chia-
velli case, but he was released in 1983 due to poor health.

EFUTU (Afutu, Fetu, Futu). 5°12' N, 1°19' W. Central Region.
The town is near Cape Coast, and its history has been influenced by that proximity. The people were originally Guan, but
they have been identified with the Fante since at least 1710.

EGALA, IMORU. 1914-1981. Wealthy Muslim politician from the
Tumu area of the Upper Region-West. Egala was elected to
parliament in 1954 and he served as a minister in Nkrumah's
first all-African Cabinet. He was defeated in the 1956 elections,
so Nkrumah made him chairman of the Cocoa Marketing Board.
Reelected in 1959, he was soon back in the Cabinet. He held
several posts in Nkrumah's government, serving as Minister of
Industries from 1962 until the 1966 coup.

In 1969 Egala announced that he would form a political party, but he was excluded from the elections that year as a former leader of the CPP. Nevertheless, during this period he
was most active in keeping the Nkrumah movement alive.
Though banned again in 1979, he was a founding father of the
PNP, and he was instrumental in the choice of Hilla Limann as
the candidate of PNP for president. After the election of Limann, Egala became an adviser to the new President of the
Third Republic. He died suddenly on 1 April 1981.

EGUAFO. Guan coastal group known to the Europeans as Comany
or Great Komenda. Shama, at the mouth of the Pra, was an
Eguafo village. At one time the Eguafo controlled trade through

Elmina, and they were important middlemen in the gold and slave trade. In time they became part of the Fante alliance.

EGWIRA (Igwira, Igwijra). An area in the extreme western part of what is today the Western Region. It was shown on a 1629 Dutch map, which noted that the land was rich in gold. Egwira overlaps the Aowin and Sefwi lands west of the Tano.

EJA (Egya). 5°11' N, 1°06' W. A village in the Fante area near modern Saltpond. The English maintained a trade post there at one time.

EJISU. 6°43' N, 1°28' W. Town in the Asante Region just east of Kumasi on the highway and railroad to Accra. Some of the most bitter fighting of the Asante-British war took place here in 1900. The Queen Mother of Ejisu, Yaa Asantewa, was leader of the Asante cause against the English. In 1948 Ejisu had a population of 1,381. By 1960 there were 2,288 living there, and in 1970 the count was 3,346.

EJUANEMA, MOUNT. 6°34' N, 0°46' W. A peak on the southern edge of the Kwahu Plateau near Nkawkaw in the Eastern Region. It is 2,478 feet (755 m) high. Bauxite deposits are worked in the area.

EJURA. 7°23' N, 1°22' W. A town on the Great Northern Highway north of Kumasi and between Mampong and Atebubu. It is at the northern edge of the Asante Region. A road branches off to the west from Ejura and crosses the Pru valley to the Techiman-Kintampo road. The Akyem Bosome believe that they originated in Ejura. In 1911 the town had a population of 2,703. This dropped to 1,535 in 1948, but increased to 7,078 in 1960, and was 10,664 a decade later.

EKUANA. One of the principal Akan clans.

EKUMFI. A coastal Fante group of fishermen located to the west of Winneba.

ELEPHANTE GRANDE (Aliphante Grande, Big Elephant). An area in the Ankobra valley in Sefwi territory where the Portuguese reported gold and ivory could be found.

ELEPHANTS. Ivory was one of the items most sought after by Europeans on the Guinea coast. There is a debate about how many elephants there were in the sixteenth and seventeenth centuries, but the number has certainly decreased rapidly since then. Iain Douglas-Hamilton did an elephant census in Africa in 1979. He listed 4,000 elephants in the Ivory Coast, 1,700 in Upper Volta, only 80 in Togo, and 3,500 in Ghana. The greatest concentration in Ghana is located in the Western Region near the border with the Ivory Coast.

ELIZA CARTHAGO, FORT. 4°53' N, 2°17' W. A post started by the Dutch on a hill overlooking the left bank of the Ankobra in 1702. From this point the Dutch hoped to connect with the gold trade from the interior.

ELLIS, ALFRED BURDON. 1852-1894. Soldier, Colonial Administrator, and Author. He served as a lieutenant in the First West India Regiment under Sir Garnet Wolseley in the 1874 Asante campaign. From 1878 to 1879 he was District Commissioner at Keta, where he carried on a spirited campaign against smugglers. An attempt against his life by Geraldo de Lima and the Anlo was almost successful at this time. The year 1881 found him back in the army. In 1884 he was in the South African Zulu campaign, and in 1889 he was in the Bahamas. By 1893 he was a Lt. Colonel, fighting Samori's Sofas on the borders of Sierra Leone. Here he contracted a fever from which he died in 1894.

Ellis was not only a soldier, but he was an author of some note. His West African Sketches appeared in 1881, followed by The Land of Fetish in 1883, The Tshi-Speaking Peoples of the Gold Coast of West Africa in 1887, West African Stories and The Ewe-Speaking Peoples of the Slave Coast of West Africa in 1890, History of the Gold Coast of West Africa in 1893 (taking the story to 1887), and The Yoruba-Speaking Peoples of the Slave Coast was published the year he died.

ELMINA (Edina, Ednaa). 5°05' N, 1°20' W. A town at Elmina Point where a small stream drains the Benya Lagoon into the Gulf of Guinea. It is in the Central Region and was once called the "village of two parts" because part of the people were Efutu and part Eguafo. The town is dominated by San Jorge Castle, built by the Portuguese in 1482. This impressive structure was captured by the Dutch in 1637 and for over two hundred years was the Dutch headquarters on the Gold Coast. In 1872 the English purchased the Castle, which they gave to Ghana in 1957. Across town from the Castle is San Iago Fort, also an imposing reminder of the colonial era. In earlier days the town was a key outlet for gold, ivory, and slaves from Asante. Today the town is surrounded by coconut groves, salt evaporation pans, and beautiful beaches. Elmina is an important port for African fishing canoes. Within sight of Cape Coast--eight miles to the east, and on the main coastal highway, the town is one of the most popular tourist attractions in Ghana. The population of the town was 5,091 in 1911, 5,909 in 1948, 8,534 in 1960, and 11,401 when the last census was made in 1970.

ENCASSAR or ENCASSE see SEFWI

ETSI (Ati, Atti, Etsu). A small Guan group located just north of the Fante. These were among the earliest known people along the coast. The state was shown on a Dutch map in 1629. In time it became a part of Assin.

EVALUE. An Akan group in southwestern Ghana who are related to the Nzema.

EVEGBE. The Ewe language. The chief Evegbe dialect used in Ghana is Anlo, used in the coastal area of the Volta Region.

EVENING NEWS. An Accra newspaper founded by Kwame Nkrumah, with the first edition appearing 3 September 1948. It became the chief voice of the CPP, and it was on the pages of this paper that Nkrumah first launched his "Positive Action" program for independence. K.A. Gbedemah was the first editor. From time to time there were slight changes in the name, such as Ghana Evening News.

EWE. One of the major groups of people in Ghana. Most of the Ewe live east of the Volta River in Ghana and Togo. Tradition ties them to the Oyo Yoruba, Ketou in Benin (Dahomey), and Notsie (Nouatja, Nuatja) in Togo. They probably moved into their present locations soon after 1600. Eweland is the area between the Mono River in Togo and the Volta in Ghana. It runs west to east about 80 miles (129 km) and is about the same distance north to south. From 1885 to 1914 the Ewe were divided between British and German rule. Then during World War I (1914-1919) most of the Ewe were under British rule. Under a League of Nations mandate, the eastern part of Eweland became part of French-ruled Togo. The rest was administered by the British, either as a mandate or part of the Gold Coast. In 1956 a plebiscite was held in the British mandate, and a majority voted to cast their lot with the new country of Ghana. But there is still sentiment among many Ewe to form a union with Ewe in Togo as a separate nation.

Ho, Krepi, and Anlo are three of the main divisions of the Ewe in Ghana. Ghanaians call the Ewe (Evhe) the Awona. There are about a million Ewe in Ghana.

- F -

FANTE (Fanti, Fantyn). A coastal Akan group who according to their traditions moved from Techiman to their present location in the Central Region in the thirteenth century. Their original coastal settlement was called Kwaman. Later Kwaman became Mankesim. It is still their chief center. Abora, Abease, Nkusukum, Kwanyako, and Anomabo were other early Fante towns. By 1800 the Fante dominated the coast from Winneba to the Pra River. The Fante never united as one polity, but they could cooperate when threatened. The Fante often found themselves allied with the British against the Asante and Dutch.

FANTE CONFEDERACY, 1868. The Fante Confederacy was an attempt on the part of a number of coastal peoples to unite for protection and for development because they believed the British were about to leave the Gold Coast. Delegations from Fante, Denkyira, Wassa, Assin, and Twifo towns met in Mankesim and reached a basic agreement to form a confederation. Mankesim would be the seat of government. Executive and legislative authorities were to be selected, taxes were provided for, and the mobilization of an army began. Dutch and English plans to exchange posts on the coast without consulting the Africans were denounced. For a time prospects looked bright. Enthusiasm spread. New groups applied for admission to the alliance. The union has often been called the forerunner of modern Ghanaian nationalism. But it was dead by 1873. The Dutch departure from the coast in 1872 removed a threat to the Fante. The Confederation could not raise the funds necessary for defense or a program of development. Most important as the cause of the failure of the Confederation was the British opposition to the whole plan. Without British support the Fante attempt at union failed. The British then decided to set up a protectorate over the coastal region.

FEKUW. The Mfantsi Amanbuhu Fékuw (Fante National Society) was formed in 1889 at Cape Coast by John Mensah Sarbah, J.W. de Graft-Johnson, J.P. Brown, and others to build national consciousness and pride among the Fante. It was the precursor of the Aborigines' Rights Protection Society (ARPS).

FELLI, ROGER JOSEPH ATOGETIPOLI. Soldier and Member of the National Redemption Council. He was born in 1938 at Navrongo in the Upper Region, near the border with Upper Volta. He enlisted in the army in 1960, was sent to Sandhurst in England, and thereafter advanced rapidly through the ranks. He was a member of the NRC from its formation in 1972 and was one of those closest to Acheampong. He rose to be Commissioner of Foreign Affairs in the Supreme Military Council. Felli was one of those executed by Rawlings in June 1979.

FERA (Awuna). A group of Awuna who live along the border of Upper Volta in the Upper Region. Actually, the Awuna are divided into the Fera and the Nagwa subgroups.

FERGUSON, GEORGE AKEM. 1864-1897. Colonial Officer, Geographer, and Explorer. Born in Anomabo, trained in London as a surveyor, George Ferguson joined the British Civil Service in 1881. From 1884 he was engaged in mapping the interior behind the Gold Coast, and in 1886 he served on the commission that determined the boundaries between the Gold Coast and German Togo territories. After 1890 he conducted missions into the north, as far as Ouagadougou, establishing British control over as much of the territory as he could. The Papers of George Ekem Ferguson give a vivid picture of conditions in what is now the Northern Region and Upper Region in the period between

Fetish 84

1890 and 1897. On 7 April 1897 Ferguson was killed by forces of Samori near the town of Wa.

FETISH. From the Portuguese word "feitiço," meaning "something made." An object getting respect or devotion. The Akan term "asuman," meaning charm, amulet, or talisman, has an approximate meaning.

FETU see EFUTU

FEYIASE, BATTLE (Feyiasi). 6°36' N, 1°34' W. The place eight miles (13 km) southeast of Kumasi where, in November 1701, the Asante army under Osei Tutu defeated the Denkyira army under Ntim Gyakari. The King of Denkyira lost his life and the power of Denkyira was broken. Plundering lasted for several weeks after the battle.

FIA. The Ewe word for "chief." Fiaga is a paramount chief.

FIRAO (Frao, Atirri). An African name of the Volta River below the point where the Oti flows into the Volta.

FLAG. The flag of Ghana is a tricolor of red, gold, and green, with a black star in the center of the gold stripe. In 1964 Nkrumah had the colors of the flag changed to a tricolor of red, white, and green, with the black star on the center white. After the coup against Nkrumah in 1966, the old flag was returned.

FOMENA. 6°17' N, 1°31' W. A town on the Cape Coast-Kumasi highway in the Asante Region some 25 miles (40 km) north of the place where the highway crosses the Pra River. From Fomena a highway branches off westward to Obuasi, only 11 miles (17.6 km) away. Fomena is the capital of Adansi. In 1948 the population was 2,179, which dropped to just 1,896 in 1960, and rose to 2,277 by 1970.

FOMENA, TREATY OF. In February 1874, after the British under Wolseley had destroyed Kumasi, the Asante agreed to a peace treaty. The Asantehene signed a treaty at Fomena on 14 March 1874. Asante renounced claims to Denkyira, Assin, Akyem, Adansi, Elmina, and gave up rents for coastal forts. They agreed to pay a large indemnity, and the Asantehene promised to do his best to stop human sacrifice.

FOO-FOO (Fufu). A basic food in West Africa. It is usually made from cassava flour, but may be made from yams, plantains, bananas, or rice. Cassava is peeled, cut up, and placed in water a few days to soften and ferment. It is then dried, pounded into flour, and made into balls for cooking. After it is ready it is eaten with a sauce or stew.

FORESTRY ORDINANCES. The British colonial government began to consider forestry conservation controls as early as 1883, but regulations were postponed because of African opposition. A Forestry Department was created in 1909, and it brought in legislation to create forest reserves in 1910 and 1911. The bills were bitterly opposed by the ARPS and many Africans, fearing that the reserves were a subterfuge by the British to take native lands. The Forest Ordinance of 1919 gave chiefs responsibility to set aside forest reserves, but few were established. Finally, the Forestry Ordinance of 1927 empowered the government in Accra to form forest reserves, with title to the reserves and control of the reserves in the native stool authority.

FOSO (Fosu). 5°42' N, 1°17' W. A Fante market-town in the Central Region on the Cape Coast-Kumasi road 18 miles (30 km) south of the Pra crossing. It had 2,550 people in the census of 1948, 5,284 in 1960, and by 1970 the population was 7,249.

FRAFRA. Name of a small group of people in the Upper Region-East who live to the east of Bolgatanga near the border of Upper Volta.

FRANCOIS, CURT VON. 1852-1931. Member of a Prussian military family, he served in the German army during the Franco-Prussian War. Afterwards he was a member of the Grenfell-Wissmann Expedition to the Congo. In 1888 the German Foreign Office sent him to explore the hinterland of the Togo area, and between March and June of that year he visited Salaga, Yendi, Karaga, and Gambaga, crossing into the modern Upper Volta territory before returning to the coast. He signed agreements with Yendi, Karaga, and Salaga. In 1889 he was assigned to Southwest Africa, where he remained until 1895. Later he wrote several books about his African experiences.

FRASER, ALEXANDER GORDON. 1873-1962. The first principal of Achimota College. Born in Scotland and educated at Oxford, he did missionary educational work in Uganda before he was appointed to run the school at Achimota. He headed Achimota for a decade, 1924-1935.

FREDENSBORG. 5°45' N, 0°11' E. A fort built by the Danes at Great or Old Ningo around 1740. It was abandoned later, but the ruins were acquired by the English in 1850.

FREDERIKSBORG (Fort Royal). A fort built just east of Cape Coast by the Danes about 1660. It was purchased by the British and renamed Fort Royal in 1688. In 1699 it was rebuilt, but fifty years later it was abandoned.

FREEMAN, THOMAS BIRCH. 1809-1890. Missionary, writer, and government official. Freeman was born in Hampshire, England, of an African father and an English mother. In 1838 he went to Cape Coast as a Methodist missionary, and he played an important role in the expansion of the Methodists in the Gold Coast and Nigeria. He kept a journal of three trips from Cape Coast to Kumasi, and one trip to Dahomey and Nigeria between 1839 and 1843, which is an important source for information on the Guinea Coast. He served some time as Civil Commandant of the Accra District, and lived the last twenty years of his life mostly in Accra or Mankesim.

FRONT FOR THE PREVENTION OF DICTATORSHIP. A group organized during the military government campaign for a union government in early 1978. This opposition to the Supreme Military Council was headed by Victor Owusu.

FULLER, FRANCIS. 1866-1944. British official and author. He was the British Chief Commissioner in Asante from 1902 to 1920. He had entered the Colonial Service in 1884 and had served in Nigeria and other places before coming to Kumasi. He retired after his Asante service and published A Vanished Dynasty: Ashanti in 1921.

FURLEY, J.T. A member of the Colonial Service of the Gold Coast from 1902 to 1923, the last six years of which he was Secretary for Native Affairs. He retired in 1924 and began to collect materials on the history of the Gold Coast from Portugal, the Netherlands, Denmark, and England. These materials were given to the Balme Library at the University of Ghana at Legon, and the collection is called the Furley Collection.

FUTU see EFUTU

FWEMSO. A famous fetish house on the shores of Lake Bosumtwi, it was suppressed by the British during their rule of Asante.

FYNN, JOHN KOFI. Born 1935. Historian, politician, and professor. Fynn was born in Abura-Dunkwa in the Central Region and was educated at Mfantsipim, the University of Ghana, and the University of London, where he received his doctorate in 1964. Since then he has published many articles on the history of Asante, and in 1971 his Asante and Its Neighbors 1700-1807 appeared. He is on the faculty of the University of Ghana, and the Institute of African Studies at Legon. In the period of the Second Republic he was a leading member of the Progress Party and served in the National Assembly, 1969-1972. Later he was active in the Popular Front Party.

- G -

GA. People who live in Accra, Osu, Labadi, Nungua, Teshi, and

Tema. The Ga of Accra are called Gamashie. According to their traditions, the Ga came to the Accra Plains from Nigeria in the sixteenth century under the leadership of Okai Koi. They never united under one leader, and so were frequently at the mercy of other people. Between 1677 and 1681 they were conquered by Akwamu. They have a patrilineal society, and traditionally they have supported themselves as fishermen, but their location on the coast also gave them advantage as traders with the Europeans. The Ga are closely related to the Adangbe, who share common traditions and customs.

GA MANCHE. The principal Ga chief of Accra.

GA SHIFIMO KPEE. The Ga Standfast Organization. A Ga protest group organized in 1957 to protest the large influx of outsiders who began to move into Accra and threaten the Ga inhabitants of Accra after independence.

GAMASHIE. The Ga of Central Accra.

GAMBAGA. 10°32' N, 0°26' W. The ancient Mamprusi capital, it is located in the Northern Region just below the Gambaga Scarp. It is 80 miles (128 km) northeast of Tamale. Gambaga was occupied by a British force under Captain Donald Stewart on Christmas Eve in 1896. It became a popular hill station for the English and served as their seat of government from 1897 to 1907 for the Northern Territories. At one time Gambaga was an important commercial town, and the Mole-Dagbani have always looked upon it as their spiritual home, but its population has never been large. It was reported to have 1,567 inhabitants in 1911. By 1960 the number had increased to 2,936, and in 1970 the figure was 3,730.

GAMBAGA SCARP. The erosion escarpment or drop at the southern face of the Gambaga Plateau in northeastern Ghana. At some points the fall in the surface is over 1,000 feet (305 m).

GARDINER, ROBERT KWEKU ATTA. Born 1914. Government official. Gardiner graduated from Cambridge in economics in 1941 and got his masters from Oxford a year later. During the period 1943-1946 he was a lecturer in economics in Sierra Leone and from 1947 to 1949 he was employed in the UN Trusteeship Department. From the UN he moved to Nigeria to become the Extramural Studies Director at the University of Ibadan. Then he returned home to Ghana to be Director of Social Welfare and Community Development (1953-1955), Secretary to the Ministry of Housing (1955-1957), and Head of the Ghana Civil Service (1957-1959). Then he joined the Economic Commission for Africa from 1959 to 1961. He served twice in the UN operation in the Congo, in 1961 and again from 1962 to 1963. From 1963 to 1975 he was Executive Secretary of the UN Economic Commission for

Africa. In 1975 he returned home once again to become Commissioner for Economic Planning for the SMC, a position he resigned in May 1978 because of ill health.

GARI. Toasted cassava flour that is the staple dish consumed by the poor in Ghana and much of West Africa.

GBANYA (Gbanyito). Guan language spoken in Gonja.

GBEDEMAH, KOMLA AGBELI. Born 1912. Journalist, businessman, politician. His parents were Ewe from the Volta Region, but he was born at Warri in Nigeria. He attended secondary school in Cape Coast, and then attended Achimota, 1929-1933. He then taught a few years in Akuapem and Accra before going into business. In 1948 he was chairman of the Committee on Youth Organizations. He joined the UGCC and became a founding member of the CPP in 1949. While Nkrumah was in prison, Gbedemah ran the CPP and edited the Evening News. He was the organizer of the CPP election victory in 1951 in which he won a seat in the Legislative Assembly. In 1951-1952 he was Minister of Health and Labor, from 1952 to 1954 he headed Commerce and Industry, and from 1954 to 1961 he was Finance Minister. As Nkrumah moved toward the left politically, he and Gbedemah became estranged. Gbedemah objected to the President's effigy being put on the Republic's new bank notes. Gbedemah finally resigned in a dispute over control of the budget. He was briefly assigned to his old position in the Ministry of Health, but in September 1961 Nkrumah fired him, and he went into exile for five years, until after the overthrow of the CPP in 1966. He devoted himself to business interests until the 1969 elections, when he organized the National Alliance of Liberals and was elected to the National Assembly as leader of the opposition. Denied his seat, he returned to his business activities. After the coup of January 1972 the NRC appointed Gbedemah a roving ambassador. By 1977 Gbedemah had broken with the military authorities and come out in opposition to the SMC's referendum on union government. He was arrested by the military in 1978, but soon released. He was banned from taking part in the 1979 elections.

GBEHO, PHILIP. Born 1905. An Ewe was taught at Achimota and composed the national anthem, "God Bless Our Homeland Ghana." During the colonial period he was active in the struggle for Ewe unification. Under Nkrumah he served a term as Director of the Arts Council.

GBEWA (Bawa, Nedega). Grandson of Tohajie, and son of Kpogonumbo, he founded a Mole-Dagbani state at Pusiga, near Bawku. His daughter Yennega (Nyennega, Yantaure) started the Mossi dynasties; his son and grandson, Sitobu and Nyagse, founded Dagomba; another son, Tohogo, founded Mamprugu or Mamprusi;

son Nnantombo (Yantambo) founded Nanumba; and other children founded lesser Mole-Dagbani states.

GBONLANA. The eldest son of the ruler of Dagomba at Yendi. He served as regent during an interregnum.

GBUGBLA. The people of Prampram, an Adangbe coastal town.

GBUIPE. The Gonja Division whose chief town was Buipe, a town just above the Black Volta on an old trade route from Kumasi and Kintampo to Daboya, and ultimately Jenne in modern Mali.

GEMI HILL. A hill in the Volta Region above Ho and near Amedzofe. It is famous for a victory of Krepi forces on the hill over the Asante and Akwamu in 1869.

GHANA. An ancient Mande kingdom located in the Sahel north of the Niger on the edge of the Sahara. The kingdom began to decline after it was conquered by Almoravids in 1076. By 1235 it was replaced by Mali as the chief power in the Sahel. In the 1920s a popular tradition developed in the Gold Coast that the people of ancient Ghana had moved south from the Sahel after the destruction of ancient Ghana. It is generally agreed that J.B. Danquah deserves credit for the suggestion that the Gold Coast name be changed to Ghana when independence came in 1957.

GHANA COLLEGE. A school organized in the Oddfellows Hall, Cape Coast, by Nkrumah in July 1948 for secondary schoolboys who had been dismissed from their regular school due to a strike in February.

GHANA CONGRESS PARTY (GCP). A political party formed in 1952 by J.B. Danquah and other leaders of the old UGGC, and intelligentsia such as K.A. Busia. In 1954 the GCP was replaced by the National Liberation Party, and this in turn was followed by the United Party in 1957. Each in its own way tried to find a formula to check the power of Nkrumah.

GHANA NOTES AND QUERIES. A publication of the Historical Society of Ghana which began in 1961 and has appeared irregularly since then.

GHANA PATRIOTIC MOVEMENT (GPM). A group organized by Alex Quaison-Sackey in 1977 in support of the SMC's union government without political parties.

GHANA PEACE AND SOLIDARITY COUNCIL (GPSC). One of the groups which were organized in 1977-1978 to campaign in support of the SMC plan for union government without political parties.

GHANA PEOPLE'S REPRESENTATIVE ASSEMBLY. A meeting, called by Nkrumah, at the West End Arena in Accra in November 1949 to oppose changes in the government suggested by the Coussey Commission.

GHANAIAN TIMES. A state-owned Accra daily newspaper published from 1958. The Sunday edition is called the Weekly Spectator.

GHARTEY IV (also known as Kwamin Akyempong). Ca. 1820-1897. President of the Fante Confederation, 1868-1873; King (Odefa) of Winneba, 1872-1897. R.J. Ghartey was an important merchant on the coast during the second half of the nineteenth century.

GHOFAN DESERT. The area between the forest area and the savanna between Kintampo and Buipe. It was an area with very few people in the nineteenth century.

GOKA, F.K.D. Born 1921. Goka was from the Volta Region. He was a member of the assemblies from 1954 to 1966 as a leading member of Nkrumah's CPP. He was a teacher before entering political life. He was regional commissioner of the Volta Region, 1959-1960. In 1960 he became Minister of Trade, and in the following year he was K.A. Gbedemah's successor as Finance Minister. During his tenure as Finance Minister to 1965 his austerity budgets were unpopular.

GOLD COAST. European name for the coastal area between the Ivory Coast and Togo. In 1874 the English adopted the name for the area under their "protection," and as their rule extended over Asante and the Northern Territories the name came to be applied to those areas also. In 1957 the name became Ghana.

GOLD COAST NEWSPAPERS. A number of newspapers published along the coast incorporated the Gold Coast name in their titles. The Gold Coast Aborigines was published at Cape Coast from 1898. Its motto was "For the safety of the Republic, and the welfare of the Race." Its first editor was a Methodist minister named F. Egyir-Asaam, one of the early Gold Coast nationalists. The Gold Coast Chronicle began in Accra in September 1890, edited by J. Bright Davies. The Gold Coast Echo was successor to another paper called The Western Echo. The Gold Coast Echo appeared between 1888 and 1890 at Cape Coast, and was edited by J.E. Casely Hayford. The Gold Coast Express and Gold Coast Free Press were both newspapers that appeared in the 1890's, as was Dr. F.V. Nanka-Bruce's Gold Coast Independent. J.E. Casely Hayford's Gold Coast Leader was published at Cape Coast from 1902 to 1929. The Gold Coast Methodist Times was a Cape Coast journal edited by Methodist ministers. The Gold Coast Nation was the ARPS paper, published during the World War I period by such able men as J.D. Abraham and J.P. Brown. The Gold Coast News was published by an English law-

yer, W.C. Niblett, but it survived only a few months in 1885.
Mensah Sarbah's The Gold Coast People, promising to be a
"mouthpiece" for the people, began in 1891. The Gold Coast
Spectator, and the Gold Coast Times round out the list. The
latter paper was founded in 1874 by Prince James Brew. It became a weekly in 1881, and for many years it was the voice of
merchant opinion at Cape Coast.

GOLD COAST YOUTH CONFERENCE. A nationalist movement organized by J.B. Danquah and others in 1929. It held its first conference at Achimota in April 1930. In 1948 the Gold Coast Youth
Conference was absorbed by the United Gold Coast Convention.

GOLDEN STOOL. (Sika Dwa) The symbol of Asante. This creation
of Osei Tutu and Okomfo Anokye is believed by the Asante to
embody the soul of their nation. Today it is one of the symbols
of Ghana.

GOLD WEIGHTS. Objects made from bronze or other metals by the
lost wax method. At one time the weights were used in a balance to weigh gold, but they are also prized as art objects.
Many gold weights represent African proverbs.

GOMOA (Gomua). The Akan who live between the Ga and Fante in
the Winneba area. They were once called the Akraman.

GONJA (Gongya, Gonya). The western part of the Northern Region.
The state of Gonja was founded by people said to have come
from Mali in the seventeenth century. Yagbum was the capital,
and Buipe the most important commercial center. Ndewura Jakpa
is the traditional founding father. Headmen use the name of
their town with the suffix "-wura" added. In time Salaga became the major trade city, and today the paramount chief of
Gonja lives at Damongo. The mass of the people use the Vagala
language, which belongs to the Gur or Grusi classification. The
upper classes use a Guan dialect, akin to Akan speech. The
history of Gonja is vague. During the seventeenth century they
expanded eastward at the expense of Dagomba. The Asante
conquered Gonja in the eighteenth century and placed it under
heavy tribute. Asante call Gonja "Ntafo." The French, Samori's forces, the Zabrama, and the British all arrived at the end
of the nineteenth century. When the scramble ended, Gonja was
part of the Northern Territories of the Gold Coast.

GOOD HOPE, FORT (Goede Hoop). A Dutch post set up in 1667 at
Senya Beraku, a short distance down the coast to the east of
Winneba. The Dutch built the fort in 1706.

GOULDSBURY, VALESIUS SKIPTON. British Surgeon-Major and
Colonial Administrator. Dr. Gouldsbury visited Yendi in 1876
as a British Commissioner, becoming the first Englishman to reach

the middle Volta Basin. He visited Salaga on this trip. From 1877 to 1884 he was Administrator of The Gambia. During this period, he visited the hinterland of the Gambia-Futa Jallon-Sierra Leone in 1881. Then, from 1891 to 1897, he was Commissioner of Saint Lucia in the Lesser Antilles.

GOVERNMENT GAZETTE. The official journal of the government of the Gold Coast.

GRANT, FRANCIS CHAPMAN. 1825-1908. Merchant. Son of a Scottish father and an African mother, he was educated in England. By the 1860s he was one of the leading merchants at Cape Coast. He played a role in the organization of the Fante Confederation, 1868-1873, and he served several terms on the Gold Coast Legislative Council.

GRANT, "PA" GEORGE ALFRED. 1878-1956. Merchant. Grandson of Francis Chapman Grant, he became wealthy as a timber merchant during the first four decades of the twentieth century. In 1947 he was one of the founders of the United Gold Coast Convention, of which he was the first president.

GREAT AKANNY (Akanni). This area is shown on a 1629 Dutch map as Great Acanij, and on the 1729 Anville map as Akanni, "formerly very powerful." The territory overlaps the Adansi-Assin area of today.

GREAT INKASSA (Ahasia, Enkassar Iggina). A gold-producing area west of Wassa, shown on 1629 and 1729 maps near modern Sefwi.

GREAT KOMENDA. 5°03' N, 1°29' W. The capital of the Eguafo polity, on the coast west of Elmina.

GREAT NORTH ROAD. The road north from Kumasi to Mampong, Ejura, Atebubu, Yeji, Salaga, Tamale, Bolgatanga, Navrongo, and the border with Upper Volta.

GRIFFITH, WILLIAM BRANDFORD, SR. 1824-1897. British Governor. Born in Windsor, Barbados, where he was a member of the Legislative Assembly from 1861 to 1874. By 1880 he was in the Gold Coast as the Lieutenant Governor, a position he held until he became Governor. As Governor from 1885 to 1895 he did much to extend British responsibility on the Gold Coast. Boundaries with the Germans and French were defined, departments of roads, education, telegraph, and prisons were created, the first African joined the Legislative Assembly, and the first census was taken. Griffith was interested in the diversification of agriculture, but had little success in this area. It was during his administration that much of the Northern Territory began to recognize British control.

GRIFFITH, WILLIAM BRANDFORD, JR. 1858-1939. Colonial Administrator. Like his father the governor, William Brandford, Jr. was born in Barbados. Following his father to the Gold Coast, he became Queen's Advocate, then District Commissioner, then Attorney-General, and finally Chief Justice of the Gold Coast, 1884 to 1911. He compiled the Ordinances of the Gold Coast Colony in 1887, 1898, and 1903. In 1934 he published a <u>Digest of Gold Coast Law Reports</u>, and in 1935 <u>Note on HIstory of Courts and Constitution of Gold Coast Colony</u>.

GROMETTOES. Term meaning African mercenaries.

GROSS FRIEDRICHSBURG (Prince's Town). 4°47' N, 2°08' W. This fort was built in 1683 by the Brandenburgers. From 1717 to 1725 it was held by John Konny, and the Dutch then took over the fort.

GRUSI. A general term used for several small groups in the Northern Region and the Upper Region. The Kasena, Mo, Nunuma, Sisala, Tampolense, and Vagala are usually identified under this rubric, but the term is of doubtful value. In the 1880's these poor people were often raided by the forces of Samori and of Babatu. In some sources Grusi appears as Gourounsi, Grunshi, Grunsi, Gurunsi, etc. These people live not only in Ghana, but also in Upper Volta.

GUAN (Guang, Gwan). An ancient group of people who now live in a great curve from Gonja in the Northern Region to Krakye, to Larteh in the Eastern Region, to Senya Bereku and Efutu in the Central Region. The Guan language is related to the language of the Akan.

GUGGISBERG, FREDERICK GORDON. 1869-1930. Governor of the Gold Coast. Born in Toronto, Canada, he joined the army in 1889. He did survey work in the Gold Coast, 1902-1908, then he became Surveyor-General of Nigeria, serving there from 1910 until the outbreak of World War I. During the war he served in France. After the war he was appointed Governor of the Gold Coast, a position he held with great distinction from 1919 to 1927. He was later Governor of British Guiana, 1928-1930.

At the beginning of his tenure as Governor of the Gold Coast, Guggisberg offered a Ten-Year Development Program to the Legislative Council. He suggested first the improvement of transportation in the Gold Coast--harbors, railroads, and roads. Then, in order of priority, he listed water supply, drainage, hydroelectric projects, public buildings, town improvements, schools, hospitals, prisons, communication lines, and other improvements. He also set a goal of having half the technical departments staffed with Africans as soon as they could be trained. It was the most ambitious program ever proposed in West Africa to that time. Takoradi Harbor, Achimota College, Korle Bu

Hospital, completion of the Accra-Kumasi railroad, the return of the Asantehene from exile, the Constitution of 1925, and the Provincial Councils of Chiefs were a monument to his industry.

GUR. The Voltaic language category of the Gurma, Tem, Mole-Dagbani, Grusi, Lobi, and other Ghanaian groups.

GURMA. People who live in northeastern Ghana near the Togo border. Basare, Kyamba, Bimoba, Moaba, and Konkomba are some of the groups in this classification.

GURENSE see GRUSI

GYADAM (Jedem). 5°56' N, 1°02' W. The old capital of Akyem Kotoku from 1824 to 1860. It was located in the Birim gap. In 1860 the capital was moved to Nsuaem after the old capital was destroyed in a war with Akyem Abuakwa.

GYAKARI, NTIM. Ca. 1670-1701. Ruler of Denkyera from about 1692 to 1701, when he was killed in the battle of Feyiase with the Asante. When he became Denkyerahene, Denkyera was the most powerful of the Akan states. His death marked the rise of Asante to the position of dominant Akan power.

GYAMAN. An Akan Abron group who founded a kingdom about 1690. They fell under Asante domination about 1740 and did not free themselves until 1875, but there were frequent revolts, and they often refused to pay their tribute. In July 1893 England and France divided the area, with the principal town, Bonduku, going to the French and being incorporated into the Ivory Coast. Samori and his forces occupied the region for a time in 1895.

GYASEHENE (Gyaasehene). The head of the palace personnel of the Asantehene.

- H -

HALF ASSINI. 5°03' N, 2°53' W. A town in the extreme southwestern corner of Ghana, just across the border from the Ivory Coast. Here a historic meeting between presidents Kwame Nkrumah and Felix Houphouet-Boigny took place 19 September 1960. Half Assini is a small port for timber, rubber, and cocoa brought down the Tano River. In 1948 its population was only 2,733. In 1960, when the historic meeting between the two heads of state took place, the census showed 4,575 people. By 1970 there were 5,429 people.

HAMALE. 10°59' N, 2°44' W. Border town in the extreme northwestern corner of Ghana in the Upper West Region, near Upper

Volta and the Black Volta River. The 1948 population was 1,087, 2,659 in 1960, and 2,526 in 1970.

HAMARI see **AMARIA**

HANO, ALFA DAN TADANO. The first Zerma or Zabrama (Zaberma) leader. About 1860 Hano led a group of horsemen and footmen from Zerma, in modern Niger, to Dagomba. Tradition has it that Hano was deeply religious, that he had made a pilgrimage to Mecca, and that he studied in a Koranic school at Salaga. Some time after the Zabrama arrived in the Volta area they began a series of raids northwards into the lands between the Black and White Voltas. After the death of Hano, about 1870, Alfa Gazare dan Mahama became the leader of the Zabrama and consolidated the power of these people over a wide area of what is today northern Ghana and western Upper Volta.

HANSEN, JOHNNY. Radical politician. During the Second Republic, Hansen emerged as leader of the People's Popular Party (PPP), a left-wing socialist group with ties to Nkrumah's old CPP. This close connection to former supporters of Nkrumah got the PPP banned in 1971. By March 1975 he was in trouble with the Supreme Military Council for activity of the Ghana Peace and Solidarity Council, said to be "organizing people for subversion." The SMC kept him in prison for some time, but he was released in 1978, and in January 1979 he was leader of the People's Revolutionary Party (PRP), a militant socialist group. The PRP merged into the People's National Party by the time elections were held later in the year. During the Third Republic he headed a movement called the Kwame Nkrumah's Revolutionary Guard. At the end of 1981 a coup ended the Third Republic and established the Provisional National Defense Council (PNDC). Hansen became Secretary of Internal Affairs in the PNDC. In March 1983 he was demoted to the post of Secretary of Labor and Social Welfare. Three months later he was dismissed from that post.

HANTE see **AHANTE**

HARE, WILLIAM FRANCIS. Born 1906. Earl of Listowel. Hare was appointed as the Governor-General of the new country of Ghana on 23 June 1957, and took his oath 13 November. He was the second and last Governor-General of Ghana, a position he lost when Ghana became a republic in July 1960. Earlier, Hare served as the last Secretary of State for India and Burma. From 1948 to 1950 he was Minister of State for Colonial Affairs.

HARLLEY, JOHN WILLIE KOFI. Born 1919. Policeman and politician. He was born into an Ewe family at Akagla, near Akwamu, in the Eastern Region, and attended Presbyterian schools, Accra Academy, and the Metropolitan Police College in England. He joined the Gold Coast Police in 1940, and advanced through the ranks until he became Inspector-General of Police in 1966. Shortly thereafter he became Deputy Chairman of the National Liberation Council, 1966-1969, and Deputy Chairman of the Presidential Commission in 1969. After the Second Republic was established, he retired.

HARMATTAN. The desiccating northeast trade winds which blow down from the Sahara from December to February. These winds bring a red dust-fog which dries plants, soils, and humans.

HAUSA. People from northern Nigeria and Niger who are major traders in the Volta area. Their language is the language of commerce and trade for large parts of West Africa. Many Hausa live permanently in Ghana. Hausa is also a general term for any soldier or member of the constabulary who comes from the north.

HECCANYS see AKAN

HELIGOLAND TREATY. On 1 July 1890 the British ceded Heligoland, in the North Sea, and Ho, Kpandu, and part of Peki in the Volta area to the Germans in exchange for territories in East Africa.

HENDERSON, FRANCIS B. 1859-1934. British Naval Officer. In November 1896 Lt. Henderson was sent into the area above Asante to save as much of the area as possible from the French, Germans, and Samori. After several engagements with the forces of Samori, he was captured and later allowed to return to the coast.

-HENE. An Akan suffix signifying chief or ruler. It is equivalent to -wura in Gonja, -na in Dagomba, and -manche in Ga.

HERALD. The Accra Herald was founded in September 1857 by Charles Bannermann. It became the West African Herald the following year after being moved to Cape Coast.

HO. 6°36' N, 0°28' E. The chief town of the Volta Region, it is located in the Kaba hills about 45 miles (72 km) northeast of the Adomi Bridge across the Volta. This Ewe town was once the German headquarters in the region, and it was an important missionary town in the colonial era. The population of the town was 5,840 in 1948, 14,519 in 1960, and had jumped to 24,199 by 1970. Ho is 100 miles (165 km) from Accra, and less than 15 miles (24 km) from the Togo border.

HODGKIN, THOMAS LIONEL. 1910-1982. Marxist-Leninist scholar who was an avid supporter of Nkrumah. He came from England to teach at the University of Ghana in 1958, and Nkrumah appointed him as the first director of the Institute of African Studies at Legon in 1962. He often published articles under the pseudonym of Kwasi Robinson. His wife, Dorothy Mary Crowfoot, won the Nobel Prize for Chemistry in 1964.

HODGSON, FREDERIC. 1851-1925. Colonial officer. He joined the British Colonial Service in 1869, was Colonial Secretary of the Gold Coast in 1888, acting Governor in 1889, and Governor of the Gold Coast from 1898 to 1900. He then was Governor of Barbados from 1900 to 1904, and Governor of British Guiana, 1904-1911. He retired in 1911, and was appointed to the West African Lands Committee.

HODSON, ARNOLD WIENHOLT. 1881-1944. Colonial officer. Hodson saw service in Transvaal, Bechuanaland, Somaliland, and Ethiopia before being appointed Governor of the Falkland Islands, 1926-1930. He was Governor of Sierra Leone, 1930-1934, and Governor of the Gold Coast, 1934-1941. He retired at the end of his administration of the Gold Coast.

HOHOE. 7°09' N, 0°28' E. An important Ewe town in the Volta Region between Kpandu and the Togo border on the eastern route to Yendi. It is located in the midst of beautiful hills and waterfalls. In 1948 some 5,665 people lived at Hohoe. By 1960 the population was 9,502, and by 1970 the census showed 14,775 citizens in Hohoe.

HOMOWO FESTIVAL. A Ga-Adangbe homecoming festival in which people return to their hometown to be together, greet new members of the family, and remember the dead. It is also a time to forgive and settle disputes.

HORTON, JAMES AFRICANUS BEALE. 1835-1883. Army physician. Born in Sierra Leone of Ibo ancestry, Horton went to the British Isles in 1853 and studied medicine there. Returning to West Africa as an army physician, he finally retired from British service as a lieutenant general. From 1859 to 1881 he was often stationed on the Gold Coast. He published many books about West Africa. His Political Economy of British West Africa, published in 1865, and West African Countries and Peoples, 1868, influenced the people who tried to form the Fante Confederation, 1868-1873. He suggested dividing the British Gold Coast into a Fante kingdom and Accra republic.

HUNI VALLEY. 5°28' N, 1°55' W. Railroad junction village in the Western Region north of Tarkwa. One rail line runs from Sekondi-Takoradi to Kumasi, one to Achiasi and Accra-Tema, and a short line runs to Prestea. There were 1,591 people in Huni Valley in 1948, 1,577 in 1960, and 1,646 in 1970, when the last census was taken.

HUTTER, PAUL. Missionary, merchant, and hermit. Hutter started his career as a Swiss missionary at Ada in 1892. In 1896 he became a trader on the Volta, exchanging salt from Ada for guinea corn, Mossi blankets, and shea butter at Krakye. In 1903 he settled near Krakye and became famous as a hermit.

HUTTON-MILLS, THOMAS. 1865-1931. Lawyer and nationalist leader. Born in Accra, his African name was Korle Na. He was a grandson to James Bannerman, a former Lieutenant-Governor of the Gold Coast. Hutton-Mills studied law in England, 1891-1894. He was an active member of the Aborigines' Rights Protection Society and was the first president of the National Congress of British West Africa. He was a member of the Legislative Council, 1898 to 1904, and again from 1909 to 1919.

HUTTON-MILLS, THOMAS. Lawyer and politician. Active in the early campaign for independence from colonial rule in the period after World War II, he was a Prison Graduate, and early member of the Convention Peoples' Party. In 1951 he was elected from Accra with Nkrumah as CPP members of the Legislative Assembly. He served in Nkrumah's first government as Minister of Commerce, Industry, and Mines, and then as Minister of Health and Labor. He was dropped from the Cabinet in 1954, replaced by Imoru Egala.

HUZA. Land tenure among the Adangbe, especially the Krobo and Shai. The land is owned by a group of people and is subdivided into individual holdings. In the Manya-Yilo-Osudoku area some of the lines of compounds are more than a mile in length.

HWELA (Huela, Vuela, Weela). Dyula farmers who live along the Black Volta. About half of these people are Muslim.

- I -

IGWIJRA see EGWIRA

INDIRECT RULE. System of government introduced into British colonies which employed traditional rulers as agents of the colonial government. Groups of native states were combined as districts, under District Commissioners (DC), and these were combined as provinces within the Colony (Gold Coast Colony), Asante, the Northern Territories, and Togoland.

INFUMA. 4°48' N, 1°57' W. Town in the Western Region, Ahanta, on the coast west of Sekondi. It is also known as Dick's Cove or Dixcove. The English established a base here about 1691 and built Fort Metal Cross.

INKASSA (Incassa, Iggina). On a 1626 Dutch map are two divisions in what is today the Ahafo area with the names "Incassa" and "Great Inkassa." On the 1729 Anville map these two divisions are again shown. The region was said to be a gold-producing area.

INKORANZA see NKORANZA

INSAMANKOW, BATTLE OF see NSAMANKOW and BONSASO

INSOKO (Insokko, Nsoko, Socco, Begho, Nsawkaw). 7°52' N, 2°19' W. An area in the Brong-Ahafo Region. It is shown on a 1629 Dutch map as "Insoco" and on the 1729 Anville map as "Insokko." It was described as a place where they had horses and very fine clothes.

INSTITUTE OF AFRICAN STUDIES. The Institute of African Studies at Legon, on the campus of the University of Ghana, was formally opened in October 1963 by President Kwame Nkrumah. Thomas Hodgkin, an English supporter of Nkrumah, was the first Director. The Institute was created to study, preserve, and protect African culture.

INSUTA see NSUTA

INTA (Entaa). A place on a 1629 Dutch map and the 1729 Anville map, located to the north of Asante and below Insoko. Gonja.

ISALA see SISALA

ISSINI see ASSINI

IUFFER (Kuifor, Quiforo). Area shown on a 1629 Dutch map and the 1729 Anville map near the Pra river in Assin country.

- J -

JAKPA LANTA (Sumaila Ndewura). Ca. 1622-1666. Ruler of Gonja. According to Gonja tradition, Jakpa was the grandson of Nabaga, the founder of Gonja. Jakpa expanded Gonja to include all the area between the Black and white Voltas. He established the administrative divisions of Gonja under Nbanya chiefs. Jakpa was mortally wounded at Brumasi, south of the confluence of the Black and White Voltas, while fighting the Brong. According to tradition, he was buried at Buipe.

JAMAN see GYAMAN

JAMASI (Gyamase). 6°58' N, 1°28' W. Village in the Asante Region on the Great Northern Highway north of Kumasi on the way to Mampong. It had a population of 1,993 in 1948, jumped to 3,862 by 1960, and had reached 4,892 people by 1970.

JAMES, CYRIL LIONEL ROBERT. 1901- . Trotskyist historian who was born in Trinidad and was a long-time friend of George Padmore. They founded the International African Service Bureau (IASB) to advance the cause of African nationalism. James and Padmore had a great influence on Kwame Nkrumah. James was author of many books about Black heroes and revolutions. One of them was <u>Nkrumah and the Ghana Revolution</u>, 1977. He was a journalist and teacher in the West Indies until 1932, when he went to England. He lived in England until 1938. Between 1938 and 1953 he lived in the United States. Since 1953 he has lived in England, except for two years, 1958-1960, when he returned to the West Indies.

JAMES FORT (Accra). The English established a post here about 1650, and it was being called a fort by 1679. The building was almost destroyed by an earthquake in July 1862. Today it is a prison.

JASIKAN (Dzasikan). 7°24' N, 0°28' E. Town in the Volta Region north of Hohoe, about equal distance between Lake Volta and the Togo border. Its importance has increased rapidly since Lake Volta was completed. The population was only 1,839 in 1948, but it jumped to 4,989 in 1960, and was up to 6,403 by 1970.

JIBOWU REPORT. A Commission of Enquiry into the Affairs of the Cocoa Purchasing Company was established under the chairmanship of Olumuyiwa Jibowu. It reported on 21 June 1956 that there was gross misuse of public funds by members of the CPP. This was one of the earliest signs of corruption in Nkrumah's party.

JIMAN. 8°37' N, 0°06' E. Site on the Oti River above Lake Volta and just south of Bimbila where evidence of habitation as early as 10,450 B.C. has been found. This Middle Stone Age site is the earliest reported habitation in Ghana.

JOB 600. The contract for building the Palace of African Unity, better known as the State House, for a meeting of the OAU in 1965. This huge complex off Castle Road in Accra was built and furnished in less than ten months at immense expense. It is a prime example of an expensive prestige project of the Nkrumah era.

JUABEN   see   DWABEN

JUKWA. 5°16' N, 1°20' W. A village in the Central Region 14 miles (23 km) NNW of Cape Coast. Jukwa was the chief Denkyira town from 1824 to 1873. Here on 5 June 1873 the Asante army defeated the Fante and Denyira armies. Jukwa was destroyed by the Asante, but later rebuilt.

JUNE 4 MOVEMENT. A group formed in 1980 to support Jerry Rawlings and to overthrow the Third Republic.

JUSTICE PARTY (JP). One of the groups formed to oppose the Busia government. Its leader, Erasmus R.T. Madjitey, supported the 1972 coup of the military to end the Second Republic. The party was an outgrowth of a merger of the National Alliance of Liberals (NAL), the People's Action Party (PAP), the United Nationalist Party (UNP), and the All People's Republican Party (APRP) in 1970.

JUULA   see   DYULA

- K -

KABAKABA MOUNTAINS. Mountains in the Volta Region Togo Range around Ho.

KABES, JOHN. Died 1734. Komenda merchant. By 1680 Kabes was one of the leading merchants in Komenda. He was a leading producer of maize and salt, and he operated a fleet of canoes along much of the Gold Coast. He dealt with both the Dutch and British, but was partial to the English. Kabes helped the English built a fort at Komenda in 1698.

KABESTERRA (Abrambo, Cabesterra). A state shown on the 1729 Anville map just north of Efutu. By that time it was under the domination of the Fante.

KADE. 6°05' N, 0°50' W. Town in the Eastern Region near the Birim River. It is in a diamond mining area and is the terminal of the Central Railroad. It had a population of 2,102 in 1948, 6,274 in 1960, and 6,627 in 1970.

KADJEBI (Kadzebi). 7°32' N, 0°28' E. A town in the Volta Region mountains just north of Jasikan and between Lake Volta and the Togo border. In 1948 it had 2,460 people. By 1960 the population had grown to 7,491, and by 1970 the population was 7,194.

KAFABA (Kaffaba). 8°29' N, 0°44' W. An important crossing place on the Volta in the Northern Region southwest of Salaga about 15 miles (24 km). It is on the east bank of the Volta, a short distance below where the Black and white Voltas join. When Louis Binger crossed the Volta here 13 November 1888, he reported the river to be 350 meters wide.

KAKA, BATTLE OF. 8°10' N, 1°36' W. At this small village just northeast of Kintampo in what is now the Brong-Ahafo Region, Osei Bonsu in 1801 crushed forces of Gyaman and Gbuipe which were working to restore Osei Kwame to the Golden Stool of Asante.

KALABULE (Gyinabu). A term used in Ghana which means corruption or antisocial activities. Graft, smuggling, hoarding, embezzlement, black marketeering, and currency dealing are only some of the activities covered by the word. It began to be used in Ghana about 1974, but it especially was associated with activities during the Third Republic, 1979-1981.

KAMBONSE (sing. Kambona). The people of the north used this term, meaning "men with guns," as their name for the Asante.

KAMMANA. Name of a state on a 1629 Dutch map. On the 1729 Anville map it becomes Kamana. The area seems to correspond to the modern Krobo area.

KANJAGA see BUILSA

KAPOK. The silk-cotton tree. The silky material around the seeds of this tree is used as a fiber, and oil is extracted from the seeds.

KARAGA. 9°55' N, 0°26' W. One of the divisional Dagomba towns in the Northern Region. It was destroyed in 1898 in a battle between the British and the Zabrama.

KARAMOKO. A Muslim. A member of the literate class.

KARITE see SHEA

KASENA. A Grusi group who live in the Paga and Navrongo area of the Upper Region and across the border from Paga in Upper Volta.

KATAMANSO (Akantamasu). 5°44' N, 0°05' W. Place in the Eastern Region some 15 miles (24 km) northeast of Accra where a great battle took place on 7 August 1826. Asante was defeated by a coalition of the Akyem, Aquapem, Assin, Denkyira, Twifo, the British, and others. The battle is also sometimes called the Battle of Dodowa.

KEDZI. 5°59' N, 1°01' E. Village in the Volta Region just northeast of Keta on the road along the coast to Aflao and the Togo border. The population was 2,623 in 1948, 5,015 in 1960 and 4,349 in 1970.

KENTE CLOTH. Cloth woven in long bands which are about four inches wide. These are sewn together to form a cloth worn by men as a toga. The patterns are colorful, and each design has its own name. Kente cloth has become one of the symbols of Ghana. Both the Ewe and Asante pride themselves on their Kente weaving. Kpetoe, near Ho, is the Ewe center of Kente weaving. Bonwire, near Kumasi, is the Asante center.

KETA (Quita, Quittah). 5°55' N, 0°59' E. Anlo-Ewe commercial town in the Volta Region on an isthmus between the Keta Lagoon and the Atlantic. It is often threatened by the sea, and in September of 1983 a major project was launched to prevent the town from being washed away. The name literally means "on top of the sand."

Keta was founded in the seventeenth century by Togbi Wenya. The Danes established a post in the early eighteenth century, only to be replaced by the Dutch. The Danes returned in 1737 and built a fort in 1784. This was bought by the British in 1850. The British withdrew, but returned in 1874. Keta became an administrative and commercial center under the British. The area is rich in seafood, vegetables, pineapples, coconuts, plantain, poultry, goats, and pigs. Sixty-five thousand gallons of palm oil were exported from Keta in 1855. Off-shore the sharks are reported to be ravenous. In 1911 the population was just 3,630, by 1948 the figure was 11,358, in 1960 it had jumped to 16,719; but by 1970, with the sea a growing problem, the population had fallen to 14,446.

KETA LAGOON. Large lagoon in the Volta Region near the sea which is up to eight miles (13 km) wide and twenty miles (32 km) long. A narrow spit, on which Anloga, Keta, and other Anlo towns are located, separates it from the ocean.

KETE-KRAKYE (Krachi). 7°46' N, 0°03' W. The old towns were located about a mile apart. Krakye was a Volta River port, located just above the Oti confluence with the Volta, and across from where the Sene entered the Volta. Krakye was located above the Dabunga-Gyimator Cataracts of the Volta. It was the terminal for canoes coming up the river with salt for the north. A ferry also crossed the river here to Nsunua, on the right or west bank. Krakye was also home of a famous shrine which was located in a cave on the wooded bluff overlooking the river. Dente (Odentee) Bossumfo is an awesome oracle whose prophecy is sought by high and low from all over West Africa. Krakye was the chief city of the Krakye people, and for a time it was the capital of the Brong Confederation. Kete was the market for Krakye, usually filled with traders from faraway places. Ten thousand people were resident in Kete in 1895.

The Volta River Project doomed old Kete-Krakye. The rapids, the Dente's cave, and the towns disappeared beneath Lake Volta in 1966. Kete-Krakye was the largest settlement in the flooded area. The twin towns had to be resettled a short distance back at Kantankufri. A new town emerged. In 1970 the new town overlooking Lake Volta had a population of 5,097. And the oracle is hard at work again, a scant two miles from his old site.

KIBI (Kibbi, Kyebi). 6°10' N, 0°33' W. The capital of Akyem Abuakwa since about 1815. It is located in the Atewa Hills in the

Eastern Region, 15 miles (24 km) northwest of Koforidua, 60 miles (96 km) above Accra. A Basel Mission was opened here in 1861. In 1948 4,427 people lived in Kibi. There were 5,069 listed in Kibi in 1960, and 5,408 in 1970.

KIBI "RITUAL" MURDER TRIAL. After the death of Nana Ofori Atta I in 1944, a relative was beheaded, dagger thrust through both cheeks and tongue, in the traditional manner. A jury found eight persons guilty of murder, even though J.B. Danquah was one of the defense lawyers.

KINTAMPO. 8°03' N, 1°43' W. Market town in Brong-Ahafo on the Western route from Kumasi to the north. It is about 25 miles (40 km) from the Black Volta. It was once an important market for the Asante-Hausa trade. The first Englishman reached Kintampo in 1884. Krause, a German, was there in 1887. Louis Binger, a Frenchman, spent five days there in November 1888. The population was 2,809 in 1911, 2,829 in 1948, 4,678 in 1960, and 7,149 in 1970.

KINTAMPO CULTURE. Archaeological name of an early culture which developed in Ghana as early as 1300 B.C. Sites have been unearthed by archaeologists from Christian's Village (5°38' N, 0° 13' W), near Accra, to Ntereso (9°07' N, 1°12' W), in the Northern Region. The sites are concentrated around Kintampo. Evidence found at these places points to domesticated animals and early agriculture.

KITAB GHUNJA. An early chronicle, written in Arabic, in the middle of the eighteenth century by Muhammad Ibn Al-Mustafa and 'Umar Kunandi Ibn 'Umar. "The Book of Gonja" deals with the history of Gonja from the sixteenth to the eighteenth centuries.

KOBINA AMAMFI (Kwabia Amanfi). Ca. 1600-1630. Younger brother and successor to Chu Mientwi, traditional founder of the Oyoko royal line. Kobina Amamfi was succeeded by Oti Akentin, who was followed by Obiri Yeboa, founder of Kumasi.

KOFI KARIKARI (Kakari). Ca. 1837-1884. Asantehene, 1867-1874. His reign began with campaigns east of the Volta, 1867-1871. In 1873 the Asante invasion of the south ended in the Sagrenti War, 1873-1874, and the British destruction of Kumasi. Kofi Karikari was destooled in 1874 for rifling the royal mausoleum at Bantama. The Asante empire began to disintegrate. He conspired to regain the Golden Stool in 1883, but died suddenly on 24 June 1884.

KOFORIDUA. 6°05' N, 0°15' W. Capital of the Eastern Region, cocoa center, and chief town of New Dwaben (Juaben). It is located on the highway and railroad from Accra to Kumasi. The railroad reached Koforidua in 1912, and the town grew rapidly thereafter. In 1901 the census was 1,406, in 1911 it was 3,891, and by 1921 it was 5,364. In 1931 the population of Koforidua was 10,529, in 1948 up to 18,941; by 1960 it had jumped to 34,856, and in the census of 1970 the count was 46,235, making it one of the largest cities in Ghana.

KOKOFU. 6°30' N, 1°32' W. Village in the Asante Region near Lake Bosumtwi, and ten miles (16 km) south of Kumasi. It was one of the founding villages in the Asante Confederacy.

KOLA (Cola, cola nitida, gora). A nut grown on trees in central Ghana. The pinkish-purple nut is about the size of a chestnut. Its caffeine is a mild stimulant with a crisp, bitter taste that can cut hunger and thirst. It is called the "poor man's tranquilizer." It is very popular with people in West Africa, especially Islamic people, and it attracted traders form many miles to Asante.

KOMENDA (Commendo, Guoffo, Kommani, Kommenda, Coomendah). 5°03' N, 1°29' W. A town in the Central Region just west of Elmina. It was the chief town of the old Eguafo polity, and it was there when the first Europeans arrived. The English established a base there in 1663, the Dutch built Vredenburg there in 1688, the French were also there briefly in 1688, but by 1782 the English were back. There were 3,394 inhabitants in 1948, 4,261 in 1960, and 5,966 by 1970.

KONADU, SAMUEL ASARE (pen-name: Kwabena Asare Bediako). Born 1932. Author and publisher. Born near Kumasi at Asamang, Konadu is the author of many popular novels. The Wizard of Asamang (1964), The Lawyer Who Bungled His Life (1965), Shadow of Wealth (1966), A Woman in Her Prime (1967), Night Watchers of Korlebu (1968), and Ordained by the Oracle (1969) are among his better known works. Konadu has worked for Ghana Information Service, Ghana News Agency, and has headed Anowuo Publications and Anowuo Educational Publications.

KONGENSTEN FORT (Konigstein). A Danish fort built at Ada about 1783. It became English in 1850. None of the original structure remains.

KONKOMBA (Komba). A Gurma group who live along the Oti River on the Togo border in northeastern Ghana. They are a stateless group who have often been subjects of Dagomba. They call themselves the Bekpokpam, their language Lekpokpam, and their territory Kekpokpam. They are enemies of the Nanumba, and in 1981 they killed hundreds of Nanumbas.

KONNY, JOHN (Counie, Kony). Ca. 1660-1732. Merchant Prince. Konny was one of the great merchants on the Gold Coast in the early eighteenth century. For some time he was an ally of the Brandenburg African Company, and from 1711 to 1724 he was commander of the Prussian fort of Gross Friedrichsburg at Pokoso or Prince's Town, some 27 miles (43 km) southwest of Takoradi. He is sometimes called the "Last Prussian Negro Prince," and sometimes the "Brandenburg Caboceer." For over a decade he was the chief go-between for the Asante-German trade. After the Germans pulled out of Ahanta, Konny held off the Dutch for over six years, but the Dutch took Gross Friedrichsburg away from him in 1724.

KONONGO. 6°37' N, 1°13' W. Town on the Accra-Kumasi highway in the Asante Region. It is a twin town of Odumase. It became an important mining and cocoa-buying center after the railroad reached there in 1923. In 1948 it had a population of 6,547; in 1960 the census had jumped to 10,771, and in 1970 it was 10,881.

KONOR. The paramount chief of the Krobo.

KORANTENG-ADDOW COMMITTEE. A committee set up by the SMU in January 1977 to draw up proposals for a union government of the military and civilians. The committee presented its report 4 October 1977. It recommended an executive president selected by adult suffrage from a list presented by an electoral college. It also suggested a 140-member legislature of people who would run as independents without connection to a political party. Political parties would be prohibited. The chairman of the committee was Dr. Gustav G. Koranteng-Addow, who at the time was Attorney General and also Commissioner of Justice.

KORLE BU. The General Hospital of Accra. Founded in 1925, during the administration of Governor Gordon Guggisberg, it was the first teaching hospital in the Gold Coast.

KORMANTIN (Kormantan, Kormanti, Great Kromanti, Cormantyne). 5°12' N, 1°05' W. A coastal village in the Central Region between Anomabo and Saltpond. The Dutch were here before 1600, but by 1638 the English were building a fort on a hill nearby. In 1665 the Dutch captured the English fort and named it Fort Amsterdam. The British held it again from 1782 to 1785. The Asante took the Fort and plundered it in 1807, and the people of Anomabo destroyed it in 1811. By then the Europeans had already outlawed the Atlantic slave trade. The ruins were regained by the British in 1868. In the 1950s a restoration project was undertaken, but it was never completed.

-KORPE. Suffix denoting village. Also Akuraa, kurom, etc.

KORSAH, KOBINA ARKU. 1894-1967. Lawyer, Judge, Nationalist leader. Born in Saltpond, educated at Mfantsipim, Fourah Bay College, and the universities of Durham and London, Korsah became one of the more distinguished early nationalist leaders.

He was active in the Aborigines' Rights Protection Society and the National Congress of British West Africa. He was the municipal member of the Legislative Council from Cape Coast from 1928 to 1940. In 1942 he was a member of the Executive Council. Appointed a judge in 1945, he became Chief Justice of the Gold Coast in 1956, and the following year became the first Chief Justice of Ghana. In 1963 he presided over the treason trials of Tawia Adamafio and others charged with trying to kill Nkrumah. When the defendants were acquitted, President Nkrumah removed Korsah from office. He died three years later.

KOTEI, R.E.A. Died 1979. Soldier. One of the leaders of the military government from 1972 to 1979. He was Commissioner of Works and Housing from 1972 to 1975, and of Information in 1975. He then became Chief of Staff. He was executed by Rawlings and the AFRC in June 1979.

KOTOKA AIRPORT, ACCRA. Ghana's International Airport, located on the northeastern end of Accra just off Liberation Road. It is only a fifteen-minute drive to Tema via the Nkrumah Freeway. The Airport was named for General Emmanuel K. Kotoka, who was killed at the airport in April 1967.

KOTOKA, EMMANUEL KWASI. 1926-1967. Soldier. Kotoka was born an Ewe in the little village of Alakple, near Keta, in the Volta Region. He was reared a Presbyterian, but became a Catholic while attending Catholic schools. He enlisted in the Gold Coast Regiment in 1947 and attended Infantry School at Teshie. By 1951 he was a sergeant-major. Commissioned in November 1954, he served for a time in England and Germany. By 1959 he was a captain. In 1960 and 1962 he went to the Congo (Zaire) as a member of the UN Emergency Force. By 1965 he was commander of the First Brigade of Infantry at Kumasi. There he helped plan the coup which removed Nkrumah from power, 24 February 1966. He was 39 years old and a colonel by then. After the coup, Kotoka became a member of the National Liberation Council and Commander of the Ghana Armed Forces, with the rank of major-general, soon to be lieutenant-general, and Minister of Defence, Health, Labor, and Social Welfare. He was killed during an unsuccessful countercoup 17 April 1967 by Lt. Moses Yeboah in front of the Accra Airport. A statue of General Kotoka was erected on the spot where he fell, and in 1969 the airport was named for him.

KOTOKO. The Privy Council of Asante. It was made up of the Asantehene, the Queen Mother, the chiefs of Dwaben, Bekwai, and Mampong, and selected nobles of Kumasi. It could enstool or destool the Asantehene, declare war, and it was the court of last resort.

KOTOKO UNION SOCIETY. An organization formed by educated Asantes in 1916 to foster Asante pride and interests.

KOTOKU AKYEM (Akyem Oda). One of the branches of the Akyem. Most of the Kotoku Akyem live in the Eastern Region near the Birim River.

KPANDU. 7°00' N, 0°18' E. An Ewe town on the left or east bank of Lake Volta about 90 miles (144 km) inland from the coast and 20 miles (34 km) from the Togo border. It is now an administrative unit of the Volta Region, but it was once the center of German kola plantations. It has become a busy port since Lake Volta was finished. The population was 4,193 in 1948, 8,070 in 1960, and in 1970, after the Lake was filled, the town expanded to 12,842.

KPEDZE. 6°50' N, 0°30' E. Border town in the Volta Region about 18 miles (29 km) north of Ho. It had a population of just over 5,062 in 1970.

KPEMBE (Pembi). 8°33' N, 0°30' W. Gonja divisional capital which is located just two miles (three km) east of Salaga. It was captured by the Asante about 1744. Europeans began to arrive from 1876, and the chief of Kpembe signed a treaty with British Agent G.E. Ferguson in September 1894. A German force under von Zech occupied the town in 1896. After that a period of decline began. The population was only 718 in 1948, and just 1,056 in 1970.

KPESI (Kpeshi). Guan people along the coast in the Tema area who were in the Accra Plains before the Ga and Adangbe arrived.

KPETOE. 6°33' N, 0°42' E. Village in the Volta Region near the Togo border and 17 miles (27 km) southeast of Ho. It is famous as a center for the production of Ewe Kente cloth.

KPONE (Kponi). 5°41' N, 0°04' E. Small Ga-Adangbe village some five miles (eight km) east of Tema on the coast. The census was 1,142 in 1948, and in 1970 it was 3,269.

KPONG (Pong). 6°09' N, 0°04' E. Manya Krobo town in the Eastern Region on the Volta River between Senchi and Akuse. It is 18 miles (30 km) downstream from Akosombo Dam and about 50 miles (80 km) northeast of Accra. The town was burned in the Anlo-Ada War in 1865. It became an important emporium for the palm oil trade during the early days of European trade. In 1880 Governor Ussher said it was "a receptacle for all the rascals in the eastern division." Both the Basel and Wesleyan missionaries organized schools in the area. It also served as headquarters for some of the early exploration of the Volta River. Today the University of Ghana has an agricultural station at Kpong, and it is a veterinary center. In November 1977 a power project was started on the river nearby, and the first unit of this enterprise went into operation in 1981. In 1911 around 4,213 people lived in Kpong. That figure had dropped by half in 1948; was 3,251 in 1960, and was 4,975 in 1970.

KRA (Okra). The spark of life that comes from Onyame--the Akan supreme being. Kra enters the body at conception and departs the body at death. It determines the inexorable destiny of the individual it inhabits.

KRAKYE (Krachi). People who belong to the Guan classification. They live mostly on the peninsula between the main Volta and the Oti arm of Lake Volta. Their chief town is Kete-Krakye.

KRAMO. The Muslim middle class of Gonja.

KRAUSE, GOTTLOB ADOLF. 1850-1938. German explorer. He made his first trip to Africa in 1869, and between 1879 and 1881 he explored the Sahara and North Africa. On 12 May 1886 he left Accra to follow a route to the Niger. He was in Salaga from 18 June to 7 July, when he joined a caravan which was taking kola nuts to Timbuktu. The caravan followed the left bank of the White Volta northward, passing through Dagomba to Walewale, and on into what is today Upper Volta. He reached the Mossi capital at Ouagadougou 24 September, and remained there almost a month before heading north again. In December he returned to the Mossi capital, not having gone all the way to the Niger. Early in 1887 he returned south again, visiting Wa, Bole, and Kintampo, before reaching Salaga again in April. After this trip he settled in Togo for several years as a merchant, but returned to Germany as a result of World War I.

KREPI. An Ewe group who live in the Volta Region between Ho and Asikuma. Peki (6°32' N, 0°14' E) is the chief town of these people. Their ruler is called the Fia. At one time they were dominated by Akwamu, but they broke away in 1833. The English purchased a claim to the area from Denmark in 1850, but during the Scramble for Africa by the Europeans it ended in German hands. In 1914 the British got the area again.

KROBO (Klo). Adangbe group who live along the right bank of the Volta. Odumasi, Kpong, and Akuse are the chief towns in their area. The two major Krobo groups are the Manya and the Yilo, each under a chief called the Konor. The area at one time was subject to Denmark, but the British dominated the region after 1850.

KROBO HILL. 6°05' N, 0°03' E. Famous Krobo position just southwest of Akuse, near the Tema-Akosombo highway. It was almost impregnable, except for lack of good water supplies. The Krobo often held out here against their enemies.

KRONTIHENE (Kontihene). The commander of an Akan military force. In Asante the Bantama stool had priority for the position.

KUDUO. Metal pots or containers which were highly prized by the Akan.

KUHNE, JOHANNES see RAMSEYER, FRIEDRICH AUGUST

KUIFORO. Area shown on a Dutch map of 1629. It was just east of Wassa. It is also shown as Iuffer, Kuifor, Quiforo. Today it would be Twifo.

KUJANI GAME RESERVE. Land on the peninsula between the Afram and Sene tributaries of the Volta in the Afram Plains which has been set aside as a game sanctuary.

KULPAWN. Major tributary of the White Volta. The Kulpawn rises in the Upper Region West near the border of Upper Volta, northwest of Tuma, and near Kapulima (10°56' N, 2°02' W). It then flows southeast to a point east of Ducie from which it turns to a northeasterly direction, intermittently forming the border between the Northern and Upper regions. It joins the White Volta at 10°21' N, 1°05' W, in the Northern Region.

KULUNGUGU. 11°09' N, 0°13' W. Village near Bawku and the Upper Volta border in the Upper Region East where an attempt was made on the life of President Nkrumah, 1 August 1962. Hundreds of people in the area were arrested afterwards.

KUMASI (Kumase, Coomassie). 6°41' N, 1°37' W. The capital of Asante. Founded about 1680 by Osei Tutu near an earlier village of Tafo, known as a very old market. At one time the town was called Kwaman. It is sometimes called Oseikrom, the city of Osei, and in the 1930s Kumasi was called the Garden City of West Africa. Kum-ase means "under the okum tree." Kumasi is the commercial and transportation center of central Ghana.

The first half of the nineteenth century was the golden age of Kumasi. It was the capital of the richest and most powerful state in that part of West Africa. By 1850 the population may have been more than 30,000, and visitors reported on the vitality of the city. But the city was occupied by the British in 1874. The palace of the Asantehene was destroyed (it had been built in 1816), and much of the city was burned. Recovery had not been completed before the English returned in 1896. Once again much of the town was destroyed, and this time the Asantehene, Prempe, was carried away. By 1897 the British had built a fort in the center of the town, and foreign troops patrolled the streets. Kumasi had reached its nadir. The population was less than 3,000. In 1900 the Asante revolted and laid siege to the British in their fort. Once again the city suffered, and the Asante lost the last of their claims to independence. In 1901 Asante became a part of the Gold Coast Administration.

The British connection brought modern transportation to Kumasi. Highways to Accra, to Cape Coast, and to Obuasi and

Dunkwa in the south were improved. The Great Northern Road through Mampong, Atebubu, Salaga, and Tamale to Bolgatanga and Navrongo was also improved. The railroad from Sekondi arrived in 1903, and the tracks from Accra in 1923. A railroad to the north was planned, but never built. By 1911 the population of Kumasi was 18,853, and in 1921 the city was a thriving metropolis of almost 24,000. Prempe was allowed to return in 1924, the same year that Wesley College opened. The Central Market was opened in 1925 just across Zongo Road from the Catholic Cathedral and Railroad Station.

Electricity was installed in 1927, and piped water came in 1934. The census in 1931 showed the population to be almost 36,000. A Town Council was established in 1943 and that became a Municipal Council in 1954. The University of Science and Technology opened in 1952, and in 1953 Kumasi acted as host to the Sixth Pan-African Conference. In 1948 there were nearly 78,000 citizens in the Garden City. By 1960 that figure had climbed to the fantastic figure of 180,000, a count which would jump still 80,000 more in the next decade.

KUMAWU. 6°54' N, 1°17' W. A town in the Asante Region some ten miles (16 km) southeast of Nsuta or 30 miles (48 km) northeast of Kumasi. By tradition this town was founded by Asante who came from the village of Asantemanso. The population was 2,585 in 1948, and by 1970 it had grown to 6,670.

KUSASI (Kusase, Kusae). A Mole-Dagbani group who live in the Upper Region East of Ghana and in Upper Volta and Togo. Bawku is their chief town. Their language is called Kusal.

KUSI OBODUM (Kusi Bodum, Kwesi Bodom). Asantehene, 1750-1764. He was an old man when his reign began. His predecessor, Opoku Ware, had selected a prince named Dako as his heir. Kusi Obodum was enstooled and Dako began a civil war. Dako was ultimately defeated and executed. Later a campaign in the east against Oyo and Dahomey turned out to be a disaster, and Kusi Obodum, old and almost blind, abdicated. He died a short time later. His body was not placed in the royal mausoleum at Bantama.

KWA. Language classification which includes the languages of the Akan, Guan, Ewe, Ga, and Adangbe.

KWABIA AMANFI see KOBINA AMAMFI

KWABRE. The area northeast and east of Kumasi toward the Afram basin.

KWAHU (Kwawu, Quahoe). The area and the Akan people who live between the Afram River to the north, the Onyim River on the northwest, the Pawnpawn on the east, and the Accra-Kumasi railroad on the south. Abetifi, Mpraeso, and Nkawkaw are important Kwahu towns. During the eighteenth and nineteenth centuries Kwahu was counted in the Asante sphere.

KWAHU ESCARPMENT. The watershed between the Afram River and its tributaries on the north and the tributaries of the Tano, Pra, and Densu. The fall line runs roughly from Wenchi, through Mampong to Koforidua.

KWAKU ADUSEI   see   OPOKU WARE II

KWAKU DUA I (Fredua Agyeman). Ca. 1797-1867. Asantehene, 1834-1867. He took part in the Gyaman campaign in 1818-1819 and was a division Commander in the battle of Katamanso (Akantamansu or Dodowa) in 1826. He was elected Asantehene in 1834 without opposition. After his reign began he adopted a policy of peace, trade, and open roads. He persuaded the Dwaben refugees to return to their old homes in 1841. In that same year he sent troops north into Gonja and Dagomba in a campaign that lasted until 1844. In 1863 his armies occupied considerable territory in the south which was under British protection, and relations with the British steadily declined from 1863 until Kwaku Dua died on 27 April 1867.

KWAKU DUA II (Kwaku Dua Kuma, Agyeman Kofi, Quacoe Duah). Ca. 1860-1884. Asantehene, 27 April-10 June 1884. He was enstooled during a period of great turmoil in Kumasi, and during his short reign he tried to massacre all his enemies. He died of smallpox after a reign of six weeks. An interregnum followed his death, 1884-1888.

KWAKU DUA III   see   PREMPE I

KWAMAN (Kwaaman). The early name of Kumasi, during the time of Obiri Yeboa, and before Osei Tutu and Okomfo Anokye established Kumasi.

KWAME MENSA   see   MENSA BONSU

KWAME NKRUMAH IDEOLOGICAL INSTITUTE, WINNEBA. An institute established by Nkrumah at Winneba to produce Ghanaian Nkrumahist socialists and African freedom fighters. The cornerstone was placed 18 February 1961. The first director was Kwodwo Addison, a former trade union official and friend of John Tettegah. Addison was head of the Ghana-Soviet Friendship Society, and the President of the USSR attended the ceremonies opening the Institute. A collection of theorists from communist countries were appointed to the first faculty. They could barely communicate with their students. The two-year course was a failure from the start. Addison was soon fired for inefficiency, and on 5 November 1965 Nkrumah assumed personal charge of the administration. The coup a few weeks later in 1966 ended the Institute. In 1983 the PNDC talked of reviving the idea of training revolutionaries at Winneba.

KWAMISA, MOUNT. 7°08' N, 1°53' W. High point in the Brong-Ahafo Region, near the border with Asante. It is near Bechem and about halfway between Sunyani and Kumasi. The altitude is 2,516 feet (767 m).

KWAWU see KWAHU

KWEKU AKA (Quaqoh Accah). Around 1832 when Kweku Aka became the chief of Nzema he held the funeral customs for his predecessor and over a 150 persons were sacrificed so that their spirits could keep the spirit of the dead chief company. Later he frequently held traders prisoner, and he forced the English out of their post at Beyin. In 1835 George Maclean launched an attack against the Nzema, forcing them to submit to British control.

KYAMBA (Tchamba). A Gurma group, sometimes called the Basare. Their language is called Tobote and some live in Togo. Of those who live in Ghana, 23 percent live in the Volta Region, 20 percent in Asante, 17 percent in the Eastern Region, and 19 percent in the Northern Region. The rest are scattered in the other four regions.

KYEBI see KIBI

KYEREPONG (Cherepong). A Guan group most of whom live in the Eastern Region. They have several villages in the Akuapem Hills around Adukrom.

- L -

LABADI (Labade). 5°33' N, 0°09' W. Ga coastal town which was one of the original seven Ga settlements. It appeared on a Dutch map in 1629. Today it is an eastern suburb of Accra.

LADOKU. A coastal Adangbe state which once existed east of Accra and between the Dodowa and Volta rivers. The state was also known as Ningo. The town of Ladoku was conquered by the Akwamu in 1679, and it was destroyed in 1702. The area supplied fish, salt, and livestock to Gold Coast markets.

LAMPTEY, EMMANUEL ODARQUAYE OBETSEBI. 1902-1963. Ga attorney and politician. A native of Accra, he graduated in law from London University in 1939 and returned home to practice law and be elected as municipal member of the Legislative Council from his hometown. Lamptey was one of the founders of the

UGCC and was one of the famous Big Six arrested after the riots of 1948. He was a member of the Coussey Commission, which drew up plans for constitutional reform in 1949, but he was defeated in the 1951 elections. He then became one of the leading opponents of Nkrumah, helping to form the Ghana Congress Party in 1952, the National Liberation Movement in 1956, and the United Party in 1957. In 1961 he went into exile in Togo, where he plotted against the CPP and Nkrumah. After Nkrumah offered an amnesty to his opponents, Lamptey returned home, but was arrested 5 October 1962 and sent to Nsawam prison, where he died the following January of cancer.

LAMPTEY, JONATHAN KWESI. Born 1909. A native of Sekondi, Lamptey attended the Methodist Mission School in his hometown, Mfantsipim School at Cape Coast, Wesley College at Kumasi, Achimota, the University of Exeter (England), and London University Returning to the Gold Coast, he became a science teacher at Mfantsipim, and became an early member of the CPP. He was acting deputy chairman of the CPP in 1950. He was elected to the Legislative Assembly in 1951 on the CPP ticket and became Junior Minister of Finance in Nkrumah's first government. But before 1951 was over, Lemptey broke with Nkrumah and returned to teaching, this time in Sekondi. He soon entered politics as a member of the Ghana Congress Party. In September 1954 he followed K.A. Busia into the National Liberation Movement, and then into the United Party. After the coup of 1966 he became Head of the State Gold Mining Corporation. When political parties were allowed again in 1969, he became a lieutenant of Busia in the Progress Party. He won a seat in the National Assembly of the Second Republic, 1969-1972. He was a member of Busia's Cabinet, first as Minister of Defense, and then as Minister of Parliamentary Affairs. He acted as Prime Minister on several occasions while Busia was out of the country. After the coup of 1972 he retired to Sekondi once again.

LANDS BILL OF 1894. A measure introduced into the Legislative Council on 14 November 1894. The bill would have vested waste lands, forest lands, and minerals in the Crown of England. The object was to control exploitation of timber and mineral resources of areas under British protection. Opposition developed at once and the measure never became law.

LANDS BILL OF 1897. A bill introduced in the Legislative Council on 10 March 1897. It gave the British Crown rights of administration of public lands, but did not claim Crown ownership. Africans could make land grants to Europeans only with the Governor's express permission. Opposition to the bill developed at once, and the Gold Coast Aborigines' Rights Protection Society grew out of the agitation. The bill was withdrawn in 1898. A Concessions Ordinance was enacted in 1900 which accomplished most of what the British wanted to do in the land acts, namely give security to titles for concession-holders, and protection against fraud to the African landowners. But the land issue had created an uproar, and it had shown the Africans how they could force the British to back down when confronted with determined opposition.

LANTA see JAKPA LANTA

LARABANGA. 9°13' N, 1°51' W. Village in the Northern Region about 12 miles (19 km) north of Damongo. It is near the Mole Game Reserve, and in the heart of Gonja. It was built in the second half of the seventeenth century in the Sudanese style with flat-roofed buildings. It has a famous mosque. In 1948 it had a population of 1,263, down to 1,040 in 1970.

LARTE (Larteh, Late). 5°56' N, 0°04' W. Town in the Akuapem area of the Eastern Region, some 32 miles (51 km) northeast of Accra. Most of the population is Guan. The town is famous for its Akonnedi Shrine. In 1911 the population of Larte was 6,507, a figure which has been pretty constant ever since. In 1970 the census was 6,725.

LATE see LARTE

LAWRA (Lorha). 10°39' N, 2°52' W. Village in the extreme northwest of the Upper Region on the Western Road only a short distance from the Black Volta and the Upper Volta border. Kwame Nkrumah was held in detention here by the British in March and April 1948. The place had a population of 1,050 in 1911, and in 1948 there were 2,189 in the village. In 1970 the census showed 2,709 inhabitants.

LEAGUE OF GHANA PATRIOTS. The inner circle of Nkrumah lieutenants in the CPP.

LEGISLATIVE COUNCIL. In 1850 when the Gold Coast was established as a separate dependency of the British Crown, the Legislative Council was created to advise the Governor. Members were appointed by the Governor for the first seventy-five years of the history of the Council. Africans were appointed from the beginning, James Bannerman serving on the first Council. Guggisberg's reforms of 1925 provided for the election of a member each by Accra, Cape Coast, and Sekondi; and six members to be elected by councils of chiefs. The Burns Constitution of 1946 provided for an African majority for the first time and gave representation to Asante. The 1950 changes provided for an assembly of seventy-five, plus six special members. This body would select its own Speaker. The Northern Territories were also represented.

LEGON. 5°39' N, 0°11' W. The location of the University of Ghana, some eight miles (13 km) north of Accra.

LEGON OBSERVER. The journal of the Legon Society on National
Affairs. It began publication in July 1966 as a fortnightly, and
has been published intermittently as political conditions have allowed. Yaw Twumasi and Kwame Arhin are two of the more
famous editors. It is the sometime voice of the political science
faculty of the University of Ghana. In the 1969 elections it
tried to stay between Gbedemah and Busia by creating a "Third
Force" which supported Dr. John Bilson. It was banned by
Acheampong's NRC from 1974 to 1978.

LEGU (Lago). 5°13' N, 0°47' W. Small coastal village in the Central
Region some 35 miles (56 km) east of Cape Coast and 45 miles
(72 km) west of Accra. The English began trading here in the
mid-sixteenth century.

LENNOX-BOYD CONSTITUTION, 1957. The compromise constitution
which was supported by the British Secretary of State, Lennox-Boyd. This was the constitution under which the Gold Coast
became independent Ghana.

LEVER BROTHERS (Unilever). Trading firm which was founded by
William Leverhulme (1851-1925) in 1884. It entered the West African market in 1896, with special interest in palm oil and
coca. By 1929 it was diversified into mines, timber, and almost
every area of commerce. In 1929 the Unilever interests created
the United Africa Company.

LEWIS REPORT. In 1953 the Gold Coast government requested W.A.
Lewis of Manchester University to investigate the possibilities of
industrialization in the Gold Coast. Lewis suggested creating a
favorable climate for industry, improvements in agriculture, expansion of basic services, and gradual expansion of exports.

LEYDSAAMHEID, FORT. 5°17' N, 0°44' W. A fort started by the
Dutch at Apam, just west of Winneba, in 1697. It became British in 1868, and today it is used as a police station.

LIBERATOR. National Liberation Movement (NLM) newspaper which
began publication in 1955 and lasted only to 1957. It opposed
Nkrumah's Convention People's Party (CPP).

LIGBI (Ligby). One of the earliest Dyula groups of merchants to
trade along the Black Volta. They were involved in the kola
and gold trade at one time. There are still descendants in the
Brong area west of Wenchi living as farmers today.

LIKPE. A small Central Togo group who live in the Volta Region
east of Lake Volta.

LIMANN, HILLA. Born 1934. President of the Third Republic, 24
September 1979 to 31 December 1981. A native of the Sisala area

of the Upper Region, Limann paid for his education by earnings from hunting and by scholarships. He became one of the most highly educated persons in Ghana, earning an economics degree from the London School of Economics, a history degree from the University of London, and a doctorate in political science and law from the Sorbonne. After returning to Ghana, he was a teacher awhile before joining the diplomatic service. He was a member of the CPP and called himself a Nkrumahist before the coup of 1966. Later he was a member of the commission which wrote the constitution for the Second Republic.

In April 1979 he was nominated by the People's National Party (PNP) as their candidate for president. This was due in part to his being a nephew to Imoru Egala, chief founder of the PNP, but by his own right, Hilla Limann was a highly qualified candidate. His vice presidential candidate, J.W. de Graft-Johnson, was also an attractive candidate. They easily defeated their opposition, and were sworn in 24 September 1979. As President, Limann was a cautious pragmatist who deliberately attacked the economic problems of Ghana. But the problems would have overcome any leader, and Limann lacked charisma. He could never compete with the popular appeal of Jerry Rawlings. On 31 December 1981 Jerry Rawlings and his cohorts seized power for a second time. Limann was arrested and held in protective custody until September 1983.

LITTLE KOMENDA   see   KOMENDA

LOBI (Lo, Lober). A Mole-Dagbani group who inhabit the extreme northwestern section of Ghana. Some also live in Upper Volta. The Birifor, Miwo, Lo Dagaba, Lowili, and Yangala are related groups.

LOCAL GOVERNMENT ORDINANCE, 1951. A CPP-sponsored ordinance which was enacted by the Legislative Assembly in November 1951. It provided for local councils with two-thirds the members selected by popular vote, and one-third appointed by the chiefs. The chairman of the local council would be an elected member, and he would be the real authority at the local level.

LOGBA. A small Central Togo group in the mountains of the Volta Region.

LOLOBI. A small Central Togo group in the Volta Region.

LONGORO. 8°11' N, 1°53' W. A small village on the Black Volta in the Brong-Ahafo Region which used to be the limit to which canoe traffic could come. Goods were once unloaded here for Kintampo.

LONSDALE, RUPERT LA TROBE. A British officer who traveled widely in the Gold Coast-Asante-Northern Territories area in the

1880s. In October 1881 he left Accra for Kumasi, and from Kumasi he went on to Salaga, Yendi, Krakye, and Krepi, before returning to Accra. In a report made 18 March 1882, he outlined the commercial possibilities of trade in the north. From April to August 1882 he went on a mission to Asante and Gyaman, returning through Sefwi and Denkyira to Cape Coast. He made a third trip to Kumasi in 1887. Lonsdale reported on the internal dissensions tearing Asante apart, and he recommended that consuls be stationed at various points in the interior. Lonsdale died in 1888.

- M -

MACARTHY, CHARLES. 1768-1824. British General and Administrator. Son of a French father and Irish mother, he first joined the French army, but after the French Revolution he changed to the British. In 1812 he was placed in charge of British forces in Senegal, and in 1814 he was transferred to be first acting Governor, and in 1816 Governor of Sierra Leone. When the Company of Merchants was dissolved in 1821, he became responsible for the British settlements on the Gold Coast as well. He is remembered as one of the better administrators of Sierra Leone.

In the Gold Coast Macarthy quickly developed an antipathy to the Asante, and he formed the coastal peoples into an alliance against the Asante. In 1823 the Asante executed a Fante in British service, and Macarthy moved against the Asante. On 21 January 1824 he was killed in a skirmish near Bonsaso. The Africans call the engagement Insamankow or Nsamankow. The Asante called Macarthy "Mankata."

MACLEAN, GEORGE. 1801-1847. British Administrator. He went to Africa as a lieutenant in the Royal African Colonial Corps in Sierra Leone in 1826. On 15 February 1830 he became President of the Council of Merchants at Cape Coast, a position he held until 13 February 1844. From 1843 until his death in 1847 he was Judicial Assessor. During his service in the Gold Coast he maintained the peace between the Fante and Asante, and trade increased threefold as a result of this policy.

MADJITEY, ERASMUS (ERIC) RANSFORD TAWI. Born 1920. He was born near Krobo Odumasi. He was Commissioner of Police under Nkrumah, 1958-1964, but was sacked when a constable tried to kill the President. From then until the 1966 coup he was held in prison under preventive detention. He was Ghana's High Commissioner to Pakistan, 1966-1969, during the NLC period. When political parties were allowed again he was one of the leaders of the National Alliance of Liberals (NAL), and was elected to the National Assembly for Manya Krobo, and became Leader of the Opposition to Busia in the parliament. He was arrested in April 1978 by the SMC, but was released by the coup of the following June.

MAKOLA. The three major markets of Accra are called Makola I, II, and III. They are between Independence Avenue and Liberation Avenue. On 18 August 1979 these markets were razed by AFRC troops.

MAMPA (Mompa). An old polity between the Ankobra and Pra above Ahanta. It is shown on a 1629 Dutch map, and on the 1729 Anville map.

MAMPELLE. The language of Mamprusi.

MAMPONG AKUAPEM (Mampon Akwapim). 5°55' N, 0°08' W. Town in the hills of Akuapem where the Basel missionaries experimented with cocoa seedlings first in 1859. Tetteh Quashie planted his first cocoa near here in 1878 and had his first harvest in 1883. The hospital at Mampong is named for Tetteh Quashie. The population of the town in 1970 was 5,818.

MAMPONG ASANTE (Mampon Ashanti). 7°04' N, 1°24' W. Town on the Great Northern Road from Kumasi to Tamale, 30 miles (48 km) northeast of Kumasi. It is one of the founding states of the Asante Union, and the Mamponghene is second only to the Asantehene in importance in the Union. He occupies the Silver Stool. It was settled by migrants from Adansi. Mampong and Nsuta are twin towns, located only a short distance apart. In 1948 the census showed only 3,933 persons in Mampong. By 1970 there were 13,895 people living there.

MAMPONG ESCARPMENT. The southern elevated edge of the Volta basin is the principal watershed of Ghana. The line runs from Wenchi in the northwest to Koforidua in the southeast. The watershed is called the Mampongtin Range by some, the Kwahu Escarpment by others.

MAMPRUGU. This is the old capital of Mamprusi. It was located in the area of Gambaga and Naleregu, the present chief city of the Mamprusi. The name of the old capital is sometimes used as the name of the Mamprusi people.

MAMPRUSI. One of the Mole-Dagbani states in the Northern Region. It was founded by conquerors who came from the east in the fourteenth or fifteenth century. The dynasty was founded by Gbewa of Pusiga. His son, variously spelled Tohagu, Tohogo, or Tohugu, founded the town of Mamprugu. Gambaga and Naleregu are the chief villages of Mamprusi. The Mamprusi are Muslim in theory, but they do not follow traditional Muslim practices. They signed a treaty of friendship with the British 28 May 1894. There were about 55,000 Mamprusi in 1960.

MANCHE (Mantse). A paramount chief of the Ga and Adangbe.

MANCHESTER PAN-AFRICAN CONGRESS. The Fifth (or Sixth) Pan-

African Congress was the first such Congress attended by large numbers of Africans. Kwame Nkrumah, Joe Appiah, and J.C. de Graft-Johnson were among the Ghanaian delegation. It was at this Congress that Nkrumah first came into contact with many of the men who soon would become leaders in the movement for African independence. Nkrumah organized his West African Secretariat at Manchester in order to promote the idea of a West African Federation.

MANHYIA (Menhia). The section of Kumasi where the palace of the Asantehene and the Asanteman Council Hall are located. It is to the northeast of the Central Market.

MANKATA see MACARTHY, CHARLES

MANKATASA WAR. The name the Asante used for the conflict with the coastal states from 1823 to 1826.

MANKESIM (Mankessim, Mankesemu). 5°16' N, 1°01' W. Important Fante "Great Town" in the Central Region about 20 miles (32 km) northeast of Cape Coast on the highway towards Accra. It is the location of the great Fante Oracle, Naanam Mpow, and the Fante Confederation was started here in 1867. The population was only 1,240 in 1948. This grew to 2,604 in 1960, and 4,142 in 1970.

MANKUMA. 9°11' N, 2°29' W. A small village on the Bole-Wa road in the Northern Region, just east of the Black Volta and 12 miles (19 km) north of Bole. It is the location of the mausoleum of the chiefs of Yagbon (Gonja). In 1970 there were only 268 inhabitants of Mankuma.

MANSO (Mansu). 5°31' N, 1°10' W. The Assin Apemanim capital, on the Cape Coast-Kumasi highway in the Central Region. Located some 30 miles (40 km) north of Cape Coast, it was once an important collection point for slaves being brought down from Asante for sale on the coast.

MANYA KROBO. A branch of the Adangbe; these Eastern Krobo live in the Volta Plains and have a capital at Odumasi (Odumase).

MATE KOLE, EMMANUEL. 1860-1939. Konor or paramount chief of the Manya Krobo, he was born at Odumasi. Once a teacher in Basel mission schools. He was elected Konor in 1892. During his rule he pushed agricultural development, and he built many miles of roads. In 1911 he became the first paramount chief to be appointed to the Gold Coast Legislative Council, on which he served several terms.

MAWU. The supreme deity of the Ewe, creator of the world, and source of all power.

MENSA BONSU. Ca. 1840-1896. Asantehene. He became Asantehene after Kofi Karikari was deposed in September 1874. He began to try to restore the power of Kumasi. He defeated Dwaben in November 1875, and tried to regain control of trade to the north. He reorganized the civil service and the military in order to bring them more closely under his control. In March 1883 he was deposed. Attempts had been made to do this earlier in 1877 and 1880. The British arrested Mensa Bonsu in early 1896, and he died a short time later.

MENSAH, JOSEPH HENRY. Economist, politician. Born in 1928, and educated at Achimota, Legon, London School of Economics, and Stanford University. He was a teacher and did research at Legon, 1953 to 1958, then was an economist for the UN from 1958 to 1961. He then returned to Ghana to work for the National Planning Commission, 1961-1965. From 1965 to 1969 he was with the Economic Commission for Africa. In 1969 he joined Busia's Progress Party, was elected to the National Assembly, and was Minister of Finance, 1969-1972. The National Redemption Council sent him to prison in 1975 for causing disaffection from their rule. Released in 1978, he was banned from politics the following year, but was an active supporter of the Popular Front Party, the old Busia coalition, in the 1979 elections. Later going into exile in England, in August 1983 he headed a group in opposition to the Rawlings-Tsikata PNDC.

METAL CROSS (Metalen Kruis). The Dutch name for Dixcove Fort. The post was built by the English at the end of the seventeenth century, but the Dutch held it from 1868 to 1872, and during this brief period it was known as Metalen Kruis. The fort was restored in the 1950s and is now used as government offices.

MFANTSE. The language of the Fante-Akan, spoken in the Central and Western coastal areas of Ghana.

MFANTSIPIM. One of Ghana's most famous secondary schools. It was started in 1876 as a Wesleyan mission at Cape Coast. It became a secondary school in 1909. Many of Ghana's most distinguished sons are products of its classes.

MIGRANTS. Perhaps as much as one-eighth of the population of Ghana has at least one parent not native to Ghana. Hausa, Mossi, Igbo, Yoruba, Mande, Fulani, Songhai, and many other West Africans live and work in Ghana.

MILNER-SIMON AGREEMENT, 10 July 1919. The agreement between the British and French over the boundary of their areas of Togoland. England gained control of Eastern Dagomba and part of the Ewe territory. This was confirmed by a League of Nations mandate in 1922.

MIM (Mmem). 6°54' N, 2°34' W. A mining town in Brong-Ahafo about ten miles (16 km) north of Goaso. It had a census of 2,401 in 1948, and in 1970 the population was 9,630.

MINA COAST. The Portuguese name for the Gold Coast, which they first reached in 1471.

MISORE. The founder of the Mole-Dagbani Talensi gorup. He came from Mampurugu to settle in the Tongo Hills, above Mamprusi. He was succeeded by his son, Seyene.

MMOATIA. The legendary prehistoric first inhabitants of what is today Ghana. They were said to have been of short stature and reddish complexion. They are the "little folk" or fairies of traditions passed down in Ghana.

MO. Descendants of Grusi Sisala who migrated to the Bamboi region on the Black Volta, and also to the area around Wa.

MOABA see BIMOBA

MOAR see BIMOBA

MOBA see BIMOBA

MOGYA (Bogya). Akan for blood or the maternal, physical side of the family. Every Akan is thought to possess three souls: the Mogya or abusua is the blood or physical soul, connecting one to the maternal ancestors; the Ntoro is the connection to the paternal or "spirit" ancestors; and the Kra is derived from the day of the week on which one is born.

MOINSI HILLS (Adansi Hills). The hills running from Lake Bosumtwi southwest to Obuasi and Dunkwa, between the Fum and Oda rivers.

MOLE GAME RESERVE. Ghana's largest and best-developed Game Reserve. The area covers some 900 sq miles (2,331 sq km). It is located 92 miles (148 km) west of Tamale, and the entrance is near the Gonja village of Larabanga. It is named for the Mole River, which begins in the Park. Baboon, duiker, antelope, and monkeys are the most common animals found in the Park.

MOORE, GEORGE EDWARD. 1879-1950. Nationalist. A treasury clerk and Asafo captain in Cape Coast, he was one of the more radical members of the ARPS. In 1940 he was elected as Municipal Member of the Legislative Council and served there until he died in 1950.

MØRCH, FREDERICK SIEGFRED. 1800-1839. Danish Governor who

was in the Gold Coast from 1834 to 1839. He founded a plantation, called Frederiksgave, in Akuapem, where he hoped to demonstrate the agricultural potential of the Gold Coast in order to attract Danish settlers.

MORE. Language of the Mossi.

MOSHI see MOSSI

MOSSI (Moshi). Mole-Dagbani people who have common traditions with Nanumba, Dagomba, Mamprusi, Builsa, Talensi, and other groups in the Northern and Upper regions and in Upper Volta. Many Mossi migrate each year from Upper Volta and live in the northern half of Ghana.

MOURI (Moure, Mouree, Moree, Mori). 5°08' N, 1°12' W. An Asebu village on the coast in the Central Region just east of Cape Coast. The Dutch began trading here around 1594 and began Fort Nassau there in 1612. The Dutch headquarters was located here from 1612 until they moved it to Elmina in 1637. Fort Nassau was abandoned after 1815 and transferred to Britain in 1868. The population of Mouri was 10,086 in 1970.

MOWA see BIMOBA

MOXON, ROLAND JAMES. Born 1920. A native of Shrewsbury, England who has spent most of his life in Ghana. After attending Cambridge, he joined the Colonial Service in 1941. He served as DC at Koforidua, Kpandu, Akuse, and Accra. He was Director of the Information Service of the Gold Coast, and then Ghana from 1954-1960. Since then he has been in the publishing and restaurant businesses in Accra. He is one of the great expatriate characters of Accra.

MPANYIMFO. The council of elders of an Akan village or town.

MPESASO HILLS. The ridge to the west of Kumasi between the Ofin and Tano rivers. They rise to 2,467 feet (752 m).

MPRAESO. 6°35' N, 0°44' W. Commercial center on the Kwahu Scarp in the Eastern Region above Nkawkaw. It had a population of 2,785 in 1911, 3,346 in 1948, and 5,908 in 1970.

MRAMMUO. Akan for gold weights.

MUMFORD (Dwomba). 5°16' N, 0°45' W. Coastal town in the Central Region about 12 miles (19 km) west of Winneba. In 1948 there were 4,250 people living in Mumford. By 1970 the census showed 8,566.

MUNICIPAL CORPORATIONS ORDINANCE, 10 May 1858. An ordinance

which provided for municipal elections of mayors, councillors, and the establishment of municipal courts in the Protectorate. The corporation was authorized to assess house taxes. This law was repealed in 1861, after corporations had been established in James Town and Cape Coast.

MUNICIPALITIES ORDINANCE OF 1889. An ordinance which provided for Municipal Councils, to be elected by qualified voters. The Councils would deal with municipal services, and could levy a house tax to pay for these services. Opposition to the tax kept the Ordinance from ever being used.

MUSLIM ASSOCIATION PARTY (MAP). A Gold Coast Muslim Association was formed in 1932 as a welfare and social society. By 1953 the Association was involved in politics, and in 1954 it became the Muslim Association Party. Most of the leaders were anti-CPP. The Party was strong among immigrant peoples in the Zongo areas of the larger towns. They joined the United Party in opposition to the CPP in November 1957.

MUSLIMS. About 17 percent of Ghanaians are Muslim, divided about equally between the Maliki and Ahmadiya branches of Islam, with a few Shafi. Most of the Fulani, Hausa, Mande, Songhai, and Gurma peoples of Ghana are Muslim. About half of the Mole-Dagbani and the Yoruba in Ghana profess Islam.

- N -

NA, NABA (pl. Nabdema, Nanamse). Title or honorific among the Mole-Dagbani for secular rulers or chiefs.

NABAGA (Wadh Naba). The traditional leader of the Mande who established Yagbum near Bole about 1550. He was the grandfather of the great Gonja leader Jakpa Lanta (Lante).

NABTE. Language of the Namnam (Nabdom), one of the Mole-Dagbani groups of the Upper East Region.

NALERIGU. 10°32' N, 0°22' W. Mamprusi capital in the Northern Region a short distance from Gambaga. The population in 1948 was 1,477 and in 1970 the census had grown to 3,950.

NAMBALI. A small Ewe group in the Volta Region.

NAMNAM (Nabdam). A Mole-Dagbani group in the Upper East Region. Their language is Nabte, they call their land Nabrug, and by their traditions they came from Nalerigu. They are much like their neighbors the Talensi and Kusasi. Their chief town is Nangodi (Nangoot).

NANA. An honorific or term of respect. A grandparent.

NANAANOM MPOW. The sacred grove of the Fante at Mankesim. Here are buried the patriarchs of the Fante, who are said to have come to the coast from Techiman.

NANDOM. 10°51' N, 2°45' W. A village in the extreme northwestern edge of the Upper West Region on the Western Road, just east of the Black Volta and the border with Upper Volta. It is 16 miles (26 km) north of Lawra. There were 3,236 people there in 1970.

NANKA-BRUCE, FREDERICK VICTOR. 1878-1953. Medical physician, journalist, and secretary of the National Congress of British West Africa. He studied medicine at Edinburgh University. In addition to his medical practice in Accra, he was a planter and shipper of cocoa and actively involved in politics. He was a member of the ARPS, and was Municipal Member of the Legislative Council for a time.

NANKANSI. Mole-Dagbani group in the Upper East Region. They call themselves Gurense, and their language is Gureni. They are indistinguishable from the Fra Fra. They are surrounded by the Kasena, Builsa, and Talensi.

NANUMBA (Nanum, Nanune). A Mole-Dagbani group in the Northern Region with the Daka River on their western border, and the Oti on the east. Their kingdom is related to Mamprusi and Dagomba. It was founded by Nnantombo, son of Na Gbewa and brother of Sitobu. The principal town is Bimbila. In 1960 there were 13,610 people in the Nanumba area.

NAPOLEON. An experimental farm begun by Col. George Torrane in 1807. It was revived in the 1830s by James Swanzy, and later continued by T.B. Freeman in the 1840s. The Wesleyans changed the name to "Beulah" after they took over the operation. Cotton, coffee, grapes, limes, oranges, guavas, and mangoes were all tried out here. The farm was operated until about 1860. It was located near Cape Coast.

NASA, BATTLE OF. 10°09' N, 2°21' W. The battle took place in the Upper West Region northeast of Wa in 1890. Babatu and his Zabrama defeated the Wala army. Afterwards the Wa Na committed suicide. Nasa was destroyed, and Wa was taken and its elders were all executed.

NASSAU, FORT. A fortification built at Mouri about 1612. It was used as the Dutch headquarters on the Gold Coast until they took Elmina and moved their headquarters there in 1637.

NATHAN, MATTHEW. 1862-1939. Governor of the Gold Coast.

Nathan was a graduate of the Royal Military Academy at Woolwich, and he was commissioned into the Royal Engineers in 1880. He was acting Governor of Sierra Leone in 1899, Governor of the Gold Coast, 1900-1903; Governor of Hong Kong, 1903-1907; of Natal, 1907-1909; and of Queensland, 1920-1925. He held several other positions under the Colonial Service before he retired in 1930.

THE NATIONAL ALLIANCE OF LIBERALS (NAL). The chief opposition to the Busia government during the Second Republic. Its leader was K.A. Gbedemah. Eric Madjitey was its leader in the National Assembly, 1970-1972. In the Assembly Busia's Progress Party had 105 seats to 29 seats for the NAL.

NATIONAL ANTHEM. The anthem played at the Independence celebrations in March 1957 was entitled "Ghana Arise." It was written at the request of Nkrumah by an English Labor MP who had never been to Ghana. On 14 March 1958 the government approved a new national anthem taken from nine entries in a national competition. The music was composed by Philip Gbeho. It starts "God bless our homeland Ghana."

NATIONAL ASSOCIATION OF SOCIALIST STUDENTS ORGANIZATION (NASSO). A students' group organized by Tawia Adamafio for radical Ghanaian students in 1957. The organization was abolished in 1961 after Nkrumah decided to establish the Kwame Nkrumah Ideological Institute at Winneba.

NATIONAL COMMISSION FOR DEMOCRACY (NCD). A PNDC agency organized in 1982 to educate the people politically to support the PNDC and to keep the PNDC informed on conditions in the country.

NATIONAL CONGRESS OF BRITISH WEST AFRICA. An organization formed largely as a result of the efforts of J.E. Casely Hayford. In March 1920 six representatives from Nigeria, three from Sierra Leone, one from Gambia, and over forty from the Gold Coast met in Accra and created the National Congress of British West Africa. The group was created to work for cooperation among Britain's West African peoples and for increased local autonomy. Meetings were held during the 1920s, but by 1930 the movement was almost dead.

NATIONAL DEFENSE COMMITTEE. The national coordinating committee established by the PNDC in 1982 to direct the activities of the Peoples' and Workers' Defense Committees in advancing the cause of the PNDC revolution.

NATIONAL DEMOCRATIC PARTY (Demos). A party organized to contest the elections of 1951 against both the United Gold Coast Convention and the Convention Peoples' Party. Dr. F.V. Nanka

Bruce was the chief force in the organization of this conservative party.

NATIONAL DEVELOPMENT COMPANY (NADECO). A company formed and controlled by Nkrumah and the CPP in October 1957 as a means of acquiring funds to finance CPP activities. This was done through "commissions" on government contracts. Most of the directors were Nzema and Fante friends of Nkrumah.

NATIONAL LIBERATION COUNCIL (NLC). The military group which staged the overthrow of Nkrumah and which ran Ghana from 1966 to 1969. J.A. Ankrah, A.A. Afrifa, and J.W. Harlley were the leaders of the NLC.

NATIONAL LIBERATION MOVEMENT (NLM). Political movement formed in Asante in September 1954 under the leadership of K.A. Busia and made up of those in favor of a federal decentralized form of government as opposed to the centralized power which Nkrumah wanted. In October 1957 it joined other opposition parties in the United Party.

NATIONAL REDEMPTION COUNCIL (NRC). The military group which overthrew the Second Republic. Col. I.K. Acheampong, J.H. Cobbina, Major A.H. Selormey, and Major R.M. Baah were leaders of this group. In 1975 Acheampong organized a Supreme Military Council, to which the NRC was subordinated.

NATIONAL SERVICE CORPS. A group created in 1969 by the Second Republic to replace Nkrumah's Workers' Brigade. The National Service Corps was voluntary and undertook many public service projects. It lasted only a short time.

NATIONAL UNION OF GHANAIAN STUDENTS (NUGS). A highly politicized organization of university students which sooner or later generally clashes with every Ghanaian government.

NATIVE ADMINISTRATION ORDINANCE OF 1927. This Act of the Legislative Council contained 129 sections. The positions of native rulers and councils were defined, and procedures for elections and destoolment were outlined. Jurisdiction of native government under customary law was defined. Provincial Councils, established in 1925, were established as courts. The Ordinance expanded the powers of chiefs, recognized the Oman councils as the highest authority within each jurisdiction to decide stool disputes, and made Provincial Councils the appeal court in stool and inter-tribal disputes. The Governor retained power as the final authority.

NATIVE AUTHORITY ORDINANCE OF 1944. This Ordinance required that all organs of local authority had to be recognized by the Central Government in Accra.

NATIVE JURISDICTION ORDINANCES. There were several NJOs approved by the Legislative Councils of the Gold Coast. In 1878 an Ordinance attempted to define the relation of the British government to chiefs in the Protectorate, and to define the powers of chiefs and their councils in civil and criminal matters. It was never implemented and was replaced in 1883.

NATIVE JURISDICTION ORDINANCE OF 1883. The powers of chiefs in civil and criminal affairs was defined and decisions of native tribunals was subject to appeal to British courts. The British maintained the right to dismiss recalcitrant chiefs. The 1883 Ordinance was the basis of native jurisdiction until 1927. But it was amended in 1910 and 1924.

NATIVE STATES. This is the term used after the Native Administration Ordinance of 1927 for traditional states or kingdoms in the Gold Coast. They often were used as districts for administrative purposes. In 1946 there were 13 native states in the Northern and Upper Region, 24 in Asante, and 71 in the Eastern, Central, and Western regions, for a total of 108 native states. In 1957 there were 63 in the three southern regions, 25 in Asante, and 21 in the north, for a total of 109 native states.

NAVRONGO. 10°54' N, 1°06' W. Town on the Great Northern Road in the Upper Region northwest of Bolgatanga, and near the border of Upper Volta. It is a Kasena (Grusi) village. The White Fathers of Upper Volta opened a school here in 1907 and built a Cathedral in 1920.

NAWEN. The chief Lobi deity.

NAYIRI. Paramount chief of the Mamprusi.

NBANYA. The Dyula conquerors who established Gonja. The descendants of the Malians who founded Yagbum.

NCHUMURU see NTWUMURU

NEDEGA. The Mossi name for Gbewa or Bawa, the ancestor of the Mole-Dagbani peoples. Traditions say that he came from Gurma, in modern Upper Volta, and that he settled in Pusiga in what is now the extreme northeast of the Upper East Region.

NEUTRAL ZONE. Territory defined in an Anglo-German agreement of 1888 as a neutral zone where neither country was to acquire a protectorate or special influence. The northern limits of the zone followed the 10th parallel of latitude, and the latitude of the confluence of the Volta and Daka rivers was the southern limits. The western side was 1°27' W, and the eastern side was 0°33' E. Yapei, Yendi, Salaga, Tamale, Yeji, and Bimbila were all in the zone. The agreement lasted until 1899, when the zone was divided between the two countries.

NEW DWABEN. On 21 October 1875 Asante invaded Dwaben. Many of the people of Dwaben emigrated to Koforidua in Akyem, where they founded the new oman of New Dwaben.

NEW JUABEN   see   NEW DWABEN

NEW TAFO   see   TAFO, NEW

NEWTOWN. 5°05' N, 3°05' W. A small coastal village in the Western Region west of Half Assini. It is between the Gulf and Juen Lagoon. Its wharf is called Newtown Wharf (Avolienu Ahonlezo or Avlium Ahonozo). This is the most western settlement in Ghana. The town and wharf area together counted a population of 868 in 1970.

NGBANYA. Local name for Gonja.

NIFA. The right wing of an Akan army. It is under the command of a Nifahene.

NII BONNE, KWABENA TAYLOR. Wealthy merchant who was chief of the Alata quarter of Osu, Accra, and Oyokohene of Techiman. In 1948 he organized an anti-inflation committee which boycotted European goods. This caused riots, looting, and burning of shops of many Europeans and Syrians. A number of people were killed.

NINGO. Area listed on a 1629 map. It was an Adangbe state which is also sometimes shown as Ladoku.

NINGO, GREAT (Old Ningo, Nigo, Nungo). 5°45' N, 0°11' E. A coastal village where the Danes built a fort, Fredensborg (Friedensborg), about 1736. The British gained the area in 1850. Today the old fort is in ruins. Great Ningo had a population of 1,180 in 1948, 2,332 in 1960, and 5,166 in 1970.

NINGO, MOUNT (Ningo Grande, Ningo Peak). 6°03' N, 0°11' E. A hill in the Eastern Region just below Akuse in the Accra Plains. A group of Adangbe people formed the Ningo or Ladoku state on and around Mount Ningo before 1600. They quickly spread to the coast.

NINGO, NEW (Nungo, Nigo). 5°44' N, 0°10' E. Coastal town in the Eastern Region to the east of Prampram, and just west of Great or Old Ningo. The population was 1,052 in 1948, 1,940 in 1960, and 3,447 by 1970.

NKAWKAW. 6°33' N, 0°46' W. City at the foot of the Kwahu Scarp in the Eastern Region near Mpraeso. It is on the main road from Accra to Kumasi. It is an important commercial center. It had 5,043 people in 1948, which jumped to 15,627 by 1960, and to 23,219 by 1970.

NKETIA, JOHN HANSON KWABENA. Born 1921. Musicologist, folklorist, poet, and playwright. Longtime Director of the Institute of African Studies at Legon. Born at Mampong-Asante, he attended the Teacher Training College at Akuropon-Akuapem, the University of London, Columbia University, Northwestern University, and Juilliard School of Music. He has taught on the faculty of several universities, including the University of London, University of Ghana, and the University of California, Los Angeles. He is one of the world's greatest authorities on African music.

NKONYA. Guan people who mostly live in the Volta Region.

NKORANZA (Nkoransa). 7°34' N, 1°42' W. Town in the economic heart of the Brong-Ahafo area. It was located 60 miles (96 km) north of Kumasi and was one of the leading Brong towns. Nkoranza was one of the leaders of the Brong rebellion against Asante 1892-1893. The population of Nkoranza in 1970 was 7,101.

NKRAMO (sing. Kramo). Muslims.

NKROFUL (Nkrofo, Nkrofro). 4°58' N, 2°19' W. Nzema village in the Western Region. It is located some ten miles (16 km) northwest of Axim. This is the birthplace of Kwame Nkrumah and the place of his burial on 9 July 1972.

NKRUMAH, FATHIA HALEN RITZK. Egyptian wife of Kwame Nkrumah. She was a relative of Gamal Nasser. She married Prime Minister Nkrumah at Government House, Accra, in 1958. At the time she was 26 and the Prime Minister was about 48. She was permitted to go to Cairo to live after the coup in February 1966, returned briefly for Nkrumah's funeral in 1972, and returned permanently in 1975, when Ghana gave her a pension. She and Nkrumah had three children.

NKRUMAH, FRANCIS KWESI. Born 21 April 1935 in Elmina. Educated at St. Augustine's, Cape Coast, Würzburg and Berlin universities in Germany, and Harvard. He received the MD degree from Berlin, and a masters in Public Health from Harvard. He is a Ghanaian physician and son of President Nkrumah.

NKRUMAH, KWAME (Osagyefo, Kantamanto, Mbrantsehene, Show Boy, Deliverer of Ghana, Black Star of Africa). 1909-1972. Creator of Ghanaian independence. Prime Minister and President. He was born at Nkroful, in the Western Region, and educated at the Roman Catholic School at Half-Assini, Achimota, Lincoln University, the University of Pennsylvania, London University, and the London School of Economics. In London he was active in the West African Students' Union, and he attended the Pan-African Congress at Manchester in 1945. It was in this period that he got to know George Padmore, T.R. Makonnen, W.E.B. Du Bois, Bankole Awooner-Renner, and others who would help shape his future. One of his companions in Pennsylvania and in London was Ako Adjei. It was Adjei who later suggested to J.B. Danquah that Kwame Nkrumah be invited to return to Ghana to become the general secretary of the United Gold Coast Convention (UGCC). Nkrumah accepted the position. He returned home at the end of 1947.

His tenure as Secretary of UGCC was a stormy one. In March 1948 he was arrested and detained as one of the Big Six. After his release he was increasingly at odds with the pace of the intelligentsia who had founded the UGCC. All of the Big Six except Nkrumah were invited to join the Coussey Committee to make recommendations for a new form of government. Nkrumah, K.A. Gbedemah, Kojo Botsio, and the "verandah boys" began to demand "Self-Government Now." On 12 June 1949 the Convention People's Party, with Nkrumah as Chairman, was born at the Arena in Accra. "Positive Action" and civil disobedience, strikes, boycotts, and noncooperation became the program of the CPP. On 21 January 1950 Nkrumah was arrested again, for promoting an illegal strike. He was sentenced to a total of three years' imprisonment. He spent a year in prison before being elected to the Legislative Assembly in the CPP sweep of February 1951. He was released from prison 12 February 1951, and on the 23 February he became Leader of Government Business in the Assembly. A year later his title was changed to Prime Minister. On 10 July 1953 he made his "Motion of Destiny," calling for independence within the British Commonwealth. In June 1954 the CPP consolidated its position. During 1955 and 1956 there was bitter debate over the form an independent government would take, but Nkrumah was firmly in control. On 15 November 1956 the Assembly endorsed Nkrumah's plan for a unitary constitution. Ghana was born less than four months later. But from the beginning Nkrumah conceived of himself as more than just the leader of Ghana. He thought of himself as the leader of all Africa.

As Nkrumah began to think of himself as more than a Ghanaian leader, his impatience with opposition began to grow. In July 1958 the Preventive Detention Act gave Nkrumah the power to imprison those who questioned his actions. By April 1959 the opposition began to be expelled from the National Assembly. In 1960 Ghana became a Republic. In the presidential election, Nkrumah overwhelmed J.B. Danquah by 1,016,076 to 124,623. In 1961 it became illegal to insult the President. Nkrumah began to dismiss his old comrades. Hundreds of opponents went to prison or into exile. In 1962 the National Assembly made Nkrumah President for Life. In February 1964 Ghana became a one-party state. In 1965 the President took over direct control of the army, and all senior officers were required to take an oath of allegiance to the President. On 21 February 1966 Nkrumah left for a trip to China. Three days later a military coup ended his administration of Ghanaian affairs.

On 2 March 1966 Nkrumah was welcomed to Guinea by Sekou Toure, who proclaimed Nkrumah to be co-president of Guinea. In Guinea he plotted a return to power, and he wrote his apologia, Dark Days in Ghana. He had six years of life left. He lived long enough to hear that Busia's Republic was also destroyed by a military coup. Then in April 1972 he died in a Bucharest, Rumania, hospital. At first his body was put to rest in Guinea, but finally, in July, the embalmed body was flown to Accra. There the body rested in state in the Conference Hall of the State House while Ghanaians and the world paid tribute. The following day the body of the Osagyefo was returned to Nkroful.

NKWATIA. 6°38' N, 0°44' W. Town on the Kwahu Plateau in the Eastern Region. It had a population of 3,547 in 1948 and 6,285 in 1970.

NNANTOMBO. Son of Gbewa of Pusiga, Nnantombo was the traditional founder of the Mole-Dagbani state of Nanumba.

NORTHCOTT, HENRY. Died 1899. British officer. He was the first British Commissioner and Commandant in the Northern Territories. Appointed in September 1897, Northcott was to occupy any place in the hinterland of the Gold Coast not occupied by some other European power. He established his headquarters at Gambaga in June 1898, and accompanied by a former Mossi king, he marched with an English force into the area that is now Upper Volta. On 30 June 1898 he was met by a French force at Kombissiri, and he turned back with the news that an agreement had ceded the area to France. During the rest of 1898 and early 1899 Northcott organized local government in the Northern Territories and planned a transportation network for the region. Later in 1899 he went to South Africa to take part in the war there. He was killed shortly after he got to South Africa.

NORTHERN PEOPLE'S PARTY (NPP). A political group organized under the leadership of Simon Diedong Dombo, traditional Chief of Duori in the Upper Region. Its purpose was to protect the interests of the northerners. It contested the 1954 and 1956 elections and then merged with other opposition parties against the CPP in November 1957.

NORTHERN REGION. The Gonja, Mamprusi, and Dagomba savanna lands between the Volta borders of Brong-Ahafo and the Upper Regions. Houses are generally round with grass-thatch roofs, and they are formed into compounds. Tamale is the administrative center. It included the Upper Regions until they were separated 29 June 1960.

NORTHERN TERRITORIES. The hinterland of the Gold Coast north of the Asante lands of the Ahafo and Brong. The area was annexed to the British crown under the Governor of the Gold Coast as of 1 January 1902. The headquarters was at Gambaga from Christmas 1896, but it was moved to Tamale in 1907. The area was not represented in the Legislative Council until 1950.

NORTHERN TERRITORIES RAILROAD. In 1926 the British Under-Secretary for Colonies recommended that the railroad at Kumasi be extended to Navrongo, a distance of around 350 miles (563 km). The great depression of the 1930s killed any chance for the line to be built.

NOTSIE (Nouatja). A town on the railroad in Togo from which the Ewe trace their origins. Traditions give the date of dispersal from Notsie as 1720.

NSAKI, BATTLE OF. On a stream just north of Accra a coalition of people under the leadership of Frimpon Manso, ruler of Akyem Kotoku, defeated the Akwamu in 1730. This forced the Akwamu to retreat across the Volta to the area they now occupy east of that river.

NSAMANKOW (Nsamanko, Insamankow) see **BONSASO**

NSAWAM. 5°48' N, 0°21' W. City on the highway and railroad from Accra to Koforidua in the Eastern Region. In 1911 it had a population of 2,596. By 1948 the population was 12,263, and in 1970 that had grown to 25,518. The town is on the Densu River.

NSAWKAW. 7°52' N, 2°19' W. Town located near the site of the old trade center of Begho.

NSUAEM (5°55' N, 0°59' W) see **ODA**

NSUMANKWAAHENE. The head of the scribes and physicians, and therefore the shrine priests, priestesses and the Muslims (Nkramo) in Kumasi.

NSUTA (Insuta). 7°01' N, 1°23' W. One of the major Asante metropolitan towns. It was founded about the same time as Kumasi. The town submitted to the British on 30 January 1896.

NTAFO. Asante name for Gonja and the people north of Asante. The ancestors of the Akan, said to have come down the Volta from the north.

NTERESO (Nterso). 9°07' N, 1°13' W. Place in the Northern Region just west of Yapei and the White Volta. An archaeological site near here seems to have been occupied by 1300 B.C. Oliver

Davies excavated a Kintampo culture site here, showing evidence of early pastoralism.

NTETEA. Akan name day or outdooring. Eight days after birth Akan infants are given a name by some member of their paternal family. This personal name comes from the father's side of the family.

NTORO (Nton). The Akan are divided into maternal and paternal descent groups. The Ntoro is the paternal spirit in each infant at birth.

NTRUBU (Ntruber). One of the small Volta-Togo groups in the Volta Region east of Krakye.

NTWUMURU (Nchumuru, Nchumbulung). Guan group closely allied to the Krakye. There are some on each side of Lake Volta.

NUMU (Ton, Tonfo). Artisans--blacksmiths, sandal-makers, woodworkers, potters, etc.--who are animists and related to the Ligbi and Hwela. They are scattered along the Black Volta from Bole to Salaga.

NUNGUA (Nungwa). 5°36' N, 0°04' W. Coastal village between Teshi and Tema. It was one of the seven original Ga towns. In 1948 it had a population of only 1,101, but it has grown rapidly as Tema and Teshi developed, and by 1970 it had a population of 13,839.

NUNUMA (Nanoumba). A small Grusi group.

NYAGSE. Son of Sitobu and grandson of Gbewa. The first Ya-Na of Dagbon or Dagomba. Tamakloe dated Nyagse at 1416 to 1432. Fage says 1476-1492.

NYAKROM (Nyaakrom). 5°37' N, 0°47' W. Town in the Central Region which was the first capital of Agona. It is said to have been founded about 1660. In 1921 it had 6,257 people. By 1970 the census figure was 11,252.

NYAMASI. The subject people or common people of Gonja.

'NYAME see ONYAME

'NYAME AKUMA. God's axes. Stone relics dated from neolithic times which have been found all over Ghana. They may have been used as hoes in ancient times. They are associated with Kintampo culture.

NYANAWASE (Nyanaoase). 5°47' N, 0°23' W. The old Akwamu capital before 1730, when the Akyem drove Akwamu out of the Akuapem area.

NYANGBO. Volta-Togo group in the Volta Region.

NYANOA (Nyanga, Nyango, Yagbum). 9°15' N, 2°23' W. Place in the Northern Region a few miles northeast of Bole which was the home of the Yagbumwura, paramount chief of the Gonja from about 1700 to 1942, when the Gonja headquarters was moved to Damongo.

NYANTROBI, BATTLE OF. In 1660 the armies of Akwamu defeated Okai Koi of Accra, who committed suicide after the battle. The battle took place 12 miles (19 km) north of Accra.

NYARKO KWEKU (Nyarko Eku). The founder of the Agona State with its seat at Nyakrom. He lived in the latter part of the seventeenth century and was killed by the Akwamu in 1693.

NYENDAAL, DAVID VAN. Dutchman who was the first known European to go to Kumasi. He went to the Asante capital in 1701, soon after the Asante defeated Denkyira at Feyiase, eight miles (13 km) southeast of Kumasi. He stayed about a year and died in 1702, shortly after his return to the coast. He never had the chance to write an account of his experiences in the Asante capital.

NZEMA (Nzima). Coastal people in the Western Region between the Tano and Ankobra rivers. Europeans often called the area Apollonia (Appolonia). Kwame Nkrumah was a Nzema from Nkrofro, just a short distance above the coast. The British built Fort Apollonia at Beyin, in Nzema territory about 1768.

- O -

OBIRI YEBOA MANU. Ca. 1660-1693. Leader of the Asante Oyoko matriclan. He was a nephew of Oti Akenten. The uncle had moved the Asante into the Kwaman area around the old trading town of Tafo. This had involved quite a bit of fighting, and the fighting continued during the rule of Obiri Yeboa. Obiri Yeboa was followed as head of the Oyoko matriclan by his nephew, Osei Tutu, who created Kumasi in Kwaman and established the Asante Union.

OBOSOM (pl. Abosom) see ABOSOM

O'BRIEN, CONOR CRUISE. Born 1917. Irish diplomat, academician, author, and politician. O'Brien was employed by the Irish Department of External Affairs, 1944-1964. From 1956 to 1960 he was a member of the Irish delegation at the UN. Then for a time he was attached to the UN Mission in the Congo (Zaire). He was an admirer of Nkrumah's socialism and anti-imperialism, and Nkrumah invited him to come to Ghana as Vice-Chancellor of the University of Ghana, 1962-1965. He then served on the faculty of New York University for four years, before returning to Ireland, where he was elected to the Dail. He was Irish Minister of Posts and Telegraphs from 1973 to 1977. He then was a member of the Irish Senate for a time.

OBUASI. 6°12' N, 1°40' W. City in the Asante Region about 39 miles (63 km) south of Kumasi. It is located in the richest mining area of Ghana. Gold mining began there in 1897. By 1911 Obuasi had a population of 5,626. In 1948 the census had grown to 15,724, in 1960 it was 22,818, and in 1970 there were 31,005 people in Obuasi. The city is located on the Sekondi-Kumasi railroad.

OBURONI (pl. Abrofoo). Akan for a European or Caucasian.

OCANSEY, ALFRED JOHN. 1879-1943. Born in Ada, he became a leading merchant, journalist, and nationalist. As a merchant he introduced electric generators, motion pictures, record players, radios, and automobiles to the Gold Coast. As the owner of the African Morning Post he brought Nnamdi Azikiwe to Accra as his editor. He was an admirer of Marcus Garvey. He was an advocate of Gold Coast nationalism, and he constantly did things that harassed the colonial government. He was one of the forces behind the cocoa holdup of 1930-1931.

OCRAN, ALBERT KWESI. Born 1929. Born in Brakwa, Central Region, he was educated at the Roman Catholic School in Accra. He joined the army in 1947 and went to Officers' Training School, Teshi. He then went to England and attended Eton Hall, several military programs, and the British Staff College at Camberley. Commissioned in 1954, he was attached to the British army in West Germany for a time in 1955. After home duty in Kumasi and Accra, he was sent to the Congo.

In 1966 Ocran was an active participant in the coup against Nkrumah, and he wrote a book, A Myth Is Broken (1968) about the coup, and another book, Politics of the Sword (1977) about the military government that came after the coup. He was a member of the National Liberation Council, responsible for the Works, Housing, Transport, and Communications ministries. In May 1967 he became Commander of the Ghanaian army, and in November 1968 he was acting Chief of the Ghanaian Defense Staff. In 1969 he joined Afrifa and J.W.K. Harlley as a member of the brief Presidential Commission.

ODA (Insuaim, Nsuaem). 5°55' N, 0°59' W. Capital of Akyem Kotoku. It was founded in 1863 as Nsuaem, and the name was changed to Oda in 1922. It is a commercial and administrative center on the railway from Sekondi to Kade. A ferry across the Birim is located here. Oda is in a diamond-producing region. The population in 1948 was 8,354; it grew to 20,957 by 1970.

ODEHYE. A member of the royal blood of the reigning Stool in an Akan state.

ODEKURO (pl. Adekurofo). The headman of a village.

ODONKO see DONKO

ODUMASI (Odumase). 6°08' N, 0°01' W. The capital of the Manya Krobo after 1892. It is 50 miles (80 km) northeast of Accra. The Basel Mission opened a school here as early as 1857. In 1970 Odumasi had a population of 6,343.

ODWIRA (Odwire). The national purification festival of the Akan. It is the most important day of the year in Asante. The Odwira is held in September at the time of the harvest of the new yams. It is a day of purification in which allegiance to authority is renewed, the spirits of ancestors are propitiated, and the Asantehene visits the royal mausoleums. In the past many people were sacrificed on this day. "Dwira" means "to clean."

OFORI ATTA I (Aaron Eugene Boakye Danquah). 1881-1943. Omanhene of Akyem Abuakwa, 1912-1943. Half brother of J.B. Danquah. Educated in Basel Mission schools and the Basel Mission Theological Seminary at Akuropon, he spent several years as a clerk. He then joined the West African Frontier Force in 1900, and served in the Yaa Asantewa War. Returning to clerical jobs in Accra and Kibi, he was elected Omanhene of Akyem-Abuakwa in 1912. From then until his death he was the most influential traditional ruler in the Gold Coast. From 1916 he was a member of the Legislative Council, and just before his death he was appointed to the Executive Council of the Colony.

OFORI ATTA II (Daniel Opoku Akyempon). 1899-1973. Paramount Chief of Akyem Abuakwa. Educated in Basel Mission schools in Kibi and Begoro, and Albert Academy in Sierra Leone. From 1928 to 1943 he was an employee of the Akyem Abuakwa Native Authority, and in September 1943 he was selected to succeed his uncle, Ofori Atta I, as paramount chief of Akyem Abuakwa. He was President of the Joint Provincial Council of Chiefs from 1948 to 1954, and a member of the Legislative Assembly from 1951 to 1954. He was a member of the Coussey Committee. His opposition to Nkrumah resulted in an investigation of his administration of Akyem Abuakwa. The government then destooled Oforo Atta II, and forcibly brought him to Accra in September 1958. Only after the NLC came to power was he allowed to return to Kibi. Once again he was allowed to become ruler of Akyem Abuakwa.

OFORI ATTA, JONES. Born 1937. Economist and politician. Educated at Kibi, Achimota, Legon, and the University of Ottawa, Canada. He worked for a time as teacher and journalist.

Elected to the National Assembly for the Second Republic, he also served in the Ministry of Finance and Economic Planning, and in the Prime Minister's office. After the coup of 1972 he spent some time in prison. After his release he became a professor in the economics department at Legon. In 1978 he was arrested again by the SMU, for opposition to the Union Government plans. He was released after the SMC was toppled.

OFORI ATTA, WILLIAM. Born 1910. Lawyer, teacher, politician. Son of Ofori Atta I of Akyem Abuakwa. He was educated at Kibi, Mfantsipim, Achimota, and Cambridge. He taught at Achimota, 1933-1943, worked for the Akyem Abuakwa Native Authority for several years, and was Headmaster of Abuakwa State College, 1947-1952. He was one of the founders of the UGCC, and one of the "Big Six" held in detention after the riots of 1948. He was elected to the National Assembly in 1951, but defeated for reelection in 1954. He became one of the leaders of the opposition to the CPP, being associated with the Ghana Congress Party in 1952, the National Liberation Movement in 1954, and the United Party in 1957. After the overthrow of Nkrumah the NLC made him a member of their Political Committee, the Constitutional Commission, and he was made Chairman of the Cocoa Marketing Board. He was a member of the Constituent Assembly in 1968, and was elected to the National Assembly as one of the leaders of the Progress Party. In the Second Republic he was first Minister of Education, Culture, and Sports, and then Minister of Foreign Affairs. He was arrested by the SMC in April 1978, but released after the coup in June of that year. In the elections of 1979 he was the candidate of the United National Convention party, doing very poorly in the returns. Afterwards, he retired from politics.

OFORI KUMA I (Kwao Safori, Sakyiama Tenten). Died 1731. First ruler of Akuapem. A member of the royal family of Akyem Abuakwa, he was the leader of a coalition which helped the Guan in their rebellion against Akwamu, 1728-1730. After the Akwamu were forced across the Volta, the Guan made Ofori Kuma their paramount chief. He died shortly thereafter.

OFORI KUMA II (Bernard Ofosu Apea Koranteng). 1879-1954. Controversial paramount chief of Akuapem from 1914 to 1919 and from 1932 to 1941. His contempt for traditions frequently got him into trouble with his subjects, and he was twice destooled. Between tours as Okuapemhene he practiced law.

OFORI PANIN. Died 1727. The fourth paramount chief of Akyem Abuakwa. Ofori Panin established the rule of Akyem Abuakwa in the Birem River valley.

OGUAA. The Fante name for Cape Coast.

OGUAA FETU AFAHYE. The major festival at Cape Coast. It commemorates the purification of the fishing shrines. It occurs the first week of September, climaxing on the first Saturday of the month.

OHEMMAA (pl. Ahemmaa). Queen Mother.

OHENE (pl. Ahene). King, ruler, paramount chief, etc. The head of something. The Akan chiefs belong to a particular clan, and they trace descent through the female line. They are "father" to their people; responsible for their secular and religious welfare. Their person is sacred, but their duties are strictly defined at the time of enstoolment. They may not act without advice from the queen mother and council. Abuse of power may result in destoolment.

OIL PALM (Elaeis guineensis). A tree which is grown over most of the area of Ghana south of the Black Volta. Its oil is used as a cooking oil, for margarine, and for soap. It is tapped for sap from which wine is made. Oil palms are often killed by Weaver birds.

OKAI KOI. Ca. 1610-1660. Chief of Great Accra. He went a long way toward uniting the seven Ga groups under his power. His capital was at Ayawase, a few miles inland from the coast. He was the Ga ruler who allowed the English, Danes, Dutch, and Swedes to build trading posts along the coast at Accra. He was defeated by the Akwamu at Nyantrobi, north of Accra, in 1660, and is said to have committed suicide shortly after the battle.

OKOMFO (pl. Akomfo). Priest.

OKOMFO ANOKYE   see   ANOKYE, OKOMFO

OKOMFO ANOTCHI   see   ANOKYE, OKOMFO

OKOMFO MAA. Priestess.

OKRA (gumbo). A vegetable which is widely grown in Ghana for use in stews.

OKUAPEMHENE. The paramount chief of Akuapem (Akwapim).

OKYEAME. Linguist, spokesman, or secretary of an Akan ruler.

OKYEAME (The Spokesman). A Ghanaian literary quarterly which was started by the Ghana Society of Writers in 1961. Kofi Awooner and Christina Ama Ata Aidoo have each served a turn as editor.

OKYEHENE. The paramount chief of Akyem Abuakwa.

OKYEMAN COUNCIL. The council of chiefs of Akyem Abuakwa.

OLD TAFO see TAFO, OLD

OLLENNU, NII AMAA. Born 1906. Teacher, author, lawyer. A Ga from Labadi, he was educated at the Basel Mission School in Labadi, at Accra High School, and studied law in England. He was a teacher at Accra High School from 1929 to 1937, a member of the Accra Council, 1944-1950, a member of the Legislative Council, 1946-1950, and the Coussey Committee on Constitutional Reform in 1949. He became a High Court Judge in 1956, and a member of the Supreme Court in 1962. He was Speaker of the National Assembly of the Second Republic, 1969-1972, during which time he was briefly the acting President of the Republic. Ollennu is the author of several law books.

OMAN (pl. Aman). The community, a political unit, a district, a polity.

OMANHENE (pl. Amanhene). Head of an Oman.

ONYAME ('Nyame). The Supreme, Almighty, Creator God of the Akan. The Onyame is also called Amowia (Maker of Sunshine); Amosu (Maker of Rain); Atoapem (Alpha and Omega, the First and Last). Onyame also means "the sky."

OPERATION COLD CHOP. The code name for the coup of 24 February 1966 which overthrew Kwame Nkrumah.

OPERATION FEED YOURSELF (OFY). The policy of food self-sufficiency launched by Acheampong and the NRC in 1972. It was initially successful, but ultimately a failure.

OPOKU FOFIE. Ca. 1775-1799. Asantehene. He was the successor to Asantehene Osei Kwame, who was destooled and later killed in 1803. Opoku Fofie reigned for less than two years, most of which was spent trying to crush rebellions in the northern part of his realm. He was followed on the Golden Stool by his half brother, Osei Tutu Kwame, known as Osei Bonsu. Opoku Fofie's brief reign was from 1798 to 1799.

OPOKU FREFRE. Ca. 1760-1826. Royal Treasurer (Gyasehene) of Asante during the first quarter of the nineteenth century, he was one of the closest advisers of Asantehene Osei Bonsu, 1800-1823. He also commanded part of the Asante army in campaigns against the Fante and Gyaman. He was killed at Katamanso in the great defeat of 1826.

OPOKU, THEOPHILUS. 1824-1913. A native of Akuropon in Akuapem, he was the first African to be ordained as a minister in the Gold Coast by the Basel Mission. He travelled over much of what is today Ghana during his ministry, and his diary, published in 1884, is a valuable source on the country in the 1870s.

OPOKU WARE I. Ca. 1700-1750. Asantehene from around 1720 to 1750. He was the grandnephew of Asantehene Osei Tutu. There is a blank in the history of Asante between the reign of Osei Tutu and the reign of Opoku Ware I. It is not clear if Osei Tutu died in 1712 or in 1717 (Ivor Wilks favors 1712). There may have been a ruler between Osei Tutu and Opoku Ware I, or there may have been an interregnum. By 1720 Opoku Ware I was the Asantehene. His reign was a period of great expansion at the expense of all his neighbors. He defeated armies of the Sefwi, Aowin, Gonja, Dagomba, and Techiman, Gyaman, and Akyem. By the time of his death he had established his power over much of what is today Ghana, but he never crushed the Fante and Wassa which kept his victories from being complete, and aided rebellions in outlying provinces.

OPOKU WARE II (Barima Kwaku Adusei, J. Matthew Poku). Born 1918. Asantehene, 1970- . He was a nephew of Asantehene Prempe II. He was educated at Adisadel College, Cape Coast, and he studied law in England. He served as Commissioner of Communications in the NLC, 1968-1969, and was Ambassador-designate from the Second Republic to Rome when elected Asantehene. He became Asantehene 6 July 1970 with the name Opoku Ware II.

OPON ENIM. The traditional founder of the Adansi state, sometime after 1500. The Adansi claim to be the senior Akan state. The first capital was Adansimanso in the Kwisa and Moinsi hills.

OPON-MANSI HILLS. Hills between Tarkwa and Dunkwa.

OPON, SAMPSON. Ca. 1884-1960. Evangelist. A native of the Brong-Ahafo Region, near the Ivory Coast border, who was converted to Christianity in 1920 and became a famous preacher who claimed prophetic powers.

ORANGE, FORT. Fort built by the Dutch at Sekondi about 1640. It was plundered by the Ahantas in 1694 but later rebuilt. It serves as a lighthouse today.

OSEI BONSU   see   OSEI TUTU KWAME

OSEI KWADWO (Osei Kojo, Osei Kuma). Ca. 1735-1777. Asantehene from 1764 to 1777. In 1765 he joined the Fante in fighting Wassa, Twifo, and Akyem. The Akyem were defeated and all their leading chiefs committed suicide. The Asante and Fante soon fell out, and Akyem renewed its war with Asante. Akyem was defeated again, but when the Asante attacked the Krobo, the Krobo forced the Asante to retreat. Campaigns were conducted in Gyaman and Banda, and the Asante army attacked Dagomba in 1772 and brought back many slaves. Osei Kwadwo surrounded himself with a powerful bodyguard, and he sent Asante commissioners to keep an eye on conquered peoples.

OSEI KWAME. Ca. 1764-1803. Asantehene from 1777 to 1798. Son of a Mamponghene, he was forced on the electors in Kumasi when he was hardly 13 years old. An attempted coup against Osei Kwame in 1790 was crushed. In 1797 opposition to his reign forced him to leave Kumasi, and when he did not appear for the Odwira festival in 1798 he was destooled. Some said the chief opposition to his rule was because he was favorable to the Muslims of the north. There were movements for his restoration, but in 1803 he was executed by strangulation at his own request.

OSEI TUTU (Sai, Zay, Zaay). Ca. 1660-1712 or 1717? Asantehene, ca. 1680-1712 or 1717. Nephew of Obiri Yeboa, Oyoko leader and Kwamanhene. Osei Tutu completed the pacification of the peoples around Kwaman which had been begun by his uncle. With the aid of his friend, Okomfo Anokye, he established Kumasi, the Odwira festival, the tradition of the Golden Stool, and the Asante Union. He also established the precedents that came to stand as the Asante constitution. The Asante Union, though, was based primarily on the Asante army and its organization. Around 1698 he began the campaign against Denkyira which climaxed in 1701 with the defeat of Denkyira at Feyiase. This left Asante the most powerful Akan state. The defeat of Denkyira also opened a way to the coastal trade for Asante. Osei Tutu was killed in a campaign against Akyem Kotoku at a crossing of the Pra River. The date is disputed, either 1712 or 1717.

OSEI TUTU KWAME (Osei Bonsu, Osei Tutu Kwamina Asibe). Ca. 1779-1823. Asantehene from 1800 to 1823. At the start of his reign he halted a rebellion in the northern part of Asante. In 1807 he led his army against the Fante in the south. He returned again in 1811 and 1816 and had it not been for the Europeans he would have established firm Asante control of the coastal regions. He came to be called "Bonsu" signifying "whale," the master of the seas. Most of the coastal people were willing to admit Asante supremacy, but not the British. The British had committed themselves to end the slave trade, and the Asante were a threat to that commitment. The British preferred trade through the Fante, but the Asante had ties to the Dutch. In 1817 the British sent T.E. Bowdich to Kumasi to negotiate with Osei Bonsu. In 1819 Joseph Dupuis also visited the Asantehene. In both cases the Asante were willing to concede almost everything except their claims over the Fante.
In the meantime rumors reached the English at Cape Coast that, in connection with his mother's funeral, Osei Bonsu had had thou

sands of souls dispatched to keep his mother's soul company in the world of spirits. Charles Macarthy, British General and Governor, arrived at Cape Coast in 1823 and set about organizing an alliance against the Asante. Osei Bonsu began to advance against Wassa and Denkyera. Osei Bonsu died before the issue was resolved.

OSEI YAW AKOTO. Ca. 1800-1833. Asantehene from 1824 to 1833. Half brother of Asantehenes Osei Bonsu and Opoku Fofie. He inherited a war with the British and British allies in which the Asante had just defeated a British force under the command of Governor Charles Macarthy, who was killed, at Nsamankow (Bonsaso or Insamankow) 21 January 1824. The war continued, called by the Asante the Mankatasa War, into 1826. The British mobilized the coastal peoples against the Asante, and on 7 August 1826 a showdown took place between Dodowa and Katamanso (Akantamasu). Asante was defeated, its battered army retreated to Kumasi. The Asante Union was shaken. Tremendous pressure was brought for Osei Yaw Akoto to resign, but he persisted in making peace with the enemy, and in restoring order in Asante affairs. On 27 April 1831 a treaty was reached with the British. British priorities in the south were recognized. The claims of Asante over Akyem, Wassa, Denkyira, Assin, Fante, and Ga was renounced. In return the British guaranteed the Asante free access to coastal trade. At home he tried to consolidate his position. He executed many of those who opposed him in Kumasi, and he sent troops against those who questioned his policies in the provinces. When rebellion brewed in Dwaben, the town was occupied and mostly destroyed. The Dwabenhene and most of the people of Dwaben fled, some into Akyem territory where they found British protection. But Osei Yaw Akoto ruled less than a decade. He died in 1833.

OSU (Orsaky, Christiansborg). One of the original Ga coastal villages, it is today a part of Accra. The Swedes were trading here as early as 1652. In 1661 the Accra ceded a spot to the Danes, who began to build a castle which they named for Christian IV of Denmark. The Castle changed hands several times over the years. The Portuguese called it St. Francis Xavier, 1679-1683. Christiansborg Castle was bought from the Danes by the English in 1850. They moved their headquarters to the Castle in 1874, and in 1957 it became the seat of government for Ghana. It came to be called Government House.

OTI RIVER (Sabran). The major eastern tributary of the Volta River. It drains 18 percent of the Volta Basin, and in a normal year it contributes 30 to 40 percent of the annual flow. It rises in the Atakora Mountains of Benin, flows northwards to the Upper Volta border, then turns sharply to the west, and then flows southwest. It is known as the Pendjari until it enters Togo. Then it becomes the Oti. For some distance it forms the border between Togo and Ghana before cutting across the Northern Region and the Volta Region to enter Lake Volta some 15 miles (24 km) southeast of Bimbila.

OTI AKENTEN. Ca. 1630-Ca. 1660. The third generation Oyoko Royal of the Asante. The first generation were joint leaders, known as Twum and Antwi. They were followed by Kobina Amanfi, who was an uncle of Oti Akenten. Oti Akenten began to establish the Asante in the Kwaman. He was succeeded by his nephew, Obiri Yeboa.

OTU, KWESI. Died 1852. Ruler of Abora, one of the Fante states, from 1820 to 1852. He was one of the allies of the British at Dodowa (Katamanso) in 1826 against Asante. He was a friend of Thomas Birch Freeman and other missionaries, and he became a convert who promoted Christianity and western ways among the Fante.

OWARE (Aware). The national game of the Akan. It is a game for two players who use a board with two parallel rows of six holes. Pebbles are moved between the holes.

OWOKO see OYOKO

OWUSU, VICTOR. Born 1923. Lawyer and politician. Native of Agona-Asante. He was educated at the universities of Nottingham and of London and was called to the English Bar, Lincoln's Inn, in 1952. During the Nkrumah years Owusu developed a reputation as an outstanding lawyer. He was President of the Ghana Bar Association from 1964 to 1967. After the coup of 1966 the NLC made him both Attorney General and Commissioner of Justice. He helped organize the Progress Party and became its national Vice-Chairman. In the 1969 elections he was elected to the National Assembly from the Agona-Kwabre district, and during the Second Republic he was first the Minister for External Affairs, and then the Minister of Justice and Attorney General. The coup of 1972 resulted in his detention along with many of the PP leaders, but in 1978 he helped organize the Front for the Prevention of Dictatorship to campaign against the Union Government plans of the SMC. The movement was banned and Owusu found himself in prison again. After Acheampong was forced out in July of 1978, Owusu was released, but he was disqualified from standing for election or holding office because of "abuse of office." In spite of this, he joined other former Progress Party members in forming a new party, the Popular Front Party (PFP), and he was the presidential candidate of that party. He came in second in the first round of voting, but was defeated by Hilla Limann in the second vote. During the Third Republic Owusu continued as the leader of the PFP. He worked hard to combine all the opposition parties in preparation for the 1983 and 1984 elections. By early December 1981 he had put together the All People's Party (APP). But at the end of the month the PNDC and Jerry Rawlings ended the Third Republic and politics for the moment at least.

OYOKO. One of the principal Akan clans. Osei Tutu, founder of the Asante Union, was a member of this clan, so it is the royal clan of Kumasi.

OYOKO STATES. These are the Asante states which are ruled by members of the Oyoko matriclan. Kumasi, Dwaben, Bekwai, Kokofu, and Nsuta all were ruled by members of the Oyoko matriclan. This gave a sense of fraternity and cohesion to the Asante Union. Mampong was an exception. Its leader was always a member of the Beretuo or Bretuo matriclan.

- P -

PADMORE, GEORGE (Malcolm Nurse). 1903-1959. A native of Trinidad, he attended Fisk, New York, and Howard universities in the United States. He became a member of the Communist Party and adopted the name of George Padmore. In 1929 he went to the Soviet Union and received instruction in working with black workers. From there he went to Germany in 1931 and he became editor there of the Negro Worker. In a short time, though, he was deported, going to England. In England Padmore made contact with many radicals from Commonwealth countries and emerged as a leader in the Pan-African movement. It was in London in 1945 that he met Kwame Nkrumah, and they began the collaboration that continued until Padmore died fourteen years later. After Kwame Nkrumah returned to the Gold Coast, Padmore frequently visited him. In 1953 Padmore published The Gold Coast Revolution. In 1957 George Padmore was an honored guest at the independence ceremonies. Shortly thereafter his friend appointed him head of Ghana's new African Bureau to advance the cause of African unity. When Padmore died in 1959, Nkrumah had him buried at Christiansborg Castle near where W.E.B. Du Bois would be buried in 1963.

PAGA. 10°58' N, 1°06' W. Border village in the Upper Region on the border with Upper Volta. It is 27 miles (43 km) northwest of Bolgatanga in Kasena territory. A notorious crocodile pond is located nearby.

PANYARRING. Seizing or holding a person as security for the payment of a debt. It is called Adwo in Asante.

PARAMOUNT CHIEF. A chief who is not subordinate to another chief.

PAWN. A person held as security for an obligation.

PEKI. 6°32' N, 0°14' E. The chief town of the Krepi people. It is in the Volta Region some 70 miles (112 km) northeast of Accra and near Lake Volta. The name means "later comers." It had a population of 4,158 in 1948, 5,154 in 1960, and 8,054 in 1970.

PEOPLE'S ACTION PARTY (PAP). A political party which contested the election of 1969 and won two seats in the National Assembly. Its leader was Imoru Ayarna. Much of its vote came from the Nzema area of the Western Region, Nkrumah's native area.

PEOPLE'S DEFENSE COMMITTEE (PDC). The basic unit in the government structure set up in 1982 by the PNDC. These committees were to maintain national discipline, supervise national resources, and allow everyone to participate in government. All PDCs were under a National Co-ordinating Committee.

PEOPLE'S MOVEMENT FOR FREEDOM AND JUSTICE (PMFJ). A group organized in January 1978 to oppose the SMU's Union Government proposals. Some of its members were Jones Ofori-Atta, William Ofori-Atta, A.A. Afrifa, Adu Boahen, and Komla A. Gbedemah. It was banned after a few months, and many of its members went to prison.

PEOPLE'S NATIONAL PARTY (PNP). The dominant political party of the Third Republic. Some of its leaders were people, such as Kojo Botsio and Imoru Egala, who had once been close to Nkrumah. Most of the members had been in opposition to Busia during the Second Republic. They had not been unsympathetic to Acheampong, the NRC-SMU, and the idea of Union Government. Their executive candidates, Hilla Limann, nephew of Imoru Egala, and Joseph William Swain de Graft-Johnson, were elected in June 1979. The PNP won 71 of the 140 seats in the National Assembly at the same time.

PEOPLE'S POPULAR FRONT (PPF). A small radical party organized in 1971.

PEOPLE'S POPULAR PARTY (PPP). One of the small parties organized in 1969. Its leaders were Willie Lutterodt and Johnny Hansen. It was left-wing socialist. At first it was disqualified as an attempt to revive Nkrumah's CPP, but the ban was later lifted. In 1979 it became the People's Revolutionary Party (PRP).

PEOPLE'S REVOLUTIONARY PARTY (PRP). A political party organized in 1979 by Johnny Hansen and others to advance the cause of radical socialism. The same group had called themselves the PPP in 1969. The party was disqualified before the balloting in 1979.

PETROLEUM. In mid-1983 Ghana was producing small amounts of oil from a field ten miles (16 km) offshore from Saltpond. Prospect ing was underway in the Gulf of Guinea off Keta, Accra, and Half Assini. The cost of petroleum since 1972 has been a major cause of Ghana's balance-of-payments problems. Ghana operates a refinery at Tema.

PILAPILA. A Gurma group who are scattered all over Ghana, with the greatest numbers in the Eastern and Asante regions.

PINEAPPLE. A popular fruit grown all over southern Ghana.

PIONEER. A newspaper started in Asante at Kumasi in 1939. It was banned by Nkrumah and later by the NRC-SMU. It also was published as the Ashanti Pioneer.

PLANTAIN. A tropical tree with a fruit that resembles a banana. It is one of the major foods of Ghana. The fruit is roasted, boiled, and fried. It is also dried and ground into a meal which is used in cooking.

POLL TAX OF 1852. On 19 April 1852 an assembly of chiefs and elders meeting at Cape Coast Castle with the British Governor and his Council, agreed to an ordinance establishing a poll tax of a shilling on every man, woman, and child in the area under British protection. The proceeds were to be used as salaries for the chiefs and for public services. A similar plan was worked out with chiefs at Accra, but chiefs around Keta refused to agree to a tax. By 1854 general opposition to the tax had developed. The ordinance was amended in May 1858, but after 1862 there was no longer any real attempt to collect the tax.

PONG TAMALE. 9°41' N, 0°49' W. A village on the Great Northern Road in the Northern Region between Tamale and Bolgatanga. It is about 20 miles (32 km) due north of Tamale. In 1948 there were only 409 people living there, but by 1970 the population had grown to 3,222. The chief veterinary center in northern Ghana is located here.

POPULAR FRONT PARTY (PFP). A political party organized in 1979 under the leadership of Victor Owusu, Joseph Mensah, Jones Ofori-Atta, and other former colleagues of K.A. Busia from the Progress Party of the Second Republic. The party was in favor of free enterprise, and was pro-West. The PFP won 42 seats in the June 1979 elections, and their candidate for president came in second. Victor Owusu, the candidate, came in first in Asante, Brong-Ahafo, and the Northern regions, and went into the runoff with Limann (PNP), who won. In the July runoff the PFP got 38 percent of the vote. In late 1981 the PFP merged into the coalition called the All People's Party (APP). A few days later the PNDC and Rawlings ended political activity.

POSITIVE ACTION. In October 1949 Kwame Nkrumah published a

pamphlet, "What I Mean by Positive Action," calling for strikes, boycotts, and noncooperation unless the British granted immedaate self-government to the Gold Coast. He announced that the campaign was beginning in January 1950.

THE POST. A bimonthly publication started by the Ghanaian government Information Services 2 January 1980. At that time the Information Services also published The Ghana Review, a quarterly pictorial magazine, and Today in Ghana, a booklet on aspects of life in Ghana. In addition to these, in 1980 the Information Service published eight Ghanaian language newspapers each month.

POSUBAN. Fante altars.

PRA. River which, with its tributaries, the Ofin, the Oda, the Fum, and the Birim, drains much of southern Ghana. It flows into the Gulf of Guinea near Shama, about eight miles (13 km) east of Sekondi. It is crossed by a suspension bridge six miles (ten km) inland, near Beposo. The river serves as a boundary between Asante and three other regions. It has played an important role in the history of the Akan peoples.

PRAMPRAM (Gbugbla). 5°42' N, 0°07' E. Coastal Adangbe Village in the Eastern Region a short distance east of Tema. It is about 30 miles (48 km) east of Accra. The Dodowa River enters the Gulf just east of town. The British built Fort Vernon here at the start of the nineteenth century, but abandoned it by 1820. The population of Prampram in 1970 was 3,729.

PRANG. 7°59' N, 0°53' W. Town in the Brong-Ahafo Region on the Great Northern Road, about half way between Atebubu and the ferry across Lake Volta at Yeji. It is close to the Pru branch of Lake Volta. It is a major stopping place on the cattle drives from Upper Volta to Kumasi.

PRASU (Praso). 5°56' N, 1°22' W. The name means "Pra water." It is a key town, located on the Pra River, on the Cape Coast-Kumasi highway, halfway between these two cities. For many years this was the border between Asante and British protected territories.

PREMPE I (Kwaku Dua III, Agyeman Prempeh, "Tubby"). Ca. 1873-1931. Asantehene, 1888-1931. Exile, 1896-1924. He was a brother of Kwaku Dua II, who died in 1884, beginning an interregnum of four years. In March 1888, at sixteen, he became Asantehene-designate as Kwaku Dua III. Kokofu, Mampong, and Nsuta objected, and civil war resulted. The rebels appealed to the British for support. He was finally enstooled in June 1894, with Mampong and Kokofu taking part in the ceremony, but there was much discontent in Asante territories, and frequent campaigns were necessary to maintain order. The British used the turmoil as justification for intervention into Asante affairs, and in January 1896 the British invaded Asante and occupied Kumasi 17 January 1896. Prempe was arrested, and the Asante state was declared dissolved by the British. Prempe and his family were taken first to Elmina, then Sierra Leone, and finally to the Indian Ocean Seychelles Islands, from which Prempe I was not allowed to return until 1924. At first the British treated him as a private citizen, but in 1926 they did recognize him as Kumasihene. He died in 1931.

PREMPE II (Edward Prempe Owusu, Kwame Kyeretwie, Osei Agyeman Prempeh). 1892-1970. Kumasihene, 1931-1935. Asantehene, 1935-1970. He was a nephew of Prempe I. Before he became Kumasihene he was a storekeeper in Kumasi, but he was one of the founders of the Asante Kotoko Union Society in 1916, and he played an active role in the campaign for the return of his exiled uncle to the Gold Coast. After the death of Prempe I in 1931, he became Kumasihene, and in 1935, after the British allowed the restoration of the Asante Union, he became the Asantehene. From that time until his death in 1970 he was an important influence in Gold Coast affairs. He often was opposed to British policy, but he was also opposed to moves that might create disorder and revolution. He never trusted Kwame Nkrumah and the CPP Veranda Boys, and his relations with Nkrumah were always strained. After independence Nkrumah quickly centralized power over Ghana in his own hands. Half of Asante was sliced away as the Brong-Ahafo Region. From that time on Prempe II withdrew from national politics, though he was elected President of the National House of Chiefs in 1969 a short time before his death.

PREMPEH COLLEGE. Secondary school founded in Kumasi in 1949. It is located in the western outskirts of the town, just off the Western By-Pass and the Sunyani roads.

PRESIDENT'S OWN GUARD REGIMENT (POGR). This military group was first established 1 October 1960 as an honor guard, but within a year it had become a private army, supervised in part by officers from Communist countries. By 1965 the POGR had two battalions with 50 officers, 1,100 men, and the most modern equipment in the Ghanaian army. It was directly responsible to the President rather than the regular military commanders. The POGR was abolished after the 1966 coup toppled President Nkrumah.

PRESTEA. 5°26' N, 2°09' W. Mining town located 20 miles (32 km) northwest of Tarkwa in the Western Region. It is near the Ankobra River and is the terminal of a rail line from Sekondi. Oil palms are important to the economy of the area. The population of the town in 1948 was 6,293. By 1960 it had grown to 13,246, and in 1970 the census stood at 15,143.

PREVENTIVE DETENTION ACT (PDA). The bitter relations between members of the NLM and CPP made it dangerous for CPP members, even if they were officers of the government, to enter Asante, especially Kumasi. This bitterness caused the CPP to introduce the PDA in July of 1958. The PDA empowered the government to arrest and detain any enemy of the state or any person who was a threat to state security, for up to five years. The PDA was renewed in June 1962 and in May 1964. It ended with the coup of 1966.

PRINCE'S TOWN (Pokesu, Pokoso). 4°47' N, 2°08' W. Ahanta coastal town in the Western Region just west of Cape Three Points and some 47 miles (76 km) west of Sekondi-Takoradi. It was an outpost of Brandenburg by 1682, and they built Friedrichsburg Castle here about 1684. This was acquired by the Dutch by 1725. They called it Fort Hollandia. Some restoration has been done on the Fort in recent times.

PRINSENSTEN, FORT (Prinzenstein). The Danes established a post at Keta in the early eighteenth century. The Dutch soon replaced the Danes, but in turn were forced out by Akwamu in 1731. The Danes returned in 1737, but Prinsensten was not built until 1784. It was purchased by the British in 1850.

PROGRAM FOR WORK AND HAPPINESS. A plan to build a socialist Ghana introduced by Nkrumah and the CPP in 1962. The first stage of the program was launched in March 1964.

PROGRESS PARTY (PP). The dominant political party of the Second Republic, 1969-1972. The party was organized in 1969, mostly of people who had once been members of the United Party (UP). Kofi Abrefa Busia, Victor Owusu, William Ofori-Atta, and much of the Akan middle-class belonged to the PP. The PP won an impressive victory in August 1969, with 105 seats in the National Assembly to 29 seats for the opposition National Alliance of Liberals (NAL), and five other seats for minor parties. Busia became Prime Minister in the Second Republic. The coup of 1972 ended his administration.

PROTECTORATE. Territory under protection of the British. It meant different areas at different times. Before 1874 it was limited to coastal areas. After 1902 it meant the Northern Territories.

PROVINCIAL COUNCILS OF CHIEFS. In March 1918 the chiefs of the Eastern Province of the Gold Coast began to meet for mutual consultation. The 1925 constitutional changes provided for three Provincial Councils of Chiefs. The Western Council, with 20 paramount stools, could elect one member of the Legislative Council; the Central Province, with 27 paramount stools, could have two members of the Legislative Council; and the Eastern Council

with 13 paramount stools, was allowed three members of the
Legislative Council. The Provincial Councils gave chiefs a
chance to consult together, and to make their positions known
to the British. The first meetings under the 1925 provisions
were held in May 1926.

PROVISIONAL NATIONAL DEFENSE COUNCIL (PNDC). The central
committee of the government established by Flight Lieutenant
Jerry Rawlings the night of 31 December 1981. It was made up
of three soldiers--a flight lieutenant, a brigadier, and a sergeant; and three civilians--a priest, a trade union leader, and
a student leader. Rawlings had replaced most of these within
a year.

PRU. Tributary of the Volta which rises on the border of Brong-Ahafo and Asante near Bechem. Most of the Pru's tributaries
rise between Wenchi, Techiman, and Bechem and flow northeast.
The Pru reaches Lake Volta just below the ferry at Yeji. Many
of these streams are dry from November to March.

PUSIGA. 11°05' N, 0°07' W. Village in the Upper East Region some
eight miles (13 km) east of Bawku, and near the borders of
Togo and Upper Volta. It is here that Gbewa founded the Mole-Dagbani dynasty that founded many states in northern Ghana
and Upper Volta. The Kusasi, who live in Pusiga, are one of
these Mole-Dagbani peoples. The Mossi, Mamprusi, Dagomba,
Nanumba, etc., trace their origins to Pusiga. In 1970 there
were fewer than 2,000 persons in the village.

- Q -

QUAHOE (Quahu) see KWAHU

QUAISON-SACKEY, ALEX. Born 1924. Attorney, politician, diplomat, author. A native of Winneba, Quaison-Sackey was educated at Mfantsipim, Achimota, Exeter, Oxford, London School
of Economics, Tours, and read law at Lincoln's Inn. He was
employed in the Gold Coast-Ghana Civil Service until appointed
Ghanaian representative in the UN, 1959-1965, during which
time he was also Ghana's ambassador to Cuba and Mexico. He
was Africa's first President of the UN General Assembly, 1964-1965. He was Foreign Minister of Ghana in 1965 and until the
1966 coup. In 1963 he published Africa Unbound. In 1977 he
organized the Patriotic Movement to support the SMCs Union
Government without political parties plan. Acheampong, in January 1978, appointed him as ambassador to Washington.

QUAQUA. The area to the west of the Gold Coast-Ghana. The
Ivory Coast.

QUAQUE, PHILIP (Quacoe). 1741-1816. A native of Cape Coast, he was sent to England to be educated by the Society for the Propagation of the Gospel in 1754. He was ordained an Anglican priest while still in London in 1765, and he married an English girl. In 1766 he returned to Cape Coast as a missionary and schoolmaster. He also served as chaplain at Cape Coast Castle until he died in 1816.

QUASHIE, TETTEH (Tete Kwashi, Tetti Quashi, Tetteh Kwashi, Tetteh Quarshie). 1842-1892. Born at Osu, he was trained as a blacksmith at a Basel Mission. In 1870 he went to Fernando Poo (Bioko, Equatorial Guinea) and worked on a cocoa plantation for eight years. Returning home in 1878, he brought some cocoa pods, which he planted at Mampong in Akuapem. He made his first harvest in 1883. The Basel Misison had planted cocoa pods in Akuapem two decades earlier, but little developed from their efforts. The Ghanaian cocoa industry was to develop from Tetteh Quashie (Quarshie) and his efforts.

QUIFORO see TWIFO

QUIST, EMMANUEL CHARLES. 1880-1959. A native of Christiansborg who was of Ga-Dutch extraction; he was educated at Basel Mission schools at Christiansborg and Akuropon. He went on to England and read law at the Middle Temple. Returning to Accra, he served on the Town Council there from 1919 to 1929. He became the first African to be a Crown Counsel in 1914. He was a member of the Legislative Council in 1925 and 1934, and served as President of the Legislative Council from 1949 to 1950. He then became the first Speaker of the Gold Coast-Ghana National Assembly, 1951-1957.

- R -

RAILROADS. Ghana has a rail system with a route length of just under 600 miles (966 km). The Western Line from Sekondi to Kumasi is the oldest, built between 1898 and 1903, and partly rebuilt between 1919 and 1926. A branch from Tarkwa to Prestea was added, 1908-1911. The track from Sekondi to Kumasi covers just under 170 miles (274 km). The Eastern Accra-Kumasi line was started in 1909 and not finished until 1923. The distance for the Eastern is 188 miles (303 km). A Central line was run 99 miles (160 km) from the Huni Valley junction with the Western line to Kade between 1922 and 1927. In 1956 the triangle from Accra to Sekondi to Kumasi was completed with a line from Achiasi, below Oda, to Kotoku, below Nsawam. This tied the Western and Eastern lines. A final rail line from Achimota to Tema and the Shai Hills was opened in 1954. There were elaborate plans for lines north of Kumasi in 1927. Plans were for a great circle from Kumasi to Tamale to Naga to Navrongo, and from Naga to Wa to Bole, and back to Kumasi. The depression of the 1930s and World War II ended all such dreams. As of 1983, the whole rail system of Ghana is in a state of disrepair. Equipment and roadbeds are worn out.

RAMSEYER, FRIEDRICH AUGUST, and JOHANNES KUHNE. Two Germans who were captured by the Asante at Anum in Peki in 1869 and held as hostages in Kumasi, with M.J. Bonnat, until 1874. They wrote an account of their adventures, Four Years in Ashantee.

RATTRAY, ROBERT SUTHERLAND. 1881-1938. Colonial officer, anthropologist, folklorist, and ethnographer. Rattray was a Scotsman, born in India. In 1906 he joined the Gold Coast Customs Service on the Volta River. In 1911 he became assistant District Commissioner at Ejura, on the Great Northern Road, above Mampong in Asante. By 1914 he had learned both Mossi and Akan (Twi). He went on to become a DC, but administration had lost its appeal, and in 1921 he was appointed the one and only head of the Anthropological Department of Asante. He retired from that position nine years later, and he was killed while flying a glider in 1938. All told, he published twelve volumes of ethnography and folklore. His books on the Asante and the people of the Asante hinterland are masterpieces from which all study of northern Ghana must begin.

RAWLINGS, JERRY JOHN. Born 1947. Of mixed Ewe-Scottish background, Jerry John Rawlings was born in Accra 22 June 1947, attended Achimota, and was enrolled at the Military Academy at Teshi in 1968. He was commissioned a lieutenant in 1969, took flight training at Takoradi, and became a flight lieutenant in 1978. He took part in an attempted coup 15 May 1979 against the SMC and was arrested. He was released from prison by another coup on 4 June 1979, and he became chairman of the Armed Forces Revolutionary Council (AFRC), which ruled Ghana only until 24 September 1979, when he turned the reins of power over to an elected government. In that brief period of less than four months the AFRC undertook a systematic purge of the SMU leaders. Three former heads of state and many high-ranking officers were executed, and many people were sent to prison after summary trials. After Limann became President of the Third Republic, he nominated Rawlings to serve on the Council of State, but Rawlings refused the appointment. On 27 November 1979 Rawlings was retired from the army on the grounds that his position as a flight lieutenant was not compatible with his status as a former head of state. Relations between Limann and Rawlings were increasingly strained as the problems of Limann and his PNP grew in magnitude. Rumors of a new plot for a coup by Rawlings and his friend, Kojo Tsikata, abounded. On 31 December 1981 they destroyed the Third Republic with almost no effort, and they established the rule of the Provisional

National Defense Council. Once more Jerry John Rawlings became head of state.

RED VOLTA. A stream which begins to the northwest of Ouagadougou in Upper Volta and enters Ghana in the Upper Region northeast of Bolgatanga. A short distance from Gambaga it joins the White Volta. Its course in Ghana is just over 30 miles (48 km).

REGIONS. Before 1951 the Gold Coast was divided into the Gold Coast Colony, Ashanti (Asante), and the Northern Territories Protectorate. These three parts were administered from Accra, Kumasi, and Tamale. The Colony had been created in 1874, with part of the Togo Trust Territory added to the Colony in 1919. Ashanti was created in 1901, and the Northern Territories Protectorate was also organized in 1901. The North also got part of the Togo Trust in 1919.

From 1951 a new system of divisions began to emerge. Trans-Volta-Togo Region was created in 1952, to be managed from Ho. It would become the Volta Region. The Colony was divided into an Eastern and a Western Region and Greater Accra. Brong-Ahafo was separated from Ashanti in 1958. The Regions of Ghana Act of 29 June 1960 adjusted all the boundaries and created the Central Region from the Western Region, and the Upper Region from the Northern Region. In 1982 the PNDC divided the Upper Region into Upper West and Upper East.

REINDORF, CARL CHRISTIAN. 1834-1917. Son of a Danish father and Ga mother, Reindorf was born at Prampram. He became a minister and teacher with the Basel Misison. He took part in a project to translate the Bible into Ga, published in 1912. His greatest work was History of the Gold Coast and Asante, completed in 1889, and published by the Basel Mission in 1895. The history is based on the oral traditions of the Akan, and it is the first history of a West African area written by an African.

RELIGION. In 1960 some 60 percent of Ghanaians who answered the census takers professed to be Christian. Sixteen percent said they were Catholic, with about the same number saying they were Methodist. About 14 percent claimed to be Presbyterian, and 6 percent Anglican. Seventeen percent answered that they were Muslim, 8.7 percent Maliki, 7.6 percent Ahmadiya, and less than one percent Shafi. Traditional religion (Animism) got only 15.9 percent response and 6.9 percent said they had no religion. As might be expected, the Muslims and traditionalists were strongest in the north. Islamic faith was also strong among those peoples who had come from Nigeria. The Catholics were strongest in the Volta Region, where the Presbyterians were also strong. In recent years there has been a rapid growth of what is called the "Spiritual Churches." These groups mix Christianity with traditional beliefs. They believe in faith healing, the use of drums, cymbals, dancing, bearing witness, and total involvement of the entire congregation in worship. Some of the syncretic sects are the Aladuras, the Church of the Lords, the Light of the Worlds, Olumba Olumbas, and Musama Disco Christo.

RODGER, JOHN PICKERSGILL. 1851-1910. Governor of the Gold Coast, 1904-1910. He was a graduate of Eton and Christ Church, Oxford, and was called to the bar at the Inner Temple in 1877. He served in the Malay States for several years before going to the Gold Coast as its Chief Executive. He died in office.

ROWE, SAMUEL. 1835-1888. Governor of the Gold Coast, 1881-1884. He was an army surgeon who was posted to Lagos in 1862. He took part in the Asante campaign of 1873, was Lieutenant-Governor of the West African Settlements in 1875, Administrator of the Gambia, 1875-1877, Governor of the West African Settlements, 1877-1881, Governor of the Gold Coast, 1881-1884, and Governor of Sierra Leone from 1885 until he died in office, 1888. Rowe believed in indirect rule through the chiefs.

ROYAL AFRICAN COMPANY. A joint-stock company chartered in 1672. On the Gold Coast it operated Cape Coast Castle and a number of subordinate trade posts. It had a monopoly until 1698, but expenses were high, and the government offered it subsidies after 1730. After 1751 the African Company of Merchants took over control of Gold Coast trade, even though the Royal African Company continued to own its properties until the properties were assumed by the Crown in 1821.

ROYAL WEST AFRICAN FRONTIER FORCE (RWAFF). A West African military force created by the Colonial Office in 1897. At first called the West African Frontier Force, the Royal was added to the name in 1928. During World War I, the Gold Coast Regiment of the WAFF saw service in Togo, the Cameroons, and East Africa. In 1940 it was sent to Kenya, Italian Somali, and Ethiopia. In 1943 the Gold Coast Regiment went to Burma. The WAFF was originally created to act as a constabulary force. Most of the recruits, especially in the Gold Coast, came from Muslim peoples in the Northern Territories, so they were often called Hausa, because the Hausa were usually identified as Muslim. By 1957, when the RWAFF became the Ghanaian army, about 10 percent of the officers were Africans. Headquarters for the Ghanaian troops was at Burma Camp, Accra, from World War II.

RUYGHAVER, FORT. A base built by the Dutch in 1653 some 60 miles (96 km) up the Ankobra River. The Dutch hoped to control the gold trade of the area from this point. The fort was named for the Dutch Director-General on the Gold Coast at this time. His name was Jacob Ruyghaver. Unable to maintain a garrison so far from the coast, the Dutch destroyed their own building in 1658. The location of the site is not far from modern Prestea in the Western Region.

- S -

SABARI (Sabare). 9°17' N, 0°16' E. Village in the Northern Region 23 miles (37 km) southeast of Yendi on the old Hausa caravan route to Salaga. It was near a crossing of the Oti River. Muhammad Zangina had a Mosque built here, and it became a Muslim center.

SABOE   see   ASEBU

SABRAN   see   OTI

SAFORI   see   OFORI KUMA I

SAGBADRE WAR. The struggle between Anlo and Denmark in 1783 caused by an Anlo attack on a Danish trader. Anlo was defeated, and a peace treaty was signed in 1784. The Danes built several forts near the mouth of the Volta to maintain the peace after this.

SAGRENTI WAR. The Asante name for the campaign between the British and Asante in 1873-1874. Sagrenti was the Akan name for the British Commander, Sir Garnet Wolseley. The British invasion was also called the Toto War, in imitation of the sound of English guns.

SAHWI   see   SEFWI

SAINT JOHN RIVER. European name for the Pra River.

SALAGA (Saharah). 8°33' N, 0°31' W. A village in the eastern Gonja area of the Northern Region which flourished from around 1800 to 1874. Its reason for existence was the slave and kola trade between Asante and peoples along the Niger. It started as a small Nanumba village, grew into a busy Gonja trade center, and declined rapidly as Asante withered from British attacks. Dr. V.S. Gouldsbury, an Englishman, was the first European to see Salaga. He reached Salaga in 1876, shortly after Salaga began to die. There were still traces of the former prosperity. The Frenchman Louis Binger arrived twelve years later, after the decline was far advanced. Binger described Salaga as a ruined city. The Germans actually did destroy the place in 1896, but the British made a feeble attempt to restore it after 1898. There were 2,059 people there in 1911, by 1960 this was up to 4,200, and in 1970 the census showed over 6,400 inhabitants.

SALLAH CASE. In 1970 the Busia government dismissed E.K. Sallah from his position as a manager of the Ghana National Trading Corporation. The courts ruled that Sallah was illegally dismissed and ordered the government to reemploy Sallah. Busia refused, and the opposition used the case to denounce the PP and Busia's regime.

SALTPOND (Nankesidu). 5°12' N, 1°04' W. Coastal town in the Central Region Fante area between Anomabo and Ankoful. The town was a focal point for political meetings in the period just before independence. The population was 3,540 in 1911, 6,968 in 1948, 9,869 in 1960, and had reached 11,849 by 1970.

SAM, ALFRED. Ca. 1880-Ca. 1934. An Akyem merchant who started a movement to encourage Afro-Americans to move to the Akyem area of the Gold Coast during the period just before and during the early part of World War I. The movement was not a success.

SAMAN (pl. Asaman). A ghost or ancestral spirit. The form the dead take when becoming visible to living humans.

SAMORI (Samori Toure, Samory). Ca. 1830-1900. Dyula leader who came originally from Guinea. In the 1860s he built a state around Bisandugu in Guinea and began to expand into the area of modern Mali. His state had elements of an Islamic theocracy. By the late 1880s the expansive designs of Samori clashed with the plans for expansion of the French. So in 1894 Samori moved his center of operations to Dabakala in modern Ivory Coast. From here he planned to build a new nation by expanding north and east. To make his position stronger he offered an alliance to Prempe I of Asante. In reply, in October 1895, Prempe asked Samori to help the Asante reestablish their former power in the Gold Coast. The British moved quickly to head off such an association. In January 1896 a British expeditionary force occupied Kumasi, and Prempe was sent into exile. Samori's forces, under his son Sarankenyi-Mori, crossed the Black Volta and moved freely back and forth in the area between Bole and Tumu. For a time there was even a possibility of cooperation between Samori and Babatu against the Europeans. In November 1896 the British sent forces toward Wa to clear the east bank of the Black Volta of the forces of Samori. In fighting during March and April 1897 Samori's troops had the upper hand. They captured the English commander, Francis Henderson. But by May Samori moved his army into western Upper Volta, and the threat to what is today the Northern and Upper West regions of Ghana diminished. Months later Samori was captured by the French and exiled to Gabon, where he died in 1900. Today he is remembered as a tyrant in the lands he conquered, but to African nationalists he is a hero of the resistance to European imperialism.

SAMPA. 7°57' N, 2°42' W. Town on the Ivory Coast frontier in the Brong-Ahafo area. The Tain River rises nearby. The population in 1948 was 1,687. By 1970 the population had grown to 3,906.

SAMPSON, MAGNUS JOHN. 1900-1958. Teacher and writer. He was a member of the Coussey Committee on Constitutional Reform in 1949, and the Legislative Assembly, 1951-1954. His Gold Coast Men of Affairs, published in 1937, is his best-known work. A Political Retrospect of the Gold Coast, 1860-1930 (n.d.) and West African Leadership: Public Speeches Delivered by J.E. Casely Hayford (1940) were examples of the growing interest in local history in the Gold Coast on the eve of independence.

SAMREBOI. 5°36' N, 2°34' W. Town in the Western Region located at the junction of the Tano River and one of its tributaries, the Samre. The town is in the heart of a timber region, and a plywood factory is located here. In 1948 the population was 2,141. By 1970 the census showed 7,151 people in Samreboi.

SAN ANTONIO (Santo Antonio de Axem). This fort was the second base established by the Portuguese on the Gold Coast. The Portuguese were first here in 1503, but the triangular fort was started about 1515. It was taken by the Dutch in 1642 and became British in 1872. The structure was restored in the 1950s, and today it is used by the town of Axim as council and police offices.

SAN JAGO (San Iago, Coenraadsburg). The Portuguese first built a structure here on a hill in Elmina at the start of the sixteenth century. The Dutch fort was built in the 1650s and enlarged in 1671. San Jago or Coenraadsburg became British in 1872. Today it is maintained by the Museum and Monuments Board.

SAN JORGE (São Jorge de Mina, St. George's, Elmina Castle). This is the oldest and most impressive of all the structures standing in Ghana today. The location and some of the site preparation took place at Edinaa (Ednaa) in 1480 or 1481. In December 1481 more than 600 men sailed from Portugal under the command of Diogo de Azambuja for the Gold Coast. Bartholomew Diaz was one of those with the fleet. Christopher Columbus may have been part of the expedition. The fleet brought much of the building material from Portugal. The Castle served as the Portuguese headquarters from 1482 to 1637, then it served the Dutch as their trade center from 1637 to 1872, when it became British. Many changes have been made over the years.

SAN SEBASTIAN. Fort San Sebastian was built by the Portuguese at Shama around 1560. This was east of modern Sekondi, and near the mouth of the Pra. It was soon taken by the Dutch, who enlarged it between 1640 and 1642. It was acquired by the

English in 1872 and restored in the 1950s. It is used for offices today.

SANKANA. 10°12' N, 2°35' W. Place in the Upper Region West where Samori's son, Sarankenyi-Mori, and Babatu met in August 1896.

SANTEMANSO see ASANTEMANSO

SANTROKOFI. A small Central Togo-Volta group. About 3,000 live in the Buem-Krakye area of the Volta Region.

SARANKENYI-MORI (Sarangue Mori, Sarangye Mori, Sarantye More). The son of Samori Toure and leader of Samori's army in what is today the Northern Region and Upper West Region, 1896-1897.

SARBAH, JOHN MENSAH (Kofi Mensah). 1864-1910. He was born at Cape Coast and was the son of one of the outstanding merchants of the Fante coast. He was educated in law at Lincoln Inn in London, and he became the first Gold Coaster to be licensed to practice law. He founded the Gold Coast People, which he published from 1891 to 1898. He was one of the founders of the Gold Coast Aborigines' Rights Society in 1897. He published his Fanti Customary Laws in 1897, Fanti Law Reports in 1904, and the Fanti National Constitution in 1906. He was most interested in education, was active in founding and supporting the Collegiate School at Cape Coast, and helped create Mfantsipim School in 1904. He was a member of the Legislative Council from 1901 until his death. Mensah Sarbah Hall at the University of Ghana, Legon, is named in his honor.

SARI, SARKIN. The chief of a zongo or strangers quarter in a town.

SASA. An invisible, destructive power which can work evil.

SASABOR WAR, 1693. A war between Agona and her Fante neighbors in which Agona was defeated.

SASRAKU ANSA I. Died 1689. The seventh paramount chief of Akwamu. He was the ruler of Akwamu at its point of greatest expansion. He conquered the Ga and began the subjection of Ladoku.

SAVELUGU. 9°37' N, 0°49' W. Farm center in the Northern Region on the Great Northern Road some 20 miles (32 km) north of Tamale. It is one of the three chief divisional towns of Dagomba. The census of 1948 showed a population of 5,878. By 1970 there were 9,895 listed as living in Savelugu.

SEDITION ORDINANCE, 1934. This expansion of the definition of sedition by the Legislative Council in 1934, during the depression, stirred up a great protest in Accra and Cape Coast.

SEFWI (Sahwi, Sehwi, Encassar, Inkassa). Anyi-Bawle Akan group which once covered much of what is today the Western Region north of the Aowin and Wassa. Today they are mostly located between Wiawso and Bibiani between the Tano and Ankobra rivers. They were dominated by Denkyira during the latter part of the seventeenth century and by Asante after 1717. In 1717 the Sefwi invaded Asante and sacked Kumasi. Members of the royal family, including the Asantehene Opoku Ware's mother, were murdered. The royal mausoleums were plundered. In response the Asante conquered all of Sefwi and annexed it to Asante. Sefwi continued to be a part of Asante until 1887. There are three divisions of Sefwi today: Sefwi Anwiawso (Anhwiaso), located near the source of the Ankobra River at 6°20' N, 2°16' W; Sefwi Bekwai, the smallest division, located at 6°11' N, 2°19' W; and Wiawso, on the Tano River at 6°12' N, 2°29' W.

SEKONDI. 4°56' N, 1°42' W. A coastal city in the Ahanta part of the Western Region. It is the twin city of Takoradi. Today they are regarded as one town. At one time Sekondi was regarded as an important port, but after the modern port was opened at Takoradi the Sekondi docks were no longer important. The Dutch built Fort Orange at Sekondi in 1640. Today the fort is a lighthouse. The town is the terminus of the railroads to Kumasi and Accra. In 1948 there were 26,571 people in Sekondi and 43,700 in Sekondi and Takoradi together. By 1960 there were 34,513 in Sekondi and 120,793 in both Sekondi and Takoradi together.

SEKYERE. A district of Asante north and northeast of Kumasi between the upper Ofin river and the Afram river. Dwaben and Mampong are in this area.

SEKYI, WILLIAM E. (Kobina Sekyi). 1892-1956. He was born in Cape Coast, where his father was the headmaster of the Wesleyan School. He attended Mfantsipim and the University of London and became a lawyer in 1919. He was president of the ARPS for many years and was an active nationalist who advocated the ideas of Marcus Garvey and was active in the National Congress of British West Africa. He was a member of the Coussey Committee on constitutional reform in 1949. In 1918 he wrote The Anglo-Fante, the first English language novel written in the Cape Coast. His play, The Blinkards, a satire on Africans who try to act like Europeans, was published posthumously in 1974.

SENCHI RAPIDS. 6°12' N, 0°05' E. This is the limit of navigation on the Volta in the wet season. The Senchi Ferry, operated by the United Africa Company from 1920 to 1956, was once a famous institution. Ebenezer Cato and subsequently his son, James Cato, were captains. The Ferry closed in 1956 when the Adomi Bridge opened to traffic.

SENYA. A Guan group who live on the coast in the Gomoa district at Senya Beraku.

SENYA BERAKU (Bereku). 5°23' N, 0°29' W. A Gomoa coastal village east of Winneba in the Central Region. The Dutch built a post here in 1667 and started to build Fort Goede Hoop (Good Hope) in 1706. From time to time the British took over the Dutch post, and it was transferred to the British in 1868. The village was long famous for its iron and gold smiths who produced fine jewelry, chains, weapons, and metalwork. The population was 9,921 in 1970.

SEVEN-YEAR PLAN FOR WORK AND HAPPINESS. A plan introduced by President Nkrumah in 1961. It declared socialism to be the national objective of Ghana. Nkrumah promised self-sustaining industrial growth by 1967.

SHAI. An Adangbe group who are related to the Ada and Krobo. Most of the Shai live in the Accra District or the Eastern Region between Accra and the Volta Region.

SHAI HILLS. Inselbergs or hills in the Accra Plain above Tema, and between Dodowa and Senchi. The Adangbe live in this area.

SHAMA (Samma). 5°01' N, 1°38' W. Eguafo coastal town in the Western Region near the mouth of the Pra River and about six miles (ten km) to the east of Sekondi. The Portuguese bought gold here in 1472, and reported that the village had 800 inhabitants. For a decade, until Elmina Castle was finished, Shama was the chief Portuguese trade post. San Sebastian was started around 1560. The Dutch took the place in 1640 and rebuilt San Sebastian in 1666. It became British in 1872. The population of the town was 5,155 in 1948 and 7,739 in 1970.

SHEA TREE (Karite). The Butyrospermum parkii is most important tree in the Northern and Upper regions. The fruit resembles a yellow plum and contains a sweet pulp which is edible when ripe. Shea butter is obtained from oil in the kernels of the nuts. Shea oil is used for cooking, as an illuminant, as an ointment, and as a hairdressing.

SHIENE HILLS see ZABZUGU HILLS

SIKA DWA see GOLDEN STOOL

SILK-COTTON TREE (Kapok). The Ceiba pentandra is one of the monarchs of Ghanaian forests. It can grow to a height of 200 feet (60 m) and is highly regarded for making canoes.

SILVER STOOL. Stools of Mampong, Techiman, and the Asante Queen Mother.

SINGELENBURGH, FORT. A Dutch fort built at Keta in 1734 and blown up in 1737.

SISALA (Isala, Sissala, Pasala). A Grusi group in the Upper West Region on the Upper Volta border and between the Kulpawn and Sisili rivers. Dr. Hilla Limann, President in the Third Republic, came from this group. The Vagala and Kasena are closely related to the Sisala.

SISILI (Sissili). A tributary of the Kulpawn that flows intermittently from the Upper Volta border southward to join the Kulpawn at 10°16' N, 1°15' W, near the village of Yagaba, and on the border between the Upper and Northern regions.

SITOBU (Sitobo). One of the sons of Gbewa of Pusiga and the father of Nyagse of Dagomba. Sitobu lived probably in the fifteenth century. One brother, Tohogo, founded Mamprusi. Another brother, Nnantombo, founded Nanumba. Sitobu settled awhile at Gambaga, and then lived at Savelugu, north of Tamale. He is buried at Bagale at the mausoleum of the Dagomba Nas. His son Nyagse was the first ruler of Dagomba.

SKIN. Symbol of authority in northern Ghana comparable to the Stool among the Akan or a throne in Europe.

SLATER, ALEXANDER RANSFORD. 1874-1940. Governor of the Gold Coast. He attended King Edward's School in Birmingham and Emmanuel College, Cambridge. He was Colonial Secretary of the Gold Coast from 1914 to 1922. During this period he was acting governor several times. He was Governor of Sierra Leone, 1922 to 1927, and of the Gold Coast from 1927 to 1932. During his administration he was most interested in expanding the transportation system of the Gold Coast, but little was accomplished because of the depression. After he left Accra he served as Governor of Jamaica, 1932-1934.

SLOAN, PATRICK. English Marxist who joined the staff of Kwame Nkrumah's Ideological Institute at Winneba in 1961. He became an adviser to Nkrumah. Late in 1964 he suggested that all materials critical of socialism be purged from Ghana. This resulted in the establishment of a committee of nine, under Professor William E. Abraham of the University at Legon, in November 1964. The committee began work on a system to identify and remove anti-socialist literature.

SMITH, JOHN HOPE. The last Chief Agent of the Company of Merchants Trading to Africa at Cape Coast. He replaced Joseph Dawson in January 1817, and he held the position as President of the Council of Merchants at Cape Coast until the charter of the company was revoked by the Crown. He was replaced by Governor Charles Macarthy of Sierra Leone in March 1822. During Smith's stay at Cape Coast the Bowdich mission to Kumasi in 1817 and the Dupuis mission of 1820 opened direct contact between the British and Kumasi for the first time. Asantehene Osei Bonsu agreed to allow a British Resident at Kumasi and to recognize the British as mediators in Asante-Fante relations. The English were to guarantee Asante trade on the coast. Misunderstandings persisted throughout the period. Osei Bonsu was willing to admit subservience to the British so long as the British would recognize Asante dominion over the Fante. Smith refused to recognize Asante sovereignty over the coastal people or responsibility for Asante. Smith and his council at Cape Coast refused to even deal with the Asantehene's ambassadors and began to prepare for a showdown. Meantime the English Parliament abolished the company and placed the Gold Coast settlements under the Governor of Sierra Leone. War between the Asante and the British soon followed.

SOBORE. The chief deity of Sefwi.

SOCCO see BEGHO

SOCIAL DEMOCRATIC FRONT (SDF). A political party in the 1979 elections. The party was a merger of trade union people and social democrats who during the Second Republic had been members of the National Alliance of Liberals and the Justice Party. The party called for the creation of a socialist state. The SDF was dominated by northerners, and their candidate for president in the 18 June 1979 election was a Dagomba, Dr. Ibrahim Mahama. Alhaji M.A. Issifu was the party leader. The SDF won three seats in the Assembly and their candidate for president came in fifth.

SOCIETE COMMERCIALE DE L'OUEST AFRICAIN (SCOA). Swiss commercial firm which purchased cocoa in Gold Coast for the Swiss chocolate industry from 1914 until after 1957.

SOGAKOFE (Sogakope, Sogakorpe). 6°00' N, 0°36' E. Town on the Volta River about 25 miles (40 km) north of Ada. It is at the bridge over the Volta, on the Accra-Lome highway, some 50 miles (80 km) from the Togo border. In 1948 there were only 365 people at Sogakofe. By 1970 the population had grown to 3,099.

SOMANYA. 6°06' N, 0°01' W. The chief village of the Yilo Krobo; it is located on the Accra-Akosombo highway near Kpong and

Akuse. The village had a population of 2,485 in 1948, and 9,326 in 1970.

SONGAW LAGOON. 5°49' N, 0°28' E. Salt marshes and lagoon west of the Volta near Ada. The area is famous for its birds.

SONGO HILLS. 10°55' N, 0°30' W. The watershed between the Red and White Voltas in the Upper East Region above Gambaga.

SOPHIE LOUISE, FORT. Trade post built at Cape Three Points or Takrama, on the coast, Western Region. It was built by the Brandenburgers in 1690. The Dutch took over the place in 1717, calling it Fort Maria Luisa. Not much remains of the building today.

SORLIYA. The original na or paramount chief of Wa.

SOUTHWEST MONSOON. The winds from the South Atlantic that blow to the coast of Ghana. These winds are also called the tropical maritime or equatorial air mass. These currents are generally cool and moist. The Southwest Monsoon is opposed by the Northeast trades or the Harmatten, which blow down from the Sahara, and are dry.

SPARK. A fortnightly journal started by Nkrumah in December 1962 in imitation of Lenin's Iskra. It carried articles on socialist themes.

SPECTATOR. Accra paper from 1948. Sunday edition of The Ghanaian Times.

SPOKESMAN. An opposition newspaper to Busia and the Progress Party government during the Second Republic. It was edited by Kofi Badu, who had been a CPP editor in the First Republic and became a supporter of the NRC, and Commissioner of Consumer Affairs under the SMC.

SRI II, TOGBI (Cornelius Kofi Kwakume). 1862-1956. Paramount Chief of Anlo, 1907-1956. He modernized Anloga, promoted the Bremen Missions and western ideas, and was an advocate of Ewe unification. He was a member of the Gold Coast Legislative Council, 1916-1938.

STANDARD. Accra Catholic weekly published from 1938. It was often critical of the government of the day.

STAR. The newspaper of K.A. Busia and the Progress Party during the Second Republic.

STOOL. The Akan symbol of authority, the office of chief or king.

STEWART, DONALD. 1860-1905. British officer. He entered the British army in 1879 and served in Afghanistan, the Transvaal, and the Sudan. He was the political officer with the Asante expedition in 1896 and served as British Resident at Kumasi, 1896-1902, and Chief Commissioner of Asante, 1902-1904. In December 1896 he made a trip northward to occupy Gambaga for the British. From there he went to Tenkodogo, in modern Upper Volta, where he met Lieutenant Paul Voulet (1866-1899) of the French army. They agreed upon a temporary border between British and French interests. In 1904 Stewart went as Commissioner to British East Africa.

SUHUM. 6°02' N, 0°27' W. Town in the Eastern Region on the Accra-Kibi highway. It was the center of the cocoa boycott in 1937 and 1938. Suhum had a population of 5,099 in 1948, 10,193 in 1960, and 12,421 in 1970.

SUMAN (pl. Asuman). A charm, talisman, fetish, or totem believed to have magical power for good or evil.

SUNSUM. The elan, libido, drive, psyche, or spirit of a human being. It is intangible and it can leave the physical body in dreams or fantasies at will. It can change in mood from one mood or state to another. The sunsum represents the real personality of an individual.

SUNYANI. 7°20' N, 2°20' W. The capital of the Brong-Ahafo Region. Sunyani was a small village of 1,184 in 1911. In 1948 it had grown to 4,558. Since the creation of the Brong-Ahafo Region it has grown rapidly. In 1960 the census showed 12,160, and in 1970 the figure was 23,780. Sunyani is connected to other regional capitals by air.

SUPREME MILITARY COUNCIL I. I.K. Acheampong came to power in January 1972 as head of the National Redemption Council (NRC). On 9 October 1975 he reorganized his government and created the Supreme Military Council (SMC). This group ruled Ghana under Acheampong until it forced Acheampong to resign 5 July 1978.

SUPREME MILITARY COUNCIL II. On 5 July 1978 Acheampong's associates in the SMC persuaded him to resign. He was replaced as head of state by Lt. Gen. Frederick W.K. Akuffo. The second SMC ruled Ghana until 4 June 1979, when it in turn was ousted by the Armed Forces Revolutionary Council (AFRC) of Jerry John Rawlings.

SUTHERLAND, EFUA THEODORA. Born 1924. She was born at Cape Coast and her maiden name was Morgue. She is one of Ghana's most famous poets and playwrights. She was one of the first African women to attend Cambridge in England, and she married an American, William Sutherland, in 1954. She is author of many plays, and she has been connected with the University of Ghana's School of Drama for many years. Edufa and Foriwa are two of her better-known plays.

SUTRI RAPIDS. The falls of the Tano River. The rapids are located between the villages of Tanoso and Asuaso near Sunyani in the Brong-Ahafo Region.

SWANZY COMPANY, F. AND A. A mercantile business founded by Frank and Andrew Swanzy in the middle of the nineteenth century. By the 1890s it operated stores in almost every village in the Gold Coast. In 1919 it became part of the Eastern Trade Corporation, which in turn was consolidated into the United Africa Company.

SWEDISH AFRICA COMPANY. A company organized by a group of Dutch merchants in the seventeenth century. They financed Henry Caerlof, a native of Poland, in trade activities on the Gold Coast. Caerlof had formerly worked for the Dutch West India Company. Caerlof was instrumental in establishing several stations along the coast in the 1640s and 1650s. Caerlof later betrayed his Dutch supporters and worked for the Danes.

SWEDRU (Agona Swedru). 5°32' N, 0°42' W. The chief commercial center of the Agona area of the Central Region. It is located on the road between Oda and Winneba, about 15 miles (24 km) north of Winneba and the coast. In 1921 the population of Swedru was 2,582. By 1948 the population had grown to 10,913, and in 1970 the census showed 21,522 people in Swedru.

SWINTON, LORD (Philip Lloyd-Greame to 1924, Phlip Cunliffe-Lister to 1935). 1884-1972. Member of the British Parliament, 1918-1935. President of the Board of Trade of England, 1922-1923, 1924-1929, 1931. Secretary of State for Colonies, 1931-1935. Secretary of State for Air, 1935-1938. Cabinet Minister Resident in West Africa, 1942-1944. Minister for Civil Aviation, 1944-1945. Secretary of State for Commonwealth relations, 1952-1955. In 1942 the British government recognized the necessity of coordinating all allied war activities in West Africa at one place. Lord Swinton was appointed Cabinet Minister Resident in West Africa and established his headquarters at Achimota College in July 1942. For the next three years Achimota became the central command post for all West Africa. Swinton was replaced by Harold Harington Balfour in 1944, and Balfour held the responsibilities at Achimota until the end of World War II. Swinton's memoirs of his public life, I Remember, were published in 1948 by Hutchinson.

SWISS AFRICAN TRADING COMPANY (SAT). A small Swiss trading company which had its headquarters at Kumasi from 1922 to purchase cocoa for the Swiss chocolate industry. It was bought out by UAC in 1936.

SWOLLEN SHOOT. A virus spread by mealy bugs that was first reported in the Gold Coast in 1936. The only known remedy was cutting out infected trees. Attempts to cut the diseased trees aroused resentments among the growers.

- T -

TAFI. One of the small Volta-Togo groups, almost all of whom live in the Volta Region. The Tafi live near the Avatime and the Nyangbo.

TAFO, NEW. 6°13' N, 0°22' W. Town in the Eastern Region on the railroad northwest of Koforidua. It is the home of the Cocoa Research Institute. New Tafo had a population of only 3,217 in 1948. But by 1970 the census showed 11,114 residents.

TAFO, OLD. 6°44' N, 1°37' W. A very old town on the ancient trade route from Begho through Adansi to the Guinea coast. It was near here that the Asante founded Kwaman and then Kumasi.

TAFOE (Tafu). This area is shown on a 1629 Dutch map to the north of Kwahu. Mountains are shown on the map with the notation that gold mines are located there. The state is still shown, as Tafu, on the D'Anville map of April 1729.

TAIN RIVER. The southernmost tributary of the Black Volta. It enters the Black Volta just a few miles west of the Bamboi Ferry. It forms a curve in western Brong-Ahafo around the region where ancient Begho was located. It rises on the border of the Ivory Coast. The chief tributaries of the Tain are the Nimpeni, the Chen, and the Tombe.

TAKORADI. 4°53' N, 1°45' W. Twin city of Sekondi, located on the coast in the Western Region. The Swedes were trading here as early as 1650. The beach was contested by the Swedes, Danes, Dutch, and the English, and in 1659 the Dutch built Fort Witzen here. They abandoned Witzen in 1818. The Brandenburgers also tried once to establish a base in Takoradi around 1684. The major port of the Gold Coast was opened there in 1928. The headquarters of the Gold Coast railroads was moved there in 1934, and an airport was built a short time later. The Bureau of African Industries was located there in 1934, and the city became an important industrial center, with cocoa processing, lumber, paper, tobacco, plywood, and salt production. Takoradi is one of the best planned cities in Ghana. In 1960 the population of Takoradi alone was about 41,000, but Sekondi and Takoradi together had a population of over 120,790.

TAKRAMA. A place on Cape Three Points on the Ahanta coast of the Western Region where the Brandenburgers built a fortified lodge in 1690. It was called Fort Sophie Louise. It was sold to the Dutch in 1717, and the Dutch called it Fort Maria Luisa. Only a trace of the foundations were left in 1960.

TAKYIMAN see TECHIMAN

TALENSI (Talene, Tallensi). A Mole-Dagbani group who live in the Upper East Region above the Mamprusi and below the Frafra. Their society is called Tale, their country is Taleland, their language is Talene or Talen.

TAMAKLOE, EMMANUEL FORSTER. British clerk. He began his career as a German interpreter at Kete Krakye, 1897-1907, but then joined the British service and was a census clerk in 1910. Later he was a clerk at Yendi, where he collected local history and folklore. In 1931 his A Brief History of the Dagbamba People was published by the government printer in Accra. That same year his "Mythical and Traditional History of the Dagomba" appeared as a chapter in Tales Told in Togoland, edited by Allan Cardinall. Tamakloe also collaborated with H.A. Blair in producing a Dagbane dictionary and grammar.

TAMALE. 9°24' N, 0°50' W. Regional capital of the Northern Region. It is the administrative, financial, commercial, and transportation center for all the northern part of Ghana. It is on the Great Northern Highway from Kumasi to Bolgatanga, has one of Ghana's better airports, and is only 27 miles (43 km) from Yapei or Tamale Port, located on Lake Volta. Tamale became the British administrative headquarters of the Northern Territories in 1907. At that time the population was 1,435. A primary school opened there in 1909, and a secondary school was established in 1927. Trade schools and mission schools were created in the 1920s. Lloyd Shirer and his wife, of Pennsylvania, operated a school here for many years to train teachers. By 1970 Tamale had five secondary schools and two teacher training colleges. The average annual rainfall in Tamale is 43 inches (109 cm), most falling from June to October. The dry season is from November to June. February and March are the hottest months, and the rainy season, especially August, is the coolest time. The population of Tamale was 432 in 1901, 2,138 in 1911, almost 3,900 in 1921, about 13,000 by 1931, over 17,000 in 1948, 40,443 in 1960, and in 1970 the census showed 83,653 in Tamale.

TAMALE PORT (Yapei). 9°10' N, 1°10' W. A port on the northern end of Lake Volta. It was first established as the terminus for river traffic on the White Volta in 1908. It is 27 miles (43 km) from Tamale. A bridge crosses the lake at this point. One road goes on to Damongo, and another road turns south and goes to Kintampo, Techiman, and Kumasi.

TAMPOLENSE (Tampolensi). Grusi group who live in the Northern Region above Gonja, south of Mamprusi, and west of the White Volta and the Dagomba. They are much like the Sisala and Vagala.

TANO OBOASE (Tano beneath the rock). A place near the source of the Tano River, not far from Techiman in Brong Ahafo. It is the center of worship of Tano (Ta Kora), the Akan Obosom or god upon earth.

TANO RIVER. The most sacred river of the Akan. It rises in the Brong Ahafo Region near Techiman and flows in a southwesterly direction into the Western Region, by Wiawso, to the border of the Ivory Coast, and through the Juen Lagoon to the ocean. It is navigable to the falls near Tanoso (7°17' N, 2°15' W), where the Bechem-Sunyani road crosses the river. The Bain, Suhien, Samre, Yoyo, Suraw, Famuna (Pamunu), Srani, Amama, and other tributaries drain the section of Ghana which has the greatest rainfall.

TARKWA (Tarquah). 5°18' N, 1°59' W. Mining, commercial, and administrative center on the railroad in the Western Region about 50 miles (80 km) north of Dixcove. Governor Ussher reported a population of above 7,000 in 1880. It was one of the first two interior towns where the British stationed a DC. The town is surrounded by low hills where today there are many derelict mines, but a gold refinery is located in Tarkwa, and it is a lumber center. In 1911 the population was reported as only 2,426, up to 7,707 in 1948, 13,545 in 1960, and the census figure showed 14,702 in 1970. Kwame Nkrumah made his first important political speech in Tarkwa in 1948 soon after he returned to the Gold Coast.

TARO. A tropical plant with a tuberous root. It is also called cocoyam. The leaves are used as greens and are rich in minerals, vitamins, and protein.

TAVIEVI. Area in the Volta Region east of Lake Volta and some 15 miles (24 km) northeast of the Krepi lands. In 1875 the Krepi massacred a number of Tavievi people, and in 1888 the Tavievi took their revenge. The Krepi called upon the British for support. The British sent a force into Tavievi country and suffered an ambush in which there were several casualties. The British then sent in a larger force and the Tavievi were forced to submit to the British.

TECHIMAN (Takyiman). 7°35' N, 1°56' W. A town in the Brong Ahafo Region some 18 miles southeast of Wenchi. It was an important kola market for many years. In 1948 it had only 2,581 people, but by 1970 the population was 12,068. The Fante have a tradition that their ancestors came from Techiman. The town

Techimantia

is very old and once played an important part in the trade with the Dyula. It was taken by the Asante in 1722-1723.

TECHIMANTIA (Takyimantia, Techimentia). 7°11' N, 2°02' W. A Brong Ahafo town near Bechem. It had a population of 7,207 in 1970.

TEFLE. 5°51' N, 0°59' E. Town in the Volta Region near Sogakofe. It is just above the Volta Delta, some 23 miles (37 km) above Ada on the Accra-Lome highway. There was once a famous ferry here across the Volta, but the river is now crossed by a bridge.

TEKYIMAN see TECHIMAN

TEMA. 5°37' N, 0°01' W. One of the original seven Ga coastal towns. It has been turned into Ghana's most modern port and industrial city. It is 17 miles (27 km) east of Accra and is part of the Greater Accra Region. Tema is still an important fishing harbor, but today it is also home of the Valco plant, an oil refinery, the home docks of the Black Star Line, car assembly plants, meat processing plants, cocoa processing plants, and many other industries built to take advantage of the power from the Akosombo Volta Electric Project, located some 45 miles (72 km) to the north. Tema also boasts one of the largest planned industrial communities in Africa. It is connected to Accra by a coastal road, a freeway, and a railroad.

TEMPERATURES. Annual mean temperatures in Ghana are 79°F (26°C) to 84°F (29°C). It is cooler on the coast and warmer in the Upper Region. February and March are the warmest months, and August is coolest in daytime. However, nights are coolest in the north in January, and coolest in the south in August. Highs of 106°F (41°C) are recorded in the Upper Region, while lows of 53°F (12°C) are recorded at Kumasi.

TEN' DANA (pl. Ten'dama). The person in charge of religious welfare and the land in the Northern and Upper regions. The land priest.

TENSOB. The Ten'dana or earth priest of the Lobi.

TENZUGU SHRINE. A famous religious shrine in the Tong Hills of the Upper Region near Zuarungu and Bolgatanga. The British destroyed the shrine in 1911 and again in 1915, but people continued to make pilgrimages to the shrine. The shrine is a large natural temple in a rock cavern. R.S. Rattray visited the shrine in May 1928, and he wrote an account of a service there.

TESHI (Teshie). 5°35' N, 0°06' W. One of the seven original Ga coastal settlements. It is ten miles (16 km) east of Accra, and it is part of Greater Accra. The Dutch were trading here by the 1730s, and the Danes built Fort Augustaborg at Teshi in 1787. It was bought by the British in 1850. The British established the Royal West African Frontier Force Training School at Teshi, and many of West Africa's leading military men were trained at this school. The Ghanaian military academy is located here.

TETTEGAH, JOHN KOFI BARKU. Born 1930. He was born at Denu, near the Togo border, in the Volta Region. He attended Catholic schools and Secretarial College in Accra. For a time he was employed with G.B. Ollivant, where he became secretary of the employees' union. From there he became active in trade union activities. By 1954 he was General Secretary of the Gold Coast TUC and a member of the general board of the International Conference of Trade Unions. In the meantime he became a member of the Central Committee of the CPP and a close associate of Tawia Adamafio and the radical wing of the CPP. In 1959 Tettegah headed Nkrumah's Workers' Brigade for a brief period. Then in July 1960 he was appointed a Roving Ambassador. While an employee of the government, he continued his connection with the TUC, and was Secretary-General of the All-African Trades Union Federation, 1964-1966. After the fall of Nkrumah he left Ghana, not returning until the coup that ended the rule of Busia. Later in 1973 Tettegah was arrested by the NRC, along with Kojo Botsio, and they were sentenced to death for plotting against the military government. The sentences were commuted to life in April 1974, and Tettegah was finally released in November 1978. In 1983 the PNDC appointed him as their Ambassador to Russia.

THIRD FORCE (TF). This was a group created during the later days of the NLC in 1969 in opposition to both the leading parties, Busia's Progress Party and Gbedemah's National Alliance of Liberals. The Legon Observer supported this "middle way" for a time. Some of the Third Force supporters organized the All People's Congress. John Bilson, MD, of Kumasi was leader of the APC. The Third Force appeared again in 1979, when Bilson ran for president as candidate of the Third Force Party (TFP) and came in a poor sixth. In 1981 the Third Force merged into the All People's Party, but political activities were cut short by the coup which ended the Third Republic.

THOMAS, THOMAS SHENTON WHITELEGGE. 1879-1962. Governor of the Gold Coast, 1932-1934. He was educated at St. John's School, Leatherhead, and Queen's College, Cambridge. He served the Colonial Service in Kenya, Uganda, Nigeria, and was Colonial Secretary of the Gold Coast before becoming Governor of Nyasaland, 1929-1932, the Gold Coast, 1932-1934; and of Malaya, 1934-1942. He was then interned by the Japanese during World War II and retired in 1946.

THOMPSON, AUGUSTUS WILLIAM KOJO (Kojo Thompson). 1880-1950. Accra lawyer and politician. He was born at Winneba and educated at Mfantsipim and Wesleyan schools in Accra and Nigeria. He then went to London and qualified for the bar at Lincoln's Inn in 1914. He spent the rest of his life practicing law in Accra. He became active in Accra politics, being active in the Youth Conference and the Mambii political group. Among his close associates in the 1930s were Alfred Ocansey, Nnamdi Azikiwe, and I.T.A. Wallace Johnson. In the 1920s he failed in campaigns for election to the Legislative Council from Accra, but in 1935 his radical attacks on the British government helped him defeat the more conservative F.V. Nanka-Bruce. As a member of the Legislative Council he became famous for his attacks on colonial rule, traditional rulers, and European businesses, especially the United African Company. In 1941 he was member of a committee, with J.B. Danquah, which recommended reforms in the Legislative Council which were partly incorporated in the Burns reforms of 1946. In 1944 Thompson was convicted in an extortion case. This ended his political career.

THORBURN, JAMES JAMIESON. 1864-1929. Governor of the Gold Coast from 1910 to 1912. Educated at Edinburgh Collegiate School, he joined the Colonial Service in Ceylon in 1886. He was assigned to Nigeria for several years before coming to the Gold Coast. He retired after his term in Accra.

TINDANA (pl. tindamba)   see   TEN'DANA

TINTEINTINA. The Ten'dana or earth priest among the Sisala. There are many variations to the title. Tendagena among the Dagomba, Tegatu among the Awuna (Grusi).

TOGOLAND, BRITISH. After World War I the League of Nations entrusted or mandated the western part of the former German colony of Togoland to England. The total area placed under British control amounted to 13,041 square miles (33,777 sq km). The northern part of this area was 7,196 square miles (18,638 km), and it was placed under the jurisdiction of the Northern Territories of the Gold Coast. The southern section of 5,845 square miles (15,139 sq km) was governed as part of Trans-Volta-Togoland Region. In 1945 the whole Togoland Mandate of the British became a United Nations Trust Territory. The southern section held a plebiscite in May 1956 over the question of joining Ghana when independence came. This created much bitterness between the Ewe, who favored an independent Ewe nation, and those people who favored union with Ghana. Those who wanted union in a free Ghana won, and in 1957 the southern section of the Togoland Trust Territory became the Volta Region of Ghana.

TOGOLAND CONGRESS PARTY (TCP). A political party active in the 1950s. The TCP wanted unification of the Ewe in the British and French Trust Territories as a separate Ewe state. The party was defeated in the May 1956 plebiscite over unification with the Gold Coast-Ghana. It won two seats in the July 1956 Gold Coast elections, but did not last long after that.

TOGOLAND REMNANTS. The many small groups who were the original inhabitants of the lands which the Ewe occupied when the Ewe moved into the areas the Ewe now occupy. There are many of these small tribes. They were pushed into the remote mountain areas to the east of the Volta River in what after 1957 became the Volta Region. These small groups are sometimes known as the Central Togo tribes. The Avatime, Buem, Adele, Nyangbo, and Logba are among the thirteen tribes that the 1960 Ghanaian census classified as Central Togo tribes.

TOGOLAND UNION. Ewe group created during World War II in 1943 to work the unification of the Ewe, and an independent Ewe nation to be formed from the British and the French-mandated territories of Togoland.

TOHAJIE (Tohajiye). The legendary progenitor of the Mole-Dagbani peoples. Traditions vary, but Tohajie was called the "Red Hunter." He lived in what is today modern Niger. He and a wife named Pagawolga had a son named Kpogonumbo. This son migrated to Gurma, in what is today Upper Volta. Kpogonumbo and a wife named Soyini or Solyini had a son named Gbewa in some traditions, Bawa in the Mamprusi traditions, and Nedega in the Mossi traditions. Gbewa (Bawa, Nedega) in turn moved west again, to Pusiga, in the modern Kusasi country of Ghana. Gbewa had a daughter and many sons, and these children created a number of Mole-Dagbani states.

TOHOGO (Tohugu, Tohagu, Tusugu). Son of Gbewa of Pusiga and brother of Sitobu, whose son founded Dagomba, and Zirile, who followed his father as ruler at Pusiga, and a sister and other brothers who founded Mole-Dagbani states. After Zirile disappeared on a campaign in Gurma, the council at Pusiga selected Tohogo as their leader. This touched off a bitter fight between the sons of Gbewa, and Tohogo fled to his mother's town of Mamprugu, where he founded the Mamprugu or Mamprusi state. Tohogo probably lived in the middle of the fifteenth century.

TOKYO JOES. Unemployed school-leavers in Accra in 1957. Their leader called himself "Zorro." His real name was Emmanuel Oko Bruce. They played an important role in causing discontent against Nkrumah and the CPP among the Ga because of the crowded conditions created in Accra by the thousands of outsiders being attracted into the city.

TOMATOES. A popular vegetable imported into the Gold Coast from the Americas in the seventeenth century about the same time tobacco began to be brought in. Tomatoes play an important role in the cooking of Ghanaians today.

TON TON. Dyula name for the Brong-Ahafo area around Wenchi.

TONG HILLS. A low range of hills in the Upper Region near Bolgatanga. The Tenzugu Shrine is located in these hills. Large flocks of wild guinea fowl once lived here.

TONGU. Volta River fishermen.

TOROGBANI, MOUNT. Peak in the Volta Region mountains near the town of Pampawie and the Togo border. The peak is 2,862 feet (873 m) high.

TORRANE, GEORGE. President of the Council of Merchants at Cape Coast from October 1804 to 1807. He experimented with coffee and other crops at Cape Coast in an attempt to develop the economy. He also adopted a policy of collaboration with the Asantehene Osei Bonsu which recognized Asante claims to suzerainty over the Assin and the Fante that amounted to a betrayal of people who were British friends. He divided the people of Anomabo with the Asante, and the people were sold into slavery. Torrane was convinced that peace and trade were more likely if the Asante were allowed to control the coast.

TOWN COUNCILS. In 1858 Municipal Councils were elected at James Town (Accra) and Cape Coast. Support for the idea collapsed when the Councils tried to collect taxes. Councils were established in Accra in 1896, at Sekondi in 1904, at Cape Coast in 1905, and at Kumasi in 1943. The Municipal Corporations Bill of 1924 provided for a majority of elected members on the councils and broadened the vote to allow all who owned or rented houses taxed at five pounds to cast a ballot for members of the councils.

TRADES UNION CONGRESS (TUC). Workers' unions began to be organized in the Gold Coast in the 1930s. In September 1945 various unions came together at Sekondi and organized the TUC. This Congress collapsed after the general strike of January 1950. It was not until 1953 that the movement reunited, and in September 1954 John Tettegah was elected full-time secretary of the group. From then until the fall of Nkrumah in 1966 the TUC was an important adjunct of the CPP. Every employed person in Ghana was required to pay dues to the TUC. After the fall of Nkrumah, Tettegah went into exile and the TUC has had a checkered career since then. Under the NLC and Second Republic the TUC was suspect because of its close ties to the CPP. Benjamin Bentum was leader of the TUC during this period.

Under Busia the government closed the TUC and halted compulsory dues. Under the NRC relations between the TUC and the government improved somewhat for a time, but after 1974 depressed economic conditions have worked against the labor movement in Ghana. A.M. Issifu was the TUC leader in the middle 1970s. He supported Acheampong during the Union Government referendum, but when Frederick Akuffo replaced Acheampong as Head of State the TUC and the SMC parted ways.

TRANS-VOLTA-TOGOLAND REGION (TVT). A region established in 1952 to administer the area now called the Volta Region.

TROPASSA. Tropassa and Little Tropassa are shown on the 1729 Anville map to the northwest of Asante.

TRO TRO. A mammy lorry. A truck with seats in the back for passengers. They often have slogans painted across the back. They are the most common form of transportation in Ghana.

TROWO. Lesser spirits of the Ewe. Each trowo has priests and priestesses.

TSATSADU FALLS. Cascades in the hills between Kpandu and Hohoe.

TSETSE. There are 21 species of African bloodsucking flies. They transmit several diseases, especially sleeping sickness.

TSHI see TWI

TSHIKAPA MUTINY. In January 1961 the Third Battalion of the Ghanaian Army, stationed at Tshikapa in Kasai, Congo (Zaire) rebelled and their commander, David Hansen, was severely beaten.

TSIBOE, JOHN WALLACE. 1904-1963. A native of Assin Attandaso who was educated at Wesleyan in Kumasi. He then opened a store in Kumasi and became a wealthy merchant. He founded the Abora Printing Company, and in 1939 he founded the Ashanti Pioneer. The paper became a major mouthpiece for Asante interests. Tsiboe was an early member of the United Gold Coast Convention. In 1949 he briefly joined the CPP, but was soon in the opposition to Nkrumah. In 1950 he failed in an attempt to organize the Gold Coast Labour Party. He then joined the Ghana Congress Party and then the NLM in 1954. In the 1956 elections he was NLM candidate for the Legislative Assembly from his home Abora district, but he was defeated. In 1957 he helped organize the United Party. After independence the Ashanti Pioneer became the leading critic of the CPP government. Nkrumah banned the paper in 1962. John Tsiboe's wife, Nancy Tsiboe, worked closely with her husband. She was a candidate of the Congress Party in 1954. She joined the NLM in 1954, and she was later the National Treasurer of the United Party.

TSIKATA, KOJO. A former captain in the Ghanaian army whom Kofi Awooner once called a "student of world revolution." He was arrested by the SMC in November 1975 and tried for his connection with the "Ewe Plot" to kill the SMC leaders. He was sentenced to death, but released in August 1978. During the period of the Third Republic he was a constant critic of President Hilla Limann and he claimed that he was arrested and tortured by Military Intelligence. He was one of the founders of the 4 July Movement of Rawlings supporters. After the coup that ended the Third Republic, Tsikata became a special adviser to the PNDC and head of state security. In 1982 he was implicated in the murders of three judges and a retired military officer, but the Attorney General refused to proceed against him.

TUMU. 10°52' N, 1°59' W. Kasena town in the Upper West Region near the Upper Volta border. It is 86 miles (138 km) west of Bolgatanga. It had a population of 1,561 in 1948, 2,773 in 1960, and 4,366 in 1970.

TUSUGU see TOHOGO

TUTUOJIRAM (Tutuodgiram). 6°37' N, 0°48' W. A mountain in the Eastern Region on the southern edge of the Kwahu Plateau. It is 2,500 feet (762 m) above sea level. It is not far from Mpraeso.

TWI (Akan, Tshi, Odschi, Oji). Some five million people speak one or more varieties of Akan or Twi. Akuapem, Asante, and Fante are the chief dialects. Asante is used by the greatest number.

TWIFO (Twifu, Cuifferoe). One of the Akan states in the Pra valley on the trade route between Asante and the Fante. The name means Twi people. Their capital was north of Elmina.

- U -

UNILEVER. The conglomerate which started as Lever Brothers in 1884. Lever Brothers entered the West African trade in 1896 and rapidly bought out many smaller companies. By 1925, when the founder, William Leverhulme died, Unilever was made up of more than two hundred firms.

UNION GOVERNMENT (Unigov). A proposal of the SMC in 1977 to combine civilian and military rule. Justice Koranteng-Addow was chairman of the committee that wrote the plan. The idea was to create an elected government of military and civilian officials who would hold office without alliances in political organizations. A referendum on the plan was held in March 1978, and the SMU claimed that the electorate had approved Union Government by large margins. But opposition was so great that the plan was never put into operation.

UNITED ACTION FRONT (UAF). A coalition of dissident political factions put together by Frank G. Bernasko at the end of 1981. It was stillborn since political parties were outlawed by the PNDC shortly thereafter.

UNITED AFRICA COMPANY. In March 1929 the African Association, the Eastern Company, and the Niger Company merged to form the United Africa Company (UAC). By 1932 Unilever had gained controlling interest in the stock of UAC. UAC was the most important business firm in the Gold Coast at independence.

UNITED GHANA FARMERS' COUNCIL. A farmers' group founded in 1953 and recognized by the CPP as the sole representative of farmers in September 1957. It was banned after the coup of 1966. Martin Appiah-Danquah was the secretary-general of the United Ghana Farmers' Co-operative Council.

UNITED GOLD COAST CONVENTION (UGCC). The first true political party in the Gold Coast to talk of self-government "in the shortest time possible." It was founded 4 August 1947. The key founders were A.G. Grant (chairman), R.S. Blay, J.B. Danquah, R.A. Awoonor-Williams, William E. Ofori Atta, E.A. Akufo Addo, J.W. de Graft-Johnson, and Obetsibi Lamptey. Its immediate aim was to replace chiefs on the Legislative Council with educated people. The UGCC hired Kwame Nkrumah as its general secretary at the suggestion of Ako Adjei. The UGCC was defeated by a party Nkrumah organized in June 1949 after he broke away from the UGCC. Nkrumah had served as general secretary from January to September 1948. The UGCC was defeated in the general election of February 1951, and it dissolved the following year.

UNITED NATIONAL CONVENTION (UNC). A political party formed in 1979 by William Ofori Atta and other former supporters of K.A. Busia and the Progress Party (PP). The UNC was the moderate party of academics, professional people, and businessmen. The party won 13 seats in the National Assembly elected in the June 1979 elections, and the UNC candidate for president, William Ofori Atta, came in a poor third behind Hilla Limann (PNP), the winner, and Victor Owusu (PFP), the candidate with the second highest vote. In the beginning of the Third Republic the PNP and UNC agreed to cooperate, but the alliance lasted only a short time. In August 1980 the UNC walked out of the National Assembly in a dispute over the appointment of judges. At the end of 1981 the UNC was negotiating for a merger of opposition parties when the PNDC coup ended political activities and the Third Republic.

UNITED NATIONALIST PARTY (UNP). A small political party which contested the 1969 elections. Its leader was Joe Appiah. The UNP won only two seats in the National Assembly. The next year it merged into the Justice Party (JP).

UNITED PARTY (UP). A coalition of groups opposed to the CPP which was organized 3 November 1957 in Accra at a rally presided over by K.A. Busia. J. Hutton-Mills, J.A. Braimah, Nancy Tsiboe, S.D. Dombo, Joe Appiah, and J.B. Danquah were among the leaders of this anti-Nkrumah movement. The Preventive Detention Act of 1958 worked havoc with the UP. Busia went into exile in June 1959, leaving S.D. Dombo as leader of the opposition in the Assembly. In the 1960 elections the UP ran J.B. Danquah as their candidate for president against the CPP leader, Nkrumah. Nkrumah got 1,016,076 to only 124,623 for Danquah. In 1961 Danquah and many of the last UP stalwarts went to prison. By the following year, for all practical purposes, Ghana was a one-party state.

UNIVERSITY OF CAPE COAST. The youngest of Ghana's universities, it was founded in 1961 to train teachers for secondary schools and teachers' colleges.

UNIVERSITY OF GHANA. The University College of the Gold Coast was founded in 1948 near Achimota around Legon Hill. It had a special relationship with the University of London, and all degrees were issued in the name of the University of London until 1961. From 1948 to 1957 the principal of the university was David Mowbray Balme, a classical scholar, who was a graduate of Cambridge. He played the key role in organizing the university along Cambridge lines, with residence halls, faculty rule, and intellectual elitism. The library at the university is named for him. At independence in March 1957 the name change to the University College of Ghana. Then in October 1961 it became the University of Ghana, granting its own degrees, and breaking its ties with the University of London. By 1970 the University of Ghana had six faculties--agriculture, arts, law, science, social studies, medicine. There were twenty-seven departments.

UNIVERSITY OF SCIENCE AND TECHNOLOGY. The University of Science and Technology at Kumasi started in 1952 as the Kumasi College of Technology. In August 1961 it was given full university status as the Kwame Nkrumah University of Science and Technology. In February 1966 it assumed its present name. It has faculties of agriculture, engineering, pharmacy, science, art, and architecture.

UPPER REGIONS. The Upper Region was created from the Northern Region 29 June 1960. It was made up of many small Grusi, Mole-Dagbani, and Gurense peoples. In 1982 the PNDC divided the Upper Region into Upper West Region and Upper East Region.

USSHER, HERBERT TAYLOR. Died 1880. Governor of the Gold Coast. Ussher's first experience in West Africa was as private secretary to the Governor of Lagos in 1864. In 1866 he became Collector of Customs for the Gold Coast and from that position he was promoted to be the Administrator of the Gold Coast, 1867-1872. These were turbulent years during which the Dutch and English tried to exchange posts on the Gold Coast; the Asante army threatened the coastal regions, and the Fante tried to organize a federation. In 1872 the decision was made that England would take over all the Dutch possessions on the Gold Coast. Ussher was transferred to Tobago (near Trinidad) as Governor from 1872 to 1875. Then he was sent to the other side of the world, to Labuan (off Malaysia) as Governor from 1875 to 1879. In 1879 he was returned to the Gold Coast as Governor. He died at Christiansborg Castle on 1 December 1880, and he is buried at James Town, Accra.

USSHER FORT. The Dutch opened a lodge in 1642 at Accra which within a decade they enlarged and named Fort Crevecoeur. This structure was badly damaged by an earthquake in 1862. Six years later it was turned over to the British. They rebuilt it and named it after the administrator of the Gold Coast at the time, Herbert Taylor Ussher. It became a prison, but in 1975 it was turned over to the Museums and Monuments Board for historical preservation.

- V -

VAGALA (Vigala, Vagele). Grusi group related to the Mo, Sisala, and Tampolensi. They live in the Gonja area northeast of Bole.

VERANDA BOYS (Verandah). Men who lounge on the porches of patrons, waiting to run errands for the boss. Early supporters of Nkrumah.

VERNON, FORT. A small fort built by the English at Prampram around 1806, but abandoned within a few years.

VICTORIA, FORT (Phipp's Tower). An early structure was started about 1702 at Cape Coast by the British that was called Phipp's Tower. It was rebuilt in 1837 and called Fort Victoria.

VODZA. 5°57' N, 1°00' E. Anlo town on the Keta Lagoon where Geraldo de Lima carried on slave trade in the 1850s and 1860s. On 13 May 1871 the British bombarded de Lima's deserted residence at Vodza. The Anlo promised to turn de Lima over to the British if he showed himself. He stayed away for many years, but on 7 January 1885 he was lured back to Vodza and captured.

VOLTA. The Volta River begins as three branches in Upper Volta, the Black, Red, and White Voltas. A fourth branch begins in Benin as the Pendjari, which becomes the Oti after it enters Togo. From the source of the Black Volta to the Gulf of Guinea at Ada is a distance of about a thousand miles (1609 km). The entire system drains an area of 150,000 sq mi (388,500 sq km) in Benin, Togo, Upper Volta, Ivory Coast, and Ghana. Within Ghana the Volta drains 61,000 sq mi (157,990 sq km), which is 67 percent of the country.

The African name for the river after it becomes one stream below Kete-Krakye is Firao (Frao) or Atirri. "Volta" was the name given the river in the fifteenth century by the Portuguese on account of its meandering course. For four centuries Europeans were blocked from the Volta by the dreaded bar near Ada. Finally, in 1861, an English expedition under Edward Bullock Andrews crossed the bar in surf boats and ventured up the river, portaging around rapids, for a distance of almost 120 miles (193 km). In 1868 the Eyo became the first steamer to cross the Ada bar. From the bar it is possible to move up the river to the tidal limit at Akuse, which is 55 miles (88 km) above Ada. This is the end of navigation in the dry season save for canoes. In the wet season small-draft vessels may venture a few miles more to the Senchi Rapids. Here portage is required even for canoes. The river is at its lowest in March and at its highest at the end of September.

The Volta is about a mile wide at Ada. A ferry crosses at this point to Anyanui, on the left bank from Ada. Bridges cross the river at Tefle and at Adomi. Hydroelectric projects were completed across the river at Kpong (1981) and the Ajena Gorge (1964). On 19 May 1964 the gates of the dam across the Ajena Gorge were closed, and Lake Volta began to form.

VOLTA ALUMINUM COMPANY (VALCO). A corsortium of aluminum interests created by Edgar Kaiser of Kaiser Aluminum in 1959. By an agreement reached with Nkrumah in 1960, the consortium agreed to build an aluminum smelter at Tema. VALCO was given special electric and tax rates in exchange for a commitment to purchase up to 74 percent of the current produced at the Akosombo Dam for a period of 30 years. This guaranteed payments on the loans made to build the dam. The smelter was completed in 1966 and full production was reached by 1968. An expansion project was added in 1976. Hopes that VALCO would use Ghanaian bauxite were not realized by 1983 because bauxite could be imported from Jamaica at a lower cost.

VOLTA BASIN. The Volta Basin in Ghana is the area between the Gambaga Scarp on the north, the Konkori Scarp on the west, the Mampong or Kwahu Scarp on the south, and the Togo border on the east.

VOLTA DAM. The Volta or Akosombo Dam was started in 1961 and the gates to the dam were first closed in May of 1964. The dam is an earth and rock fill structure 370 feet (113 m) high, and 2,100 feet (640 m) long at its crest. The dam is rockfill rather than concrete as a protection against earthquakes.

VOLTA DELTA. In the extreme southeastern corner of Ghana is a flat, featureless area with many lagoons which pushes out into the Gulf of Guinea. Sandbars block the exit of the river and create several channels. The Songaw and Keta lagoons are both saltwater. The Avu and Ke lagoons are freshwater. The lagoons and river are a source of fish and salt. Coconut and oil palms grow well in the delta; and shallots, cassava, maize, and other truck crops are cultivated. There are large areas of tideland grass.

VOLTA REGION. Before the Gold Coast became Ghana, this region was named the Trans-Volta-Togo Region. It consisted of small areas which had once been part of the Gold Coast Colony, plus the southern part of the old Togo Trust Territory. It became the Volta Region in 1959. Ho is the administrative center, and the region is divided into Anlo North and South, Keta, Tongu, Ho, Kpandu, and Buem-Krakye.

VOLTA RIVER see VOLTA

VOLTA RIVER AUTHORITY (VRA). The agency established in 1961 to manage the Volta River hydroelectric project. It succeeded the Volta River Project. The first responsibility of the VRA was to move the 80,000 people living in the area to be flooded by Lake Volta and resettle them in new homes and villages. This mission was carried out with almost spectacular success. From 1966 the VRA has directed the operation of the Akosombo and Kpong hydroelectric stations and their distribution networks. Transmission lines to Togo and Dahomey were opened in 1972.

VOLTA RIVER PROJECT (VRP). Planning on the project to develop the Volta River began years before the dam of the Ajena Gorge was actually built. Albert Kitson, head of the Gold Coast Geological Survey Department, marked the Gorge as an excellent place for a dam 24 April 1915. Later Kitson also spotted Bui, on the Black Volta, as another place that could be developed. Planning on the project began in earnest in 1951. The Volta dam was started in 1961, finished in 1965, and dedicated by President Nkrumah just before he was deposed in 1966. Lake Volta, created by the Volta Dam, covers 3,276 sq mi (8,485 sq km), is 250 miles (402 km) long, and has a shoreline of 4,500 miles (7,241 km).

VOLTA RIVER TRANSPORT SERVICE. In 1902 the British organized
a fleet of canoes to transport supplies form Ada up the Volta to
Longoro, on the Black Volta near Kintampo, and Yeji, on the
White Volta below Salaga. After Tamale became administrative
center in the north in 1907, the canoe transport was extended
to Yapei or Tamale Port. By 1930 improvements in the road
network of the Gold Coast made canoe traffic obsolete.

VREDENBURG, FORT (Vreedenburgh). Both the English and Dutch
built bases at Komenda in the seventeenth century. Even the
French were interested in the location for a while. The Dutch
began Vreedenburgh about 1688. Almost a century later the
fort was taken and destroyed by the British. The Dutch rebuilt in 1785. In 1872 the Dutch ceded the place to the English.

- W -

WA. 10°03' N, 2°29' W. Important early trade depot of the Dyula
on the western route from the coast to Jenne. The Black Volta
and the border with the Ivory Coast are just a short distance
to the west. It is in the Upper West Region. Southward the
road goes to Bole, northward to Lawra, eastward to Yagaba or
Daboya. The city today is a cosmopolitan town of many peoples.
The Wala, Dagaba (Dagarte), and Lobi, and many Muslims.
There are two impressive mosques, and the most important festival, the Damba, is the birthday of Muhammad. In 1948 the population of Wa was just 5,156. By 1970 the census listed a population of 21,374. Wa is the regional capital of the Upper West
Region.

WADH NABA see NABAGA

WAFF see ROYAL WEST AFRICAN FRONTIER FORCE

WALA (sing. Walo, Oule, Walba, Wile). People of the Wa state.
Their language is Wale or Wali. They are a Mole-Dagbani group
who came from Mamprusi in the seventeenth century and established their rule over the Dagaba and Lobi who were already in
the area. The traditional leader of the journey to Wa was
Soalia. Power was divided between groups that settled in several small places in and around Wa. The Wala have often been
attacked by other peoples. The Gonja have attacked several
times. In the late 1880s Babatu's Zabrama attacked the Wala,
destroyed a mosque in Wa, and executed many of the local Muslim leaders. The Wa Na committed suicide after a bloody defeat
at Nasa. The Wala, searching for security, signed a treaty for
protection with the British in 1894, and with the French the
following year. These treaties initially did them little good because the area was soon devastated by Samori's forces. Only
after Samori left the area did the British venture back.

WALEMBELE. 10°30' N, 1°58' W. Sisala town on a branch of the Kulpawn in the Upper West Region. It is 27 miles (43 km) south of Tumu. In the late nineteenth century this region was under the rule of the Zabrama. In 1970 the population of the village was 1,568.

WALEWALE. 10°21' N, 0°48' W. Town in the Northern Region on the Great Northern Highway, 28 miles (45 km) due south of Bolgatanga and about the same distance southwest of Gambaga. Louis Binger, the French explorer, reported being here 10 August 1888 to 17 September 1888. Walewale had a population of 3,821 in 1948, 4,493 in 1960, and 5,302 in 1970.

WAMFIE. 7°18' N, 2°42' W. Town in the Brong Ahafo Region some 23 miles (37 km) southwest of Sunyani near the source of the Bia River. The population in 1948 was 1,524, but by 1970 the town had grown to 6,025.

WANGARA. Mande merchants who were attracted to the Black Volta area from Mali in search of gold and kola. They made important settlements at Begho (in Brong Ahafo) and at Wa (in the Upper West Region). They are often called the Dyula.

WANKI see WENCHI

WANQUIE see WENCHI

WARD, WILLIAM ERNEST FRANK. Born 1900. After attending Lincoln College, Oxford, and Ridley Hall, Cambridge, Ward became a member of the first faculty at Achimota in 1924. He remained in the Gold Coast until World War II, spending his spare time in the study of African music, folklore, and history. In 1935 he published A Short History of the Gold Coast. In the seventh edition this became A Short History of Ghana, 1957. In 1940 William Ward finished a fuller account of the history of the Gold Coast. This was just before he left the Gold Coast to go to Mauritius. That second book was not published until after the war, in 1948; it appeared as A History of the Gold Coast. After independence this was revised and became A History of Ghana, 1958. Both these books have gone through many editions. In 1940 Ward went to Mauritius as Director of Education. After the war he returned to England as Educational Adviser to the Colonial Office, 1945-1956, and editor of Overseas Education, 1946-1963. He continued to write. Educating Young Nations appeared in 1959; Fraser of Trinity and Achimota and Government in West Africa both were published in 1965. The Royal Navy and the Slavers: The Suppression of the Atlantic Slave Trade followed in 1969. In addition he helped with a history of East Africa, a history of Africa, and publications on education in the non-European world.

WARSHAS see WASSA

WASIPE. 8°32' N, 2°12' W. Village in the Northern Region on the western road between Bamboi and Bole, and just a short distance from the Black Volta. Alluvial gold was once found in the area. Old pits can be found between Wasipe and Bole. At some point the Wasipe-wura moved from Wasipe to Daboya. Daboya is the divisional capital of the Gonja Wasipe division.

WASSA (Warshas, Wasa, Wasaw, Wassaw). One of the major groups of the Akan. They are shown on a 1629 map as Wassa, and a 1729 map as Warshas or Wassa. Wassa today is in the Western Region. The Nzema and Ahanta are their southern neighbors, Aowin and Sefwi are on the west and north, and the Denkyira and Fante are on the east. Wassa is divided into two divisions, the Upper or Amanfi, and the Lower or Fiaso. Wassa was conquered by Denkyira in the latter half of the seventeenth century. After 1715 Wassa and Asante were often at war, and all during the eighteenth century the Asante conducted campaigns against Wassa in their attempts to keep routes to the coast open. The British worked to keep Wassa at odds with Asante, and Asante campaigns were directed against Wassa in 1715-1723, the 1750s, the 1770s and 1780s, and most of the nineteenth century until 1873. Throughout the Wassa tried to ally with the coastal people. In 1871 they were associated with the Fante confederacy movement.

WATER WORKS ORDINANCE, 1934. An ordinance that would have required the citizens of towns that had water systems to pay for their water, which had been furnished free. This ordinance was suggested at the same time that the Sedition Ordinance was proposed in the Legislative Assembly. A delegation under J.B. Danquah was sent to England to protest. The ARPS sent a separate delegation. Both groups demanded that people in the Gold Coast be given more participation in the government of the Gold Coast, but they did not entirely agree on how this would be done.

WATSON REPORT. Economic and political conditions in the Gold Coast created much discontent after World War II. Early in 1948 a Ghanaian merchant, Nii Kwabena Bonne III, organized a boycott of European goods. On 28 February unarmed veterans were fired on as they marched toward Government House. Two men died. Rioting and looting spread across Accra and into a number of towns, and before order was restored some thirty persons were dead, many were injured, and millions in property had been destroyed. Six leaders of the UGCC were arrested and detained at distant places in the north. These men became the famous "Big Six." Governor Gerald Creasy then asked for the Secretary of State for the Colonies to appoint a commission to come out from England to investigate the causes for the riots and discontent.

Andrew Aiken Watson was chairman of the Watson Commission. The Commission remained in the Gold Coast several weeks conducting hearings, and the Watson Report was released in August 1948. It recommended a greater role for educated Africans in the government of the Gold Coast by expanding the legislative branch of the government and by including five African ministers on the Executive Council, with departments responsible to the legislature. It also suggested that chiefs should take no part in political affairs, but should be limited to their traditional roles. The government then decided to test African opinion, so an all-African committee was appointed under the leadership of Sir Henley Coussey. There were thirty-eight members, including five of the "Big Six" who had been sent into detention a few months before.

WELBECK, NATHANIEL A. Born 1915. Teacher and politician who was one of the original members of the Central Committee of the CPP. He went on to be one of Nkrumah's most trusted lieutenants. He was propaganda secretary to the CPP, and after being elected to the Legislative Assembly in 1954 he became Minister of Works. Over the years until Nkrumah's fall he held various posts in the Cabinet and the party. He supervised the initial stages of the organization of the Workers' Brigade in 1957. He was a hard-working General Secretary of the CPP. He also was Minister of Information, and last of all the Minister of State for Party Propaganda. Nkrumah tried to turn him into a diplomat, but Welbeck was too loose-mouthed for that. When Welbeck was sent to Guinea in 1958, Sekou Toure soon sent him home. In 1960 when he was sent to the Congo (Zaire), he was run out of the country. In the end, when Nkrumah went off to China in February 1966, the President left Welbeck in charge of Accra. That was when the NLC ended Nkrumah's rule. Welbeck could not have saved his master. But he did go to prison with a degree of dignity, and while many of his former colleagues outdid themselves in denouncing their former leader, Welbeck remained silent.

WENCHI (Wanque). 7°44' N, 2°06' W. Important town in Brong Ahafo 18 miles (29 km) northwest of Techiman and 95 miles northwest (152 km) of Kumasi. It is on one of the old caravan routes from the coast to Begho and beyond, and the whole area attracts archaeology buffs in search of the past. Prime Minister Kofi Abrefa Busia was born in Wenchi. In 1948 the population was 3,812. In 1960 it had jumped to 10,672, and in 1970 it was 13,836.

WENYA, TOGBI. Leader of the Ewe who fled from Notsie (Nouatja, Nuatja) in modern Togo into the area of the modern Volta Region. This was probably early in the eighteenth century.

WESLEY COLLEGE, KUMASI. A prestigious secondary school established in Kumasi by the Wesleyans in 1924. It is located on the northern side of Kumasi on the Mampong Road.

WEST AFRICA. Weekly publication from London which is probably the best single source for information on English-speaking West Africa. It was first published 3 February 1917. David Williams was the editor for three decades. Kenneth Makenzie was editor in 1981. In 1984 the editor is Kaye Whiteman.

WEST AFRICAN AIRWAYS CORPORATION (WAAC). A joint project of the English-speaking countries of West Africa organized in 1947. The British, Gambia, Sierra Leone, Gold Coast, and Nigeria cooperated in the airline.

WEST AFRICAN COCOA RESEARCH INSTITUTE. An institute established at Tafo in 1938 to do research on cocoa. After Ghanaian independence it became the Cocoa Research Station.

WEST AFRICAN CONFERENCE. A movement which developed at the end of World War I to try to get the West African English-speaking colonies to work together for self-determination. J.E. Casely Hayford, T. Hutton Mills, W.E.G. Sekyi, and F.V. Nanka Bruce were the Gold Coast leaders. The headquarters at first were at Sekondi. In March 1920 the West African Conference evolved into the National Congress of British West Africa.

WEST AFRICAN FRONTIER FORCE (WAFF) see ROYAL WEST AFRICAN FRONTIER FORCE (RWAFF)

WEST AFRICAN NATIONAL SECRETARIAT (WANS). Group formed in London after the Manchester Pan-African Congress in 1945. The object was to follow up on the ideas of the Manchester Congress and to work for self-determination and a federation of West Africa. Isaac Theophilus Akunna Wallace Johnson was chairman, Kwame Nkrumah was the secretary. George Padmore and Bankole Awooner Renner were members.

WEST AFRICAN PRODUCE BOARD. An agency created by the British in 1942, during World War II, to push for an increase in the production of materials considered necessary for the war. In the Gold Coast the Produce Board encouraged production of food products, rubber, cocoa, minerals, palm kernels, and timber.

WEST AFRICAN REGIMENT (WAR). An African constabulary established in Sierra Leone in 1898. On occasion it was used in the Gold Coast.

WEST AFRICAN STUDENTS' UNION (WASU). An organization of Africans in London founded in 1925. J.B. Danquah and Edward O. Asafu-Adjaye of the Gold Coast were early leaders. Almost every Gold Coast student in London after 1925 was affiliated with WASU. Marcus Garvey gave the WASU a hostel in 1928. He also helped finance WASU publications. Blacks from all over the world were brought together at WASU meetings. WASU was a union of the Gold Coast Students' Union, the Nigerian Progress Union, and the Association of Students of African Descent.

WEST AFRICAN TIMES (later the Times of West Africa). Newspaper started in Accra by J.B. Danquah in 1931.

WEST AFRICAN YOUTH LEAGUE (WAYL). An organization founded in 1934 by Isaac Theophilus Akunna Wallace Johnson, a communist and Pan-Africanist from Sierra Leone who moved to the Gold Coast in 1933, and Bankole Awooner Renner, also an active communist. The WAYL's goal was to advance the cause of self-determination and the overthrow of British rule. Nnamdi Azikiwe used the African Morning Post in Accra as a mouthpiece for the WAYL. The colonial authorities expelled I.T.A. Wallace Johnson from the Gold Coast in 1938 and the League soon collapsed. This was the first radical movement organized in the Gold Coast to call for complete freedom from the British.

WEST INDIA COMPANY, DUTCH. A Dutch company created in 1621 to trade in the West Indies and on the coast of Africa. It was reorganized in 1674 and continued to operate until it went bankrupt and had to dissolve in 1791. They took Elmina from the Portuguese in 1637 and Axim in 1642. For many years after that they dominated all the trade west of Elmina, and for a few years, from 1642 to 1674, came close to dominating all the trade on the Gold Coast. In 1717 they acquired the property of the Brandenburgers, but the company had already lost its commanding edge to the British by then. After 1791 the Netherlands' government assumed control of Dutch interests along the Gold Coast, and trade continued until all the posts were sold to the British in 1872.

WEST INDIA AND GUINEA COMPANY (WIGC). A Danish Company which traded with West Africa in the seventeenth and eighteenth centuries. The company resulted from the union of Gluckstadt and Copenhagen trading groups and was never very successful. It was abolished in 1754 and the Danish crown took over its assets. The British purchased all Danish claims in 1850.

WESTERN ECHO. A Cape Coast newspaper founded by James Brew in 1885. It pushed the idea of representative government for the Gold Coast. Its last issue appeared in December 1887, but it was soon replaced by the Gold Coast Echo, edited by a nephew of James H. Brew, J.E. Casely-Hayford.

WESTERN REGION. The southwestern part of the old Gold Coast Colony. It includes Sefwi, Aowin, Nzema, Ahanta, and Wassa.

The administrative center is at Sekondi. The present boundaries were established in 1960. The census of 1970 showed a population of 770,087.

WHITE VOLTA. Tributary of the Volta that rises in the Yatenga section of Upper Volta, flows east of Ouagadougou about 30 miles (48 km), and crosses into the Upper East Region of Ghana some 12 miles (19 km) west of Bawku. At the Gambaga Scarp it turns sharply west, is joined by the Red Volta near the village of Gambaga, continues on west for some 38 miles (61 km) more, and then turns sharply southward, traveling down the center of Ghana until it enters Lake Volta above Yapei.

WIASE (Wiasi). 7°43' N, 0°42' W. Village in the Brong Ahafo Region about 20 miles (32 km) east of Atebubu on the road to Kete-Krakye. It is located near the Paba, a tributary of the Sene.

WIAWSO (Weoso). 6°12' N, 2°29' W. An important town in the Sefwi area of the Western Region. It is on the Tano River. The British opened an agricultural station here in 1915. This encouraged cocoa cultivation in the area.

WIAWSO HILLS. Hills in the Western Region between Enchi and Bibiani. At their highest point they are about 1,998 feet (609 m). The valley of the Tano divides these hills.

WILKS, IVOR G.H. Born 1928. A native of Coventry, England, who was educated at the University of Wales and Cambridge. He was on the faculty of the University College of the Gold Coast-University of Ghana from 1953 to 1961, on the staff of the Institute of African Studies, Legon, 1961-1966, and since 1966 has been on the faculty of Northwestern University. He is the author of Asante in the Nineteenth Century (1975) and many other important works on the Asante and the people of Ghana. His graduate students have made a great contribution to the detailed study of many areas of Ghana.

WILLIAM, FORT. One of the outforts in the fortifications around Cape Coast Castle. It was first built around 1820 and called Smith's Tower. It was refurbished in 1831 and the name was changed to Fort William. After 1835 it was used as a lighthouse.

WINNEBA (Winnebah, Simpa). 5°20' N, 0°37' W. Important coastal town in the Central Region some 35 miles (56 km) west of Accra. The traditional founder was Simpun. It is an important Efutu center. The English were trading here by 1633 and built a fort from which to trade in 1694, but no trace of Winneba Fort is left today. In the 1920s it was an important resort and residence for Europeans. It was the third most important port on the coast, and an outlet for cocoa and palm oil produced in the interior. Winneba was once famous for the canoes made on its beaches and for its fishermen, but the port was closed in 1961. When Kwame Nkrumah laid the foundation stone for the Kwame Nkrumah Institute of Ideology 18 February 1961 the President of the USSR attended the ceremonies. The Institute lasted less than six years, but in 1983 the PNDC talked of opening it again. The National Academy of Music is located at Winneba. Winneba had a population of 4,238 in 1891, 5,842 in 1911, 10,926 in 1931, 25,376 in 1960, and by 1970 the census had grown to 30,778.

WINNIETT, WILLIAM. Died 1850. Naval officer who was Lt. Governor at Cape Coast, 1846-1849, and Governor in 1850. His first major act on the Gold Coast was to conduct an expedition against the Chief of Apollonia, who had killed many people and had offered gold for the heads of strangers brought to him. Winniett imprisoned the Chief at Cape Coast Castle. In September 1848 he became the first British Governor to go to Asante, visiting with Asantehene Kwaku Dua until 26 October. He kept "a Journal of a Visit to Ashanti" (Winniett to Earl Henry George Grey, 15 November 1848). He took part in the negotiations with the Danes to buy their rights on the Gold Coast, and in March 1850 he toured the newly acquired territory. Winniett became full Governor after the Gold Coast was separated from Sierra Leone in 1850. He also selected James Bannerman, a Scottish-African, to be Civil Commandant at Christiansborg in 1850, after that Castle was acquired from Denmark. When Winniett died at the end of December 1850, Bannerman became Lt. Governor.

WITZEN, FORT. The Swedes established a post at Takoradi in 1650, but the Danes took the Swedish post, only to be replaced by the Dutch. The Dutch then built Fort Witzen. It was abandoned in 1818.

WLI FALLS (Afegame, Agumasato). 7°08' N, 0°36' E. Spectacular waterfalls east of Hohoe in the Volta Region and on the Togo border at Mount Agumasato. The falls are nearly a thousand feet (305 m) high.

WOFA. A maternal uncle. The mother's brother is most important in any matrilineal society such as Akan society.

WOLSELEY, SIR GARNET JOSEPH. 1833-1913. Military commander. Commissioned in 1852, he served in Burma, the Crimea, India, China, Canada, Zululand, and Egypt before being sent to the Gold Coast. In 1873 Wolseley was vested with supreme civil and military command in the Gold Coast. He reached Cape Coast 2 October 1873 and quickly prepared to march against Asante. He entered Kumasi on 4 February 1874, and two days later the city was destroyed. The Asantehene was forced to renounce the allegiance of Denkyira, Assin, Akyem, Adansi, and Elmina with its allies. An impossible indemnity was imposed on the Asante. Many of the provinces of Asante declared their freedom from Asante. Wolseley soon departed from the Gold Coast and returned to England the conquering hero. The Asante (Sagrenti) campaign made Wolseley famous. He was made a major general at 40.

WORKERS' BRIGADES. Organized as Builders' Brigade in December 1957, they were units to provide work for unemployed youth and to mobilize political support for the CPP. Base camps were set up in each region of Ghana. In 1964 the Brigades began to receive training as paramilitary units. They were often assigned security duties and were used to swell crowds at CPP functions and public affairs. The brigades were divested of their military functions in September 1968.

WORKERS' DEFENSE COMMITTEE (WDC). On 1 January 1982, the morning after the Provisional National Defense Council seized power, Jerry John Rawlings announced that "Power belongs to the People." PNDC policy guidelines provided for a strategy to single out the less articulate members of society for leadership roles. These guidelines stated that "The December Revolution aims at ensuring that power is exercised by the people organised from the grassroots." The PNDC promised to radically transform the socioeconomic institutions of Ghana. To offer those at the bottom of society a chance to participate in making decisions the PNDC created the Peoples' Defense Committees (PDCs), Workers' Defense Committees (WDC), Citizens' Vetting Committees (CVC), Regional Defense Committees (RDC), and the National Defense Committees (NDC). All these organizations were to be involved in community projects, community decisions, and individual members were to expose corruption and unsocial activities. Mawuse Dake was made the Secretary to the National Defense Committee, charged with making the whole structure work. The WDCs have been especially active since 1982 in taking over management of businesses from management. Many foreign-owned factories were taken over by WDCs. Unilever Soap, Valco, Ghana Textiles Printers, and Juapong Textiles are factories in which WDCs clashed with management.

WORLD WAR I, 1914-1919. Britain declared war on Germany 4 August 1914. The following day Major von Doering, acting Governor of Togoland, offered neutrality to the Gold Coast and to the French in Dahomey. France and England declined the German offer and immediately crossed into German territory. The Togo capital at Lome, just across the border from Aflao, was occupied without bloodshed. Lome was occupied on 7 August, Yendi on the 14th, and Ho on the 17th. The only real fighting took place as the British and French moved to take the German wireless station at Kamina. But that campaign was brief, and German forces in Togo surrendered on 26 August. The two allies divided Togo between themselves.

At the start of the war the Gold Coast Regiment of the West African Frontier Force consisted of 49 British and 1,584 African troops. The Northern Territories Constabulary had two British officers and 321 African troopers. Recruitment of Africans into British service was voluntary throughout World War I. From 1914 to 1918 over 3,000 men of the Gold Coast Regiment and more than a thousand auxiliary personnel were sent to the Cameroons and East Africa for service outside the Gold Coast. Many more joined the colonial military and police services for duty within the Gold Coast. Troops were sent to the Cameroons in September 1914 and remained there until May 1916. The Gold Coast Regiment embarked for East Africa in July 1916, took part in the campaigns in both the German and Portuguese areas, and returned to the Gold Coast in September 1918.

Wartime licensing, inflation, shortages, and strenuous economy in government expenditures caused serious problems. Muslim unrest and sympathy for their fellow Muslims in Islamic areas allied to Germany caused apprehension among colonial officials. There were some disorders in Asante and the Central Province in 1914; at Bongo, near the Upper Volta border, in 1916; and at Great Ningo and in Gonja in 1917; but at no time was there danger of a major revolt in the Gold Coast during World War I. Generally most of the people sided with the allied cause. But there was a sharp rise in national consciousness in the Gold Coast during World War I. Allied rhetoric about democracy and self-determination did not go unheeded in Africa. People in the Gold Coast began to hear W.E.B. Du Bois and Marcus Garvey. And for the first time the Colony, Asante, and the Northern Territories began to develop a sense of unity.

WORLD WAR II, 1939-1945. World War II weakened the British Empire and the elan of the English. With the fall of France in June 1940 hegemony of Europe began to disintegrate. The Gold Coast found itself completely surrounded by territory ruled by Vichy France. The very existence of England was threatened, and England would have collapsed in 1941 had it not been for the United States and Russia. This had profound repercussions on the British Empire everywhere. The Gold Coast Brigade of the Royal West African Frontier Force (RWAFF) was sent off to Kenya to drive the Italians out of East Africa at the beginning of World War II. With that mission accomplished, the troops were returned home, reorganized, and in June 1943 sent off to Burma. Conscription was resorted to in 1941, and during World War II some 65,000 persons from the Gold Coast saw service in one of the various allied units.

In 1942 the British began a program of appointing Africans to senior positions in the government. A new constitution with majority representation in the Legislative Assembly was promised after the war. The British launched major campaigns for increased production of food, oils, minerals, timber, and rubber.

Income taxes were introduced. And obligations were incurred by the British that would make concessions inevitable after the war.

Accra and Achimota became the command center for the allies in West Africa. The US Air Force opened a major air base at Accra Airport in 1941 to ferry planes and supplies to North Africa and the Middle East. An auxiliary base was established at Takoradi. During 1942 and 1943 an average of 200 to 300 planes refueled each day at Accra. Headquarters for West Africa were established at Achimota in July 1942 to coordinate war efforts for the British, Free French, Belgians, and Americans in that theater of operations. Lord Swinton (Philip Cunliffe-Lister), with the title of Cabinet Minister Resident in West Africa, commanded at Achimota from 1942 to 1944, when he was replaced by Harold Balfour.

WULOMO. The Ga high priest who presides over Ga communities. He exercises both political and religious authority. The wulomo of Accra was the commander of the Ga military confederation in the early days.

WURA. The suffix for chief in Gonja. It is equivalent to na in Dagbani areas, hene among the Akan, and manche among the Ga.

- X -

XAVIER, FORT SAN FRANCISCO (Saint Francis Xavier). In 1661 the Danes were ceded a piece of land on the beach at Osu by the King of Accra, and they began what became Christiansborg Castle. Mutineers took the new fortifications in 1679 and sold it to the Portuguese, who renamed the place San Francisco Xavier. By 1683 the Portuguese realized that they could no longer compete on the Gold Coast, so they sold the station back to the Danes.

- Y -

YAA ASANTEWAA (Ya Asantiwah). Died 1921. Edwesohemaa. The Queenmother of Ejisu (Edwese), a town ten miles (16 km) east of Kumasi. She rallied the Asante against the British in 1900, and the war which resulted was named for her. She was sent into exile in the Seychelles Islands after the war, in May 1901, and she died in exile in 1921.

YAA ASANTEWAA WAR, 1900-1901. The last conflict between the Asante and the British started as a result of demands by British Governor Arnold Hodgson for the Golden Stool. The British quickly gained the upper hand. Yaa Asantewaa and fourteen others were sent into exile, and Asante was placed under a British Chief Commissioner.

YAGABA (Yariba). 10°14' N, 1°16' W. Village in the Northern Region on the Kulpawn River, about 50 miles (80 km) north of Daboya. This was on an old trade path that ran from Kintampo to Buipe to Daboya to Yagaba, and then on north, across the Kulpawn to Boromo and Safane (in modern Upper Volta), and finally to Jenne. The village had a population of about 2,000 in 1898.

YAGBUM see NYANOA

YAGBUMWURA. The paramount chief of Gonja. In the beginning his seat was at Nyanoa or Yagbum, northeast of Bole.

YAKUBA. The twenty-seventh Ya Na of Dagomba. He was the son of Na Andani, and he ruled in the middle of the nineteenth century. He was the ruler of Dagomba at the time the Zabrama horsemen came to Dagomba under Alfa dan Tadano Hano from Zerma (modern Niger).

YAMS (Inhame, dioscorea). The staple vegetable of much of Ghana.

YAM FESTIVAL see AHUBAW and ODWIRA

YA NA. The paramount chief of Dagomba.

YANKEY, AMBROSE. A Nzema and distant relative of Kwane Nkrumah who was very close to Nkrumah during the First Republic. He was head of Nkrumah's special presidential body guard after 1962. When his son got into trouble about taking bribes from Lebanese merchants, Nkrumah ordered the case dropped. Yankey often used the Workers' Brigade for security duties and to line the routes of official parades.

YANKEY, AUGUSTUS KWESI. Born 1936. Labor leader. He served several years as General Secretary of the General Transport, Petroleum, and Chemical Workers Union. At the Ghana Trades Union Congress at Kumasi on 16 December 1983 he was elected to replace A.M. Issifu (who had resigned earlier) as Secretary-General of the TUC.

YANTAMBO see NNANTOMBO

YANTAURE see YENNENGA

YAPEI (Tamale Port). 9°10' N, 1°10' W. Village in the Northern Region on the northern end of Lake Volta just south of where the Mole River enters the Volta. Yapei is some 28 miles (45 km) southwest of Tamale. The northern port of Lake Volta is

located here, and a bridge crosses the Volta at this location.
The population was just 233 in 1948, and by 1970 it was only
1,203. Jakpa and the Gonja defeated the Dagomba here in the
early seventeenth century. The Ya Na at the time was Dariziegu, the eleventh of his line.

YARIBA see YAGABA

YARSE (sing. Yarga). Itinerant merchants from the north who
formerly came to the area of modern Ghana for slaves, gold,
and kola. They still come for kola. They frequently drive
livestock south. There are several terms used for traders from
the north such as Dyula, Wangara, and Kantosi.

YAW AKOTO see OSEI YAW AKOTO

YEJI. 8°13' N, 0°39' W. Village in the Brong-Ahafo Region where
the Great North Road from Kumasi to Tamale crosses the Lake
Volta Ferry. Before the impoundment of the lake, the river
was about 600 yards (549 m) wide at this point. Today the
ferry crosses a wide lake. The road from Yeji through Salaga
to Tamale was paved in 1907. Yeji is located just above where
the Pru River enters Lake Volta. It is about 20 miles (32 km)
to Salaga, and 85 miles (136 km) to Tamale. Yeji had a population of 1,351 in 1948, 2,198 in 1960, and in 1970 the census
figure was 5,485.

YENDI. 9°26' N, 0°01' W. The capital of the Dagomba, Yendi is
in the Northern Region, 55 miles (88 km) east of Tamale, and
45 miles (72 km) north of Bimbila. It was once a Konkomba
town, named Chare, but the Dagomba established themselves
here in the early seventeenth century. From 1745 to 1873 the
Dagomba owed tribute to Asante. The Europeans began to arrive in Yendi shortly after the Dagomba began to free themselves from Asante. For several hundreds of years Yendi was
an important depot on the trade routes to Hausaland. In 1824
Dupuis reported that Yendi was four times the size of Kumasi.
Dr. Gouldsbury visited Yendi in 1876, followed by Lonsdale
a few years later. The German, Von Francois was there in
1888, followed by Von Carnap. G.E. Ferguson was in Yendi
in August 1894. Yendi almost got destroyed by the Germans
5 December 1896, and after the British and Germans divided
Dagomba, Yendi fell to the Germans. It became British in August 1914. The population of Yendi in 1948 was 7,691. In
1960 the population had grown to 16,096, and by 1970 it was
22,072.

YENDI DABARI (Dapali, Dipali). 9°48' N, 0°57' W. "The Ruins
of Yendi" are located near the modern village of Dapali, in the
Northern Region, 30 miles (48 km) north of Tamale. The first
Ya Na of Dagomba, Nyagse, established his capital here. About

1713 the Gonja threatened Dagomba, and the capital was moved eastward to modern Yendi.

YENNENGA (Kachiogo, Yantaure, Yalanga, Yenenga, Nyennega). Daughter of Na Gbewa (Nedega) of Pusiga. Gbewa is the traditional progeniter of all the Mole-Dagbani peoples of the Volta basin. His oldest child was his only daughter, Yennenga. Tradition says that Gbewa did not want her to marry, so she ran away and mated with a Busansi hunter named Rialle (Riale). Their son, Ouedraogo (Ouidiraogo, Wedraoge, Widiraego, etc.) is the ancestor of the Mossi nobility. Yennenga had many brothers, Sitobu, Tohogo, Nnantombo, Zirile, and others.

YENTUA BROADCAST. On 5 February 1972 I.K. Acheampong gave a radio address to the people of Ghana. He announced that the NRC had adopted a policy of Yentua, "We Shall Not Pay," towards debts owed to four British companies. This was a repudiation of 66 million British pounds ($94 million US). It was an extremely popular announcement in Ghana, but it did not help Ghana's credit rating with the international banking community.

YILO KROBO. One branch of the Krobo Adangbe. Their chief town is Somanya, located just west of Akuse and the Volta River. They once lived on Krobo Mountain with the Manya Krobo. They still live in the eastern part of the Accra Plains. They are closely related to the Ada and Shai people. All the Adangbe believe that they first came from near Lolove Hill.

YINI. The word meaning God to many of the peoples of the Upper and Northern regions of Ghana. Winnam, Winde, Zid' winde, Wene, Nwendo, Wea, and Ouende are variations. The term also means sun, thus "Sun God," or "Supreme God."

YIRI. A family compound in the Upper and Northern regions of Ghana. The compound is home of a family headed by a Yi-dana.

YO NA. The Chief of Savelugu. He is an important figure in the hierarchy of the Dagomba because Savelugu was in the center of the Dagomba realm before the Dagomba were forced eastward to Yendi in the seventeenth century. Savelugu was near Yendi Dabari and Yoggo.

YOGGO (Yogo, Yoggu). 9°29' N, 1°06' W. Village in the Northern Region northwest of Tamale. This was the head village for the Dagomba before the descendants of Gbewa, Sitobu and his son, Nyagse, arrived. Na Nyagse, first ruler of Dagomba, died here. It is still the home of the head animist priest of Dagomba.

YOUNG, WILLIAM ALEXANDER GEORGE. Died 1885. A British naval officer who served briefly as Governor of the Gold Coast between Samuel Rowe and William Brandford Griffith. He died 24 April 1885 and is buried next to Governor Herbert Taylor Ussher at James Town, Accra.

YOUNG PIONEER MOVEMENT (YPM). An organization established by the CPP and Kwane Nkrumah in 1961 to replace the Boy Scout Movement in Ghana. Members were taught to deify Nkrumah, and to report parents, teachers, or others who expressed anti-government opinions. The YPM inculcated blind obedience to the Osagyefo and Nkrumahism.

YOUNGMAN. Literally, any Ghanaian who is not of royal blood, or is not considered to be one of the elders.

YOUTH STUDY GROUP (YSG). A group founded in 1948 by K.A. Gbedemah, Kojo Botsio, and others who broke away from the UGCC and began to support Kwame Nkrumah as their leader in opposition to the lawyers who ran the UGCC. The YSG organized mass-meetings for Nkrumah. One of these mass-meetings at the West End Arena in Accra organized the CPP, 12 June 1949.

- Z -

ZABARIMA   see   ZABRAMA

ZABERMA   see   ZABRAMA

ZABERMAWA   see   ZABRAMA

ZABRAMA (Zabarima, Zaberma, Zabermawa, Djerma, Zerma, Songhai). People speak the Djerma dialect of the Songhai language. In the 1860s a group of horsemen came from the area of modern Niger to serve the ruler of Dagomba. The leader of this group of Zerma was Alfa dan Tadano Hano. Tradition says that Hano was a very religious Muslim and that he spent some time in a Koranic school in Salaga. In time these men began to raid into the Animist areas between the White and Black Voltas. Trade in captives from these raids was so profitable that Hano determined to establish an Islamic state in the area. Hano died about 1870, and he was followed by Alfa Gazari dan Mahama. Gazari consolidated the power of the Zerma (now known as the Zabrama) in a large area north of the Kulpawn in what is today the Upper West Region of Ghana and the western part of Upper Volta. Gazari was succeeded by Babatu in 1883. Gazari encountered rebellion among his followers, a threat from the troops of Samori, and encroaching white men. In 1897 the French defeated Babatu at Gandiaga in March and at Doucie in June. Babatu retreated into Dagomba, where he joined his former allies, the Dagomba, in resistance to British advances.

Babatu died about 1900. Hamma Zaza, a son of Gazari, was the last leader of the Zabrama.

ZABZUGU HILLS. 9°17' N, 0°22' E. Also called the Shiene Hills. These low hills are between the Oti River and the Togo border in the Konkomba area of the Northern Region southeast of Yendi. There is iron ore in this area.

ZAZA, HAMMA. A son of Alfa Gazari who became leader of the Zabrama in Dagomba about 1900 after the death of Babatu. He lived in the part of Dagomba over which the Germans had established control.

ZANGBERESE (sing. Zangbeo). A name for the Hausa in northwestern Ghana.

ZANGINA, MUHAMMAD. The seventeenth Ya Na of Dagomba. He was a nephew of his predecessor, Gungobili. He converted to Islam during his reign and invited many mallams into Dagomba. Before he was converted his name was Wumbei. He ruled at a time, at the beginning of the eighteenth century, when many Hausa and Dyula Muslims were trading in Dagomba. Gonja invaded Dagomba near the end of the reign of Zangina, and the Gonja came within 20 miles (32 km) of Yendi before they were halted and defeated at Sang. Zangina was a son of Na Tutugri and grandson of Na Luro, who had moved the Dagomba capital to Yendi. When Zangina's uncle, Na Gungobili, died there was a dispute over the succession. The ruler of Mamprusi was invited to settle the dispute and selected Zangina. The method of solving the succession created bitterness that divided Dagomba during the war with Gonja. According to one tradition, Zangina abdicated in 1713 to allow his cousin, Andani Sigili (Zighli), to unite Dagomba against Gonja. Zangina died a short time later at Agbandi, a short distance southeast of Yendi near the Oti River.

ZERILE see ZIRILE

ZERMA see ZABRAMA

ZIRILE (Sirili, Zerile, Zirili, Zitiri). Son of Na Gbewa of Pusiga. Brother of Yennenga (Kachiogo), Tohogo, Sitobu, Nnantombo (Ngamtambo), and Kufogo. Zirile was the oldest son of Gbewa, but Gbewa wanted Kufogo to rule after him. Zirile killed his brother and took the skin of Pusiga. The children of Na Gbewa founded the Mole Dagbani states.

ZONGO. The strangers' quarters or section of a town.

ZOY. The first radio station on the Gold Coast. It was established at Accra in 1935.

ZUARUNGU. 10°47' N, 0°48' W. Town in the Upper East Region just east of Bolgatanga. The architectural decoration of compounds in the area are interesting.

ZULANDE. The Second Ya Na of Dagomba. He was a great-grandson of Na Gbewa, a grandson of Sitobu, and son of Nyagse. Three of Zulande's sons followed him as Ya Nas of Dagomba.

BIBLIOGRAPHY

CONTENTS

A.	Bibliographies and Guides	200
B.	General Information	204
C.	Serials	206
D.	Government Publications	208
E.	Archaeology	211
F.	General History	214
G.	History before 1840	215
H.	History 1840-1956: Colonialism	218
I.	History Since Independence	229
J.	Regional Studies	242
K.	Travel	255
L.	Geography	258
M.	Arts	260
N.	Literature and Press	262
O.	Language	267
P.	Culture and Social Life	270
Q.	Economics	277
R.	Religion and Philosophy	285
S.	Education	288

A. BIBLIOGRAPHIES AND GUIDES

Adams, Cynthia. A Study Guide for Ghana. Boston: Boston University African Studies Center, 1967. 95 p.

Afre, S.A. Ashanti Region of Ghana: An Annotated Bibliography, from Earliest Times to 1973. Boston: G.K. Hall, 1975. 494 p.

Aguolu, Christian Chukwunedu. Ghana in the Humanities and Social Sciences, 1900-1971: A Bibliography. Metuchen, N.J.: The Scarecrow Press, 1973. 469 p. Indispensable.

Agyemang, H.D., comp. Legon Theses; A Checklist of Theses and Dissertations Accepted for Higher Degrees by the University of Ghana, Legon, 1964-1977. Legon: Balme Library, 1978. 33 p.

Amanquah, S.N. A Bibliography of University of Ghana Staff Publications, 1948-73. Legon: University of Ghana, 1974. 256 p.

Amedekey, E.Y. The Culture of Ghana; a Bibliography. Accra: Ghana Universities Press, 1970. 215 p.

Aning, B.A. "An Annotated Bibliography of Music and Dance in English-Speaking Africa." Legon: Institute of African Studies, 1967. Mimeographed.

Asiedu, Edward Seth. Public Administration in English-Speaking West Africa, 1945-1975: An Annotated Bibliography. Boston: G.K. Hall Reference Books, 1977. 366 p.

Boyo, Osmanu Eshaka; Thomas Hodgkin; and Ivor Wilks, comps. Check List of Arabic Works from Ghana. Legon: Institute of African Studies, University of Ghana, Dec. 1962.

Brand, Richard Robert. A Selected Bibliography of Accra, Ghana, a West African Colonial City (1887-1960). Monticello, Ill.: Council of Planning Librarians, 1970. 27 p.

Bridgman, Jon, and David E. Clarke. German Africa: A Select Annotated Bibliography. Stanford: Stanford University Hoover Institution Bibliographical Series, 19, 1965.

Brokensha, David, and S.I.A. Kotei. "A Bibliography of Ghana: 1958-1964." African Studies Bulletin, 10, 2 (1967), 35-79.

Cardinall, Allan Wolsey. A Bibliography of the Gold Coast. (Issued as a Companion Volume to the Census Report of 1931.) Accra: Government Printer, Gold Coast Colony, 1932. 384 p.; Rpt. Westport, Conn.: Greenwood Press for Negro Universities Press, 1970; and Ann Arbor, Mich.: University Microfilms-Xerox, 1970. Indispensable.

Carson, Patricia. Materials for West African History in the Archives of Belgium and Holland. Oxford: Athlone Press, 1962. 86 p.

Chazan, N. "Ghanaian Political Studies in Transition: A Reflection on Some Recent Contributions," Development and Change, July 1978, pp. 479-503.

Cochrane, T.W. Preliminary Bibliography of the Volta River Authority Programme. Accra: Volta River Authority, 1968.

Dadson, Theresa. Index to the Legon Observer, vols. 2-9 (1967-1974). Boston: G.K. Hall, 1979. 180 p.

De Heer, A.N., comp. A List of Ghanaian Newspapers and Periodicals. Accra: Ghana Library Board, 1970. 16 p.

Duignan, Peter. Guide to Research and Reference Works on Sub-Saharan Africa. Stanford: Stanford University Hoover Institution Bibliographical Series 46, 1972, pp. 443-459.

Easterbrook, David L. Africana Book Reviews, 1885-1945: An Index to Books Reviewed in Selected English-Language Publications. Boston: G.K. Hall Reference Books, 1979. 247 p.

Fage, John Donnelly. "On the Reproduction and Editing of Classics of African History," Journal of African History (London), 8, 1 (1967), 157-178. On Cass editions of Bowdich and Dupuis.

_____. "Some General Considerations Relevant to Historical Research in the Gold Coast," Transactions of the Gold Coast and Togoland Historical Society, 1 (1952), 24-29.

_____. "Some Notes on a Scheme for Investigation of Oral Tradition in the Northern Territories of the Gold Coast," Journal of the Historical Society of Nigeria (Ibadan), 1, 1 (Dec. 1956), 15-19.

Ghana, University of. Early Africana (1556-1900) in the Balme Library. Legon: University of Ghana Press, 1972. 70 p.

Halstead, John P., and Serafino Porcari. Modern European Imperialism: A Bibliography of Books and Articles, 1815-1972. Vol. 1. Boston: G.K. Hall, 1974, pp. 188-194.

Havinden, M.A. The History of Crop Cultivation in West Africa: A Bibliographical Guide. Exeter: Department of Economic History, University of Exeter, 1970. 20 p.

Henige, David P. "The National Archives of Ghana: A Synopsis of Holdings," The International Journal of African Historical Studies (Boston), 6, 3 (1973), 475-486.

Hogg, Peter C. The African Slave Trade and Its Suppression. London: Frank Cass, 1973. 409 p. A classified and annotated bibliography of the slave trade.

Hunwick, J.O., ed. Proceedings of a Seminar on Ghanaian Historiography and Historical Research. Legon: University of Ghana, 1977. 290 p.

International Council on Archives. Guide to the Sources of the History of Africa. Vol. 3. Sources de l'Histoire de l'Afrique au Sud du Sahara dans les Archives et Bibliothèques Françaises. 1-Archives. Zug, Switzerland: Interdocumentation Company, 1971.

_____. Guide to the Sources of the History of Africa. Vol. 4. Sources de l'Histoire de l'Afrique au Sud du Sahara dans les Archives et Bibliothèques Françaises. 2-Bibliothèques. Zug, Switzerland: Interdocumentation Company, 1976.

Jahn, Janheinz, and Claus Peter Dressler. Bibliography of Creative African Writing. Millwood, N.Y.: Kraus Thomson, 1975. 446 p.

Johnson, Albert F. A Bibliography of Ghana, 1930-1961. Accra: Longman, Green for the Ghana Library Board, 1964. 210 p.; Evanston, Ill.: Northwestern University Press, 1964. Important.

Jones, Ruth. West Africa: General, Ethnography, Sociology, Linguistics. London: International African Institute, 1958.

Joucia, Edmond Antoine. Bibliographie de l'Afrique Occidentale Française. Paris: Société d'Editions Geographiques, Maritimes et Coloniales, 1937. 712 p.

Kafe, Joseph Kofi. Ghana: An Annotated Bibliography of Academic Theses, 1920-1970 in the Commonwealth, the Republic of Ireland, and the United States of America. Boston: G.K. Hall Reference Publications, 1973. 219 p. Important.

Kagan, Alfred, and Michael Sims. American and Canadian Masters and Doctoral Theses on Africa, 1886-1974. Waltham, Mass.: African Studies Association, 1975.

Kaplan, Irving, et al. Area Handbook for Ghana. 2nd ed. Washington, D.C.: U.S. Government Printing Office, 1971. 449 p.

Krzysztof, Zielnica. Bibliographie der Ewe in Westafrica. Acta Ethnologica et Linguistica, 38, Series Africana 11. Vienna: Institut für Volkerkunde der Universität Wien, 1976. 178 p.

Lawrence, Arnold Walter. "Some Source Books for West African History," Journal of African History, 2, 2 (1961), 227-234.

Levtzion, Nehemia. "Early Nineteenth Century Arabic Manuscripts from Kumasi," Transactions of the Historical Society of Ghana, 8 (1965), 99-119.

_____, and J.F.P. Hopkins. Corpus of Early Arabic Sources for West African History. London: The International Academic Union by Cambridge University Press, 1981. 492 p.

Low, Victor N., ed. African Histories and Societies to 1914: A Critical Survey of Relevant Books. Vol. 2. West Africa Region by Region. London: Frank Cass, 1981.

McIlwaine, J.H. St. J., comp. Theses on Africa, 1963-1975, Accepted by Universities in the United Kingdom and Ireland. London: Mansell, 1978. 123 p. Supplements 1964 list of theses between 1920 and 1962.

Matthews, Noel. Materials for West African History in the Archives of the United Kingdom. Guides to Materials for West African History, European Archives, 5. London: Athlone Press, 1973. 225 p.

Pitcher, G.M., comp. Bibliography of Ghana, 1957-1960. Kumasi: Library of the University of Science and Technology, 1962. 111 p.

Reindorf, Joe. Scandinavians in Africa: A Guide to Materials Relating to Ghana in the Danish National Archives. New York: Columbia University Press, 1980; Oslo: Universitets-forlaget, 1980. 140 p.

Ryder, Alan Frederick Charles. Materials for West African History in Portuguese Archives. London: Athlone Press, 1965. 92 p.

Rydings, H.A. The Bibliographies of West Africa. Ibadan: Ibadan University Press, 1961.

Smith, H.M., comp. Ghana in Non-Ghanaian Serials and Collective Works 1974-1977: A Bibliography. Legon: Balme Library, University of Ghana, 1981. 90 p.

Smit, Hettie M. Hidden Items on Ghana in the Monograph Collection of the Balme Library. 2 vols. Legon: The Balme Library, University of Ghana, 1981-1982.

Tetty, Charles, comp. Medicine in West Africa, 1880-1956: An Annotated Bibliography. Accra: University of Ghana Medical School Library, 1975. 547 p.

Travis, Carole, ed. Periodicals from Africa: A Bibliography and Union List of Periodicals Published in Africa. Boston: G.K. Hall Reference Books, 1977. 620 p.

Witherell, Julian W., and Sharon B. Lockwood, comps. Ghana: A Guide to Official Publications, 1872-1968. Washington, D.C.: Library of Congress General Reference and Bibliography Division, 1969. 110 p.

Wolfson, Freda. "Ghana in Books," West Africa (London), Feb./March 1957, pp. 2080-2083.

_____. "Historical Records on the Gold Coast," Bulletin (Institute of Historical Research, London University), 24, 70 (1951), 121-240.

Zell, Hans M., ed. African Books in Print: An Index by Author, Subject, and Title. 2nd ed., Vols. 1 & 2. Westport, Conn.: Meckler Books, 1978. 322 p. and 543 p.

_____, and Helen Silver, et al. A Reader's Guide to African Literature. New York: Africana Publishing Corp., 1971. 232 p.; London: Heinemann, 1972.

B. GENERAL INFORMATION

Adzakey, Nathaniel K., ed. Ghana Who's Who, 1972-1973. Accra: Bartels Publications, 1972. 447 p.

Ahuma, S.R. Memoirs of West African Celebrities: With Special Reference to the Gold Coast. Liverpool: Marples, 1905. 260 p.

Ajayi, J.F.A., and Michael Crowder. History of West Africa. 2 vols. New York: Columbia University Press, 1972.

Chantler, Clyde. The Ghana Story. London: Linden Press, 1971. 214 p.; Brooklyn Heights, N.Y.: Beekman, 1971.

Dodds, Maggie, ed. Ghana Talks: Ghana Past and Present. Washington, D.C.: Three Continents Press, 1976. 241 p.; First published in Accra in 1974 as History of Ghana--A Series of Lectures.

Ephson, Isaac S. Gallery of Gold Coast Celebrities, 1632-1958. Accra: Ilen Publications, 1969.

Horton, J.A.B. West African Countries and Peoples. Edinburgh: Edinburgh University Press, 1868; rpt. 1969. 281 p.

Kaplan, Irving, et al. Area Handbook for Ghana. American University Foreign Area Studies, 2nd ed. Washington, D.C.: U.S. Printing Office, 1971. 449 p.

Lipschutz, Mark R., and R. Kent Rasmussen. Dictionary of African Historical Biography. Chicago: Aldine Publishing Company, 1978. 292 p.

MacDonald, George. The Gold Coast Past and Present; A Short Description of the Country and Its People. London: Longman, Green, 1898; rpt. New York: Negro Universities Press, 1969. 352 p.

Macmillan, Allister, comp. The Red Book of West Africa. 1st ed. 1920; rpt. London: Frank Cass, 1968. Gold Coast section, pp. 139-228.

Mayer, Emerico Samassa. Ghana: Past and Present. The Hague: Levision Press, 1965; New York: Arco Publishing Co., 1968. 112 p.

Ofosu-Appiah, L.H., ed. Encyclopedia Africana: Dictionary of African Biography. Vol. 1: Ethiopia-Ghana. Algonac, Me.: Reference Publications, Inc., 1977. 367 p.

Pedler, Frederick. Main Currents of West African History 1940-1979. London and New York: Barnes and Noble, 1979. 301 p.

Pellow, Deborah, and Naomi Chazan. Ghana. Westview Profiles of Contemporary Africa Series. Boulder, Colo.: Westview Press, Forthcoming, 1985.

Rattray, Robert Sutherland. A Short Manual of the Gold Coast. n.p., 1924. 88 p.

Redmayne, Paul. The Gold Coast, Yesterday and Today. London: Chatto and Windus, 1838. 128 p.

Remy, Mylene. Ghana Today. Paris: J.A. Editions, 1977. 256 p.; New York: Hippocrene Books.

Royal Institute of International Affairs. Ghana: A Survey of the Gold Coast on the Eve of Its Independence. London: RIIA, 1957. 62 p.

Sampson, Magnus J. Gold Coast Men of Affairs; Past and Present. Ilfracombe: Stockwell, 1937. 224 p.

Semak, Michael. Image Four: Ghana. Montreal: McGill-Queen's University Press, 1969.

Strand, Paul. Ghana: An African Portrait. Millerton, N.Y.: Aperture, 1976. 159 p.

C. SERIALS

Africa. Journal of the International African Institute. London. 1928-

Africa Contemporary Record: An Annual Survey and Documents. Rex Collings, Holmes and Meier. London. 1968.

Africa Index. Oxford. 1976-

Africa Report. African-American Institute. Washington and New York. 1956-

Africa: South of the Sahara. Europa Publications. 1970-

Africa Yearbook and Who's Who. Africa Journal. London. 1977-

African Abstracts. International African Institute. London. 1950-1972.

African Affairs. Journal of the Royal African Society. London. 1901-

African Statistical Yearbook. UNECA. Addis Ababa. 1974-

African Studies Review. African Studies Association. Ann Arbor, Mich. 1958-

Africana Library Journal. Africana Publishing Corporation. New York. 1970-

Britannica Book of the Year. Chicago. 1938-

Bulletin of the Ghana Geographical Association. Accra. 1955-

Cahiers d'Etudes Africaines. Paris. 1960-

Canadian Journal of African Studies. Montreal. 1967-

Current Bibliography on African Affairs. Greenwood. New York. 1962–

Current History. Philadelphia. 1914–

Encyclopedia Americana Yearbook. New York. 1923–

Europa Year Book. London. 1959– . (Second volume each year has information on African countries.)

Facts on File. New York: 1940–

Ghana Bulletin of Theology. Department of Religion, University of Ghana. Legon. 1964–

Ghana Notes and Queries. Historical Society of Ghana. Legon. 1961–

Ghana Studies Bulletin. Issue No. 1, January 1984. Published by the Centre for West African Studies, University of Birmingham, for the Ghana Symposium, School of Oriental and African Studies, University of London. Bruce M. Haight, College of General Studies, Western Michigan University, Kalamazoo, Michigan 49008 (contact in the United States).

Ghana Who's Who. Bartels. Accra. 1972–

Ghana Year Book. Ghana Graphic Company. Accra. 1958–

International African Bibliography. Mansell Publishing Company. New York. 1980–

International Journal of African Historical Studies. Brookline, Mass. 1968–

Jeune Afrique. Paris. 1962–

Joint Acquisitions List of Africana. G.K. Hall. 1978–

Journal of African History. Cambridge. 1960–

Journal of African Studies. Washington. 1974–

Journal of Modern African Studies. Cambridge. 1963–

Journal of Religon in Africa. E.J. Brill. Leiden. 1967–

Journal of the Historical Society of Nigeria. Ibadan. 1965–

Journal of West African Languages. Cambridge. 1964–

Keesing's Contemporary Archives. London. 1931-

Legon Observer. Legon Society on National Affairs. Legon. 1966-

New International Year Book. New York. 1909-

Okyeame. Ghana Society of Writers. Accra. 1960-

Research Review. Institute of African Studies, University of Ghana. Legon. 1965-

Talking Drums. Issue No. 1, 12 September 1983. Talking Drums Publications, Madhav House, 68 Mansfield Road, London NW3 2HU. Elizabeth Ohene, a Ghanaian writer, is the editor of this news magazine.

Tarikh. Ibadan. 1965-

Transactions of the Gold Coast and Togoland Historical Society. Achimota. 1952-1957.

Transactions of the Historical Society of Ghana. Legon. 1957-

University of Ghana Law Journal. Legon. 1964-

West Africa. London. 1971-

West African Journal of Archaeology. Ibadan. 1971-

Whitaker's Almanack. London. 1869-

World Almanac. New York. 1868-

The Embassy of Ghana Information Section, 2460 16th Street, N.W., Washington, D.C. 20009, publishes Ghana News monthly.

D. GOVERNMENT PUBLICATIONS

Ghana. Census Office. Reports of the 1960 Population Census, vol. 1--The Gazeteer: Alphabetical List of Localities. Accra: Ghana Publishing Corp., 1962. 405 p.

⎯⎯⎯⎯⎯. 1960 Population Census of Ghana, vol. 2--Statistics of Localities and Enumeration Areas. Accra: Ghana Publishing Cor n.d. 707 p.

⎯⎯⎯⎯⎯. 1960 Population Census of Ghana, vol. 3--Demographic Characteristics of Local Authorities, Regions, and Total Country. Accra: Government Printer, 1964. 160 p.

_____. *1960 Population Census of Ghana, vol. 4--Economic Characteristics of Local Authorities, Regions and Total Country.* Accra: Government Printer, 1964. 270 p.

_____. *1960 Population Census of Ghana, vol. 5--General Report* by B. Gil and K.T. de Graft-Johnson. Accra: Ghana Publishing Corp., 1964. 410 p.

_____. *1960 Population Census of Ghana, vol. 6--The Post Enumeration Survey (P.E.S.) Supplementary Enquiry* by B. Gil, K.T. de Graft-Johnson, and E.A. Colecraft. Accra: Ghana Publishing Corp., 1971. 491 p.

_____. *1960 Population Census of Ghana. Special Report "A"-- Statistics of Towns with 10,000 Population of More.* Accra: Ghana Publishing Corp., 1964. 267 p.

_____. *1960 Population Census of Ghana, Special Report "E"-- Tribes in Ghana* by B. Gill, A.F. Aryee, and D.K. Ghansah. Accra: Ghana Publishing Corporation, 1964. 206 p.

_____. *1970 Population Census of Ghana, Vol. 2, Statistics of Localities and Enumeration Areas.* Accra: Ghana Publishing Corp., 1972. 971 p.

_____. *1970 Population Census of Ghana, Special Report "D"-- List of Localities by Local Authority, Ashanti Region.* Accra: Ghana Publishing Corp., 1971. 411 p.

_____. *1970 Population Census of Ghana, Special Report "D"-- List of Localities by Local Authority, Brong-Ahafo Region.* Accra: Ghana Publishing Corp., 1971. 340 p.

_____. *1970 Population Census of Ghana, Special Report "D"-- List of Localities by Local Authority, Central Region.* Accra: Ghana Publishing Corp., 1971. 158 p.

_____. *1970 Population Census of Ghana, Special Report "D"-- List of Localities by Local Authority, Greater Accra and Eastern Regions.* Accra: Ghana Publishing Corp., 1971. 213 p.

_____. *1970 Population Census of Ghana, Special Report "D"-- List of Localities by Local Authority, Northern and Upper Regions.* Accra: Ghana Publishing Corp., 1971. 197 p.

_____. *1970 Population Census of Ghana, Special Report "D"-- List of Localities by Local Authority, Volta Region.* Accra: Ghana Publishing Corp., 1971. 197 p.

_____. *1970 Population Census of Ghana, Special Report "D"-- List of Localities by Local Authority, Western Region.* Accra: Ghana Publishing Corp., 1971. 183 p.

Bibliography

_____. 1984 Population Census of Ghana. Forthcoming.

Ghana. Central Bureau of Statistics. Statistical Handbook of the Republic of Ghana. Accra: Government Printing Office, 1967- and irregular thereafter.

_____. Statistical Year Book. Accra: Government Printing Office, 1961- and irregular thereafter.

Ghana. Ministry of Information. Nkrumah's Deception of Africa. Accra: State Publishing Corp., 1967. 95 p.; also by Judiciary Committee, U.S. Senate, Washington, D.C.: U.S. Government Printing Office, 1972.

_____. Nkrumah's Subversion of Africa; Documentary Evidence of Nkrumah's Interference in the Affairs of Other African States. Accra: State Publishing Corp., 1967. 91p.; also by Judiciary Committee, U.S. Senate, Washington, D.C.: U.S. Government Printing Office, 1972.

Gold Coast Colony. Report of the Commisison of Enquiry into Disturbances in the Gold Coast. Andrew Aiken Watson, Chairman. London: H.M.S.O., 1948. 103 p.

_____. Correspondence Relating to the National Congress of British West Africa. Accra: Government Press, 1920. 61 p.

_____. Gold Coast Gazette, 1872-5 March 1957. Accra: Government Printer.

_____. The Gold Coast Handbook. Accra: Government Printer, 1923, with several editions thereafter.

Gold Coast Colony. Census Office. Report of the Census, 1891. Accra: Government Printer, 1891? 201 p.

_____. Report on the Census for the Year 1901. London: Waterlow and Sons, 1901. 66 p.

_____. Census of the Population, 1911. 3 parts. Accra: Government Press, 1912.

_____. Census Report, 1921, for the Gold Coast Colony, Ashanti, the Northern Territories, and the Mandated Area of Togoland. Accra: Government Press, 1923. 185 p.

_____. The Gold Coast, 1931; a Review of Conditions in the Gold Coast in 1931 as Compared with Those of 1921, Based on Figures and Facts Collected by the Chief Census Officer of 1931, Together with a Historical, Ethnographical, and Sociological Survey of the People of the Country. A.W. Cardinall, Chief Census Officer. Accra: Government Press, 1932. 265 p.

_____. Appendices Containing Comparative Returns and General Statistics of the 1931 Census. Accra: Government Press, 1932. 246 p.

_____. Census of Population, 1948; Report and Tables. London: Published on Behalf of the Government of the Gold Coast by the Crown Agents for the Colonies, 1950. 422 p.

Gold Coast Colony. Public Relations Department. Achievement in the Gold Coast; Aspects of Development in a British West African Territory. Accra: Government Printer, 1951. 96 p.

Gold Coast Colony. Survey Department. Atlas of the Gold Coast. Accra: Government Press, 1927. 24 maps and charts.

_____. Atlas of the Gold Coast. 5th ed. Accra: Government Press, 1949.

Great Britain. Commission of Inquiry into Disturbances in the Gold Coast, 1948. Report of. (Watson Report). London: HMSO, 1948. 103 p.

_____. The Ghana Order in Council, 1957 (Constitution of 1957). London: HMSO, 1957. 47 p.

Great Britain. Colonial Office. Statement by His Majesty's Government on the Report of the Commission of Enquiry into Disturbances in the Gold Coast, 1948. London: HMSO, 1948 14 p.

Volta River Preparatory Commission. The Volta River Project. 3 vols. London: HMSO, 1956. Includes bibliographies.

E. ARCHAEOLOGY

Ameyaw, Kwabena. "Kwawu-an Early Akan State," Ghana Notes and Queries, 9 (November 1966), 39-45.

Anquandah, James. "The Archaeological Evidence for the Emergence of Akan Civilization." Tarikh (Ibadan), 7, 2 (1982), 9-21.

_____. Rediscovering Ghana's Past. Accra: Sedco Publishing; Harlow, Essex: Longman Group, 1982. 161 p.

Bellis, James Oren. "Archeology and the Culture History of the Akan of Ghana." Ph.D. dissertation, Indiana University, 1972. 269 p.

Carter, P.L., and P.J. Carter. "Rock-paintings from Northern

Ghana." <u>Transactions of the Historical Society of Ghana</u>, 7 (1965), 1-3.

Davies, Oliver. <u>Archaeology in Ghana: Papers</u>. Edinburgh: Nelson and Sons for the University College of Ghana, 1961. 45 p.

──────. <u>Archaeology in the Volta Basin</u>. Legon: Department of Archaeology, University of Ghana, 1969. 100 p.

──────. <u>The Archaeology of the Flooded Volta Basin</u>. Occasional Papers in Archaeology, 1. Legon: Department of Archaeology and Volta Basin Research Project, University of Ghana, 1971. 34 p.

──────. <u>Excavations at Sekondi</u>. Accra: Ghana University Press, 1970. 100 p.

──────. "The Neolithic Revolution in Tropical Africa." <u>Transactions of the Historical Society of Ghana</u>, 4, 2 (1960), 14-20.

──────. "The Ntereso Culture in Ghana." In <u>West African Culture Dynamics: Archaeological and Historical Perspectives</u>, ed. by B.K. Swartz, Jr. and Raymond E. Dumett. The Hague, Paris, and New York: Mouton, 1980, pp. 205-225.

──────. <u>West Africa Before the Europeans: Archaeology and Prehistory</u>. Methuen Handbooks of Archaeology. London: Methuen, 1967. 364 p.

Effah-Gyamfi, E. "Aspects of the Archaeology and Oral Traditions of the Bono State." <u>Transactions of the Historical Society of Ghana</u>, 15, 2 (Dec. 1974), 217-227.

Flight, Colin. "The Kintampo Culture and Its Place in the Economic Prehistory of West Africa." In <u>West African Culture Dynamics: Archaeological and Historical Perspectives</u>, ed. by B.K. Swartz, Jr. and Raymond E. Dumett. The Hague, Paris, and New York: Mouton, 1980, pp. 91-100.

Kense, F.J. "Daboya: A Gonja Frontier." Ph.D. dissertation, Calgary University, 1981.

Kiyaga-Mulindwa, David. "The Earthworks of the Birim Valley, Southern Ghana." Ph.D. dissertation, The Johns Hopkins University, 1978.

──────. "Social and Demographic Changes in the Birim Valley, Southern Ghana, ca. 1450 to ca. 1800." <u>The Journal of African History</u> (London), 23, 1 (1982), 63-82.

Nygaard, Signe, and M.R. Talbot. "First Dates from Coastal Sites Near Kpone, Ghana." <u>Nyame Akuma</u> (Legon), 11 (1977), 29-30.

_____. "Interim Report on Excavation at Asokrochona, Ghana." West Africa Journal of Archaeology (Ibadan), 6 (1976), 13-19.

Ozanne, P.C. "Ghana." In The Iron Age in Africa, ed. by P.L. Shinnie. London: Oxford University Press, 1971.

_____. "Notes on the Early Historic Archaeology of Accra." Transactions of the Historical Society of Ghana, 6 (1962), 51-70.

Posnansky, Merrick. "The Archaeological Foundations of the History of Ghana." In Proceedings of the Seminar on Ghanaian Historiography and Historical Research, ed. by J.O. Hunwick. Legon: University of Ghana, 1977.

_____. "Archaeology, Technology and Akan Civilization." Journal of African Studies, 2 (1975).

Shaw, C. Thurstan. "Archaeology in the Gold Coast." African Studies, 2, 3 (1943), 139-147.

_____. Excavation at Dawu: Report on an Excavation in a Mound at Dawu, Akuapim, Ghana. London: Nelson for the University of Ghana, 1961. 124 p.

_____. "Excavations at Bosumpra Cave, Abetifi." Prehistoric Society Proceedings (London: Nelson), 10 (1944), 1-67.

Shinnie, P.L., and P.C. Ozanne. "Excavations at Yendi Dabari." Transactions of the Historical Society of Ghana, 6 (1962), 87-118.

Sutton, J.E.G. "Archaeology in West Africa: A Review of Recent Work and a Further List of Radiocarbon Dates." Journal of African History, 23, 3 (1982), 291-313.

Swartz, B.K., Jr. "An Analysis and Evaluation of the Yapei Pebble Tool Industry, Ghana." The International Journal of African Historical Studies (Boston), 5, 2 (1972), 265-270.

_____. "A Stratified Succession of Stone Age Assemblies at Hohoe, Ghana." West African Journal of Archaeology, 4 (1974), 57-81.

Wilks, Ivor. "Wangara, Akan and Portuguese in the Fifteenth and Sixteenth Centuries. I. The Matter of Bitu." Journal of African History, 3 (1982), 333-349.

York, R.N. Archaeology in the Volta Basin, 1963-1966. Legon: The University of Ghana, 1967. 45 p.

_____. "Excavations at Bui: A Preliminary Report." Bulletin of the Institute of African Studies (Legon), 1, 2 (1965), 36-39.

F. GENERAL HISTORY

Agbodeka, Francis. Ghana in the Twentieth Century. Accra: Ghana Universities Press, 1972. 152 p.

Boahen, Albert Adu. Evolution and Change in the 19th and 20th Centuries. London and New York: Longmans, 1975. 261 p. Paperback, 1979.

———. Topics in West African History. London and New York: Longman, 1966. 174 p.

Buah, F.K. A History of Ghana. London: Macmillan, 1980. 229 p. Buah was Minister of Education under Hilla Limann.

Claridge, William Walton. A History of the Gold Coast and Ashanti from the Earliest Times to the Commencement of the Twentieth Century. London: J. Murray, 1915. 649 p. and 638 p.; rpt. London: Frank Cass, 1964. 577 p. and 580 p.

Cornevin, Robert. Histoire du Togo. 2nd ed. Paris: Berger-Levrault, 1969. 554 p.

Curtin, Philip DeArmond. The Atlantic Slave Trade: A Census. Madison, Wisc.: University of Wisconsin Press, 1969. 338 p.

Decalo, Samuel. Historical Dictionary of Togo. Metuchen, N.J., and London: The Scarecrow Press, 1976. 243 p.

Dickson, Kwamina B. A Historical Geography of Ghana. Cambridge: Cambridge University Press, 1969. 379 p. paperback, 1971.

Ellis, Alfred Burdon. A History of the Gold Coast of West Africa. London: Chapman and Hall, 1893. 400 p.; rpt. New York: Negro Universities Press, 1969; rpt. Totowa, N.J.: Rowman and Littlefield, 1971.

Fage, John Donnelly. Ghana: A Historical Interpretation. Madison, Wisc.: University of Wisconsin Press, 1959. 122 p.

Flint, John E. Nigeria and Ghana. Englewood Cliffs, N.J.: Prentice-Hall, 1966. 176 p.

Forde, Daryll, and P.M. Kaberry, eds. West African Kingdoms in the Nineteenth Century. Oxford: Oxford University Press, 1967. 289 p.

Foster, Philip, and Aristide R. Zolberg, eds. Ghana and the Ivory Coast. Chicago: University of Chicago Press, 1971. 303 p.

Freeman-Grenville, G.S.P. Chronology of African History. London: Oxford University Press, 1973. 312 p.

McFarland, Daniel M. Historical Dictionary of Upper Volta. Metuchen, N.J., and London: Scarecrow Press, 1978. 217 p.

Rawley, James A. The Transatlantic Slave Trade; A History. New York: W.W. Norton, 1981. 452 p.

Reindorf, Carl Christian. History of the Gold Coast and Asante, Based on Traditions and Historical Facts, Comprising a Period of More Than Three Centuries from About 1500 to 1860. Basel: Basel Mission, 1895. 384 p.; 2nd ed. Basel: Basel Mission Book Depot, 1951; Accra: Ghana Universities Press, 1966. 349 p. Rev. Carl Christian Reindorf (1834-1917) was the first Ghanaian to write a history of his country. It is based mainly on the traditions of the Ga.

Ward, William Ernest Frank. A History of Ghana. Rev. ed. London: Allen and Unwin, 1958. 434 p.; in several editions.

_____. A History of the Gold Coast. London: Allen and Unwin, 1948. 387 p.

_____. A Short History of the Gold Coast. London and New York: Longman, Green, 1935. 241 p.; in several editions to 1956.

Wolfson, Freda. Pageant of Ghana. West African History Series. London: Oxford University Press, 1958. 266 p.

G. HISTORY BEFORE 1840

Akinjogbin, I.A. "Archibald Dalzel: Slave Trader and Historian of Dahomey." Journal of African History, 7, 1 (1966), 67-78. Dalzel was Governor at Cape Coast from March 1792 for ten years.

Bartels, Francis L. "Philip Quaque, 1741-1816." Transactions of the Gold Coast and Togoland Historical Society (Achimota), 1 (1955), 153-177.

Curtin, Philip De Armond, ed. Africa Remembered; Narratives by West Africans from the Era of the Slave Trade. Madison, Wisc.: The University of Wisconsin Press, 1967. 363 p.

_____. The Image of Africa; British Ideas and Action, 1780-1850. Madison, Wisc.: The University of Wisconsin Press, 1965. 526 p.

Daaku, Kwame Yeboa. "The European Traders and the Coastal States, 1630-1720." Transactions of the Historical Society of Ghana, 8 (1965), 11-23.

————. "John Konny: The Last Prussian Negro Prince." Tarikh (Ibadan), 1, 4 (1967), 55-64.

————. Trade and Politics on the Gold Coast, 1600-1720: A Study of the African Reaction to European Trade. London: Clarendon Press, 1970. 219 p.

Davis, K.G. The Royal African Company. London: Longmans, 1956. 396 p.; New York: Atheneum, 1970.

Fage, John Donnelly. "The Administration of George Maclean on the Gold Coast, 1830-44." Transactions of the Gold Coast and Togoland Historical Society (Achimota), 1, 4 (1954), 104-120.

————. "A New Check List of the Forts and Castles of Ghana." Transactions of the Historical Society of Ghana (Legon), 4, 1 (1959), 57-67.

Feinberg, Harvey Michael. "Elmina, Ghana: A History of Its Development and Relationship with the Dutch in the Eighteenth Century." Ph.D. dissertation, Boston University, 1969. 289 p.

————. "New Data on European Mortality in West Africa: The Dutch on the Gold Coast, 1719-1760." Journal of African History (London), 15, 3 (1974), 357-371.

————. "There Was an Elmina Note, But...." The International Journal of African Historical Studies (Boston), 9, 4 (1976), 618-630.

Furley, John T. "Notes on Some Portuguese Governors of the Captaincy da Mina." Transactions of the Historical Society of Ghana, 3, 3 (1958), 194-214.

————. "Provisional List of Some Portuguese Governors of the Captaincy of Da Mina." Transactions of the Gold Coast and Togoland Historical Society (Achimota), 2, 2 (1956), 54-62.

Grove, Jean M., and A.M. Johansen. "The Historical Geography of the Volta Delta During the Period of Danish Influence." Bulletin d'Institut Français d'Afrique Noire (Dakar), 30, 4 (Oct. 1968), 1374-1421.

Kea, Ray A. Settlements, Trade, and Polities in the Seventeenth-Century Gold Coast. Johns Hopkins Studies in Atlantic History and Culture. Baltimore: The Johns Hopkins University Press, 1982. 475 p.

Lawrence, Arnold Walter. Fortified Trade-posts: The English in West Africa, 1645-1822. London: Cape, 1969. 237 p.

_____. Trade Castles and Forts of West Africa. London: Cape, 1963. 390 p.; Stanford: Stanford University Press, 1964.

Martin, Eveline Christiana. The British West African Settlements 1750-1821: A Study in Local Administration. Imperial Studies Monographs, 2. London: Longman, Green, 1927; rpt. Westport, Conn.: Negro Universities Press, 1970. 186 p.

Meredith, Henry. An Account of the Gold Coast of Africa, with a Brief History of the African Company. London: Longman, Hurst, Rees, Orme, and Brown, 1812. 264 p.; rpt. Travels and Narratives series, Cass Library of African Studies, 20. London: Cass, 1967. Meredith was a member of the Cape Coast Council and Governor of Winneba Fort who was killed in 1812.

Müller, Wilhelm Johann. Die Africanische auf der Guineischen Gold-Cust gelegene Landschafft Fetu. Nürnberg: J. Hoffmann, 1675; Hamburg: Z. Härtel, 1676.

Nørregaard, Georg. Danish Settlements in West Africa, 1658-1850. Trans. Sigurd Mammen. Boston: Boston University Press, 1966. 287 p.

Priestley, Margaret. "The Ashanti Question and the British: Eighteenth-Century Origins." Journal of African History, 2, 1 (1961), 35-59.

_____. "Philip Quaque of Cape Coast." In Africa Remembered; Narratives by West Africans from the Era of the Slave Trade, ed. by Philip D. Curtin. Madison, Wisc.: The University of Wisconsin Press, 1967. 99-139.

_____. "Richard Brew; an Eighteenth-Century Trader at Anomabu." Transactions of the Historical Society of Ghana, 4 (1959), 29-46.

_____. West African Trade and Coast Society; a Family Study. London: Oxford University Press, 1969. 207 p.

Van Dantzig, Albert, comp. and trans. The Dutch and the Guinea Coast 1674-1743; a Collection of Documents from the General State Archive at the Hague. Accra: Ghana Academy of Arts and Sciences, 1978. 375 p.

_____. Dutch Documents Relating to the Gold Coast and the Slave Coast, 1680-1740. 2 vols. Legon: The University of Ghana, 1971.

_____. *Forts and Castles of Ghana.* Accra: Sedco, 1980. 96 p.

_____. *Les Hollandais sur la Côte de Guinée a l'époque de l'essor de l'Ashanti et du Dahomey, 1680-1740.* Paris: Société Française d'Histoire d'Outre-mer, 1980. 329 p.

Varley, William J. "The Castles and Forts of the Gold Coast." *Transactions of the Gold Coast and Togoland Historical Society* (Achimota), 1, 1 (1952), 1-17.

Vogt, John L. "The Early São Tome-Principe Slave Trade with Mina, 1500-1540." *The International Journal of African Historical Studies* (Boston), 6, 3 (1973), 453-467.

_____. *Portuguese Rule on the Gold Coast 1469-1682.* Athens, Ga.: University of Georgia Press, 1979. 266 p.

Wartemberg, J. Sylvanus. *São Jorge d'Elmina, Premier West African Settlement: Its Traditions and Customs.* Ilfracombe: Stockwell, 1951. 166 p.

Wilks, Ivor. "The Mossi and Akan States, 1500-1800." In *History of West Africa,* vol. 1, ed. by J.F.A. Ajayi and Michael Crowder. New York: Columbia University Press, 1972, pp. 344-386.

H. HISTORY, 1840-1956: COLONIALISM

Adams, C.D. "Activities of Danish Botanists in Guinea, 1783-1850." *Transactions of the Historical Society of Ghana,* 3, 1 (1957), 30-46.

Adjaye, Joseph Emmanuel Kwesi. "Asante and Britain in the Nineteenth Century: A Study in Asante Diplomatic Practice." Ph.D. dissertation, Northwestern University, 1981. 589 p.

Agbodeka, Francis. *African Politics and British Policy in the Gold Coast, 1868-1900: A Study in the Forms and Force of Protest.* Legon History Series. London: Longman; Evanston, Ill.: Northwestern University Press, 1971. 206 p.

_____. "The African Protest Movement and Its Effects on British Policy on the Gold Coast, 1868-1900." Ph.D. dissertation, University of Ghana, 1968. 537 p.

_____. "The Fanti Confederacy, 1865-69, an Enquiry into the Origins, Nature and Extent of an Early West African Protest

Movement." Transactions of the Historical Society of Ghana, 7 (1964), 82-123.

_____. "Nationalism in the Gold Coast, 1900-45." Tarikh (Ibadan), 3, 4 (1971), 22-32.

Ahuma, S.R.B. The Gold Coast Nation and National Consciousness. With an introduciton by J.C. de Graft-Johnson. 2nd ed. London: Frank Cass, 1971. 63 p.

Apter, David Ernest. Ghana in Transition. 2nd rev. ed. Princeton, N.J.: Princeton University Press, 1972. 434 p.

_____. "The Gold Coast in Transition: A Case Study of Political Institutional Transfer." Ph.D. dissertation, Princeton University, 1954. 541. Published by Princeton in 1955.

Arden-Clarke, Charles. "Gold Coast into Ghana: Some Problems of Transition." International Affairs (Oxford), 34 (January 1958), 49-56. Arden-Clarke was the last Governor of the Gold Coast.

Arhin, Kwame, ed. The Papers of George Ekem Ferguson: A Fanti Official of the Government of the Gold Coast, 1890-1897. African Social Research Documents, 7. Leiden: Afrika-Studiecentrum; Cambridge: African Studies Centre, 1974. 180 p.

Armitage, Cecil Hamilton, and A.F. Montanaro. The Ashanti Campaign of 1900. London: Sands, 1901. 278 p. Armitage was an officer in the campaign and later Chief Commissioner, Northern Territories.

Austin, Dennis. "The Working Committee of the United Gold Coast Convention." Journal of African History, 2, 2 (1961), 273-297.

Baden-Powell, Robert S.S. The Downfall of Prempeh; a Diary of Life with the Native Levy in Ashanti, 1895-96. London: Methuen, 1896. Baden-Powell was an officer with the expedition to Kumasi. He later founded the Boy Scout movement.

Baesjou, Rene, ed. An Asante Embassy on the Gold Coast: The Mission of Akyempon Yaw to Elmina, 1869-1872. African Social Research Documents, 11. Leiden: Afrika-Studiecentrum; Cambridge: African Studies Centre, 1979. 250 p.

Baldwin, Norman Cecil, comp. The Air Mails of British Africa, 1925-1932. Sutton Coldfield, England: F.J. Field, 1932. 68 p.

Bening, R. Bagulo. "Internal Colonial Boundary Problems of the Gold Coast, 1907-1951." International Journal of African Historical Studies (Boston), 17, 1 (1984), 81-99.

Bening, Raymond B. "The Definition of the International Boundaries of Northern Ghana, 1888-1904." Transactions of the Historical Society of Ghana, 14, 2 (December 1973), 229-261.

Biss, Harold C.J. The Relief of Kumasi. London: Methuen's Colonial Library, 1901. 315 p.

Bittle, William Elmer, and Gilbert Geis. The Longest Way Home: Chief Alfred C. Sam's Back to Africa Movement. Detroit: Wayne State University Press, 1964. 229 p.

Blake, John W. European Beginnings in West Africa, 1454-1578; A Survey of the First Century of White Enterprise in West Africa. London and New York: Longmans, Green, 1937. 212 p.; Westport, Conn.: Greenwood Press, 1972.

_____. Europeans in West Africa, 1450-1560. 2 vols. Vol. 1: Portuguese Discoveries, Vol. 2: English Voyages. London: Hakluyt Society, 1942; Kraus Reprint, 1967.

_____. West Africa: Quest for God and Gold, 1454-1578. Totowa, N.J.: Rowman and Littlefield; London: Curzon Press, 1977. 246 p.

Bly, Viola Mattavous. "The British Presence and Its Influence on Indigenous Gold Coast Economics, 1865-1902." Ph.D. dissertation, New York University, 1982. 315 p.

Boahen, Albert Adu. "Politics in Ghana, 1800-1874." In History of West Africa, vol. 2, ed. by J.F.A. Ajayi and Michael Crowder. New York: Columbia University Press, 1973. 167-261.

_____. "The Roots of Ghanaian Nationalism." Journal of African History, 5, 1 (1964), 127-132.

Bonne, Nii Kwabena III. Milestones in the History of the Gold Coast: An Autobiography of Nii Kwabena Bonne III. London: Diplomatist Publications, 1953. 92 p.

Bourret, Florence Mabel. Ghana: The Road to Independence, 1919-1957. Rev. ed. Stanford, Calif.: Hoover Institution Press; London: Oxford University Press, 1960. 246 p.

_____. The Gold Coast: A Survey of the Gold Coast and British Togoland, 1919-1951. Stanford, Calif.: Hoover Institution Press; London: Oxford University Press, 1952. 248 p. Revision of Bourret's 1947 dissertation at Stanford.

Boyle, Frederick. Through Fanteeland to Coomassie: A Diary of the Ashantee Expedition. London: Chapman and Hall, 1874. 411 p.

Boyle, Laura. Diary of a Colonial Officer's Wife. Oxford: Alden Press, 1968. 176 p.

Brackenbury, Henry. The Ashanti War, A Narrative. 2 vols. Edinburgh and London: William Blackwood, 1874, 1884, 1914; Rpt. by Frank Cass, 1968.

Brand, Richard Robert. "A Geographical Interpretation of the European Influence on Accra, Ghana, Since 1877." Ph.D. dissertation, Columbia University, 1972. 393 p.

Burns, Alan Cuthbert. Colonial Civil Servant. London: Allen and Unwin, 1949. 339 p. Burns was Governor, 1941-1947.

Bushoven, Cornelius. "National Law and National Courts in the Political System of the Gold Coast and Ghana, 1874-1966." Ph.D. dissertation, Duke University, 1971. 305 p.

Cardinall, Allan Wolsey. In Ashanti and Beyond: The Record of a Resident Magistrate's Many Years in Tropical Africa. London: Seeley Service, 1927; Westport, Conn.: Negro Universities Press, 1970. 288 p.

_____. "The Story of the German Occupation of Togoland." The Gold Coast Review (Accra), 2, 2 (1926); 3, 1 (1927).

Clifford, Hugh Charles. The Gold Coast Regiment in the East African Campaign. London: J. Murray, 1920. 306 p. Clifford was Governor from 1912 to 1919.

Coffee, Mary. "The Self-government Movement in the Gold Coast, West Africa." Ph.D. dissertation, Harvard University, 1954. 153 p.

Collins, Edmund. "The Panic Element in Nineteenth-Century Relations with Ashanti." Transactions of the Historical Society of Ghana, 5, 2 (1962), 79-144.

Coombs, Douglas. The Gold Coast, Britain and the Netherlands, 1850-1874. London: Oxford University Press, 1963. 160 p.

Crooks, John Joseph, ed. Records Relating to the Gold Coast Settlements from 1750 to 1874. Dublin: Browne and Nolan, 1923; Rpt. London: Frank Cass. 1973. 557 p.

Crowther, Francis. Notes for the Guidance of District Commissioners, Gold Coast Colony. Accra: Government Printer, 1916. 62 p. Crowther was Secretary of Native Affairs.

Danquah, Joseph Boakye. "Historical Significance of the Bond of 1844." Transactions of the Historical Society of Ghana, 3 (1957), 3-29.

_____. Liberty of the Subject: A Monograph on the Gold Coast Cocoa Hold-Up and Boycott of Foreign Goods (1937-38). Kibi, Gold Coast: George Boakie, 1938. 63 p.

Denzer, La Ray E. "The National Congress of British West Africa: Gold Coast Section." Master's thesis, University of Ghana, 1965.

Edsman, Björn M. Lawyers in Gold Coast Politics, c. 1900-1945: From Mensah Sarbah to J.B. Danquah. Acta Universitatis Upsaliensia, 111. Uppsala: University of Uppsala, 1979. 263 p.

Ekwelie, Sylvanus Ajana. "The Press in Gold Coast Nationalism, 1890-1957." Ph.D. dissertation, University of Wisconsin, 1971. 335 p.

Eluwa, G.I.C. "The National Congress of British West Africa." Tarikh (Ibadan), 3, 4 (1971), 12-21.

Ferguson, Phyllis, and Ivor Wilks. "Chiefs, Constitutions and the British in Northern Ghana." In West African Chiefs: Their Changing Status under Colonial Rule and Independence, ed. by Michael Crowder and Obaro Ikime. New York: Africana Publishing Corp.; Ile Ife, Nigeria: University of Ife Press, 1970, pp. 326-369.

Frimpong, Kofi. "The Joint Provincial Council of Paramount Chiefs and the Politics of Independence, 1946-58." Transactions of the Historical Society of Ghana, 14, 1 (June 1973), 79-91.

Fyfe, Christopher. Africanus Horton: West African Scientist and Patriot, 1835-1883. New York: Oxford University Press, 1972. 169 p.

Gailey, Harry A. Clifford: Imperial Proconsul. Malabar, Fla.: Krieger Publishing, 1982. 215 p. Biography of Hugh Clifford.

Gann, Lewis Henry, and Peter Duignan. The Rulers of British Africa, 1870-1914. Stanford: Hoover Institution Press, 1978. 406 p.

Gildea, Roy Y. Nationalism and Indirect Rule in the Gold Coast: 1900-1950. New York: William-Frederick Press, 1964. 34 p.

Gillespie, W.H. The Gold Coast Police, 1844-1938. Accra: Government Printer, 1955. 89 p.

Gorges, Edmund Howard. The Great War in West Africa. London: Hutchinson, 1930.

Griffith, William Brandford, Jr. The Far Horizon: Portrait of a Colonial Judge. Ilfracombe, Devon: Arthur H. Stockwell, 1951. 319 p.

Grove, Eric. "The First Shots of the Great War: The Anglo-French Conquest of Togo, 1914." The Army Quarterly and Defense Journal, 106, 3 (July 1976), 308-323.

Guggisberg, Mrs. Decima Moore, and Major Frederick Gordon. We Two in West Africa. London: W. Heinemann; New York: Charles Scribner, 1909. 368 p. Guggisberg was Governor of the Gold Coast.

Guyer, David. Ghana and the Ivory Coast: The Impact of Colonialism in an African Setting. New York: Exposition Press, 1970. 111 p.

Hailey, William Malcolm. An African Survey. London, New York, Toronto: Oxford University Press, 1938, 1957. 1,676 p.

_____. Native Administration and Political Development in British Tropical Africa. Nendeln, Liechtenstein: Kraus Reprint, 1979. 352 p.

Hatch, John. The History of Britain in Africa: From the Fifteenth Century to the Present. New York: Praeger, 1969. 320 p.

Hayford, Casely. Gold Coast Native Institutions; with Thoughts upon a Healthy Imperial Policy for the Gold Coast and Ashanti. London: Sweet and Maxwell, 1903. 418 p.; Rpt. Frank Cass, 1970.

Henige, David P. Colonial Governors from the Fifteenth Century to the Present, a Comprehensive List. Madison, Wisc.: University of Wisconsin Press, 1970. 461 p.

Henty, George Alfred. The March to Coomassie. London: Tinsley, 1874. 470 p. Henty was a famous writer and war correspondent.

Hetherington, Penelope. British Paternalism and Africa, 1920-1940. Totowa, N.J.: Frank Cass, 1978. 196 p.

Hodgson, Mary Alice. The Siege of Kumassi. London: C. Arthur Pearson; New York: Longmans, Green, 1901. 365 p. By the wife of Governor Frederic Mitchell Hodgson.

Holbrook, Wendell Patrick. "The Impact of the Second World War on the Gold Coast: 1939-1945." Ph.D. dissertation, Princeton University, 1978. 429 p.

Horton, James Africanus Beale. Letters on the Political Condition of the Gold Coast since the Exchange of Territory between the English and Dutch Governments on January 1, 1868. London: W.J. Johnson, 1870; Rpt. Frank Cass, 1970. 179 p.

Howard, Rhoda. Colonialism and Underdevelopment in Ghana. New York: Holmes and Meier, Africana Publishing Co., 1978. 244 p.

Iliasu, A.A. "The Establishment of British Administration in Mamprugu, 1898-1937." Transactions of the Historical Society of Ghana, 16, 1 (June 1975), 1-28.

Jahoda, Gustav. White Man: A Study of the Attitudes of Africans to Europeans in Ghana Before Independence. London and New York: Oxford University Press, 1961. 144 p.

Johnson, Marion. "M. Bonnat on the Volta." Ghana Notes and Queries, 10 (December 1968), 5-17.

_____, comp. "Salaga Papers." 2 vols. Legon: Institute of African Studies, University of Ghana, 1966. Mimeographed.

Johnson, Terence J. "Protest, Tradition and Change: An Analysis of Southern Gold Coast Riots, 1890-1920." Economy and Society (Oxford), 1, 2 (1972), 164-193.

July, Robert William. The Origins of Modern African Thought: Its Development in West Africa During the NIneteenth and Twentieth Centuries. New York: F.A. Praeger, 1968. 512 p.

Justesen O. "The Danish Settlements on the Gold Coast in the Nineteenth Century." Scandinavian Journal of History, 4, 1 (1979), 3-34.

Killingray, David. "The Colonial Army in the Gold Coast: Official Policy and Local Response, 1890-1947." Ph.D. dissertation, London University, 1982.

_____. "Military and Labour Recruitment in the Gold Coast During the Second World War." Journal of African History, 23, 1 (1982), 83-95.

_____. "The Mutiny of the West African Regiment in the Gold Coast, 1901." The International Journal of African Historical Studies (Boston), 16, 3 (1983), 441-454.

_____. "Repercussions of World War I in the Gold Coast." Journal of African History (Cambridge), 19, 1 (1978), 39-59.

_____. "Soldiers, Ex-Servicemen, and Politics in the Gold Coast, 1939-50." The Journal of Modern African Studies (Cambridge), 21, 3 (1983), 523-534.

Kilson, Martin. "The National Congress of British West Africa, 1918-1935." In Protest and Power in Black Africa, ed. by Robert I. Rotberg and Ali A. Mazrui. New York: Oxford University Press, 1970. 571-588.

Kimble, David B. A Political History of Ghana: The Rise of Gold Coast Nationalism, 1850-1928. Oxford: Clarendon Press, 1963. 587 p. A second volume is anticipated.

Knoll, Arthur J. Togo Under Imperial Germany, 1884-1914: A Case Study in Colonial Rule. African Colonial Studies. Stanford: Hoover Institution Press, 1978. 240 p.

Kuklick, Henrika. The Imperial Bureaucrat: The Colonial Administrative Service in the Gold Coast, 1920-1939. African Colonial Studies. Stanford: Hoover Institution Press, 1979. 225 p.

Lonsdale, Rupert La Trobe. House of Commons Blue Book, Parliamentary Papers, Report dated 24 March 1882, 46, 42 (1882), enc. 2. Report on the second British visit to Salaga.

Lucas, Charles Prestwood. The Gold Coast and the War. London: Oxford University Press, 1920. 56 p.

McCarthy, Mary. Social Change and the Growth of British Power in the Gold Coast: The Fante States, 1807-1874. Lanham, Md.: University Press of America, 1983. 208 p.

McSheffrey, Gerald M. "Slavery, Indentured Servitude, Legitimate Trade and the Impact of Abolition in the Gold Coast, 1874-1901: A Reappraisal." Journal of African History (Cambridge), 24, 3 (1983), 349-368.

Mbaeyi, Paul Mmegha. British Military and Naval Forces in West African History, 1807-1874. New York: NOK Publishers, 1978. 263 p.

Metcalfe, George Edgar. Great Britain and Ghana: Documents of Ghana History, 1807-1957. London and Edinburgh: Thomas Nelson and Sons on behalf of the University of Ghana, 1964. 779 p. This is indispensable for study of the colonial era.

_____. Maclean of the Gold Coast: The Life and Times of George Maclean, 1801-1847. West African History Series. London: Oxford University Press, 1962. 344 p.

Moberly, F.J. History of the Great War, Military Operations in Togo and the Cameroons, 1914-18. London: HMSO, 1931.

Newbury, Colin W. British Policy Towards West Africa: Selected Documents, 1786-1914. 2 vols., 1786-1874 and 1875-1914. London: Oxford University Press, 1965, 1971. 656 p. and 680 p.

Nikoi, Amon. "Indirect Rule and Government in the Gold Coast Colony, 1844-1954." Ph.D. dissertation, Harvard University, 1956. 325 p.

Nwanodi, Cyprian Wali. "Nationalism in British West Africa." Ph.D. dissertation, Claremont Graduate School, 1978. 149 p.

Okonkwo, Rina Lee. "The Emergence of Nationalism in British West Africa, 1912-1940." Ph.D. dissertation, City University of New York, 1980. 235 p.

Olorunfemi, A. "The Contest for Salaga: Anglo-German Conflict in the Gold Coast Hinterland." Journal of African Studies (Los Angeles), 11, 1 (Spring 1984), 15-24.

Olusanya, G.O. The West African Students' Union and the Politics of Decolonisation, 1925-1958. Ibadan: Daystar Press, 1982. 148 p.

Omosini, Olufemi. "The Gold Coast Land Question, 1894-1900: Some Issues Raised on West Africa's Economic Development." The International Journal of African Historical Studies (Boston), 5, 3 (1972), 453-469.

Owusu, Seth Amoako. "Political Institutions of the Coastal Areas of the Gold Coast as Influenced by European Contact." Ph.D. dissertation, University of Chicago, 1954. 107 p.

Padmore, George. The Gold Coast Revolution: The Struggle of an African People from Slavery to Freedom. London: D. Dobson, 1953. 272 p.

Patterson, K. David. Health in Colonial Ghana: Disease, Medicine, and Socio-Economic Change, 1900-1955. Los Angeles: Crossroads Press, 1981. 189 p.

_____. "The Influenza Epidemic of 1918-19 in the Gold Coast." Journal of African History (Cambridge), 24, 4 (1983), 485-502.

Pearce, R.D. The Turning Point in Africa: British Colonial Policy, 1938-48. London: Frank Cass, 1982. 223 p.

Person, Yves. Samori; une Revolution Dyula. 3 vols. Memoires de l'Institut Fondamental d'Afrique Noire. Dakar: IFAN, 1968-1975. 2377 p.

Priestley, Margaret. "The Gold Coast Select Committee on Estimates: 1913-1950." The International Journal of African Historical Studies (Boston), 6, 4 (1973), 543-564.

Ramseyer, Friedrich August. Dark and Stormy Days at Kumasi. London: S.W. Partridge, 1901. 240 p.

_____, and Johannes Kuhne. Four Years in Ashantee. London: J. Nisbet; New York: R. Carter, 1875. 320 p.

_____, and Paul Steiner. Four Years Captivity in Ashanti.
London: S.W. Partridge, 1901. 119 p.

Reade, William Winwood. The African Sketchbook. 2 vols. London: Smith, Elder, 1873.

_____. The Story of the Ashantee Campaign. London: Smith, Elder, 1874. By a war correspondent.

Ricketts, Henry J. Narrative of the Ashantee War. London: Simkin and Marshall, 1831. 221 p. An officer in the British service on the Gold Coast, Ricketts wrote this account of the 1822-31 conflict between the British and Asante.

Rohdie, Samuel. "The Gold Coast Aborigines Abroad." Journal of African History, 6, 3 (1965), 389-411.

Rooney, David. Sir Charles Arden-Clarke. London: Rex Collings; Melbourne, Fla.: Krieger, 1982. 236 p. Biography of the last Governor of the Gold Coast.

Rubens-Rathbone, R.J.A. "The Transfer of Power in Ghana, 1945-1957." Ph.D. dissertation, University of London, 1968. 416 p.

Ryan, Isobel. Black Man's Town. London: Cape; Toronto: Clarke and Irwin, 1953. 249 p. A story by a Canadian who moved to Takoradi with her husband in 1948.

Saffell, John Edgar. "The Ashanti War of 1873-1874." Ph.D. dissertation, Case Western Reserve University, 1965. 401 p.

Sampson, Magnus J. "George Eken Ferguson of Anomabu." Transactions of the Gold Coast and Togoland Historical Society (Achimota), 2, 1 (1956), 30-45.

_____. Gold Coast Men of Affairs; Past and Present. Ilfracombe: Stockwell, 1937; Rpt., London: Dawsons, 1969. 224 p.

Shaloff, Stanley. "The Cape Coast Asafo Company Riot of 1932." The International Journal of African Historical Studies (Boston), 7, 4 (1974), 591-607.

_____. "Press Controls and Sedition Proceedings in the Gold Coast, 1933-39." African Affairs (London), 71, 284 (July 1972), 241-263.

Silver, Jim. "The Failure of European Mining Companies in the Nineteenth-Century Gold Coast." Journal of African History, 22, 4 (1981), 511-530.

Simensen, Jarle. "The Asafo of Kwahu, Ghana: A Mass Movement for Local Reform under Colonial Rule." The International Journal of African Historical Studies, 8, 3 (1975), 383-406.

Spitzer, Leo, and La Ray Denzer. "I.T.A. Wallace-Johnson and the West African Youth League." The International Journal of African Historical Studies, 6, 3 (1973), 413-452.

Stanley, Henry Morton. Coomassie: The Story of the Campaign in Africa, 1873-4. London: Sampson Low, Marston and Co.: 1896. 212 p. An account by the explorer.

_____. Coomassie and Magdala: The Story of Two British Campaigns in Africa. London: Sampson Low, Marston, Low and Searle, 1874; New York: Harper and Brothers, 1874. 510 p.

Tenkorang, Samuel. "John Mensah Sarbah, 1864-1910." Transactions of the Historical Society of Ghana, 14, 1 (June 1973), 65-78.

Thomas, Roger G. "Forced Labour in British West Africa: The Case of the Northern Territories of the Gold Coast, 1906-1927." Journal of African History, 14, 1 (1973), 79-103.

_____. "The 1916 Bongo 'Riots' and Their Background: Aspects of Colonial Administration and African Response in Eastern Upper Ghana." Journal of African History (Cambridge), 24, 1 (1983), 57-75.

Tordoff, William. "Brandford Griffith's Offer of British Protection to Ashanti in 1891." Transactions of the HIstorical Society of Ghana, 6 (1962), 32-49.

Townsend, Mary Evelyn. The Rise and Fall of German's Colonial Empire. New York: Columbia University Press, 1930.

Twumasi, Yaw. "J.B. Danquah: Towards an Understanding of the Social and Political Ideas of a Ghanaian Nationalist and Politician." African Affairs (London), 77, 306 (January 1978), 73-88.

Walker, Howard Kent. "The Constitutional Debate Between Opposition and Government Nationalists in the Gold Coast on the Eve of Independence." Ph.D. dissertation, Boston University, 1968. 338 p.

Wallerstein, Immanuel. The Road to Independence: Ghana and the Ivory Coast. The Hague: Mouton, 1964. 200 p.

Ward, John Paul. "The Journalistic Frontier of Africa: Special Correspondents Covering the Sixth Anglo-Ashanti War, 1873-1874." Ph.D. dissertation, Boston University, 1971. 441 p.

Ward, William Ernest Frank. "Britain and Ashanti, 1874-1896." Transactions of the Historical Society of Ghana, 15, 2 (December 1974), 131-164.

Wight, Martin, ed. British Colonial Constitutions, 1947. Oxford: Clarendon Press, 1952. 571 p.

──────. The Gold Coast Legislative Council. Studies in Colonial Legislature, 2. Ed. by Margery Perham. London: Faber and Faber, 1947. 285 p.

Willcocks, James. From Kabul to Kumassi. Twenty-four Years of Soldiering and Sport. London: John Murray, 1904. 440 p.

Wilson, Henry S. Origins of West African Nationalism. London: Macmillan, 1969. 391 p.

Wolfson, Freda. "British Relations with the Gold Coast, 1843-1880." Ph.D. dissertation, 1952. 428 p.

──────. Pageant of Ghana. West African History Series. London: Oxford University Press, 1958. 266 p.

Wolseley, Garnet Joseph. The Story of a Soldier's Life. 2 vols. New York: Scribner's, 1903. Administrator of Cape Coast and British Commander in the Asante campaign, 1873-1874. See vol. 2, 257-370.

Wraith, R.E. "Frederick Gordon Guggisberg: Myth and Mystery." African Affairs (London), 8, 318 (January 1981), 116-122.

──────. Guggisberg. West African History Series. London: Oxford University Press, 1967. 342 p.

I. HISTORY SINCE INDEPENDENCE

Adamafio, Tawia. By Nkrumah's Side: The Labour and the Wounds. Accra: Westcoast Publishing House; London: Rex Collings, 1982. 144 p.

Addo-Fenning, Robert. "Gandhi and Nkrumah: A Study of Non-Violence and Non-Cooperation Campaigns in India and Ghana as an Anti-Colonial Strategy." The Transactions of the Historical Society of Ghana, 13, 1 (1972), 63-85.

Adjei, Mike. "Merger Misconceptions." West Africa (London), 3356 (23 November 1981), 2782-2783. Ghanaian politics just before the December 1981 coup.

Afrifa, Akwasi A. The Ghana Coup, 24th February 1966. London: Frank Cass; New York: Humanities Press, 1966. 144 p.

Agyeman-Badu, Yaw, and Kwaku Osei-Hwedie. The Political Economy of Instability; Colonial Legacy, Inequality and Political Instability in Ghana. Lawrenceville, Va.: Brunswick Publishing Co., 1982. 56 p.

Akyeampong, Henry Kwasi. The Foundations of Self-government: Selected Historic Speeches on Ghana's Independence. Accra: George Boakye Publishing Co., 1967. 51 p.

————. Ghana's Struggle for Democracy and Freedom; Speeches 1957-1969 by Dr. K.A. Busia. Legon: University of Ghana Bookshop, 1979. 300 p.

Alexander, Major General Henry Templer. African Tightrope: My Two Years as Nkrumah's Chief of Staff. London: Pall Mall Press, 1965; New York: F.A. Praeger, 1966.

Aluko, I.O. "The Influence of Foreign Aid on Ghana's External Relations, 1957-1966: A Case Study in Aid Diplomacy." Ph.D. dissertation, University of London, 1969. 674 p.

Aluko, Olajide. "After Nkrumah; Continuity and Change in Ghana's Foreign Policy." Issue, 5, 1 (1975), 55-62.

————. The Foreign Policies of African States. London: Hodder and Stoughton, 1977. 243 p.

————. Ghana and Nigeria 1957-70: A Study in Inter-African Discord. London: Rex Collings; New York: Barnes and Noble, 1976. 275 p.

————. "Ghana's Foreign Policy Under the National Liberation Council." Africa Quarterly (New Delhi), 10, 4 (January-March 1971), 312-328.

Ames, Sophia Ripley. Nkrumah of Ghana. Chicago: Rand McNally, 1961. 184 p.

Amonoo, Benjamin. Ghana, 1957-1966; Politics of Institutional Dualism. Winchester, Mass.: Allen and Unwin, 1981. 242 p.

Appiah, Joe. The Man, J.B. Danquah. Accra: Academy of Arts and Sciences, 1974. 51 p.

Armah, Kwesi. Africa's Golden Road. London: Heinemann, 1965. 292 p.; Humanities Press, 1966. The author was once a key adviser to President Nkrumah.

Arnold, Guy. "A New Start in Ghana." Africa Report, 24, 6 (November-December 1979), 43-46.

Asamoa, Kofi Vovonyo. "A Comparative Study of the Political Thoughts and Policies of Kwame Nkrumah and Kofi Abrefa Busia." Ph.D. dissertation, Howard University, 1977. 396 p.

Assensoh, A.B. Kwame Nkrumah-Six Years in Exile, 1966-1972. Ilfracombe, Devon: Stockwell, 1978.

Austin, Dennis. Ghana Observed: Essays on the Politics of a West African Republic. New York: Holmes and Meier, Africana Publishing Co., 199 p.

_____. Politics in Ghana, 1946-1960. London and New York: Oxford University Press for the Royal Institute for International Affairs, 1964. 459 p.

_____, and Robin Luckham. Politicians and Soldiers in Ghana, 1966-72. London and Totowa, N.J.: Frank Cass, 1975. 332 p.

Awooner, Kofi. "Kwame Nkrumah: Symbol of Emergent Africa." Africa Report, 17, 6 (June 1972), 22-25.

Balogun, Kolawole. Mission to Ghana; Memoir of a Diplomat. New York: Vantage, 1964. 73 p.

Barker, Peter. Operation Cold Chop. 2nd ed. Accra: Ghana Publishing Corp., 1979. 236 p. An account of the 24 February 1966 coup.

Barnor, Ansah. "Opposition Leaders Jockey for Position." West Africa (London), 3351 (19 October 1981), 2438-2440. An account of the political situation just before the collapse of the Third Republic.

Bartels, Charles, editor-in-chief. Ghana Who's Who, 1972-73. Accra: Bartels Publications, 1972. 454 p.

Bebler, Anton. Military Rule in Africa: Dahomey, Ghana, Sierra Leone, and Mali. London: Pall Mall; New York: Praeger, 1973. 267 p.

Bennett, Valerie Plave. "The Evolution of Civil-Military Relations in Ghana: 1945-1962." Ph.D. dissertation, Boston University, 1972. 332 p.

_____. "The 'Non-politicians' Take Over." Africa Report, 17, 4 (April 1972), 19-22. This is about the military coup which ended the Second Republic.

Bennion, Francis Alan Roscoe. The Constitutional Law of Ghana. London: Butterworth and Co., 1962. 527 p.

Beraki, Joseph. "Charismatic Leadership in the Nationalistic Movements in Ghana and Kenya: A Comparative Study." Ph.D. dissertation, United States International University (San Diego), 1980. 472 p.

Bing, Geoffrey. Reap the Whirlwind; an Account of Kwame Nkrumah's Ghana from 1950 to 1966. London: MacGibbon and Kee, 1968. 519 p. Bing was Attorney General and an adviser to Nkrumah.

Botchway, Francis A. "Political Development and Social Change in Ghana: A Study of the Influence of Kwame Nkrumah and the Role of Ideas in Rapid Social Change." Ph.D. dissertation, New School for Social Research (New York), 1970/71. 248 p.

Bretton, Henry L. The Rise and Fall of Kwame Nkrumah: A Study of Personal Rule in Africa. New York: Praeger, 1966. 232 p.

Busia Kofi Abrefa. Africa in Search of Democracy. London: Routledge; New York: Praeger, 1967. 192 p.

Card, Emily. "Ghana Prepares for Civilian Rule." Africa Report, 13, 4 (April 1968), 9-16.

_____, and Barbara Callaway. "Ghanaian Politics: The Elections and After. What Factors Explain Busia's Electorial Victory and What Are His Regime's Prospects?" Africa Report, 15, 3 (March 1970), 10-15.

Chazan, Naomi. An Anatomy of Ghanaian Politics; Managing Political Recession, 1969-1982. Boulder, Colo.: Westview Press, 1983. 350 p.

Cole, Joseph Irving. "Kwame Nkrumah: A Psychological Study." Ph.D. dissertation, New School for Social Research (New York), 1978. 169 p.

Crutcher, John Richard. "Political Authority in Ghana and Tanzania: the Nkrumah and Nyerere Regimes." Ph.D. dissertation, University of Notre Dame, 1968. 510 p.

Danso-Boafo, Alex Kwaku. "The Political Biography of Dr. Kofi Abrefa Busia." Ph.D. dissertation, Howard University, 1981. 343 p.

Dapaah, Kwabena. "What Does Rawlings Offer?" West Africa, 3364 (25 January 1982), 222-223.

Davidson, Basil. Black Star; A View of the Life and Times of Kwame Nkrumah. London: Allen Lane, 1973. 225 p.

Decalo, Samuel. Coups and Army Rule in Africa: Studies in Military Style. New Haven: Yale University Press, 1976. 294 p.

Dei-Anang, Michael. The Administration of Ghana's Foreign Relations, 1957-1965: A Personal Memoir. London: The Athlone Press, University of London; Atlantic Highlands, N.J.: Humanities Press, 1975. 96 p. Dei-Anang was Principal Secretary at the Ministry of Foreign Affairs, 1959-1961, and head of the African Affairs Secretariat, 1961-1966.

──────. Ghana Resurgent. Accra: Waterville Publishing House, 1964. 248 p.

Donkoh, C.E. Nkrumah and Busia of Ghana. Accra: New Times Corp., 1972. 147 p.

Dowse, Robert Edward. Modernization in Ghana and the U.S.S.R.; a Comparative Study. London: Routledge, 1969. 107 p.

Drake, St. Clair, and Leslie Alexander Lacy. "Government Versus the Unions; the Sekondi-Takoradi Strike, 1961." In Politics in Africa: 7 Cases, ed. by Gwendolen M. Carter. Harcourt Casebook in Political Science. New York: Harcourt, Brace, and World, 1966, pp. 67-117.

Du Bois, Shirley Graham. What Happened in Ghana? The Inside Story. New York: Freedomways Associates, 1966. 223 p.

Duffield, Ian. "Makers of the 20th Century: Marcus Garvey and Kwame Nkrumah." History Today, 31 (March 1981), 24-30.

Dzirasa, Rev. Stephen. The Political Thought of Dr. Kwame Nkrumah. Accra: Guinea Press, 1962. 133 p. Dzirasa was a close associate of President Nkrumah.

Edoh, Anthony Adem. "Decentralization and Local Government Reforms in Ghana." Ph.D. dissertation, University of Wisconsin, 1981. 412 p.

Elias, Taslim Olawale. Ghana and Sierra Leone: The Development of Their Laws and Constitutions. Vol. 10 of The British Commonwealth: The Development of Its Laws and Constitutions. London: Stevens, 1962. 334 p.

Fitch, Robert Beck, and Mary Oppenheimer. Ghana: End of an Illusion. New York: Monthly Review Press, 1966. 130 p. Also published as a special edition of the Monthly Review, vol. 2, 1966.

Frimpong, J.H.S. "The Ghana Parliament, 1957-1966; a Critical Analysis." Ph.D. dissertation, University of Exeter, 1970. 426 p.

Goldschmidt, Jenny. "Ghana Between the Second and the Third Republican Eras: Recent Constitutional Developments and Their Relation to Traditional Laws and Institutions." African Law Studies (Columbia, Univ.), 18 (1980), 43-62.

Goldsworthy, David. "Ghana's Second Republic: A Post-Mortem." African Affairs (London), 72, 286 (January 1973), 8-25.

Gordon, Gerald Lewis. "The Impact of Charisma on West African Political Development: A Case Study." Ph.D. dissertation, The Catholic University of America, 1981. 174 p.

Gray, Paul S. Unions and Leaders in Ghana. Buffalo, N.Y.: Conch Magazine, 1981. 238 p.

Greenstreet, D.K. "Public Corporations in Ghana During the Nkrumah Period, 1951-66." African Review (Accra), 3, 1 (1973), 21-31.

Grundy, Kenneth W. "The Negative Image of Africa's Military." Review of Politics (Notre Dame), 30, 4 (October 1968), 428-439.

──────. "The Political Ideology of Kwame Nkrumah." In African Political Thought: Lumumba, Nkrumah, and Toure, ed. by W.Z.E. Skurnik. Denver: University of Denver, 1968.

──────. "Theories and Ideologies of West African Underdevelopment and Development." Ph.D. dissertation, Pennsylvania State, 1963.

Gutteridge, William F. The Military in African Politics. London: Methuen, 1969. 166 p.

──────. Military Institutions and Power in the New States. London: Pall Mall; New York: Praeger, 1965. 182 p.

──────. Military Regimes in Africa. London: Methuen, 1975. 195 p.

Hansen, Emmanuel, and Paul Collins. "The Army, the State, and the Rawlings Revolution in Ghana." African Affairs (London), 79, 314 (January 1980), 3-24.

Harris, D.J. "The Recent Political Upheavals in Ghana." World Today, 36 (June 1980), 225-32.

Hart, David. The Volta River Project: A Case Study in Politics and Technology. Edinburgh: Edinburgh University Press, 1980. 132 p.

Hart, Keith. "The Politics of Unemployment in Ghana." African Affairs, 75, 301 (October 1976), 488-497.

Harvey, William Burnett. Law and Social Change in Ghana. Princeton, N.J.: Princeton University Press, 1966. 453 p. Harvey was Dean of the Law Faculty at the University of Ghana, 1962-64. In 1964 Nkrumah had him deported for subversive activities.

Hevi, Emmanuel John. An African Student in China. London: Pall Mall Press, 1963. 220 p. Hevi was once secretary-general of the African Student's Union of Ghana.

Hodgkin, Thomas. African Political Parties. Harmondsworth: Penguin, 1962. 217 p. Hodgkin was a pro-Nkrumah Englishman.

Hoeane, Patricia Masilo. "Economic Aid as an Instrument of Soviet Foreign Policy: The Case of Ghana, 1957-1966." Ph.D. dissertation, Western Michigan University, 1981. 157 p.

Holm, John Dwight. "Marxism and Nkrumahism: Some Problems of Ideological Adaptation in a Mobilizing System." Ph.D. dissertation, University of California at Los Angeles, 1969/70.

Hooker, James R. Black Revolutionary: George Padmore's Path from Communism to Pan-Africanism. New York and London: Praeger, 1967. 168 p.

Howell, Thomas A., and Jeffrey P. Rajasooria, eds. Ghana and Nkrumah. Interim History Series. New York: Facts on File, 1972. 205 p.

Hyde, Emmanuel A. "The Role of Ghana in the Congo Crisis: A Study of a Small State's Involvement in a Post-Colonial System." Ph.D. dissertation, University of Pennsylvania, 1970/71. 498 p.

Ikoku, Samuel Gomsu. Le Ghana de Nkrumah; Autopsie de la 1ère République, 1957-1966. Trans. from English by Yves Bénot. Paris; Maspero, 1971. 244 p. The author was a Nigerian Communist on the staff of the Ideological Institute at Winneba.

Irvine, Keith. "Ghana After Nkrumah." Current History (Philadelphia), 52, 307 (March 1967), 149-153, 181-182.

_____. "Ghana: The Black Star State." Current History, 40, 234 (February 1961), 88-92.

James, Cyril Lional Robert. Nkrumah and the Ghana Revolution.

Westport, Conn.: Lawrence Hill and Co., 1977. 227 p. James was a Trotskyite historian from Trinidad who was a friend of George Padmore.

Jarmon, Charles. The Nkrumah Regime: An Evaluation of the Role of Charismatic Authority. Third World Monograph Series. Lawrenceville, Va.: Brunswick Publishing Co., 1981. 24 p.

Jeffries, Richard. Class, Power, and Ideology in Ghana: The Railwaymen of Sekondi. African Studies Series, 23. London and New York: Cambridge University Press, 1978. 244 p.

_____. "The Ghanaian Elections of 1979." African Affairs, 79, 316 (July 1980), 397-414.

Jenkins, Amelia Viven. "The Role of Culture and Power Conflict in the Development of the African State of Ghana: A History and an Analysis of a Series of Conflict Episodes." Ph.D. dissertation, New York University, 1961. 399 p.

Jones, Peter. Kwame Nkrumah and Africa. London: Hamilton, 1965. 128 p.

Jones, Trevor. Ghana's First Republic, 1960-1966: The Pursuit of the Political Kingdom. Studies in African History Series. London: Methuen, 1976. 366 p.

Jopp, Keith. Tema: Ghana's New Town and Harbour. Accra: Ministry of Information, Development Secretariat, 1961. 51 p.

Kanu, Genoveva. Nkrumah the Man; A Friend's Testimony. Enugu, Nigeria: Delta Publications, 1982. 143 p.

Kenworthy, Leonard. "Ghana: Problems and Progress." Current History, 35, 215 (July 1959), 17-22.

Kinsey, Winston Lee. "The United States and Ghana, 1951-1966." Ph.D. dissertation, Texas Tech. (Lubbock, Texas), 1969. 425 p.

Kraus, Jon Peter. "Cleavages, Crises, Parties, and State Power in Ghana: The Emergence of a Single-Party System." Ph.D. dissertation, The Johns Hopkins University, 1971. 299 p.

_____. "The Crisis Continues." Africa Report, 23, 4 (July-August 1978), 14-21. The 1978 Referendum.

_____. "The Decline of Ghana's Military Government." Current History, 73, 432 (December 1977), 214-217, 227-229.

_____. "From Military to Civilian Regimes in Ghana and Nigeria." Current History, 76, 445 (March 1979), 122-126, 134-136, 138.

_____. "Ghana's New 'Corporate Parliament'." Africa Report, 10, 6 (June 1965), 6-11.

_____. "The Political Economy of Conflict in Ghana." Africa Report, 25, 2 (March-April 1980), 9-16.

_____. "Rawlings' Second Coming." Africa Report, 27, 2 (March-April 1982), 59-66.

_____. "The Return of Civilian Rule in Nigeria and Ghana." Current History, 78, 455 (March 1980), 115-118, 128-129, 137-138, 144.

_____. "Revolution and the Military in Ghana." Current History, 82, 482 (March 1983), 115-119, 131-132.

_____. "Strikes and Labor Power in Ghana." Development and Change, (April 1979), 259-286.

Lefever, Ernest W. Crisis in the Congo: A United Nations Force in Action. Washington, D.C.: The Brookings Institution, 1965. 215 p.

_____. Spear and Scepter; Army, Police and Politics in Tropical Africa. Washington, D.C.: The Brookings Institution, 1970. 251 p.

_____. Uncertain Mandate: Politics of the U.N. Congo Operation. Baltimore: The Johns Hopkins University Press, 1967. 254 p.

Le Vine, Victor T. Political Corruption: The Ghana Case. Stanford: The Hoover Institution Press, 1975. 169 p.

Lumsden, D. Paul. "Towards Ghana's Third Republic." Canadian Journal of African Studies (Montreal), 13, 3 (1980), 471-78.

Marais, Genoveva. Kwame Nkrumah as I Knew Him. Chichester, Sussex: Janay Publishing Company, 1972. 138 p.

Moxon, James. Volta: Man's Greatest Lake. New York: Frederick A. Praeger, 1969. 256 p.

Nayak, Sanjeeva Ramchandra. "Foreign Policy Issues in Ghana in the United Nations, 1957-1962." Ph.D. dissertation, American University, 1968.

Newbury, Colin W. The West African Commonwealth. Durham, N.C.: Duke University Press for the Duke University Commonwealth Studies Center, 1964. 106 p.

Nkrumah, Kwame. Africa Must Unite. London: Heinemann, 1965;

New York: Praeger, 1963; New York: International Publishers, 1970. 229 p.

_____. Challenge of the Congo. London: Nelson, 1967; New York: International Publishers, 1967. 304 p.

_____. Consciencism: Philosophy and Ideology for Decolonization and Development with Particular Reference to the African Revolution. London: Heinemann, 1964; New York: Monthly Review Press, 1970. 122 p.

_____. Dark Days in Ghana. London: Lawrence and Wishart, 1968; New York: International Publishers, 1969. 219 p.

_____. Ghana: The Autobiography of Kwame Nkrumah. New York: Thomas Nelson and Sons, 1957. 302 p. The best of Nkrumah's books.

_____. Handbook of Revolutionary Warfare: A Guide to the Armed Phase of the African Revolution. New York: International Publishers, 1969. 125 p.

_____. I Speak of Freedom: A Statement of African Ideology. London: Heinemann, 1961; New York: Praeger, 1961. 291 p.

_____. Neo-Colonialism: The Last Stage of Imperialism. London: Nelson, 1965; Heinemann, 1968; New York: International Publishers, 1965. 280 p.

_____. Revolutionary Path. New York: International Publishers, 1973. 532 p.

Nsarkoh, J.K. Local Government in Ghana. Accra: Ghana Universities Press, 1965. 309 p.

Ocran, Albert Kwesi. A Myth Is Broken: An Acocunt of the Ghana Coup d'Etat of 24 February 1966. London: Harlow, Longmans, 1968. 104 p.

_____. Politics of the Sword: A Personal Memoir on Military Involvement in Ghana and of Problems of Military Government. London: Rex Collings, 1977. 167 p.

Ofosu-Appiah, L.H. The Life of Lieut. Gen. E.K. Kotoka. Accra: Waterville Publishing House, 1972. 156 p.

Ohene, Elizabeth. "Is Military Rule Really the Answer?" West Africa (London), 3382 (31 May 1982), 1451-1454.

_____. "Ghana's Two Years of Civilian Rule." West Africa, 3347 (21 September 1981), 2169-2170.

Okeke, Barbara E. *4 June: A Revolution Betrayed*. Enugu, Nigeria: Ikenga Publishers, 1982.

Omari, T. Peter. *Kwame Nkrumah: The Anatomy of an African Dictatorship*. London: C. Hurst and Company, 1970; New York: Africana Publishing Corp., 1972. 229 p.

Oquaye, Mike. *Politics in Ghana, 1972-79*. Accra: Tornado Publications, 1980.

Owusu, Maxwell. "The Search for Solvency: Background to the Fall of Ghana's Second Republic, 1969-1972." *Africa Today* (Denver, Colo.), 19, 1 (Winter 1972), 52-60.

──────. *Uses and Abuses of Political Power: A Case Study of Continuity and Change in the Politics of Ghana*. Chicago: University of Chicago Press, 1970. 364 p. The book focuses on political change in Swedru, in south-central Ghana.

Owusu-Ansah, Kwabena Asare. "Local Government Under Political Integration: The Ghanaian Experience." Ph.D. dissertation, University of Southern California, 1971. 536 p.

Phillips, E.A. "Ethnicity in Ghanaian Politics." *South African Journal of African Affairs*, 9, 1 (1979), 14-21.

Phillips, John. *Kwame Nkrumah and the Future of Africa*. London: Faber and Faber; New York: Frederick A. Praeger, 1960. 272 p. John Phillips was a member of the pre-independence civil service and was Executive Secretary of Nkrumah's State Enterprises. He was one of Nkrumah's chief advisers in financial and administrative affairs.

Pieterse, Jan. "Rawlings and the 1979 Revolt in Ghana." *Race and Class*, 23 (Spring 1982), 251-274.

Pinkney, Robert. *Ghana Under Military Rule, 1966-1969*. Studies in African History. London: Methuen, 1972. 182 p.

Powell, Erica. *Kwame Nkrumah of the New Africa*. London: Thomas Nelson, 1961. 68 p. Erica Powell was the long-time private secretary and speech-writer of Kwame Nkrumah.

──────. *Private Secretary, Gold Coast*. London: C. Hurst, 1984. 228 p.

Price, Robert M. "Military Officers and Political Leadership: The Ghanaian Case." *Comparative Politics*, 3 (April 1971), 361-79.

──────. *Society and Bureaucracy in Contemporary Ghana*. Berkeley: University of California Press, 1975. 275 p.

_____. "A Theoretical Approach to Military Rule in New States: Reference Group Theory and the Ghanaian Case." World Politics, 23, 3 (April 1971), 399-430.

Quaison-Sackey, Alex. Africa Unbound: Reflections of an African Statesman. New York: Frederick A. Praeger; London: Andre Deutsch, 1963. 174 p. Quaison-Sackey served once as both the President of the U.N. General Assembly and as Foreign Minister under Kwame Nkrumah.

Radix, A. "Foreign Participation in State Enterprises: The Case of Abbott Laboratories (Ghana) Ltd." Legon Observer, 2, 23 (November 1967), 2-7.

Rathbone, Richard. "Businessmen in Politics: Party Struggle in Ghana." The Journal of Development Studies, 9, 3 (April 1973). 391-402.

_____. "Politics and Factionalism in Ghana." Current History, 60, 355 (March 1971), 164-167, 175.

Raymond, Robert. Black Star in the Wind. London: MacGibbon and Kee, 1960. 288 p.

"The Return of Jerry Rawlings." West Africa (London), 3362 (11 January 1982), 68-76.

Rothchild, Donald. "Military Regime Performance: An Appraisal of the Ghana Experience, 1972-1978." Comparative Politics, 12, 4 (July 1980), 459-79.

_____, and E. Gyimah-Boadi. "Ghana's Return to Civilian Rule." Africa Today, 28, 1 (1981), 3-16.

Rubin, Leslie, and Paul Murray. The Constitution and Government of Ghana. Law in Africa series, 1. 1st ed., 1961. London: Sweet and Maxwell, 1964. 324 p.

Saffu, E.O. "Politics in a Military Regime: The Ghana Case, 1966-69." Ph.D. dissertation, Oxford University, 1973.

St. Clair, Drake, and Leslie Alexander. "Government Versus the Unions; the Sekondi-Takoradi Strike of 1961." In Politics in Africa: Seven Cases, ed. by Gwendolen Margaret Carter. New York: Harcourt, Brace and World, 1966, pp. 67-118.

Sampson, Magnus J. Makers of Modern Ghana. Accra: Anowuo Educational Publications, 1969. 190 p.

Schiller, Edward H. "The Development and the Influence of Ghanaian Ideology in Emergent Africa, 1957-1963." Ph.D. dissertation, St. John's University, 1964.

Sekyi, H.V.H. "The Year of Revolution in Ghana." African Affairs (London), 72, 287 (April 1973), 197-201. Henry Van Hien Sekyi was Ghana's High Commissioner to the United Kingdom.

Singleton, F.S. "African States and the Congo Affair, 1960-65." Ph.D. dissertation, Yale University, 1968. 390 p.

Smith, M. Brewster. Peace Corps Teachers in Ghana; Final Report of Peace Corps Project in Ghana. Berkeley: Institute of Human Development, University of California, 1964. 195 p.

Sono, Themba. "Congruence and Dissonance in African Political Thought: An Exposition of Political Philosophy of Kwame Nkrumah and Julius K. Nyerere." Ph.D. dissertation, The George Washington University, 1979. 299 p.

Thompson, Willard Scott. Ghana's Foreign Policy, 1957-1966: Diplomacy, Ideology, and the New State. Princeton, N.J.: Princeton University Press, 1969. 462 p.

_____. "Ghana's Foreign Policy Under Military Rule." Africa Report, 14, 5-6 (May-June 1969), 8-13.

_____. "New Directions in Ghana." Africa Report, 11, 8 (November 1966), 18-22.

Tiger, Lionel Samuel. "Bureaucracy in Ghana: The Civil Service." Ph.D. dissertation, University of London, 1965.

_____. "Ghana: A Charismatic Nation." Current History, 45, 268 (December 1963), 335-340.

Timothy, Bankole. Kwame Nkrumah from Cradle to Grave. Evershot, Dorset: The Gavin Press, 1981. 258 p.

_____. Kwame Nkrumah: His Rise to Power. Foreword by Kojo Botsio. London: Allen and Unwin, 1955. 201 p. Timothy was a journalist who was expelled from Ghana during the Nkrumah period.

Tsomondo, Micah Samuel. "Kwame Nkrumah on Socialism and Continentalism as the Ideology for African Development." Ph.D. dissertation, State University of New York at Buffalo, 1971. 644 p.

Twumasi, Yaw. "Media of Mass Communication and the Third Republican Constitution of Ghana." African Affairs (London), 80, 318 (January 1981), 13-28. The author was an editor of the Legon Observer and a member of the Political Science Department of the University of Ghana.

_____. "The Newspaper Press and Political Leadership in Developing Nations: The Case of Ghana, 1964-1978." Gazette (Netherlands), 26, 1 (1980), 1-16.

Uphoff, Norman Thomas. "Ghana's Experience in Using External Aid for Development, 1957-1966." Ph.D. dissertation, University of California, Berkeley, 1970. 1011 p.

Wallerstein, Immanuel M. "The Emergence of Two West African Nations: Ghana and the Ivory Coast." Ph.D. dissertation, Columbia University, 1959. 360 p.

_____. The Road to Independence: Ghana and the Ivory Coast. London: Mouton, 1964. 200 p.

Warner, Douglas. Ghana and the New Africa. London: Muller, 1960. 181 p.

Welch, Claude E., Jr. "Ghana: The Politics of Military Withdrawal." Current History, 54 (February 1968), 95-114.

_____. "Return to Civilian Rule in Ghana." Current History, 56, 333 (May 1969), 286-291.

Williams, Michael Warren. "The Relationship Between Nkrumahism and Twentieth Century Leftist Thought in the African World." Ph.D. dissertation, University of Notre Dame, 1981. 320 p.

Woronoff, Jon. "Nkrumah--the Prophet Risen." Worldview, 16, 3 (1973), 32-36.

_____. "Le Parti de la Convention du Peuple du Ghana." Revue Française d'Etudes Politiques Africaines, 86 (1973), 34-54.

_____. West African Wager: Houphouet Versus Nkrumah. Metuchen, N.J., and London: Scarecrow Press, 1972. 357 p.

Young, Crawford. Ideology and Development in Africa. New Haven: Yale University Press, 1982. 320 p.

J. REGIONAL STUDIES

Addo-Fening, Robert, A.B. Holmes, et al. Akyem Abuakwa and the Politics of the Inter-War Peirod in Ghana. Basel Africa Bibliography, 12. Basel, Switzerland: Communications from the Basel Africa Bibliography, 1975. 166 p.

_____. "Asante Refugees in Akyem Abuakwa 1875-1912." Transactions of the Historical Society of Ghana (Legon), 14, 1 (June 1973), 39-64.

_____. "The Background to the Deportation of King Asafo Agyi and the Foundation of New Dwaben." Transactions of the Historical Society of Ghana, 14, 2 (Dec. 1973), 213-228.

Agbosu, L.K. "Land Administration in Northern Ghana." Review of Ghana Law, 12 (1980), 104-133.

Agyeman-Duah, J. Mampong. "Ashanti: A Traditional History to the Reign of Nana Sofo Kantanka. With a Note on the Traditional History of Mampong by Ivor Wilks." Transactions of the Historical Society of Ghana, 4, 2 (1960), 21-29.

Aidoo, Agnes Akosua. "Asante Queen Mothers in Government and Politics in the Nineteenth Century." Journal of the Historical Society of Nigeria (Ibadan), 9 (Dec. 1977), 1-14.

_____. "The Asante Succession Crisis of 1883-8." Transactions of the Historical Society of Ghana, 13, 2 (Dec. 1972), 163-180.

Akyeampong, Henry Kwasi. The Akim Abuakwa Crisis. With a foreword by J.B. Danquah. Accra: The Author, 1958. 63 p.

Alhasan, Malam. A Short History of the Dagomba Tribe. Trans. from a Hausa manuscript in the Library of the School of Oriental Studies by J. Withers Gill. Accra: Government Printer, n.d.

Aligwekwe, Iwuoha Edozie. "The Ewe and Togoland Problem." Ph.D. dissertation, Ohio State University, 1960. 508 p.

Amenumey, D.E.K. "The Ewe People and the Coming of European Rule, 1850-1914." M.A. thesis, University of London, 1964. 337 p.

_____. "The Extension of British Rule to Anlo (Southeast Ghana) 1850-1890." Journal of African History (London), 9, 1 (1968), 99-117.

_____. "The Pre-1947 Background to the Ewe Unification Question." Transactions of the Historical Society of Ghana, 10 (1969), 65-85.

_____. "Some Aspects of Ewe Machinery of Government with Special Reference to the Anlo Political System." Ghana Journal of Sociology (Legon), 4, 2 (Oct. 1968), 100-108.

Anafu, Moses. "The Impact of Colonial Rule on Tallensi Political Institutions, 1898-1967." Transactions of the Historical Society of Ghana, 14, 1 (June 1973), 17-37.

Anti, A.A. Akwamu, Denkyira, Akuapem, and Ashanti in the Lives of Osei Tutu and Okomfo Anokye. Accra: Ghana Publishing Corp., 1971. 100 p.

_____. The Ancient Asante King. Accra: The Volta Bridge Publishing Co., 1974. 80 p.

Arhin, P. Kwame. Asante and the Northeast. Legon: Institute of African Studies, 1970. 215 p.

_____. "The Development of Market Centres at Atebubu and Kintampo Since 1874." Ph.D. dissertation, University of London, 1969. 272 p.

_____. A Profile of Brong Kyempim. Legon: Institute of African Studies, 1979. 180 p.

_____. "Strangers and Hosts: A Study of Atebubu." Transactions of the Historical Society of Ghana, 12 (1971), 63-82.

_____. "The Structure of Greater Ashanti (1700-1824)." Journal of African History, 8, 1 (1967), 65-85.

Armitage, Cecil Hamilton. "Notes on the Northern Territories of the Gold Coast." United Empire, 4 (Aug. 1913), 634-9.

_____. The Tribal Markings and Marks of Adornment of the Natives of the Northern Territories of the Gold Coast Colony. London: Royal Anthropological Institute, 1924. 23 p.

Asare, Theodore O. The Case for a Reunited Togoland. New York, 1953.

Ayisi, E.D. "The Basis of Political Authority of the Akwapem Tribes, Eastern Ghana." Ph.D. dissertation, University of London, 1965. 395 p.

Balmer, William Turnbull. A History of the Akan Peoples of the Gold Coast. With a foreword by C.W. Welman. London: Atlantis Press: 1925. 208 p.

Beaton, Alfred Charles. The Ashantees: Their Country, History, Wars, Government, Customs, Climate, Religion, and Present Position. London: James Blackwell, 1877. 183 p.

Bening, Raymond B. "Foundations of the Modern Native States of Northern Ghana." Universitas (Legon), 5 (Nov. 1975), 116-38.

_____. "The Location of Administrative Capitals in Ashanti, Ghana, 1896-1911." The International Journal of African Historical Studies (Boston), 12, 2 (1979), 210-234.

_____. "The Regional Boundaries of Ghana, 1874-1972." Research Review (Legon), 9, 1 (1973), 20-57.

Benzing, Brigitta. Die Geschichte und das Herrschaftssystem der Dagomba. Meisenheim am Glan, Germany: Verlag Anton Hain, 1971. 285 p.

Birmingham, David. "A Note on the Kingdom of Fetu." Ghana Notes and Queries (Legon), 9 (1966), 30-33.

Boahen, Albert Adu. "The Origin of the Akan." Ghana Notes and Queries, 9 (1966), 3-10.

_____. "When Did Osei Tutu Die?" Transactions of the Historical Society of Ghana, 16, 1 (June 1975), 87-92.

Bourret, Florence Mabel. "The Gold Coast and the British Mandate of Togoland, 1919-1939." Ph.D. dissertation, Stanford University, 1947. 231 p.

_____. The Gold Coast: A Survey of the Gold Coast and British Togoland, 1919-1946. Stanford: Stanford University Press, 1949. 231 p.

Braimah, J.A. The Ashanti and the Gonja at War. Accra: Ghana Publishing Corporation, 1970. 63 p.

_____, and J.R. Goody. Salaga: The Struggle for Power. London: Longmans, Green and Co., 1967. 222 p.

Britwum, K.A. "Kwadwo Adinkra of Gyaaman: A Study of the Relations Between the Brong Kingdom of Gyaaman and Asante from c. 1800-1818." Transactions of the Historical Society of Ghana, 15, 2 (Dec. 1974), 229-239.

Brokensha, David W., ed. Awkapim Handbook. Accra: State Publishing Corp., 1972. 310 p.

_____. "Chief Akrofi of Larteh, 1885-1900." Transactions of the Historical Society of Ghana, 7 (1964), 12-23.

_____. "The Resilient Chieftaincy at Larteh, Ghana." In West African Chiefs: Their Changing Status Under Colonial Rule and Independence, ed. by Michael Crowder and Obaro Ikime. New York: Africana Publishing Corp.; Ile Ife, Nigeria: University of Ife Press, 1970. 393-406.

_____. "Social Change in Larteh." Ph.D. dissertation, Oxford University, 1962. Published by Clarendon Press, Oxford, 1966. 294 p.

Brown, David. "Anglo-German Rivalry and Krepi Politics, 1886-1894." Transactions of the Historical Society of Ghana, 15, 2 (December 1974), 201-216.

――――. "Borderline Politics in Ghana: The National Liberation Movement of Western Togoland." The Journal of Modern African Studies (Cambridge), 18, 4 (December 1980), 575-610.

――――. "Politics in the Kpandu Area of Ghana, 1925-1969. The Influence of Central Government and National Politics Upon Local Factional Competition." Ph.D. dissertation, Birmingham University, 1977.

――――. "Who Are the Tribalists? Social Pluralism and Political Idealogy in Ghana." African Affairs (London), 81, 322 (January 1982), 37-69.

Brown, Susan Drucker. Ritual Aspects of the Mamprusi Kingship. African Social Research Documents, 8. Leiden: Afrika-Studiecentrum; Cambridge: African Studies Centre, 1975. 172 p.

Buhler, Peter. "The Volta Region of Ghana: Economic Change in Togoland, 1850-1914." Ph.D. dissertation, University of California, San Diego, 1975. 227 p.

Busia, Kofi Abrefa. "The Ashanti." In African Worlds, ed. by Daryll Forde. London: Oxford University Press, 1954, pp. 190-209.

Butler, William Francis. Akim-Foo: The History of a Failure. London: Sampson, Low, Marston, Low, Searle, 1875. 300 p.

Cardinall, Allan Wolsey. Tales Told in Togoland to Which Is Added the Mythical and Traditional History of Dagomba by E.F. Tamakloe. London: Oxford University Press, 1931; Westport, Conn.: Negro Universities Press (Greenwood), 1970. 290 p.

Case, Glenna Lea. "Wasipe Under the Ngbanya: Polity, Economy, and Society in Northern Ghana." 2 vols. Ph.D. dissertation, Northwestern University, 1979. 865 p.

Chambas, Mohamed Ibn. "The Politics of Agricultural and Rural Development in the Upper Region of Ghana: Implications of Technocratic Ideology and Non-Participatory Development." Ph.D. dissertation, Cornell University, 1980. 241 p.

Coleman, James Smoot. Togoland. International Conciliation, 509. New York: Carnegie Endowment for International Peace, 1956. 91 p.

Daaku, Kwame Yeboa. "A History of Sefwi: A Survey of Oral Evidence." Research Review (Legon: Institute of African Studies), 7, 3 (1971), 32-47.

――――. Oral Traditions of Assin-Twifo, Adanse and Denkyira. 3 vols. Legon: Institute of African Studies, University of Ghana, 1969-1970.

――――. Osei Tutu of Asante. African Historical Biographies. London: Heinemann, 1976. 48 p.

Danquah, Joseph Boakye. The Akim Abuakwa Handbook. London: Forster Groom, 1928. 127 p.

――――. Gold Coast: Akan Laws and Customs and the Akim Abuakwa Constitution. London: G. Routledge, 1928. 272 p.

Dougah, J.C. Wa and Its People. Legon: Institute of African Studies, 1966. 117 p.

Duncan-Johnstone, A.C., and H.A. Blair. Enquiry into the Constitution and Organization of the Dagbon Kingdom. Accra: Government Printer, 1932. 68 p. Duncan-Johnstone and Blair were both British officials in the Northern Territories.

Dunn, John, and A.F. Robertson. Dependence and Opportunity: Political Change in Ahafo. London and New York: Cambridge University Press, 1973. 400 p.

Fage, John Donnelly. "Reflections on the Early History of the Mossi-Dagomba Group of States." In The Historian in Tropical Africa, ed. by Jan Vansina, Raymond Mauny and L.V. Thomas. London: Oxford University Press, 1964. 177-192.

Ferguson, Phyllis Stevens. "Islamization in Dagbon: A Study of the Alfanema of Yendi." Ph.D. dissertation, Cambridge University, 1973.

――――. The Organization of Islam in Yendi. Legon: Institute of African Studies, 1968.

Field, Margaret Joyce. Akim-Kotoku: An Oman of the Gold Coast. London: Crown Agents for the Colonies, 1948. 211 p.

――――. Social Organization of the Ga People. London: Crown Agents for the Colonies, 1940. 231 p.

Flight, Colin. "The Chronology of the Kings and Queenmothers of Bono-Manso: A Revaluation of the Evidence." Journal of African History. 11, 2 (1970). 259-268.

Froelich, Jean Claude. La Tribu Konkomba du Nord Togo. Memoires

Bibliography

de l'Institut Français d'Afrique Noire, 37. Dakar: IFAN, 1954. 253 p.

Fuller, Sir Francis. A Vanished Dynasty: Ashanti. London: J. Murray, 1921; London: Frank Cass, 1968. 241 p. Fuller was Chief Commissioner in Asante, 1902-1920.

Fynn, John Kofi. Asante and Its Neighbors, 1700-1807. Legon History Series. London: Longman, 1971. 175 p.

──────. Oral Traditions of the Fante States. 7 vols. Legon: Institute of African Studies, University of Ghana, 1974-1976.

──────. "The Reign and Times of Kusi Obedum, 1750-64." Transactions of the Historical Society of Ghana, 8 (1965), 24-32.

──────. "The Rise of Ashanti." Ghana Notes and Queries (Legon), 9 (1966), 24-30.

Goody, E.N. "Kinship, Marriage and the Development Cycle Among the Gonja of Northern Ghana." Ph.D. dissertation, Cambridge University, 1961. 230 p.

Goody, Jack [John Rankine]. Death, Property and Ancestors: A Study of the Mortuary Customs of the La Dagaa of West Africa. Stanford: Stanford University Press, 1962. 452 p.

──────. "The Ethnography of the Northern Territories of the Gold Coast West of the White Volta." London: Colonial Office, 1954. 59 p. Typescript.

──────. "The Mande and the Akan Hinterland." In The Historian in Tropical Africa, ed. by Jan Vansina, Raymond Mauny, and L.V. Thomas. London: Oxford University Press, 1964. 192-218.

──────. "The Over-Kingdom of Gonja." In West African Kingdoms in the Nineteenth Century, ed. by Daryll Forde and P.M. Kaberry. London: Oxford University Press, 1967. 179-205.

Gordon, James. "Some Oral Traditions of Denkyira." Transactions of the Gold Coast and Togoland Historical Society (Achimota), 1, 3 (1953), 27-33.

Greene, Sandra Elaine. "The Anlo-Ewe: Their Economy, Society and External Relations in the Eighteenth Century." Ph.D. dissertation, Northwestern University, 1981. 483 p.

Haight, Bruce Marvin. "Bole and Gonja. Contributions to the History of Northern Ghana." Ph.D. dissertation, Northwestern University, 1981. 1307 p.

_____; Nehemia Levtzion; and Ivor Wilks. Chronicle from Gonja: A Tradition of West African Muslim Historiography. London: Cambridge University Press, 1984.

Hall, Wynyard Montagu. The Great Drama of Kumasi. London: Putnam, 1939. 367 p.

Hamilton, Robert Earl. "Asante, 1895-1900: Prelude to War." Ph.D. dissertation, Northwestern University, 1978. 401 p.

Haskett, Norman Dean. "Kete-Krakye and the Middle Volta Basin, 1700-1914: Cockpit of African and European Rivalry." Ph.D. dissertation, University of California, Los Angeles, 1981. 777 p.

Henige, David P. "Abrem Stool: A Contribution to the History and Historiography of Southern Ghana." The International Journal of African Historical Studies, 6, 1 (1973), 1-18.

_____. "Akan Stool Succession Under Colonial Rule-Continuity or Change?" Journal of African History, 16, 2 (1975), 285-301.

_____. "John Kabes of Komenda: An Early African Entrepreneur and State Builder." Journal of African History, 18, 1 (1977), 1-19.

_____. "The Problem of Feedback in Oral Tradition: From Examples from the Fante Coastlands." Journal of African History, 14, 2 (1973), 223-235.

_____. "Seniority and Succession in the Krobo Stools." The International Journal of African Historical Studies, 7, 2 (1974), 203-226.

Hilton, T.E. "Notes on the History of Kusasi." Transactions of the Historical Society of Ghana, 6 (1962), 79-86.

_____. "Le Peuplement de Frafra, District du Nord Ghana." Bulletin Institute Française d'Afrique Noire (Dakar), 27, ser. B, 3/4 (July-October 1965), 678-700.

_____. "The Settlement Pattern of the Tumu District of Northern Ghana." Bulletin Institute Française d'Afrique Noire, 30, ser. B, 3 (July 1968), 868-883.

Holden, J.J. "The Zabarima Conquest of North-West Ghana, Part 1." Transactions of the Historical Society of Ghana, 8 (1965), 60-86.

Iddi, M.D. "The Ya Na of the Dagombas." Legon: Institute of African Studies, University of Ghana. Yendi Project, Report 12.

Iliasu, A.A. "The Origins of the Mossi-Dagomba States." Research Review (Institute of African Studies, Legon), 7, 2 (1971), 95-113.

Irwin, Graham W. "Precolonial African Diplomacy: The Example of Asante." The International Journal of African Historical Studies, 8, 1 (1975), 81-96.

Johnson, Marion. "Ashanti East of the Volta." Transactions of the Historical Society of Ghana, 8 (1965), 33-59.

──────. "Ashanti, Juaben, and M. Bonnat." Transactions of the Historical Society of Ghana, 12 (1971), 17-41.

Jones, D.H. "Jakpa and the Foundations of Gonja." Transactions of the Historical Society of Ghana, 6, (1962), 1-29.

Kea, Ray A. "Akwamu-Anlo Relations c. 1750-1813." Transactions of the Historical Society of Ghana, 10 (1969), 29-63.

Klein, A. Norman. "The Two Asantes: Competing Interpretations of 'Slavery' in Akan-Asante Culture and Society." In The Ideology of Slavery in Africa, ed. by Paul E. Lovejoy. Sage Series on African Modernization and Development, 6. Beverly Hills and London: Sage Publications, 1981. 149-167.

Kropp Dakubu, Mary Ester. "Linguistic Pre-History and Historical Reconstruction: The Ga-Adangme Migrations." Transactions of the Historical Society of Ghana, 13, 1 (June 1972), 87-111.

Kumah, John Kweku. "Denkyira: 1600-1730 A.D." Master's thesis, University of Ghana, 1965. 171 p.

──────. "The Rise and Fall of the Kingdom of Denkyira." Ghana Notes and Queries (Legon), 9 (November 1966), 33-35.

Kwamena-Poh, M.A. Government and Politics in the Akuapem State, 1730-1850. Evanston: Northwestern University Press, 1973. 177 p.

Kyerematen, A.A.Y. Inter-State Boundary Litigation in Ashanti. African Social Research Documents, 4. Leiden: Afrika-Studiecentrum; Cambridge: African Studies Centre, 1972. 139 p.

──────. "The Royal Stools of Ashanti." Africa (London), 39 (January 1969), 1-10.

Labouret, Henri. Nouvelles Notes sur les Tribus du Rameau Lobi: Leurs Migrations, Leur Evolution, Leurs Parlers, et Ceux de Leurs Voisins. Memoires de l'Institut Français d'Afrique Noire, 54. Dakar: IFAN, 1958. 296 p.

_____. Les Tribus du Rameau Lobi. Paris: Institut d'Ethnologie, 1931. 512 p.

Ladouceur, Paul Andre. Chiefs and Politicians: The Politics of Regionalism in Northern Ghana. London: Longmans, 1979. 320 p.

_____. "The Yendi Chieftaincy Dispute and Ghanaian Politics." Canadian Journal of African Studies (Montreal), 6 (1972), 97-115.

Levtzion, Nehemia. "Salaga--A Trading Town in Ghana." Asian and African Studies (Jerusalem), 2 (1966), 207-244.

Lewin, Thomas J. Asante Before the British: The Prempean Years, 1875-1900. Lawrence, Kan.: Regents Press of Kansas, 1978. 312 p.

Lloyd, Alan. The Drums of Kumasi: The Story of the Ashanti Wars. London: Longmans, 1964. 209 p.

Maier, Donna Jane Ellen [Donna Maier Weaver]. Priests and Power: The Case of the Dente Shrine in Nineteenth-Century Ghana. Bloomington: Indiana University Press, 1983. 258 p.

Mamattah, Charles M.K. The Anlo-Ewes and Their Immediate Neighbors. Vol. I of The Ewes of West Africa. Accra: Advent Press, Volta Research Publications, 1976. 763 p.

Meyerowitz, Eva Lewin-Richter. At the Court of an African King. London: Faber and Faber, 1962. 244 p.

_____. "Communication: The Chronology of Bono-Manso." Journal of African History, 13, 2 (1972), 348-352.

_____. The Early History of the Akan States of Ghana. London: Red Candle Press, 1974. 228 p.

_____. The Sacred State of the Akan. London: Faber and Faber, 1951. 222 p.

Naden, A.J., and R.L. Schaefer. "The Meaning of Fra-Fra." Research Review (Legon: Institute of African Studies), 9, 2 (1973), 5-12.

Northcott, Henry P. Report on the Northern Territories of the Gold Coast. London: HMSO (Harrison and Sons), 1899. 174 p. The author was the first British Commissioner of the Northern Territories.

Odonkor, Thomas Harrison. The Rise of the Krobos. Tema: Ghana Publishing Corp., 1971. 60 p. The author was Chief of Kpong, Manya Krobo.

Odotei, I. "The Ga and Their Neighbors." Ph.D. dissertation, University of Ghana, 1972.

Oroge, E.A.A. "The Rise and Fall of Asante." Tarikh (Ibadan), 5, 1 (1974), 31-45.

Painter, Colin. "The Guang and West African Historical Reconstruction." Ghana Notes and Queries (Legon), 9 (1966), 58-65.

Paternot, Marcel. Lumière sur la Volta, Chez les Dagari. Paris: Association des Missionaires d'Afrique, 1953. 254 p.

Priestley, Margaret, and Ivor Wilks. "The Ashanti Kings in the Eighteenth Century: A Revised Chronology." Journal of African History, 1, 1 (1960), 83-96.

Rattray, Robert Sutherland. Ashanti. Oxford: The Clarendon Press, 1923, 1955, 1969. 348 p.

_____. Ashanti Law and Constitution. London: The Clarendon Press, 1929, 1956, 420 p.; New York: Negro Universities Press, 1969.

_____. Tribes of the Ashanti Hinteland. 2 vols. Oxford: The Clarendon Press, 1932, 1969. 604 p.

Renehan, Margaret Anne P. "The Denkyira and the British: 1823-1874. Successful Efforts by an African Group to Gain Inclusion in the British Protectorate of the Gold Coast." Ph.D. dissertation, University of Birmingham, 1978. 505 p.

Saaka, Yakubu. Local Government and Political Change in Northern Ghana. Washington, D.C.: University Press of America, 1978. 172 p.

Sanders, James Robert. "The Expansion of the Fante and the Emergence of Asante in the Eighteenth Century." Journal of African History, 20, 3 (1979), 349-364.

_____. "The Political Development of the Fante in the Eighteenth and Nineteenth Centuries: A Study of a West African Merchant Society." 2 vols. Ph.D. dissertation, Northwestern University, 1980.

Sanderson, R.W. "The History of Nzima Up to 1874." Gold Coast Review (Accra), 1 (1925), 95 ff.

Sarbah, John Mensah. Fanti Customary Laws: A Brief Introduction to the Principals of the Native Laws and Customs of the Fanti and Akan Districts of the Gold Coast, with a Report of Some Cases Thereon Decided in the Law Courts. 2nd ed. London: W. Clowes, 1904. 317 p. (First edition was in 1897.)

Sprigge, R.G.S. "Eweland's Adangbe: An Enquiry into an Oral Tradition." Transactions of the Historical Society of Ghana, 10 (1969), 87-128.

_____. "A Note on the Ethno-Historical Background to the Ewe-speaking Villages of the Achimota-Legon Area." Ghana Notes and Queries, 11 (1970), 13-16.

Staniland, Martin. The Lions of Dagbon: Political Change in Northern Ghana. New York and London: Cambridge University Press, 1975. 241 p.

_____. "The Manipulation of Tradition: Politics in Northern Ghana." The Journal of Development Studies, 9, 3 (April 1973), 373-390.

Strevens, P.D. "Konkomba or Dagomba?" Transactions of the Gold Coast and Togoland Historical Society (Achimota), 1, 5 (1955), 211-216.

Tait, David. The Konkomba of Northern Ghana. London: Oxford University Press, 1961. 255 p. This book made use of notes by Jack Goody.

_____. "The Political System of the Konkomba." Ph.D. dissertation, University of London, 1952. 266 p.

Tamakloe, Emmanuel Forster. A Brief History of the Dagbamba People. Accra: Government Printer, 1931. 76 p. The narrative also appears in A.W. Cardinall, Tales Told in Togoland, chapter 11. Tamakloe was an interpreter in Kete Krakye, 1897-1907, and served as a Census Clerk in the Northern Territories in 1910.

Tordoff, William. "The Ashanti Confederacy." Journal of African History, 3, 3 (1962), 399-417.

_____. Ashanti Under the Prempehs, 1888-1935. London and New York: Oxford University Press, 1965. 443 p.

_____. "The Exile and Repatriation of Nana Prempeh I of Ashanti (1896-1924)." Transactions of the Historical Society of Ghana, 4, 2 (1960), 33-58.

_____. "Political History of Ashanti, 1888-1935." 2 vols. Ph.D. dissertation, University of London, 1961.

Tufuo, J.W., and C.E. Donkor. Ashantis of Ghana: People with a Soul. Accra: Anowuo, 1969. 127 p.

Verdon, Michael. "Re-defining Pre-colonial Ewe Polities: The Case of Abutia." Africa (London), 50, 3 (1980), 280-292.

Wallis, J.R. "The Kwahus-Their Connection with the Afram Plain." Transactions of the Gold Coast and Togoland Historical Society (Achimota), 1, 3 (1953), 10-26.

Weaver, Donna J.E. Maier. "The Dente Oracle, the Bron Confederation, and Asante: Religion and the Politics of Secession." Journal of African History, 22, 2 (1981), 229-244.

_____. "Kete-Krachi in the Nineteenth Century: Religious and Commercial Center of the Eastern Asante Borderlands." 2 vols. Ph.D. dissertation, Northwestern University, 1975. 578 p.

Welch, Claude E. Dream of Unity: Pan Africanism and Political Unification in West Africa. Ithaca, N.Y.: Cornell University Press, 1966. This has two chapters on Ewe unification, 37-147.

Welman, Charles Wellesley. The Native States of the Gold Coast: I Peki. London: W. Clowes, 1925. 46 p.

_____. The Native States of the Gold Coast: II Ahanta. London: W. Clowes, 1930. 88 p. The two parts were reprinted in 1969 as one volume by Dawson of London. Welman was once Secretary for Native Affairs on the Gold Coast.

Wilks, Ivor G. "Akwamu, 1650-1750: A Study of the Rise and Fall of a West African Empire." Master's thesis, University of Wales, 1959. 203 p.

_____. "Ashanti Government." In West African Kingdoms in the Nineteenth Century, ed. by Daryll Forde and P.M. Kaberry. London: Oxford University Press for the International African Institute, 1967. 206-238.

_____. "Aspects of Bureaucratization in Ashanti in the Nineteenth Century." Journal of African History, 7 2 (1966), 215-232.

_____. "The Growth of the Akwapim State; a Study in the Control of Evidence." In The Historian in Tropical Africa, ed. by J.R. Vansina, et al. London: Oxford University Press, 1964. 390-411.

_____. The Northern Factor in Ashanti History. Legon: Institute of African Studies, University of Ghana, 1961. 46 p.

_____. "The Northern Factor in Ashanti History: Begho and the Mande." Journal of African History, 2, 1 (1961), 25-34.

_____. "A Note on the Chronology and Origins of the Gonja Kings." Ghana Notes and Queries, 8 (1966), 26-28.

_____. "A Note on the Early Spread of Islam in Dagomba." Transactions of the Historical Society of Ghana, 8 (1965), 87-98.

_____. "A Note on Twifo and Akwamu." Transactions of the Historical Society of Ghana, 3, 3 (1958), 215-217.

_____. "The Rise of the Akwamu Empire, 1650-1710." Transactions of the Historical Society of Ghana, 3, 2 (1957), 99-136.

Withers-Gill, J. The Moshi Tribe: A Short History. Accra: Government Printer, 1924. 24 p.

K. TRAVEL

Anderson, Rosa C. River, Face Homeward: An Afro-American in Ghana. New York: Exposition Press, 1966. 120 p.

Barros, João de. "Extracts from the 'Decadas da India' of João de Barros," in Voyages of Cadamosto and Other Documents on Western Africa in the Second Half of the Fifteenth Century, trans. and ed. by G.R. Crone, Hakluyt Society, 2nd series, 80. London: Cambridge University Press, 1937. 114-123. Barros was at Elmina from 1522 to 1532.

Beecham, John. Ashantee and the Gold Coast: Being a Sketch of the History, Social State, and Superstitions of the Inhabitants of Those Countries. London: J. Mason, 1841; rpt. London: Dawson, 1968; rpt. New York: Johnson Reprint Corp., 1970. 376 p. A secondhand collection of facts by a Wesleyan missionary.

Binger, Louis. Du Niger au Golfe de Guinnée par le Pays de Kong et le Mossi, 1887-1889. 2nd vol. Paris: Hachette, 1892. 416 p. Fine account of the Northern area.

Bosman, William. A New and Accurate Description of the Coast of Guinea, Divided into the Gold, the Slave, and the Ivory Coasts. Utrecht: Anthony Schouten, 1704; London: J. Knapton, 1705 and later editions; London: Frank Cass, 1967. 577 p. Bosman, in Dutch service, was on the Gold Coast for 14 years. This is one of the best-known of the early accounts.

Bowdich, Thomas Edward. Mission from Cape Coast Castle to Ashantee. London: J. Murray, 1819; London: Frank Cass, 1966. 595 p. This is the earliest account by a European who had been inland to Asante.

Boyle, Frederick. Through Fanteeland to Coomasie. London: Chapman and Hall, 1874. 411 p.

Burton, Richard Francis, and V.L. Cameron. To the Gold Coast for Gold. 2 vols. London: Chatto and Windus, 1883.

Cardinall, Allan Wolsey. In Ashanti and Beyond. London: Seeley, 1927. 288 p.

Carnes, Joshua A. Journal of a Voyage from Boston to the West Coast of Africa. Boston: J.P. Jewett; Cleveland: J. Proctor and Worthington, 1852. 479 p. An American who went to the Gold Coast out of curiosity.

Crouch, Archer Philip. On a Surf-bound Coast; or, Cable-laying in the Tropics. London: S. Low, Marston, Searle, and Rivington, 1887. An interesting account by an English engineer who helped lay the cable along the west coast of Africa. 338 p.

Cruickshank, Brodie. Eighteen Years on the Gold Coast of Africa: Including the Account of the Native Tribes and Their Intercourse with Europeans. 2 vols. London: Hurst and Blackett, 1853; London: Frank Cass, 1966. Cruickshank served as Lt. Governor and acted as Governor.

Curtin, Philip D., et al., eds. Africa Remembered: Narratives of West Africans from the Era of the Slave Trade. Madison, Wisc.: The University of Wisconsin Press, 1967. 363 p.

Dupuis, Joseph. Journal of a Residence in Ashantee. London: H. Colburn, 1824; London: Frank Cass, 1966. 502 p. Dupuis was leader of a mission to Asante in 1820.

Eskelund, Karl. Black Man's Country: A Journey Through Ghana. London: Alvin Redman, 1958. 164 p.

Fage, John Donnelly. "A Commentary on Duarte Pacheco Pereira's Account of the Lower Guinea Coastlands in His Esmeraldo de Situ Orbis and on Some Other Early Accounts." History in Africa, 7 (1980), 47-80.

François, Curt von. "Bericht des Hauptmann von François über seine Reise im Hinterland des Deutschen Shutzgebiets Togo." Mitteilungen für Forschungsreisenden und Gelehrten aus den deutschen Schutzegebieten, 1 (1888), 143-171.

_____. "Bericht von Hauptmann von François über seine zweite Reise nach Salaga." Mitteilungen für Forschungsreisenden und Gelehrten aus den deutschen Schutzgebieten, 2 (1889), 33-37.

Freeman, Richard Austen. Travels and Life in Ashanti and Jaman. London: A. Constable, 1898; New York: Frederick A. Stokes, 1898; London: Frank Cass, 1967. 559 p. Richard Freeman was a medical officer who accompanied a political mission to Asante in 1888-1889.

Freeman, Thomas Birch. Journal of Various Visits to the Kingdoms of Ashanti, Aku and Dahomi in Western Africa. London: J. Mason, 1844; London: Frank Cass, 1968. 298 p. Thomas Freeman was born in England to an African Mother. He became a Methodist missionary to the Gold Coast in 1838.

Gordon, Charles Alexander. Life on the Gold Coast. London: Bailliere, Tindall, and Cox, 1874. 84 p.

_____. Recollections. London: S. Sonnenschein, 1898. 320 p. Sir Charles Gordon was a surgeon on the Gold Coast, 1847-1848.

Gouldsbury, V. Skipton. "Report of His Journey into the Interior of the Gold Coast. Accra, 27 March 1876." CO. 96.119, no. 5162/S, Enclosed in a letter to Lord Carnarvon, 30 April 1876, in Public Record Office. Gouldsbury was a surgeon in the British army medical corps. This letter is an early report on the territory from Krepi to Salaga. The photostat in the Public Records Office is 28 pages long.

Gros, Jules. Voyages, aventures et captivité de J. Bonnat chez les Achantis. Paris: Librairie Plon, 1884. 278 p.; Westport, Conn.: Negro Universities Press, 1970.

Harris, Elizabeth. Ghana: A Travel Guide. Supplementary Notes on Togo. Flushing, N.Y.: Aburi Press, 1976. 203 p.

Hutton, William. A Voyage to Africa. London: Longman, Hurst, Rees, Orme, and Brown, 1821. 488 p. William Hutton was a member of Dupuis' mission to Asante in 1820.

Huxley, Elspeth Joscelin. Four Guineas. London: Chatto and Windus, 1954. 308 p. Subtitled A Journey Through West Africa, the part on Ghana is on pages 76 to 161.

Ingrams, William Harold. Seven Across the Sahara from Ash to Accra. London: Murray, 1950. 231 p. Ingrams was Chief Commissioner of the Northern Territories, 1947-1948.

Klose, Heinrich. Journey to Northern Ghana, 1894. Inge Killick, trans. Legon: Institute of African Studies, University of Ghana, 1964.

_____. Togo unter deutscher Flagge. Berlin: D. Reimer, 1899.

Marie Louise, Princess. Letters from the Gold Coast. London: Methuen, 1926. 240 p. Letters from a Granddaughter of Queen Victoria written after a 1925 visit.

Pacheco Pereira, Duarte. Esmeraldo de Situ Orbis (Guide to Navigation). G.H.T. Kimble, trans. The Hakluyt Society. 2nd

Series, No. 74, rpt. of 1937 ed. Nendeln, Liechtenstein: Kraus Reprint, 1967. 193 p. This book was written about 1508 and was the earliest description of the Gold Coast. Pacheco Pereira was associated with Elmina from 1482, and was Governor from 1519 to 1522.

Rouch, Jane. Ghana. Lausanne: Editions Rencontre, 1964. 205 p.

Segal, Philip M. and Aaron Segal. The Traveler's Africa: A Guide to the Entire Continent. New York: Hopkinsons and Blake, 1973.

Smith, William. A New Voyage to Guinea. London: J. Nourse, 1744. 276 p. With a companion volume of drawings--Thirty Different Drafts of Guinea. Smith made a survey for the Royal African Company in 1727 along the Gold Coast.

Thompson, Thomas. An Account of Two Missionary Voyages. London: Benj. Dod, 1758. 87 p. Thompson was a missionary for the SPG who went to the Gold Coast in 1752 and stayed there for four years. The first voyage he made was to New Jersey.

_____. Memoirs of an English Missionary to the Coast of Guinea. London: Shepperson and Reynolds, 1788. 31 p. Extracted from the larger account listed above without the material on New Jersey.

Wilks, Ivor. "Travellers in the Gold Coast Hinterland: Salih Bilali of Massina, Abu Bakr, and Wargee." In Africa Remembered: Narratives by West Africans from the Era of the Slave Trade, ed. by Philip D. Curtin. Madison, Wisc.: The University of Wisconsin Press, 1967. 143-189.

Wright, Richard. Black Power; A Record of Reactions in a Land of Pathos. New York: Harper, 1954. 358 p.; London: Dobson, 1956.

L. GEOGRAPHY

Adams, David Thickens. Ghana Geography. London: University of London Press, 1960. 192 p.

Boateng, E.A. A Geography of Ghana. 2nd ed. Cambridge University Press, 1966. 212 p.

Church, Ronald James Harrison. West Africa: A Study of the Environment and of Man's Use of It. 8th ed. New York: Wiley, 1981. 560 p.; London: Longmans, Green, 1981.

Dickson, Kwamina B. "Cocoa in Ghana." Ph.D. dissertation, University of London, 1960. 303 p.

———. A Historical Geography of Ghana. Cambridge: Cambridge University Press, 1971. 379 p.

Dobson, George. "The River Volta, Gold Coast, West Africa." The Journal of the Manchester Geographical Society, 8 (1892), 18-25.

Forde, Enid Rosamund. The Populations of Ghana: A Study of the Spatial Relationship of Its Socio-Cultural and Economic Characteristics. Studies in Geography, 15. Evanston, Ill.: Department of Geography, Northwestern University, 1968. 154 p.

Gaisie, S.K. Dynamics of Population Growth in Ghana. Legon: Ghana Universities Press, 1969. 118 p.

Ghana. Information Services. Ghana at a Glance. 4th ed. Accra: State Publishing Corp., 1967. 90 p.

Gill, H.E. A Ground-Water Reconnaissance of the Republic of Ghana, With a Description of Geohydrologic Provinces. Geological Survey Water Supply Paper 1757-K. Washington, D.C.: U.S. Government Printing Office, 1969. 38 p.

Gould, Peter R. The Development of the Transportation Pattern in Ghana. Studies in Geography, 5. Evanston, Ill.: Department of Geography, Northwestern University, 1960. 163 p.

Grove, David, and Laszlo Huszar. The Towns of Ghana: The Role of Service Centres in Regional Planning. London: Oxford University Press, 1965. 128 p.

Hilling, David. Development of the Ghanaian Post System. London: Department of Geography, University of London, 1969. 350 p.

Hilton, Thomas E. The Distribution and Density of Population in Ghana. Legon: Ghana Universities Press, 1968. 60 p.

Junner, N.R. "The Diamond Deposits of the Gold Coast." Geological Survey Bulletin, 12 (1943).

———. "Geology of the Gold Coast and Western Togoland." Gold Coast Geological Survey Bulletin, 11 (1940).

Ofori-Sarpong, E. Impact of Drought in Ghana and Upper Volta, 1970-1977. Legon: University of Ghana, 1980. 23 p.

Pedler, F.J. Economic Geography of West Africa. New York: Longmans, Green, 1955. 232 p.

Route Book of the Gold Coast Colony, Ashanti, and the Northern Territories. London: War Office, 1906.

Taylor, Charles J. The Vegetarian Zones of the Gold Coast. Accra: Government Printer, 1953.

Tindall, Harold Donovan. Fruit and Vegetables in West Africa. Rpt. of 1965 ed. London: H.M.S.O., 1971. 259 p.

Udo, Reuben K. A Comprehensive Geography of West Africa. New York: Holmes and Meier, Africana Publishing Co., 1978. 303 p.

U.S. Department of the Interior, Board on Geographic Names. Ghana; Official Standard Names Approved by the United States Board on Geographic Names. Washington, D.C.: U.S. Government Printing Office, 1967. 282 p.

Varley, William J., and H.P. White. The Geography of Ghana. London: Longmans, 1958. 313 p.

M. ARTS

Antubam, Kofi. Ghana's Heritage of Culture. Leipzig: Koehler and Amelang, 1963. 242 p. Antubam was head of the Arts and Crafts Department, Achimota, before his death in April 1964.

Asihene, Emmanuel V. Understanding the Traditional Art of Ghana. Cranbury, N.J.: Fairleigh Dickinson University Press, 1978. 95 p.

Assimeng, Max J., ed. Traditional Life, Culture, and Literature in Ghana. Buffalo, N.Y.: Conch Magazine, March 1976. 200 p.

Bebey, Francis. Musique de l'Afrique. Paris: Horizons de France, 1969. 208 p.

Bennet-Clark, Margaret C. "Ghana." Encyclopedia of World Art, vol. 6. New York, Toronto, London: McGraw-Hill, 1962, pp. 298-299.

Bravmann, René A. Islam and Tribal Art in West Africa. London: Cambridge University African Studies Centre, 1974. 190 p. New ed., 1980.

_____. West African Sculpture. Seattle: University of Washington Press for the Henry Art Gallery, 1970. 80 p.

Chernoff, John Miller. African Rhythm and African Sensibility:

Aesthetics and Social Action in African Musical Idioms. Chicago: University of Chicago Press, 1979. 304 p. Chernoff spent five years in Ghana learning about drumming.

Cole, Herbert M., and Doran H. Ross. The Arts of Ghana (Exhibition Guide). Los Angeles: Museum of Cultural History, University of California, 1977. 230 p.

Coplan, David. "Go to My Town, Cape Coast! The Social History of Ghanaian Highlife." In Eight Urban Musical Cultures: Tradition and Change, ed. by Bruno Nettl. Urbana: University of Illinois Press, 1978. 96-114.

Ehrlich, Martha Judith. "A Catalogue of Ashanti Art Taken From Kumasi in the Anglo-Ashanti War of 1874." Ph.D. dissertation, Indiana University, 1981. 789 p.

Garrard, Timothy. Akan Weights and the Gold Trade. New York and London: Longman, 1980. 393 p.

Kohler, William. The Art of Goldweights: Words, Form, Meaning. Philadelphia: University of Pennsylvania Museum and Anko Foundation, 1977. 68 p.

Kyerematen, A.A.Y. Panoply of Ghana: Ornamental Art in Ghanaian Tradition and Culture. New York: Praeger, 1964. 120 p.

Lamb, Venice, and Alastair Lamb. The Lamb Collection of West African Narrow Strip Weaving. Washington, D.C.: Textile Museum, 1975. 48 p.

Littrell, Mary Ann. "Ghanaian Wax Print Textiles." Ph.D. dissertation, Purdue University, 1977. 195 p.

McLeod, Malcolm D. The Asante. London: Published for the Trustees of the British Museum by British Museum Publications, 1981. 192 p.

Nketia, John Hanson Kwabena. African Music in Ghana. Evanston, Ill.: Northwestern University Press, 1963. 148 p.

_____. Drumming in Akan Communities of Ghana. London: Nelson, for the University of Ghana, 1963. 212 p.

_____. Folk Songs of Ghana. London: Oxford University Press for the University of Ghana, 1963. 205 p.

_____. Funeral Dirges of the Akan People. New York: Negro Universities Press (Greenwood), 1969. 296 p.

_____. "Historical Evidence in Ga Religious Music." In The Historian in Tropical Africa, ed. by Jan Vansina, Raymond Mauny, and L.V. Thomas. London: Oxford University Press, 1964. 265-283.

_____. The Music of Africa. New York: W.W. Norton, 1974. 278 p.

_____. "The Musical Traditions of the Akan." Tarikh, 7, 2 (1982), 47-59.

Patton, Sharon Frances. "The Asante Stool." 2 vols. Ph.D. dissertation, Northwestern University, 1980. 599 p.

Plass, Margaret W. African Miniatures: The Goldweights of the Ashanti. London and New York: Praeger, 1967. 26 p.

Prussin, Labelle. Architecture in Northern Ghana: A Study of Forms and Functions. Berkeley: University of California Press, 1969. 120 p.

Ratton, Charles. Fetish Gold. Philadelphia: University of Pennsylvania Museum, 1975. 68 p.

Rattray, Robert Sutherland, et al. Religion and Art in Ashanti. Rpt. of the 1927 ed. New York and London: Oxford University Press, 1959. 432 p.

Sarpong, Peter. The Sacred Stools of the Akan. Tema: Ghana Publishing Corp., 1971. 83 p.

Smith, Fred Thomas. "Gurensi Architectural Decoration in Northeastern Ghana." Ph.D. dissertation, Indiana University, 1979. 365 p.

Swithenbank, Michael. Ashanti Fetish Houses. Accra: Ghana Universities Press, 1969. 68 p.

Underwood, Leon. Bronzes in West Africa. London: Tiranti, 1949.

_____. Figures in Wood of West Africa. London: Tiranti, 1964.

N. LITERATURE AND PRESS

Abbs, Akosua. Ashanti Boy. London: Collins, 1959. 256 p.

Abruquah, Joseph Wilfred. The Catechist. London: Allen and Unwin, 1965. 202 p.

———. The Torrent. London: Longmans, Green, 1968. 280 p.

Addo, Peter Eric Adotey, comp. Ghana Folk Tales: Ananse Stories from Africa. Jericho, N.Y.: Exposition Press, 1968. 51 p.

Aidoo, Christina Ama Ata. Anowa. London: Longmans, 1970. 66 p.

———. The Dilemma of a Ghost. Accra: Longmans, 1965. 50 p.

———. No Sweetness Here. London: Longmans, 1969; New York: Doubleday, 1970. 166 p.

Armah, Ayi Kwei. The Beautyful Ones Are Not Yet Born. Boston: Houghton Mifflin, 1968; Heinemann, 1969; Macmillan, 1969. 215 p.

———. Fragments. Boston: Houghton Mifflin, 1970; London: Heinemann 1974; New York: Collier-Macmillan, 1971. 287 p.

———. The Healers. London: Heinemann, 1979.

———. Two Thousand Seasons. London: Heinemann, 1979; Chicago: Third World, 1980.

———. Why Are We So Blest? New York: Doubleday, 1971; London: Heinemann, 1974.

Asare, Bediako. Majuto. Dar es Salaam: East African Literature Bureau, 1975. 145 p.

———. Mwasi. Nairobi: East African Literature Bureau, 1976.

———. Rebel. London: Heinemann, 1969. 160 p.

———. The Stubborn. Kampala: East African Literature Bureau, 1976. 161 p.

Awooner, Kofi [George Awooner-Williams]. The Breast of the Earth. New York: Doubleday, 1975. 389 p.

———. Guardians of the Sacred Word: Ewe Poetry. New York: Nok, 1974. 104 p.

———. Night of My Blood. Garden City, N.Y.: Doubleday, 1971. 96 p.

———. This Earth, My Brother. New York: Doubleday; London: Heinemann, 1971. 183 p.

———, and Geormbeeyi Adali-Mortty. Messages: Poems from Ghana. London: Heinemann, 1971. 190 p.

Bame, K.N. Come to Laugh: A Study of African Traditional Theater in Ghana. Accra: Baafour Educational Enterprises, 1982.

Casely-Hayford, Joseph Ephraim. Ethiopia Unbound. London: C.M. Phillips, 1911; Frank Cass, 1969; New York: Humanities Press, 1969.

Chick, John D. "The Ashanti Times: A Footnote to Ghanaian Press History." African Affairs (London), 76, 302 (January 1977), 80-94.

Courlander, Harold, and Albert Prempeh. The Hatshaking Dance and Other Tales from the Gold Coast. New York: Harcourt, Brace, 1947. 115 p.

Danquah, Joseph Boakye. The Third Woman. London: United Society for Christian Literature, 1943. 151 p.

_____. Liberty: A Page from the Life of J.B. Accra: H.K. Akyeampong, 1960. 35 p.

De Graft, Joe. The Secret of Opokuwa. Accra: Anowuo, 1967. 72 p.

_____. Sons and Daughters. London: Oxford University Press, 1964. 53 p.

_____. Through a Film Darkly. London: Oxford University Press, 1970. 70 p.

Dei-Anang, Michael Francis. Africa Speaks; a Collection of Original Verse. 2nd ed. Accra: Guinea Press, 1960. 104 p.

_____. Cocoa Comes to Mampong. Cape Coast: Methodist Book Depot, 1949. 47 p. Nendeln: Kraus Reprint, 1970.

_____. Ghana Glory; Poems on Ghana and Ghanaian Life. London: Nelson, 1965. 69 p. Foreword by Kwame Nkrumah.

_____. Ghana Semi-Tones. Accra: Presbyterian Book Depot, 1962. 28 p.

_____. Okomfo Anokye's Golden Stool; a Play in Three Acts. Ilfracombe, Devon: Stockwell, 1960; Accra: Waterville, 1963. 60 p.

Djoleto, Amu S. Money Galore. London: Heinemann, 1975. 182 p.

_____. The Strange Man. London: Heinemann, 1967; New York: Humanities Press, 1968. 277 p.

Duodu, Cameron. The Gab Boys. London: Andre Deutsch, 1967; Fontana-Collins, 1969. 201 p.

Ellis, Alfred Burdon. West African Stories. London: Chapman and Hall, 1890. 278 p.

Fiawoo, F. Kwasi. The Fifth Landing Stage. Trans. from Ewe. London: United Society for Christian Literature, 1943.

Fraser, Robert. The Novels of Ayi Kwei Armah. London: Heinemann, 1980. 113 p.

Hihetah, Robert Kofi. Painful Road to Kadjebi. Accra: Anawuo, 1966. 194 p.

Jahn, Janheinz, et al. Who's Who in African Literature: Biographies, Works, Commentaries. Tübingen: Horst Erdmann Verlag, 1972. 411 p.

Johnevi, Eta. Roses for Sondia. Accra: Johnevi Publications, 1972. 208 p.

Jones-Quartey, Kwatei A.B. History, Politics, and Early Press in Ghana. Accra: Afram Publications, 1975. 130 p.

_____. A Summary History of the Ghana Press, 1822-1960. Accra: Ghana Information Service, 1974. 68 p.

Kayper-Mensah, Albert. The Dark Wanderer. Tübingen: Horst Erdmann Verlag, 1970.

_____, and Horst Wolff, eds. Ghanaian Writing: Ghana As Seen by Her Own Writers As Well As German Authors. Tübingen: Horst Erdmann Verlag, 1972. 240 p.

Knipp, Thomas R. "Myth, History and the Poetry of Kofi Awoonor." African Literature Today (New York), 11 (1980), 39-61.

Konadu, Samuel Asare. Come Back Dora! Rev. ed. Accra: Anowuo, 1968. 212 p. Later published as Ordained by the Oracle. London: Heinemann, 1969. 188 p.

_____. Don't Leave Me Mercy. Accra: Anowuo, 1966. 118 p.

_____. The Lawyer Who Bungled His Life. Accra: Waterville, 1965.

_____. Night Watchers of Korlebu. Accra: Anowuo, 1968. 99 p.

_____. Shadow of Wealth. Accra: Anowuo, 1966. 173 p.

_____. The Wizard of Asaman. Accra: Waterville, 1964. 129 p.

_____. A Woman in Her Prime. London: Heinemann, 1967. 107 p.

Kotei, S.I.A., ed. Ghanaian Writers and Their Works. Accra: George Padmore Research Library on African Affairs, 1961.

Kponkpongori, C.S., et al. Gonja Proverbs. Ed. by O. Rytz. Legon: Institute of African Studies, University of Ghana, 1966. 64 p.

Kwakwa, B.S. Ghanaian Writing Today, 1. Accra-Tema: Ghana Publishing Corp., 1974. 193 p.

Kwarteng, D.K. My Sword Is My Life. Accra: Ghana Publishing Corp., 1972. 158 p.

Mensah, Grace Osei. Eight Delightful Folktales. Accra: Waterville, 1965. 57 p.

Obeng, R.E. Eighteenpence. Ilfracombe, Devon: Stockwell, 1943. 167 p.; Birkenhead: Wilmer, 1950. 167 p.; Accra: Ghana Publishing Corp., 1971. 145 p.

Quaye, Cofie. Murder in Kumasi. Accra: Moxon, 1970. 104 p.

_____. Sammy Slams the Gang. Accra: Moxon, 1970. 62 p.

Rattray, Robert Sutherland. Akan-Ashanti Folk-Tales. Oxford: The Clarendon Press, 1930. 275 p.

_____. Ashanti Proverbs. Oxford: The Clarendon Press, 1916. 190 p.; New edition, 1961.

_____. The Leopard Priestess. New York: Appleton-Century, 1934. 224 p.

Sekyi, Kobina. The Blinkards. London: Heinemann, 1974. 160 p.

Selormey, Francis. The Narrow Path. London: Heinemann, 1966. 184 p.

Sutherland, Efua Theodore. Edufa. London: Longmans, 1967. 72 p.

_____. Foriwa. Accra: State Publishing Corp., 1967. 60 p.

_____. The Story of Bob Johnson, Ghana's Ace Comedian. Accra: Anowuo, 1970. 25 p.

_____. Vulture! Vulture! Accra: State Publishing Corp., 1968. 32 p.

Zell, Hans, Helene Silver, et al. A Reader's Guide to African Literature. New York: Africana Publishing Corp., 1971. 218 p.

O. LANGUAGE

Abbott, Mary. Collected Field Reports on the Phonology of Basari. Legon: University of Ghana, Institute of African Studies, 1966. 59 p.

Ablorh-Odjidja, J.R. Ga for Beginners. Accra: Waterville, 1968. 207 p.

Akrofi, C.A., and G.L. Borchey. English-Twi-Ga Dictionary. Accra, Ghana: Waterville, 1968. 83 p.

Amankwaah, J.W.Y., et al. Gonja-English Dictionary and Spelling Book, ed. O. Ritz. Legon: University of Ghana, 1971. 273 p.

Balmer, William T., and F.C. Grant. A Grammar of the Fante-Akan Language. London: Atlantic Press, 1929. 223 p.

Bartels, Francis L. Fante Word List with Rules of Spelling. Cape Coast: Methodist Book Depot, 1944. 84 p.

Bendor-Samuel, J.T. "The Grusi sub-group of the Gur Languages." Journal of West African Languages, 2, 1 (1965), 47-55.

Beryr, Jack. English, Twi, Asante, Fante Dictionary. London: Macmillan, 1960. 146 p.

_____. The Place-names of Ghana. Accra: University of Ghana, 1958. 190 p.

_____. The Pronunciation of Ewe. Cambridge: Heffer, 1951. 28 p.

_____, and Agnes Akosua Aidoo. An Introduction to Akan. Evanston, Ill.: Northwestern University Press, 1975. 336 p.

_____, Joseph H. Greenberg, et al., eds. Linguistics in Sub-Saharan Africa. The Hague, Paris, New York: Mouton, 1971. 972 p.

_____, and Nii Amon Kotei. An Introductory Course in Ga.

Washington, D.C.: U.S. Office of Education, Institute of International Studies, 1969. 148 p.

Blair, H.A. Dagomba Dictionary and Grammar. Accra: Government Printer, 1941. 151 p.

Brew, S.H. Practical Fanti Course. Cape Coast: Wesleyan Book Depot, 1917. 132 p.

Christaller, Johann G. Dictionary of the Asante and Fante Language Called Tshi (Twi). Basel: Evangelical Society, 1933. 607 p.

_____. A Grammar of the Asante and Fante Language Called Tshi (Twi) Based on the Akuapem Dialect with Reference to the Other Dialects. Farnborough, Hampshire: Gregg International Publishers, 1964. 203 p.

Crouch, Marjorie. Collected Field Reports on the Phonology of Vagala. Legon: University of Ghana, Institute of African Studies, 1966. 44 p.

Dakubu, M.E. Kropp. Ga, Adangme, and Ewe with English Gloss. Legon: University of Ghana, 1966. 79 p.

_____. Ga-English Dictionary. Legon: University of Ghana, 1973. 248 p.

Dolphyne, Florence Abena. "Akan Language Patterns and Development." Tarikh, 7, 2 (1982), 35-45.

Froger, Fernand. Etude sur la langue du Mossi. Paris: Leroux, 1910. 250 p.

_____. Manuel pratique de langue Môré. Paris: Fournier, 1923. 326 p.

Gbedemah, Fui Fianyo Kosi. Alternative Language Policies for Education in Ghana. New York: Vantage Press, 1975. 204 p.

Ghana. Bureau of Ghana Languages. Language Guide (Akuapem-Twi). 3rd ed. Accra: Bureau of Ghana Languages, 1973. 47 p.

_____. Language Guide (Asante-Twi). 3rd ed. Accra: Bureau of Ghana Languages, 1978; rpt. 50 p.

_____. Language Guide (Dagbani). 2nd ed. Accra: Bureau of Ghana Languages, 1968. 48 p.

_____. Language Guide (Ewe). 3rd ed. Accra: Bureau of Ghana Languages, 1977. 53 p.

_____. Language Guide (Fante). 3rd ed. Accra: Bureau of Ghana Languages, 1977; rpt. 52 p.

_____. Language Guide (Ga). 3rd ed. Accra: Bureau of Ghana Languages, 1976, 50 p.

_____. Language Guide (Nzema). 3rd ed. Accra: Bureau of Ghana Languages, 1977. 60 p.

Hall, H.F. Dictionary of Practical Notes: Mossi-English Languages. Ouahigouya: Assembly of God, n.d. 78 p.

Krass, A.C. A Dictionary of the Chokosi Language: English-Chokosi. Legon: University of Ghana, Institute of African Studies, 1973. 133 p.

Kropp, Mary Ester. Adangme Vocabularies. Accra: Institute of African Studies, University of Ghana, 1970.

Lamothe, Charles. Esquisse du système grammatical Lobi. Paris and Ouagadougou: CNRS and CVRS, 1966. 168 p.

Migeod, Frederick William Hugh. The Languages of West Africa. 2 vols. Freeport, N.Y.: Books for Libraries Press, 1972; London: K. Paul, Trench, Trubner, 1911-1913. 350 p. and 419 p.

Painter, Colin. Gonja: A Phonological and Grammatical Study. Bloomington, Ind.: Indiana University Press, 1969. 523 p.

Prost, André. Contribution à l'étude des langues voltaïques. Dakar: IFAN, 1964. 461 p.

Rapp, Eugen L. An Introduction to Twi. Basel: Evangelical Society, 1948. 119 p.

Rattray, Robert Sutherland. An Elementary Mole Grammar with a Vocabulary of over 1000 Words for the Use of Officials in the Northern Territories of the Gold Coast. Oxford: The Clarendon Press, 1918. 85 p.

Redder, J.E., N. Osusu, et al. Twi Basic Course. Washington, D.C.: U.S. Foreign Service Institute, 1963. 224 p.

Schachter, Paul, and Victoria Fromkin. A Phonology of Akan: Akuapem, Asante, & Fante. Working Papers in Phonetics, No. 9. Los Angeles: University of California, 1968. 268 p.

Schaeffer, Robert. Collected Field Reports on the Phonology of Fra Fra. Legon: University of Ghana, Institute of African Studies, 1975. 43 p.

Steele, Mary, and Gretchen Weed. Collected Field Reports on the Phonology of Konkomba. Legon: University of Ghana, Institute of African Studies, 1966. 77 p.

Warburton, Irene P., Prosper Kpotufe, and Roland Glover. Ewe Basic Course. Rev. ed. Bloomington, Indiana: African Studies Program, Indiana University, 1968. 271 p.

Warren, Dennis. Bibliography and Vocabulary of the Akan (Twi-Fante) Language of Ghana. African Series, 6, Research Center for Language and Semiotic Studies. Atlantic Highlands, N.J.: Humanities Press; Bloomington, Indiana: Indiana University Research Center for Language and Semiotic Studies, 1976.

Welman, Charles Wellesley. A Preliminary Study of the Nzina Language. London: Crown Agents, 1926. 113 p.

Welmers, William Everett. A Descriptive Grammar of Fanti. Baltimore: Linguistic Society of America, 1946. 78 p.

Westermann, Diedrich Hermann. The Languages of West Africa. London: Oxford University Press, 1952. 215 p.

———. A Study of the Ewe Language. Trans. by A.L. Bickford-Smith. London: Oxford University Press, 1930. 258 p.

Wilkie, M.G. Ga Grammar, Notes and Exercises. London: Oxford University Press, 1930. 239 p.

P. CULTURE AND SOCIAL LIFE

Abraham, William E. The Mind of Africa. Chicago: University of Chicago Pres,s 1962. 206 p. Abraham, one of Nkrumah's advisers, uses the Akan as a "paradigm" or example of an African society.

Acquah, Ione. Accra Survey: A Social Survey of the Capital of Ghana, formerly called the Gold Coast, 1953-1956. London: University of London, 1958. 176 p.

Akwabi-Ameyaw, Kofi. "Ashanti Social Organization: Some Ethnographic Clarifications." Ethnology, 21 (October 1982), 325-334.

Alicoe, Thomas. The Evolution of Gold Coast Chiefship. Sheffield: Telegraph and Star, 1953.

Ankama, S.K. "The Police and Maintenance of Law and Order in Ghana." Ph.D. dissertation, University of London, 1967. 576 p.

Asante, S.K.B. Property Law and Social Goals in Ghana, 1844-1966. Accra: Ghana University Press, 1975; London: Rex Collings, 1977. 303 p.

Assimeng, Max. Social Structure of Ghana. Accra-Tema: Ghana Publishing Corp., 1981. 201 p.

Azu, Diana Gladys. The Ga Family and Social Change. African Social Research Documents, 5. Leiden: Afrika-Studie Centrum; Cambridge: African Studies Centre, 1974.

Barkan, Joel D. An African Dilemma; University Students, Development and Politics in Ghana, Tanzania and Uganda. Oxford: Oxford University Press, 1976. 280 p.

Birmingham, Walter; I. Neustadt; and E.N. Omaboe, eds. A Study of Contemporary Ghana. Vol. 1, The Economy of Ghana; Vol. 2, The Social Structure of Ghana. Evanston, Ill.: Northwestern University Press, 1966; London: Allen and Unwin for the Ghana Academy of Sciences, 1966. This study was financed by the Ford Foundation and sponsored by the Ghana Academy of Sciences.

Boamah-Wiafe, Daniel. "The Pattern and Correlates of Urbanbound Migration in Ghana." Ph.D. dissertation, University of Wisconsin-Madison, 1978. 173 p.

Bukh, Jette. The Village Woman in Ghana. Uppsala: Scandinavian Institute of African Studies, 1979. 118 p. About life in the Ewe village of Tsito, a town near Ho.

Busia, Kofi Abrefa. The Position of the Chief in the Modern Political System of Ashanti: A Study of the Influence of Contemporary Social Changes on Ashanti Political Institutions. London: Oxford University Press for the International African Institute, 1951. 233 p. Rpt. London: Frank Cass, 1968.

_____. Report on a Social Survey of Sekondi-Takoradi. London: Crown Agents, 1950. 164 p.

Caldwell, J.C. African Rural-Urban Migration: The Movement of Ghana's Towns. London: C. Hurst, 1977. 260 p.

_____. Population Growth and Family Change in Africa: The New Urban Elite in Ghana. London: C. Hurst, 1977. 224 p.

Cardinall, Allan Wolsey. The Natives of the Northern Territories of the Gold Coast: Their Customs, Religion and Folklore. London: George Routledge and Sons, 1920; New York: Negro Universities Press (Greenwood), 1969. 158 p.

Chambers, Robert, ed. The Volta Resettlement Experience. New York and London: Praeger and Pall Mall, 1970. 286 p.

Christensen, James Boyd. Double Descent Among the Fanti. Behavior Science Monographs. New Haven: Human Relations Area Files, 1954. 145 p.

_____. "The Role of the Paternal Line in Fanti Matrilineal Society." Ph.D. dissertation, Northwestern University, 1952.

_____. "The Role of Proverbs in Fante Culture." Africa (London), 28 (July 1958), 232-43.

Cleveland, David Arthur. "The Population Dynamics of Subsistence Agriculture in the West African Savanna: A Village in Northeast Ghana." Ph.D. dissertation, University of Arizona, 1980. 382 p.

Crowder, Michael, and Obaro Ikime. West African Chiefs: Their Changing Status Under Colonial Rule and Independence. New York: Africana Publishing Corp. Ile Ife, Nigeria: University of Ife Press, 1970. 453 p.

Datta, Ansu K., and R. Porter. "The Asafo System in Historical Perspective." Journal of African History, 12, 2 (1971), 279-297.

Elias, Taslim Olawale. The Nature of African Customary Law. Manchester: Manchester University Press, 1956. 318 p.

Ellis, Alfred Burdon. The Ewe-speaking Peoples of the Slave Coast of West Africa; Their Religion, Manners, Customs, Laws, Languages. London: Chapman and Hall, 1890. 331 p.

_____. The Land of Fetish. London: Chapman and Hall, 1883. 316 p.

_____. The Tshi-speaking Peoples of the Gold Coast of West Africa; Their Religion, Manners, Customs, Laws, Languages. London: Chapman and Hall, 1887. 343 p.

_____. West African Sketches. London: S. Tinsley, 1881. 326 p. Alfred Burdon Ellis, 1852-1894, went out to the Gold Coast in 1874 and spent a number of years there as soldier and government official. He wrote a number of books about the Gold Coast.

Field, Margaret Joyce. Search for Security: An Ethno-psychiatric Study of Rural Ghana. Evanston, Ill.: Northwestern University Press, 1960; London: Faber and Faber. 478 p.

_____. Social Organization of the Ga People. London: The Crown Agents for the Colonies, 1940. 231 p.

Fikry, Mona. "Wa: A Case Study of Social Values and Social Tensions as Reflected in the Oral Traditions of the Wala of Northern Ghana." 2 vols. Ph.D. dissertation, Indiana University, 1969. 1063 p.

Fortes, Meyer. The Dynamics of Clanship Among the Tallensi; Being the first part of an Analysis of the Social Structure of a Trans-Volta Tribe. London: Oxford University Press, 1945. 270 p.

────────. "Kinship and Marriage Among the Ashanti." In African Systems of Kinship and Marriage, ed. by A.R. Radcliff-Brown and Daryll Forde. London: Oxford University Press for the International African Institute, 1950. 252-284.

────────. "Primitive Kinship." Scientific American (New York), 200, 6 (June 1959), 146-158. Patrilineal and matrilineal society compared.

────────. The Web of Kinship Among the Tallensi. London: Oxford University Press, 1949. 358 p. The second part of Dynamics of Clanship Among the Tallensi.

Foster, Philip. Education and Social Change in Ghana. Chicago: University of Chicago Press, 1965. 322 p.

Gocking, Roger Stephen. "The Historic Akoto: A Social History of Cape Coast Ghana, 1843-1948." Ph.D. dissertation, Stanford University, 1981. 391 p.

Goody, Jack [John Rankine]. The Social Organization of the Lo Willi. London: H.M.S.O., 1956. 119 p.; 2nd ed. London: Oxford University Press for the International African Institute, 1967.

Howard, Rhoda. "Formation and Stratification of the Peasantry in Colonial Ghana." Journal of Peasant Studies (London), 8 (October 1980), 61-80.

Jahoda, Gustav. White Man: A Study of the Attitudes of Africans to Europeans in Ghana Before Independence. London: Oxford University Press, 1961. 144 p.

Kelly, Gail Margaret. "The Ghanaian Intelligentsia." Ph.D. dissertation, University of Chicago, 1959. 152 p.

Kilson, Marion D. African Urban Kinsmen: The Ga of Central Accra. London: C. Hurst, 1975; New York: St. Martin's, 1975. 122 p.

────────. "Urban Tribesmen: Social Continuity and Change Among the Ga in Accra, Ghana." Ph.D. dissertation, Harvard University, 1966. 235 p.

────────. "Variations in Ga Culture in Central Accra." Ghana Journal of Sociology. 3 (February 1967). 33-54.

Klein, Anatole Norman. "Inequality in Asante: A Study of the Forms and Meanings of Slavery and Social Servitude in Pre- and Early Colonial Akan-Asante Society and Culture." 2 vols. Ph.D. dissertation, The University of Michigan, 1980. 494 p.

_____. "The Two Asantes: Competing Interpretations of 'Slavery' in Akan-Asante Culture and Society." Chapt. 6 in The Ideology of Slavery in Africa, ed. by Paul E. Lovejoy. Sage Series on African Modernization and Development. Beverly Hills, Calif.: Sage Publications, 1981. 312 p.

Lubeck, Paul. Patterns of Assimilation of Hausa Families in Dagomba. Evanston, Ill.: Northwestern University Press, 1968. 55 p.

Lystad, Robert A. The Ashanti: A Proud People. New Brunswick, N.J.: Rutgers University Press, 1958. 212 p.

_____. "Differential Acculturation of the Ahafo-Ashanti of the Gold Coast and the Indenie-Agni of the Gold Coast." Ph.D. dissertation, Northwestern University, 1952. 153 p.

McCall, Daniel Francis. "The Effect on Family Structure of Changing Economic Activities of Women in a Gold Coast Town." Ph.D. dissertation, Columbia University, 1956. 125 p.

McCarthy, Mary O'Neil. "Social Change as a Prelude to Colonialism: The Fante States, 1807-1874." Ph.D. dissertation, University of Minnesota, 1980. 307 p.

Manoukian, Madeline. Akan and Ga-Adangme Peoples of the Gold Coast. Ethnographic Survey of Africa: Western Africa, pt. 1. London: International African Institute, 1950. 112 p.

_____. The Ewe-Speaking People of the Togoland and the Gold Coast. Ethnographic Survey of Africa: Western Africa, pt. 6. London: International African Institute, 1952. 66 p.

_____. Tribes of the Northern Territories of the Gold Coast. Ethnographic Survey of Africa: Western Africa, pt. 5. London: International African Institute, 1952. 104 p.

Mate Kole, Nene Azu. "The Historical Background of Krobo Customs." Transactions of the Gold Coast and Togoland Historical Society (Achimota), 1, 4 (1955), 133-140.

Meyerowitz, Eva Lewin-Richter. The Akan of Ghana: Their Ancient Beliefs. London: Faber and Faber, 1958. 164 p.

_____. Akan Traditions of Origin. London: Faber and Faber, 1952. 149 p.

_____. At the Court of an African King. London: Faber and Faber, 1962. 244 p.

_____. The Divine Kinship in Ghana and Ancient Egypt. London: Faber and Faber, 1960. 260 p.

Morrison, Minion K.C. Ethnicity and Political Integration: The Case of Ashanti, Ghana. Foreign and Comparative Studies/African Series 38. Syracuse: Syracuse University, 1982. 208 p.

Murdock, George Peter. Africa: Its Peoples and Their Culture History. New York: McGraw-Hill, 1959. 456 p.

Nukunya, G.K. "Kinship, Marriage and Family: A Study of the Influence of Contemporary Social Changes on an Ewe Tribe." Ph.D. dissertation, University of London, 1964. 385 p.

_____. Kinship and Marriage Among the Anlo-Ewe. London: Athlone Press, 1969; New York: Humanities Press, 1969. 217 p. (London School of Economics Monographs on Social Anthropology, 37.)

Opoku, A.A. "Festivals Change to Match Today's World." Africa Report, 17, 4 (April 1972), 23-26.

Opoku, Kofi Asare. "The World View of the Akan." Tarikh (Ibadan), 7, 2 (1982), 61-73.

Oppong, Christine. Growing Up in Dagbon. Tema: Ghana Publishing Corp., 1973. 79 p.

_____. Marriage Among a Matrilineal Elite: A Family Study of Ghanaian Senior Civil Servants. London and New York: Cambridge University Press, 1974. 186 p.

Osei, Osafo Kwabena. African Heritage of the Akan, Republic of Ghana. Los Angeles: By the Author, 1979. 173 p.

Pellow, Deborah. Women in Accra: Options for Autonomy. Algonac, Mich.: Reference Publications, 1977. 272 p.

Rhoda, Richard Eric. "Migration of Educated Youth from Rural Areas in Ghana." Ph.D. dissertation, University of Iowa, 1978. 228 p.

Robertson, A.F. "Anthropology and Government in Ghana." African Affairs (London), 74, 294 (January 1975), 51-59.

Robertson, Claire C. Sharing the Same Bowl; A Socioeconomic History of Women and Class in Accra, Ghana. Bloomington: Indiana University Press, 1984. 299 p.

Sandbrook, Richard, and Jack Arn. The Labouring Poor and Urban Class Formation: The Case of Greater Accra. Occasional Monograph Series 12. Montreal: Centre for Developing Area Studies, McGill University, 1977. 86 p.

Sanders, James Robert. "The Political Development of the Fante in the Eighteenth and Nineteenth Centuries: A Study of a West African Merchant Society, 1700-1806." Ph.D. dissertation, Northwestern University, 1980. 551 p.

Sarbah, John Mensah. Fanti Customary Laws. London: W. Clowes, 1897. 295 p.

_____. Fanti National Constitution and Fanti Law Report. London: W. Clowes, 1906. 273 p.; London: Frank Cass, 1968.

Schildkrout, Enid. "Government and Chiefs in Kumasi Zongo." In West African Chiefs: Their Changing Status Under Colonial Rule and Independence, ed. by Michael Crowder and Obaro Ikime. New York: Africana Publishing Corp.; Ile Ife, Nigeria: University of Ife Press, 1970. 370-392.

_____. People of the Zongo. The Transformation of Ethnic Identities in Ghana. Cambridge and New York: Cambridge University Press, 1978. 303 p.

Schott, John R., ed. An Experiment in Integrated Rural Development: The Mampong Valley Social Laboratory in Ghana. New York: International Institute of Rural Reconstruction, 1978. 252 p.

Scott, David. Epidemic Disease in Ghana, 1901-1960. London: Oxford University Press, 1965. 226 p.

Stenross, Barbara. "Customary Law, Colonialism, and the Courts: Land Law and Capitalist Class Formation in the Gold Coast Colony." Ph.D. dissertation, Indiana University, 1981. 182 p.

Tranakides, G. "Observations on the History of Some Gold Coast Peoples." Transactions of the Gold Coast and Togoland Historical Society, 1, 2 (1953), 33-44.

Von Laue, Theodore H. "Anthropology and Power: R.S. Rattray Among the Ashanti." African Affairs (London), 75 (January 1976), 33-54.

Williams, Joy E. Stewart. "The Educated and Professional Elite in the Gold Coast and Sierra Leone, 1885-1914." Ph.D. dissertation, University of California, Los Angeles, 1980. 176 p.

Wilson, Louis Edward. "The Evolution of Krobo Society: A History from c. 1400 to 1892." Ph.D. dissertation, University of California, Los Angeles, 1980. 361 p.

Q. ECONOMICS

Adedeji, Adebayo, ed. Indigenization of African Economies. New York: Africana, 1981. 413 p.

Agueman-Badu, Yaw. "Attitude of African Nations Toward American Aid: The Case of Ghana and Nigeria." Ph.D. dissertation, University of South Carolina, 1980. 266 p.

Amoah, Frank Emmanuel Kwame. "The Growth and Decline of Seaports in Ghana, 1800-1962." Ph.D. dissertation, University of California, Los Angeles, 1969. 248 p.

Andrae, Gunilla. Industry in Ghana; Production and Spatial Structure. Stockholm: University of Stockholm, Scandinavian Institute of African Studies, 1981. 181 p.

Antwi, Anthony Kwasi. Public Expenditures: The Impact on Distribution of Income-The Ghana Case. Washington, D.C.: University Press of America, 1978. 224 p.

Anyane, Seth. Ghana Agriculture: Its Economic Development from Early Times to the Middle of the Twentieth Century. London: Oxford University Press, 1963. 228 p.

Apenteng, George Aduobe. "Government Policy and the Balance of Payments in Ghana, 1956-1974." Ph.D. dissertation, University of Pittsburgh, 1979. 204 p.

Appiah, A.K. "The Development of the Monetary and Financial System of Ghana, 1950-64." Ph.D. dissertation, University of Leeds, 1967. 374 p.

Arhin, Kwame. West African Traders in Ghana in the Nineteenth and Twentieth Centuries. Legon History Series. London and New York: Longman, 1979. 224 p.

Bateman, Merrill J. "Cocoa in the Ghanaian Economy." Ph.D. dissertation, Massachusetts Institute of Technology, 1965. 230 p.

Bawuah, Kwadwo. "Some Aspects of Political-Economy of Development: The Case of Ghana, 1950-1966." Ph.D. dissertation, Virginia Polytechnic Institute and State University, 1980. 220 p.

Beckett, W.H. Akokoaso: A Survey of a Gold Coast Village. London: Lund Humphries, 1944. 95 p. An Agricultural Officer on the Gold Coast writes about a typical cocoa village.

Beckman, Bjorn. Organising the Farmers; Cocoa Politics and National Development in Ghana. Uppsala, Sweden: Scandinavian Institute of African Studies, 1976. 299 p.

Bevin, H.J., comp. Economic History of the Gold Coast, 1874-1914: Select Documents. Legon: Department of History, University of Ghana, 1960. 189 p.

──────. "The Gold Coast Economy About 1880." Transactions of the Gold Coast and Togoland Historical Society, 2 (1956), 73-86.

──────. "M.J. Bonnat, Trader and Mining Promoter." Economic Bulletin (Legon), 4, 7 (July 1960), 1-12.

Birmingham, Walter; I. Neustadt; and E.N. Omaboe, eds. A Study of Contemporary Ghana. Vol. 1, The Economy of Ghana. Evanston, Ill.: Northwestern University Press, 1966; London: Allen and Unwin for the Ghana Academy of Sciences, 1966. 472 p.

Byl, Adhemar. "Ghana's Struggle for Economic Independence." Current History (Philadelphia), 43, 256 (December 1962), 359-365.

Carlsson, Jerker. The Limits to Structural Change; A Comparative Study of Foreign Direct Investments in Liberia and Ghana, 1950-1971. Gothenburg: University of Gothenburg, Institute of African Studies, 1981. 299 p.

Chada, Geoffrey Takawira Zinyama. "Labour Protest, Group Consciousness and Trade Unionism in West Africa: The Radical Railway Workers of Colonial Ghana, 1900-1950." Ph.D. dissertation, University of Toronto, Canada, 1981.

Crisp, Jeff. The Story of an African Working Class: Ghanaian Miners' Struggles 1870-1980. London: Zed Press, 1984. 256 p.

──────. "Union Atrophy and Worker Revolt: Labour Protest at Tarkwa Goldfields, Ghana, 1968-1969." Canadian Journal of African Studies (Guelph, Ontario), 13, 1-2 (1979), 265-293.

Daaku, Kwame Yeboa. "Aspects of Precolonial Akan Economy." The International Journal of African Historical Studies (Boston), 5, 2 (1972), 235-247.

──────. Trade and Politics on the Gold Coast, 1600-1720; a Study of the African Reaction to European Trade. Oxford: Clarendon Press, 1970. 219 p. Doctoral dissertation, University of London, 1964.

Dalton, John H., Jr. "Gold Coast Economic Development: Problems and Policies." Ph.D. dissertation, University of California at Berkeley, 1955. 303 p.

Davies, P.N. The Trade Makers: Elder Dempster in West Africa, 1852-1972. London: Allen and Unwin, 1973. 526 p.

Dei-Anang, Michael Francis. Cocoa Comes to Mampong. Cape Coast: Methodist Book Depot, 1949; Nendeln, Liechtenstein: Kraus Reprint, 1970. 104 p.

Duffuor, Kwabena. "The Impact of the Post-1971 Exchange Rate System on the Economies of the Developing Countries with Specific Reference to Ghana." Ph.D. dissertation, Syracuse University, 1979. 263 p.

Dumett, Raymond E. "British Official Attitudes in Relation to Economic Development in the Gold Coast, 1874-1905." Ph.D. dissertation, University of London, 1966. 395 p.

_____. "John Sarbah, the Elder, and African Mercantile Entrepreneurship in the Gold Coast in the Late Nineteenth Century." Journal of African History (London), 14, 4 (1973), 653-679.

_____. "The Rubber Trade of the Gold Coast and Asante in the Nineteenth Century: African Innovation and Market Responsiveness." Journal of African History, 12, 1 (1971), 79-101.

Dumor, Cecilia J. "Editorial Comment and Economic Development in Ghana, 1960-1972." Master's thesis, Michigan State University, 1979. 156 p.

Dunn, John. "But How Will They Eat?" Transactions of the Historical Society of Ghana, 13, 1 (June 1972), 113-124.

Eicher, Carl K. Research on Agricultural Development in Five English Speaking Countries in West Africa. New York: Agricultural Development Council, 1970. 152 p.

Esseks, J.D. "Economic Independence in a New African State: Ghana, 1956-65." Ph.D. dissertation, Harvard University, 1967. 606 p.

Ewusi, Kodwo. Economic Development Planning in Ghana. New York: Exposition Press, 1973. 85 p.

Fage, John Donnelly. "Some Remarks on Beads and Trade in Lower Guinea in the Sixteenth and Seventeenth Centuries." Journal of African History, 3, 2 (1962), 343-347.

Feinberg, Harvey M., and Marion Johnson. "The West African Ivory

Trade During the Eighteenth Century." The International Journal of African Historical Studies, 15, 3 (1982), 435-453.

Fletcher, Robert Gary. "A Comparison of Monetarist and Keynesian Econometric Models in Ghana." Ph.D. dissertation, University of California, Los Angeles, 1971. 138 p.

Fynn, John Kofi. "Trade and Politics in Akan Land." Tarikh (Ibadan), 7, 2 (1982), 23-34.

Fry, Richard. Bankers in West Africa: The Story of the Bank of British West Africa Limited. London: Hutchinson Benham, 1976. 270 p.

Garlick, Peter Cyril. African Business Enterprise: A Study of a Group of Traders in Kumasi. Achimota: University of Ghana, Economic Research Division, 1958. 68 p.

———. African Traders and Economic Development in Ghana. London: Oxford University Press, 1971. 172 p.

———. African Traders in Kumasi. Accra: Economic Research Division, University of Ghana, 1960. 115 p.

———. "The Development of Kwahu Business Enterprise in Ghana Since 1874--An Essay in Recent Oral Tradition." Journal of African History, 8, 3 (1967), 463-480.

———. "The Ghanaian Entrepreneur: Studies in Trading in Ghana." Ph.D. dissertation, University of London, 1962. 301 p.

Genoud, Roger. Nationalism and Economic Development in Ghana. New York: Praeger; Montreal: McGill; London: Pall Mall, 1969. 245 p.

"Ghana: Donors Meeting in Paris." West Africa (London), 3460 (5 December 1983), 2789-2790.

"Ghana Road Transport Crisis." West Africa, 3453 (17 October 1983), 2404; 3454 (24 October 1983), 2447; 3455 (31 October 1983), 2504.

"Ghana: Shocks of Austerity." West Africa, 3455 (31 October 1983), 2503-2504.

Goody, Jack; John Rankine; and T.M. Mustapha. "The Caravan Trade form Kano to Salaga." Journal of the Historical Society of Nigeria (Ibadan), 3, 4 (June 1967), 611-616.

Gordon, Sara Lee. "Aspects of Economic Development in Ghana." Ph.D. dissertation, Stanford University, 1970. 405 p.

Gould, Peter Robin. "The Devleopment of the Transportation Pattern in Ghana." Ph.D. dissertation, Northwestern University, 1960. 163 p. Published by the Department of Geography at Northwestern, Studies in Geography, 5.

Gray, Paul S. Unions and Leaders in Ghana: A Model of Labor and Development. New Brunswick, N.J.: Rutgers State University, 1981. 356 p.

Grier, Beverly Carolease. "Cocoa, Class Formation and the State in Ghana." Ph.D. dissertation, Yale University, 1979. 503 p.

Handloff, Robert Earl. "The Dyula of Gyaman: A Study of Politics and Trade in the Nineteenth Century." 2 vols. Ph.D. dissertation, Northwestern University, 1982. 692 p.

Hill, Polly. The Gold Coast Cocoa Farmer: A Preliminary Survey. London: Oxford University Press, 1956. 139 p.

_____. The Migrant Cocoa Farmers of Southern Ghana: A Study in Rural Capitalism. Cambridge and New York: Cambridge University Press, 1963. 265 p.

_____. The Occupation of Migrants in Ghana. Ann Arbor: University of Michigan, 1970. 76 p.

_____. Studies in Rural Capitalism in West Africa. Cambridge: Cambridge University Press, 1970. 173 p.

Hopkins, A.G. "Economic Aspects of Political Movements in Nigeria and in the Gold Coast, 1918-39." Journal of African History, 7, 1 (1966), 133-152.

_____. An Economic History of West Africa. New York: Columbia University Press, 1973. 337 p.

Jefferies, Richard. "Rawlings and the Political Economy of Underdevelopment in Ghana." African Affairs, 81, 324 (July 1982), 307-317.

Johnson, Marion. "The Ounce in Eighteenth-Century West African Trade." Journal of African History, 7, 2 (1966), 197-214.

Kaplow, Susan Beth. "African Merchants of the Nineteenth Century Gold Coast." Ph.D. dissertation, Columbia University, 1971. 259 p.

Kay, Geoffrey B., ed. The Political Economy of Colonialism in Ghana: A Collection of Documents and Statistics, 1900-1960. Cambridge: Cambridge University Press, 1972. 431 p.

Kennedy, Paul. "The Role and Position of Petty Producers in a West African City (Accra)." The Journal of Modern African Studies (Cambridge), 19, 4 (1981), 565-594.

Killick, Tony. Development Economics in Action: A Study of Economic Policies in Ghana. London: Heinemann, 1978. 392 p.

_____. Economic Strategies of Nkrumah and His Successors. Cambridge, Mass.: Harvard University, Center for International Affairs, 1973. 72 p.

Konings, Piet. The Political Potential of Ghanaian Miners: A Case-Study of the Ashanti Goldfields Corporation Workers at Obuasi. Leiden, The Netherlands: The African Studies Centre, 1981.

Kwaku, Kenneth Kwami. "The Political Economy of Peripheral Development: A Case Study of the Volta Region (Ghana)." Ph.D. dissertation, University of Toronto (Canada), 1976.

Latorre, Joseph Raymond. "Wealth Surpasses Everything: An Economic History of Asante, 1750-1874." Ph.D. dissertation, University of California, 1978. 529 p.

Leith, J. Clark. Ghana. National Bureau of Economic Research, Foreign Trade Regimes and Economic Development, 2. New York: Columbia University Press, 1974. 216 p. Funded by the U.S. Agency for Development.

Levy, Mildred Blitt. "Interregional Labor Migration in Ghana." Ph.D. dissertation, Northwestern University, 1966. 148 p.

Lewis, William Arthur. Report on Industrialization and the Gold Coast. Accra: Government Printer, 1953. 23 p. An important report that influenced Nkrumah at one point.

Lovejoy, Paul Ellsworth. "The Hausa Kola Trade (1700-1900): A Commercial System in the Continental Exchange of West Africa." Ph.D. dissertation, University of Wisconsin, 1973. 303 p.

McCall, Daniel F. "The Koforidua Market." In Markets in Africa, ed. by Paul Bohannan and George Dalton. Evanston, Ill.: Northwestern University Press, 1968. 667-697.

McRory, Susan Tucker. "The Competition for the Merchandise Trade in the Gold Coast, 1900-1939." Ph.D. dissertation, Columbia University, 1980. 387 p.

Meillassoux, Claude, ed. The Development of Indigenous Trade and Markets in West Africa. Tenth International African Seminar, Fourah Bay College. London: Oxford University Press, 1971. 444 p.

Milburn, Josephine F. British Business and Ghanaian Independence. London: C. Hurst; Hanover, N.H.: The University Press of New England, 1977. 156 p. A history of cocoa marketing, mainly in the 1938-1947 World War II period.

Miracle, Marvin P., et al. Agricultural Cooperatives and Quasi-cooperatives in Ghana, 1951-1965. Madison: University of Wisconsin, 1968. 73 p. Funded by the U.S. Agency for International Development.

_____, and Ann W. Seidman. State Farms in Ghana. Madison: University of Wisconsin, 1968. 54 p. Funded by the U.S. Agency for International Development.

Ocansey, John Emanuel. African Trading: Or the Trials of William Narh Ocansey of Addah, West Coast of Africa, River Volta. Liverpool: B.J. Looney, ca. 1881. 92 p.

Okoso-Amaa, Kewku. Rice Marketing in Ghana. Uppsala, Sweden: Scandinavian Institute of African Studies, 1975. 102 p.

Patterson, K. David. "The Veterinary Department and the Animal Industry in the Gold Coast, 1909-1955." The International Journal of African Historical Studies, 13, 3 (1980), 457-491.

Pedler, Frederick J. The Lion and the Unicorn in Africa: A History of the Origins of the United Africa Company, 1787-1931. London: Heinemann, 1974. 343 p.

Peil, Margaret. The Ghanaian Factory Worker: Industrial Man in Africa. Cambridge: Cambridge University Press, 1972. 254 p.

Porter, R. "The Crispe Family and the African Trade in the Seventeenth Century." Journal of African History, 9, 1 (1968), 57-77.

Posnansky, Merrick. "Ghana and the Origins of West African Trade." Africa Quarterly (New Delhi), 11 (1971), 100-125.

Reynolds, Edward. Trade and Economic Change on the Gold Coast, 1807-1874. Legon History Series. London: Longman, 1974. 207 p.

Rodney, Walter. "Gold and Slaves on the Gold Coast." Transactions of the Historical Society of Ghana, 10 (1969), 13-28.

Rohdie, Samuel. "The Gold Coast Cocoa Hold-up of 1930-31." Transactions of the Historical Society of Ghana, 9 (1968), 103-118.

Rosenblum, Paul. "Gold Mining in Ghana: 1874-1900." Ph.D. dissertation, Columbia University, 1972.

Sanders, James. "Palm Oil Production on the Gold Coast in the Aftermath of the Slave Trade. A Case Study of the Fante." The International Journal of African Studies, 15, 1 (1982), 49-63.

Schwimmer, Brian. "The Organization of Migrant Farmer Communities in Southern Ghana." Canadian Journal of African Studies (Guelph, Ontario), 14, 2 (1980), 221-238.

Scott, D.A. "Growth and Crisis, Economic Policy in Ghana; 1946-1965." Ph.D. dissertation, 1967. 213 p.

Seidman, Ann Willcox. "Ghana's Development Experience, 1951-1965." Ph.D. dissertation, 1968. 467 p.

Shea, M.S.M. "The Development and Role of Trade Unions in a Developing Economy: The Case of Ghana." Ph.D. dissertation, University of Edinburgh, 1968. 372 p.

Southall, Roger J. "Cadbury on the Gold Coast; 1907-1938: The Dilemma of the Model Firm in a Colonial Economy." Ph.D. dissertation, University of Birmingham, 1975.

_____. "Polarisation and Dependence in the Gold Coast Cocoa Trade, 1890-1938." Transactions of the Historical Society of Ghana, 16, 1 (June 1975), 93-115.

Struthers, J. "Inflation in Ghana (1966-78); a Perspective on the Monetarist v. Structuralist Debate." Development and Change (London), (April 1981), 177-213.

Sutton, I.B. "The Volta River Salt Trade: The Survival of an Indigenous Industry." Journal of African History, 20, 1 (1981), 43-61.

Swanzy, Henry. "A Trading Family in the Nineteenth Century Gold Coast." Transactions of the Gold Coast and Togoland Historical Society, 2, 2 (1956), 87-120.

Uzoigwe, G.N. "The Slave Trade and African States." Transactions of the Historical Society of Ghana, 14, 2 (Dec. 1973), 187-212.

Van Dantzig, Albert. "The Ankobra Gold Interest." Transactions of the Historical Society of Ghana, 14, 2 (December 1973), 169-185.

Vercruijsse, Emile. Transitional Modes of Production: A Case Study from West Africa (Ghana). Westport, Conn.: Lawrence Hill, 1982. 224 p. An account of canoe-fishing in Ghana.

Weaver, Donna Maier. "Competition for Power and Profits in Kete-Krachi, West Africa, 1875-1900." The International Journal of African Historical Studies, 13, 1 (1980), 33-50.

Wehner, Harrison Gill, Jr. "The Cocoa Marketing Board and Economic Development in Ghana: A Case Study." Ph.D. dissertation, University of Michigan, 1964. 276 p.

Wilks, Ivor. "A Medieval Trade Route from the Niger to the Gulf of Guinea." Journal of African History, 3, 2 (1962), 337-341.

Wills, John Brian, ed. Agriculture and Land Use in Ghana. London: Oxford University Press for the Ghana Ministry of Food and Agriculture, 1962. 503 p.

R. RELIGION AND PHILOSOPHY

Affriefah, Kofi. "The Impact of Christianity on Akyem Society, 1852-1887." Transactions of the Historical Society of Ghana, 16, 1 (June 1975), 67-86.

Appiah-Kubi, Kofi. Man Cures, God Heals: Religion and Medical Practice Among the Akans of Ghana. Totowa, N.J.: Allanheld, Osmun, and Co., 1981. 173 p.

Arhin, Kwame. "The Missionary Role on the Gold Coast and in Ashanti: Reverend F.A. Ramseyer and the British Take-over of Ashanti, 1869-1894." Research Review (Legon), 4, 2 (1968), 1-12.

Baëta, C.G.K. "Prophetism in Ghana." Ph.D. dissertation, University of London, 1959. 282 p.

Bartels, Francis L. "Jacobus Eliza Johannes Capitein, 1719-47." Transactions of the Historical Society of Ghana, 4, 1 (1959), 3-13.

_____. "Philip Quaque, 1741-1816." Transactions of the Gold Coast and Togoland Historical Society, 1 (1955), 153-77.

_____. The Roots of Ghana Methodism. London: Cambridge University Press and Ghana Methodist Book Depot, 1965. 368 p.

Breidenbach, Paul S. "Maame Harris Grace Tani and Papa Kwesi John Nackabah: Independent Church Leaders in the Gold Coast, 1914-1958." International Journal of African Historical Studies, 12, 4 (1979), 581-614.

Busia, Kofi Abrefa. "Ancestor Worship, Libation, Stools, Festivals." In Christianity and African Culture. Accra: Christian Council, 1955. 17-23.

Danquah, Joseph Boakye. The Akan Doctrine of God. London: Lutterworth, 1944. 206 p.

──────. Ancestors, Heroes and God. Kibi, Gold Coast: G. Boakie, 1938. 46 p.

Debrunner, Hans W. A History of Christianity in Ghana. Accra: Waterville Publishing House, 1967. 375 p.

Field, Margaret Joyce. Religion and Medicine of the Ga People. New York: AMS Press, 1979. 214 p.; London: Oxford University Press, 1937.

Fisher, Humphrey J. Ahmadiyyah. A Study in Contemporary Islam on the West African Coast. London: Oxford University Press for the Nigerian Institute of Social and Economic Research, 1963. 224 p.

Grau, Eugene Emil. "The Evangelical Presbyterian Church (Ghana and Togo) 1914-1946." Ph.D. dissertation, Hartford Seminary. 261 p.

Haliburton, Gordon Mac Kay. The Prophet Harris: A Study of an African Prophet and His Mass-Movement in the Ivory Coast and the Gold Coast 1913-1915. London: Longman Group, 1971; Abridged version, London and New York: Oxford University Press, 1973.

Jenkins, Paul. "The Anglican Church in Ghana, 1905-1924." Transactions of the Historical Society of Ghana, Part I, 15, 1 (June 1974), 23-39; Part II, 15, 2 (Dec. 1974), 177-200.

Kalu, O.U. The History of Christianity in West Africa. London and New York: Longman, 1980. 352 p.

Kilson, Marion. Kpele lala; Ga Religious Songs and Symbols. Cambridge, Mass.: Harvard University Press, 1971. 313 p.

Levtzion, Nehemia. Muslims and Chiefs in West Africa: A Study of Islam in the Middle Volta Basin in the Pre-Colonial Period. Oxford: Clarendon Press, 1968. 228 p.

──────. "The Spread and Development of Islam in the Middle Volta Basin (Northern Ghana) in the Pre-Colonial Period." Ph.D. dissertation, University of London, 1965. 425 p.

Lewis, Ioan Myrddin, ed. Islam in Tropical Africa. London: Oxford University Press for the Fifth International African Seminar, 1966. 470 p.

Mobley, Harris Witsel. Ghanaian's Image of the Missionary: An

Analysis of the Published Critiques of Christian Missionaries by Ghanaians, 1897-1965. Leiden: Brill, 1970. 181 p. This was a Ph.D. dissertation, Hartford Seminary, 1966.

Opoku, Kofi Asare. West African Traditional Religion. Singapore: F.E.P. International Private, Ltd., 1981.

Parrinder, Edward Geoffrey. West African Religion: A Study of the Beliefs and Practices of Akan, Ewe, Yoruba, Ibo, and Kindred Peoples. London: Epworth Press, 1961. 203 p.

Pfann, Helene M. A Short History of the Catholic Church in Ghana. Cape Coast: Catholic Mission Press, 1965. 172 p.

Rattray, Robert Sutherland. Religion and Art in Ashanti. Oxford: The Clarendon Press, 1927. 414 p.; later editions, 1954, 1959, 1969, 1980.

Smith, Noel. The Presbyterian Church of Ghana, 1835-1960. London: Oxford University Press, 1966. 304 p.

Swithenbank, Michael. Ashanti Fetish Houses. Legon: Ghana University Press, 1969. 68 p.

Trimingham, John Spencer. A History of Islam in West Africa. London: Oxford University Press for the University of Glasgow, 1962. 262 p.

_____. Islam in West Africa. Oxford: Clarendon Press, 1959. 262 p.

Ward, Barbara E. "Some Observations on Religious Cults in Ashanti." Africa (London), 26, 1 (1956), 47-61.

Wilks, Ivor. "The Position of Muslims in Metropolitan Ashanti in the Nineteenth Century." In Islam in Tropical Africa, ed. by Ioan Myrddin Lewis. London: Oxford University Press for the International African Institute, 1966.

Williamson, S.G. "Akan Religion and the Christian Faith." Ph.D. dissertation, University of London, 1957. 411 p.

_____, and Kwesi Dickson, eds. Akan Religion and the Christian Faith: A Comparative Study of the Impact of Two Religions. Accra: Ghana Universities Press, 1965. 186 p.

Wiltgen, Ralph M. Gold Coast Mission History, 1471-1880. Techny, Ill.: Divine World, 1956. 181 p.

Yates, Walter Ladell. "The History of the African Methodist Episcopal Zion Church in West Africa, Liberia, Gold Coast (Ghana), and Nigeria, 1900-1939." Ph.D. dissertation, Hartford Seminary, 1967. 398 p.

S. EDUCATION

Agbodeka, Francis. Achimota in the National Setting. Accra: Afram Pubs., 1977. 208 p.

Busia, Kofi Abrefa. The Challenge of Africa. New York: Praeger, 1962. 156 p.; London: Pall Mall, 1962.

──────. Purposeful Education for Africa. The Hague: Mouton, 1964. 107 p.

Curle, Adam. Educational Problems of Developing Societies: With Case Studies of Ghana, Pakistan, and Nigeria. Expanded and Updated ed. Praeger Special Studies in International Economics and Development. New York: Praeger, 1973. 200 p.

Foster, P.J. Education and Social Change in Ghana. London: Routledge and Kegan Paul, 1963. 322 p.

Frazier, Alexander G. Achimota: Comments on the Inspectors' Report. Achimota: Prince of Wales School Press, 1932.

Graham, Charles Kwesi. History of Education in Ghana from the Earliest Times to the Declaration of Independence. London: Frank Cass, 1971. 232 p.

Grindal, Bruce. Growing Up in Two Worlds: Education and Transition Among the Sisala of Northern Ghana. Case Studies in Education and Culture, ed. by George and Louise Spindler. New York: Holt, Rinehart, and Winston, 1972. 114 p.

Hayward, Fred M. "Ghana Experiments with Civic Education: Center for Civic Education Aims to Inculcate Democratic Values." Africa Report (Washington), 16, 5 (May 1971), 24-27.

Hilliard, F.H. A Short History of Education in British West Africa. London: Nelson, 1957. 186 p.

Macartney, William M. Dr. Aggrey-Ambassador for Africa. London: SCM Press, 1949. 106 p. (Student Christian Movement Press)

McElligott, Therese E. "Education in the Gold Coast Colony, 1920-1949." Ph.D. dissertation, Stanford University, 1950. 233 p.

McWilliams, Henry O.A. Development of Education in Ghana. London: Longmans, Green, 1959. 114 p.

Ofosu-Appiah, L.H. The Life of Dr. J.E.K. Aggrey. Accra: Waterville Publishing House, 1975. 103 p.

Smith, Edwin W. Aggrey of Africa; A Study in Black and White. London: Student Christian Movement, 1929. 202 p.

Tenkorang, Samuel. "The Founding of Mfantisipim 1905-1908." Transactions of the Historical Society of Ghana, 15, 2 (Dec. 1974), 165-175.

Thomas, Roger G. "Education in Northern Ghana, 1906-1940: A Study in Colonial Paradox." The International Journal of African Historical Studies (Boston), 7, 3 (1975), 427-467.

Ward, William E.F. Fraser of Trinity and Achimota. Legon: Ghana Universities Press, 1965. 328 p.

Williams, Charles Kingsley. Achimota: The Early Years 1924-1948. London: Longmans, 1963. 158 p.

APPENDIX A: GHANAIAN PEOPLES

AKAN

Abora
Adansi
Agona
Ahafo
Ahanta
Akuapem (Akwapim)
Akwamu
Akyem Abuakwa (Akim)
Akyem Bosome
Akyem Kotoku
Aowin
Asante (Ashanti)
Assin (Asen)
Banda
Bawle (Baoule, Baule)
Brong (Abrong, Bono, Boron)
Chokosi (Chakossi, Kyokosi)
Denkyira (Dankyira, Denkera,
    Denkyera, Kankyira)
Evalue
Fante (Fanti)
Gomoa
Gyaman (Gyaaman)
Kwahu (Akwahu, Kwawu)
Nzema (Nzima)
Sefwi (Sahwi, Sehwi)
Twifu
Wassa (Wasa, Wassaw)

GUAN (GUANG)

Anum-Bosso
Atwode (Achode, Atyoti)
Awutu
Bole
Efutu
Gonja (Gongya, Gonya)
Krakye (Krachi)
Kyerepon (Cherepong)
Larte (Larteh, Late)
Nkonya
Ntwumuru (Nchumuru)
Salaga
Senya (Senya Bereku)

GA

ADANGBE (ADANGME, DANGME)

Ada
Krobo (Kloli)
Prampram (Gbugbla)
Shai

EWE (AWONA)

Anlo
Krepe (Peki)

VOLTA-TOGO

Adele
Akpafu
Akposo
Avatime
Bowli
Buem (Boem)
Likpe
Logba
Lolobi
Ntrubu (Ntruber)
Nyangbo
Santrokofi

Tafi

GURMA

Basare (Bassari)
Bimoba (Bimawba, Bmoba, Moab, Moba)
Konkomba (Komba)
Kyamba (Tchamba)
Pilapila

GRUSI

Kasena
Mo
Nunuma
Sisala (Isala, Sissala)
Tampolense
Vagala (Vagele)

MOLE-DAGBANI-GURENSE

Builsa (Kangyaga, Kanjaga)
Dagaba (Dagari, Dagarte, Dagati)
Dagomba (Dagbani)
Frafra
Gurense (Grunshi, Gurinse, Gurunsi)
Kusasi (Kusae)
Lobi (Birifor, Lober, Miwo, Yangala)
Mamprusi (Mampruli, Mampruse, Mamprussi)
Mossi (Mole, Moshi)
Namnam (Nabdam)
Nankansi (Nankanse)
Nanumba (Nanune)
Talensi (Talene, Talense, Tallensi)
Wala (Walba, Wile)

OTHERS

Busansi (Busanga, Bussansi)

Fulani (Fula)
Hausa
Igbo (Ibo)
Mande (Bambara, Diula, Dyula, Juula, Mandingo, Wangara)
Songhai
Tem (Kotokoli, Temba, Timu)
Yoruba
Zabrama (Djerma, Zaberma, Zerma)

APPENDIX B: RULERS OF ASANTE

Osei Tutu	ca. 1680-1712 or 1717
Interregnum or unknown Asantehene?	
Opoku Ware	ca. 1720-1750
Kusi Obodom	1750-1764--Abdicated
Osei Kwadwo	1764-1777
Osei Kwame	1777-1798--Destooled. Executed in 1803.
Opoku Fofie	1798-1799
Osei Tutu Kwame (Osei Bonsu)	1800-1823
Osei Yaw Akoto	1824-1833
Kwaku Dua I	1834-1867
Kofi Karikari	1867-1874--Destooled. Died in 1884.
Mensa Bonsu	1874-1883--Destooled. Died in 1896.
Interregnum	1883-1884
Kwaku Dua II (Agyeman Kofi)	1884
Interregnum	1884-1888
Prempe I (Kwaku Dua III)	1888-1931 (Exile 1896-1924)
Prempe II (Osei Agyeman)	1931-1970
Opoku Ware II	1970-

APPENDIX C: BRITISH ADMINISTRATORS OF THE GOLD COAST

GOVERNOR

George C. Strahan	1874-1876
Stanford Freeling	1876-1879
Herbert T. Ussher	1879-1880
Samuel Rowe	1881-1884
William A.G. Young	1884-1885
William Brandford Griffith	1885-1895
William Edward Maxwell	1895-1897
Frederic M. Hodgson	1897-1900
Matthew Nathan	1900-1904
John P. Rodger	1904-1910
James J. Thorburn	1910-1912
Hugh Clifford	1912-1919
Frederick Gordon Guggisberg	1919-1927
Alexander R. Slater	1927-1932
Thomas S.W. Thomas	1932-1934
Arnold W. Hodson	1934-1941
Alan C.M. Burns	1941-1948
Gerald H. Creasy	1948-1949
Charles N. Arden-Clarke	1949-1957

Appendix C

GOVERNOR-GENERAL

Charles N. Arden-Clarke   1957

William Francis Hare   1957-1960

This list is adapted from David P. Henige, <u>Colonial Governors from the Fifteenth Century to the Present</u> (Madison: University of Wisconsin Press, 1970), p. 120-121. Also in Henige for Gold Coast administrators for Denmark see p. 9, the Netherlands see pp. 215-216, Portugal see p. 263, and Sweden see p. 351.

APPENDIX D: GHANAIAN LEADERS FROM 1951

KWAME NKRUMAH: Leader of Government Business, 1951-1952; Prime Minister, 1952-1960; President, 1960-1966.

JOSEPH A. ANKRAH: Chairman, National Liberation Council, 1966-1969.

AKWASI A. AFRIFA: Chairman, National Liberation Council, 1969- ; Head, Presidential Commission, 1969-1970.

KOFI A. BUSIA: Prime Minister, 1969-1972.

EDWARD AKUFO-ADDO: President, 1970-1972.

IGNATIUS K. ACHEAMPONG: Chairman, National Redemption Council, 1972-1975; Chairman, Supreme Military Council, 1975-1978.

FREDERICK W.K. AKUFFO: Chairman, Supreme Military Council, 1978-1979.

JERRY JOHN RAWLINGS: Chairman, Armed Forces Revolutionary Council, 1979.

HILLA LIMANN: President, 1979-1981.

JERRY JOHN RAWLINGS: Chairman, Provisional National Defense Council, 1982.

APPENDIX E: EUROPEAN POSTS ON THE GOLD COAST, 1482-1808

Base	Place	Nationality	Date
Apollonia	Beyin	English	1768-70
Eliza Carthago	Ankobra River	Dutch	1702
Duma	Ankobra River	Portuguese	1623
Ruyghaver	Ankobra River	Dutch	1653
San Antonio	Axim	Portuguese	1503
Gross Friedrichsburg	Prince's Town	Brandenburg	1683
Sophie Louise	Takrama	Brandenburg	1690
Dorothea	Akwida	Brandenburg	1685
Metal Cross	Dixcove	English	1692
Batenstein	Butre	Dutch	1656
Witzen (Witsen)	Takoradi	Dutch	1659
Orange	Sekondi	Dutch	1640
Sekondi	Sekondi	English	1685
San Sebastian	Shama	Portuguese	ca. 1560
Komenda	Komenda	English	1663/1694
Vredenburg	Komenda	Dutch	1688
San Jorge	Elmina	Portuguese	1482
Carlsborg	Cape Coast	Swedes	1650-52
Cape Coast Castle	Cape Coast	English	1664
Nassau	Mouri	Dutch	1612
Anomabo	Anomabo	English	1679/1753
Kormantin	Kormantin	English	1638
Fort Amsterdam	Kormantin	Dutch	1665
Leydsaamheid	Apam	Dutch	1697
Winneba	Winneba	English	1694
Good Hope	Senya Beraku	Dutch	1706
James Fort	Little Accra	English	1672
Crevecoeur	Little Accra	Dutch	1642/1652
Ussher	Little Accra	English	1868
Christiansborg	Osu	Danes	1661
Augustaborg	Teshi	Danes	1787
Vernon	Prampram	British	1740
Fredensborg	Ningo	Danes	1734
Kongensten	Ada	Danes	1784
Prinsensten	Keta	Danes	1784